Y0-BOH-434

Survey of Applied Soviet Research in School Mathematics Education

The University of Chicago

WITHDRAWN

Soviet Studies in Mathematics Education

Volume 4

The Development of Elementary Mathematical Concepts in Preschool Children

Soviet Studies in Mathematics Education

Volume 4
The Development of Elementary Mathematical Concepts in Preschool Children

A.M. Leushina

Volume Editor,
English Language Edition

Leslie P. Steffe
The University of Georgia

Translator

Joan Teller

National Council of Teachers of Mathematics
Reston, Virginia
1991

HIEBERT LIBRARY
FRESNO PACIFIC UNIV
FRESNO. CA 93702

Research Library
AIMS Education Foundation
Fresno CA 93747-8120

Survey of Applied Soviet Research in School Mathematics Education

Izaak Wirszup, Principal Investigator
Department of Mathematics
The University of Chicago

Series Editorial Committee

Jeremy Kilpatrick, Chairman
The University of Georgia

Izaak Wirszup
The University of Chicago

Alphonse Buccino
The University of Georgia

Robert Streit
The University of Chicago

Financial support for the *Survey of Applied Soviet Research in School Mathematics Education* has been provided by the National Science Foundation.

Originally published in 1974 by Prosveshchenie, Moscow, as *Formirovanie elementarnykh matematicheskikh predstavlenii u detei doshkol'nogo vozrasta.*

English Translation © 1991 by the University of Chicago
All rights reserved

Set in Adobe Postscript Times Roman with Helvetica display.

Printed in the United States of America

Second printing 1995

Library of Congress Cataloging-in-Publication Data

Leushina, A. M.
    [Formirovanie elementarnykh matematicheskikh predstavlenii u detei doshkol 'nogo vozrasta. English]
    The development of elementary mathematical concepts in preschool children / A.M. Leushina ; volume editor English language edition Leslie P. Steffe ; translator Joan Teller.
        p.   cm. — (Soviet studies in mathematics education ; v. 4)
    Translation from Russian: Formirovanie elementarnykh matematicheskikh predstavlenii u detei doshkol 'nogo vozrasta.
    Includes bibliographical references.
    ISBN 0-87353-299-6
    1. Mathematics—Study and teaching (Preschool) I. Steffe, Leslie P.
II. Title. III. Series.
QA135.5.L4813   1991
372.7—dc20   91-3865
                                                             CIP

Contents

Series Preface

The series *Soviet Studies in Mathematics Education* is a collection of translations of books from the extensive Soviet literature on research in the psychology of mathematics instruction. It also includes works on teaching methods directly influenced by this research. The series is a product of the Survey of Applied Soviet Research in School Mathematics Education at the University of Chicago and is funded by the National Science Foundation. The final editing and preparation of manuscripts was a cooperative undertaking by the Survey and the Department of Mathematics Education at the University of Georgia, with the valuable collaboration of a team of leading scholars from around the country. The *Soviet Studies* series comprises outstanding works selected for their value to the American mathematics educator and translated for the first time into English.

In view of Soviet social and political doctrines, several branches of psychology that are highly developed in the U.S. have scarcely been investigated in the USSR. On the other hand, because of the USSR's emphasis on education and its function in the state, Soviet research in educational psychology and teaching methods has received considerable moral and financial support. Consequently, this Soviet research has attracted many creative and talented scholars who have made remarkable contributions.

Even prior to World War II the Soviets had made great strides in educational psychology. The creation in 1943 of the Academy of Pedagogical Sciences helped to intensify research efforts and programs in this field. Since then the Academy has become the Soviet Union's chief educational research and development center. One of the main aims of the Academy is to conduct research and train research scholars in general and specialized education, educational psychology, and the methods of teaching various school subjects. Members of the Academy (51 in 1987,

with another 85 associate members) are chosen from the ranks of distinguished Soviet scholars, scientists, and educators.

The Academy of Pedagogical Sciences comprises 15 research institutes,
most of them in Moscow and Leningrad. Many of the studies reported in this
series were conducted at the Academy's Institute of General and Polytechnical
Education and Institute of Psychology. In 1987 the research institutes had
available some 15 laboratory schools in which experiments were conducted.
Developments in foreign countries are closely followed by the Bureau for the
Study of Foreign Educational Experience and Information.

The Academy has its own publishing house, which produces hundreds
of books each year as well as a number of periodicals, including *Proceedings of the Academy of Pedagogical Sciences of the USSR* (Izvestiya
Akademii Pedagogicheskikh Nauk SSSR), the monthly *Soviet Pedagogy*
(Sovetskaya pedagogika), the bimonthly *Topics in Psychology* (Voprosy
psikhologii), the journal *Special Education* (Defektologiya), and the
remarkable enrichment monthly for secondary school mathematics and
science students (Grades 6-10) *Quantum* (Kvant).

Soviet psychologists have concerned themselves with the dynamics
of mental activity and the principles of the learning process. They have
investigated such areas as the development of mental operations; the
nature and development of thought; the formation of mathematical
concepts and the related questions of generalization, abstraction, and
concretization; the mental operations of analysis and synthesis; the
development of spatial perception; the relation between memory and
thought; the development of logical reasoning; the nature of mathematical skills; and the structure and special features of mathematical abilities.
Over the years, they have created a vast and impressive body of research.

This research has had a notable impact on the recent Soviet literature on
methods of teaching mathematics. Experiments have shown the student's
mathematical potential to be greater than previously assumed. Consequently, Soviet psychologists have advocated various changes in the content
and methods of mathematics instruction. They participated in designing the
revolutionary Soviet mathematics curriculum of the late 1960s and have been
actively involved in more recent school reforms. Studies conducted with the

assistance of the Survey of Applied Soviet Research in School Mathematics Education and the University of Chicago School Mathematics
Project show that Soviet and American elementary school mathematics
textbooks differ strikingly, with the Soviet books featuring many more
types of word problems, treating a more even distribution of problem
types, a much higher percentage of problems whose solution requires
more than one operation, more varied sequences of problems, earlier
introduction of multidigit addition and subtraction, and an emphasis on
methods of mental calculation for single-digit operations. Furthermore,
Soviet elementary school mathematics texts contain a continuous treatment of intuitive geometry, which by mandate comprises at least 20% of
the mathematics curriculum in grades 1-5. The Soviet textbooks have
clearly been constructed to reflect careful analyses of learning tasks and
students' responses to them.

The USSR's apparent successes in the mathematics classroom, especially in the lower grades, have spurred American interest in Soviet
research in educational psychology. One of the first opportunities to
examine that research came with the appearance of the 14-volume series
Soviet Studies in the Psychology of Learning and Teaching Mathematics.
A joint publication of the Survey of Recent East European Mathematical
Literature at the University of Chicago and the School Mathematics
Study Group at Stanford University, that series had a broad and beneficial
impact on mathematics education research in the United States and
elsewhere and led directly to a great number of influential research projects.

At the time the earlier *Soviet Studies* series was published, American
educational research was beginning to turn from its strong quantitative-ex-
perimentalist orientation toward the qualitative-interpretivist view so prominent today. The *Soviet Studies* helped bring to the attention of American
researchers a tradition in which case studies and intensive work with small
groups of children were the norm rather than the exception. Of particular
interest to Americans was the *teaching experiment*, in which children were
studied in the process of learning mathematical concepts, usually in ordinary classroom settings over a substantial period of time, and the teaching
was continually modified in the light of the children's responses to it.

American researchers were interested not only in the approaches Soviet researchers used in their research but also in the topics they studied. One volume in the series concerned the structure of mathematical abilities. It brought the seminal work of V. A. Krutetskii to the attention of English-speaking mathematics educators. Subsequent publication of Krutetskii's landmark book *The Psychology of Mathematical Abilities in Schoolchildren* by the University of Chicago Press stimulated a variety of investigations into children's memory for the problems they have solved and how they perceive problems as being related. A subsequent book by Krutetskii is included in the present series.

Another volume in the earlier series dealt with studies in the perception of three-dimensional space. In the United States this ability had long been considered relatively static and little influenced by school instruction. The Soviet research demonstrated clearly that spatial abilities could be developed; again, that work is represented in the present series.

The earlier series was drawn primarily from journal articles published prior to the mid-1960s. The present series picks up where that one left off and consists entirely of translated books, for the most part monographs, all of which underwent thorough review by experts before they were originally published. Each manuscript was recommended by a scholarly committee or editorial council of either a university, a research institute of the Academy of Pedagogical Sciences, or the Ministry of Education.

The aim of the present series is to acquaint mathematics educators and teachers with directions, ideas, and accomplishments in the psychology of mathematical instruction in the Soviet Union. This series should assist in opening up avenues of investigation to those who are interested in broadening the foundations of their profession, for it is generally recognized that experiment and research are indispensable for improving the content and methods of school mathematics.

We hope that the volumes in this series will be used not only for research by individuals but also for study, discussion, and critical analysis in teacher-training programs and in institutes for in-service teachers at various levels.

It goes without saying that a publication project of this magnitude requires the commitment and cooperation of a network of institutions and individuals. In acknowledging their contributions, we would like first of all to express our deep appreciation to the National Science Foundation. Without the Foundation's generous long-term support of the Survey of Applied Soviet Research in School Mathematics Education, these books might never have become accessible to the American education and research communities.

The Survey at the University of Chicago is very pleased that the *Soviet Studies in Mathematics Education* are being published by the National Council of Teachers of Mathematics. It has always been a major goal of the Survey to disseminate its translations to a wide audience at minimal cost. We believe that the NCTM's recognized leadership, publishing expertise, and steadfast support and encouragement have assured us of reaching that goal. We are particularly indebted to the NCTM Educational Materials Committee and the Board of Directors. Special thanks are due Ms. Cynthia Rosso, NCTM Publications Business Manager, whose expertise, counsel, and energetic efforts were critical to the publication of this series.

The Editorial Committee would like to acknowlege the special assistance provided by Steven Young and George Fowler, who made a meticulous review of the translations; Jack Kirkman of the University of Georgia, who supervised the preparation of the edited manuscripts for publication; and Birute Tamulynas, who worked tirelessly on the manuscripts at the University of Chicago. We gratefully acknowledge the dedicated efforts of the volume editors and translators whose names appear on the title pages, as well as the valued contributions of the many language editors, typists, proofreaders, and production specialists who helped bring this extraordinary research to the English-speaking public.

Jeremy Kilpatrick
Izaak Wirszup
Alphonse Buccino
Robert Streit

Introduction to the English Language Edition

Leslie P. Steffe

This monograph was originally published in 1974. Since that time, significant advances have been made in understanding the mathematical conceptual development of children and the role of schooling in that development. The task of explaining and then contrasting and synthesizing these recent advances with the work of A. M. Leushina is too extensive to be undertaken in a short introduction. Nevertheless, whenever it seems to be appropriate, selected results presented in the monograph are discussed in order to identify certain issues highlighted by the more recent work.

For example, Leushina (cf. 22 ff.) states that instruction guides or is a source of development. Following Vygotskii, the orientation is always toward the children's zone of proximal development. Development is not identified with instruction, but it is preceded and engendered by instruction. More recent work (D'Ambrosio, 1986; Steffe & Cobb, 1987) has revealed a complex relationship among cultural factors, mathematics teaching, mathematics learning, and mathematics development. One prominent issue concerning the sources of children's mathematical experiences emerges when contrasting Leushina's and D'Ambrosio's work. Following D'Ambrosio, one can see the sources as including the children's social-cultural environment. D'Ambrosio sees the mathematical experience in school as a closed system: "The big challenge I see in education . . . is how to bring this cultural diversity into curriculum design" (p. 5). In other words, how children might develop in mathematics cannot be attributed only to a closed system of school instruction that essentially ignores cultural diversity.

A second issue concerns children's mathematics knowledge. We have found that what children make of "mathematical instruction" is greatly influenced by their current mathematics knowledge and that mathematics teaching precedes mathematics development only in a partial and global sense. Mathematics teaching is understood as only harmonizing with the children's current ways and means of operating; as *responding to* as well as *provoking* learning.

A third issue concerns the relation between learning and development. As early as 1964, Piaget presented his view that learning is subordinate to development in the sense that what children may make of a certain situation is greatly influenced by their current mathematical operations, operations that were seen by Piaget as being products of development. Although what we have found is compatible with Piaget's view, there are important differences. Development to Piaget included maturation of the central nervous system as well as other factors. In our current model, mathematical development is viewed as being relative to certain schemes, and it is understood as a modification of a scheme called *metamorphic accommodation* (Steffe & Cobb, 1987). A metamorphic accommodation of a scheme is a product of learning in that it is preceded by certain engendering accommodations that occur in the use of the scheme. In this sense, learning can be said to engender development, and mathematics teaching (insofar as it provides the child with an opportunity to modify a certain scheme in the context of its use) can be also said to engender development. This is a very different relation between "instruction" and "development" than the direct, causal relation posited by Leushina.

Another issue concerns the child's zone of proximal development. The child's actual level of development can be determined by the problems he or she can solve without the help of the teacher. On the other hand, the child's zone of proximal development can be determined by the types of problems that the child can solve with the *help* of the teacher. It is the novel experiential elements that are produced by the *temporary and local or contextual modifications* of the involved schemes that determine the child's zone of proximal development. "This means that two children at the same actual level of development can have different zones of potential development" (Sinclair, 1988, p. iii), which is in contrast to Vygotskii's view that the teacher's role is to guide the child toward the adult's conception of the new problems to be mastered.

Leushina outlines six stages in the development of counting (cf. 91 ff.). These stages are viewed as being products of mathematics instruction and are embedded in the logical analysis of counting and number on which that instruction is based (cf. p. 64). The conclusion that "instruction for small children should begin not with counting using number-words but by having children actively create sets and compare them . . . so that the children gradually become familiar with equal and unequal aggregates" is based on the assumption that children can develop aggregates and their comparison through instruction. Toward this end, Leushina cogently begins by isolating unbounded "sets"—pluralities. *Set* is a word Leushina uses to indicate a collection of homogeneous entities (objects or phenomena, sounds, movements, etc.) as perceived by different analyzers (visual, tactual, kinesthetic). Leushina's analysis is compatible with how the terms *plurality, collection, lot, arithmetic lot,* and *number* are used by von Glasersfeld (1981). It is compatible because Leushina proceeds from set as plurality to set as bounded plurality—to what von Glasersfeld calls *collection.* But Leushina stops there in favor of comparing the collections thus formed. One reason for Leushina's digression is how number is viewed: "Number is an index of a class of sets, or the concept of the class" (p. 65). In this logical definition, one-to-one correspondence is essential and serves as a basis for comparing sets in Leushina's work.

Preceding the instruction of comparing sets, Leushina believes that "from an early age children must be taught not only to distinguish between 'many' and 'one' but also to form a notion of a set as a structurally integral unity [bounded plurality] and a distinct perception of the individual elements that make up a set" (p. 84). This claim accounts for only the two first composite wholes identified by von Glasersfeld and, as such, does not go far enough. Von Glasersfeld's theoretical analysis has been corroborated by an experiential analysis of children's construction of number (Steffe & Cobb, 1988). There it was found that children construct what are called *numerical composites* and *abstract composite units.* These two types of composite wholes correspond to von Glasersfeld's notions of arithmetic lot and number. In a numerical composite, the child focuses on the constituent unit items; and in a abstract composite unit, the child focuses on the composite unit as one thing. Leushina's work does not isolate these crucial abstractions involved in the construction of number. Nevertheless, it should be noted that Leushina's analysis was conducted independently of our analysis. The overlaps that are present are striking, especially when one considers the vast difference in the epistemological frameworks in which the two research programs operate. I attribute these striking overlaps to the necessity of explaining what children do mathematically, which seems to provide a basis for communicating across research paradigms.

The stages that Leushina isolates in the development of counting are connected to the logical analysis of number presented earlier in the book. These stages are as follows.

> Stage 1: Manipulations with plurality where movements of objects are accompanied by a repetition of one word: "Another . . . another . . . another. . . ."

> Stage 2: Comparison of sets.

> Stage 3: Sequential naming of number words, which begins to be included when the elements of the sets to be compared are contrasted.

> Stage 4: A correlation of the sequence of number words with each element in a set independently of the way in which the set is arranged. Children understand the significance of the last number

as the total and begin to understand that a number shows the equivalence of sets.

Stage 5: Children are taught to count sets of various unit bases where groups consisting of several objects are counted instead of the individual objects.

Stage 6: Children are taught counting by tens.

The six "stages" constitute a logical progression. But Leushina gives no indication that they satisfy four essential criteria for stages: the period criterion, the invariant sequence criterion, and the reorganization criterion (Steffe & von Glasersfeld, 1988). Stages in the development of counting have been isolated that do satisfy these four criteria, and the mechanisms of transition from one stage to another have been isolated as well (Steffe & Cobb, 1988). These mechanisms of transition are essential in specifying how learning contributes to development.

Leushina devotes Chapters 4-7 to elaborating children's notions of size, shape, mass, measurement, spatial orientation, and time; Chapter 8 to didactic principles of instruction; and Chapters 9-12 to curriculum and methods for teaching the elements of mathematics to children from 3 to 7 years of age. I focus on two didactic principles discussed in Chapter 8 because such principles of instruction are of current interest (Bauersfeld, Krummheuer, & Voigt 1985; Treffers, 1987). In the principle of developmental instruction, in spite of the logical analysis of number, Leushina believes that "instruction should by no means be reduced to shifting knowledge from an adult's mind to a child's mind" (p. 149). Furthermore, not enough attention is paid to "activating the children's thought in class and ensur[ing] that children reflect their knowledge through diverse solution methods and statements" (p. 150). These three beliefs are certainly shared by many other mathematics educators. However, there is a subtle but important distinction to be made between two interpretations of mathematics *for* children, and this distinction is not made clear in Chapters 9-12.

The mathematics *of* children can be thought of as schemes of action and operation that can be inferred from children's behavior, and mathematics *for* children can be thought of as their possible modifications (Steffe, 1988). In the latter case, the modified schemes are not models of the adult's mathematical knowledge that he or she cannot attribute to the children of current concern. They are based on the mathematics *of* the children of current concern as well as other children. Leushina does not explicitly distinguish between the mathematics *of* children and adult mathematical knowledge, so it is difficult to know the status of the substantive content presented in Chapters 9-12. It often seems that it is based on a logical analysis of adult mathematics rather than on an analysis of children's mathematics.

Of the other principles, the principle of conscious and active learning from the mastery of knowledge is of interest because, as Leushina says, it "is especially connected to the principle of developmental instruction. Its characteristic feature is that it applies less to instruction and more to learning—the child's conscious mastery of knowledge and skills during instruction" (p. 183). Interpretation of "conscious mastery" is very tricky. For example, from the perspective of a model of the types of items children can create and count, a child might be aware of only sensory signals in the visual channel and thereby create and count visual perceptual items (Steffe, von Glasersfeld, Richards, & Cobb, 1983). Sensory signals in the kinesthetic channel generated by motor activity in counting might be outside of the child's awareness. This presents a fundamental problem for the teacher of the child, for if she would insist on the child becoming aware of his or her movements as countable items that signify visual perceptual items, the likely outcome would be frustration for both. On the other hand, if she waits for the child to independently isolate his or her motor acts as countable items in the sense indicated, then there is no effort required by the teacher, and the principle essentially does not apply. So, just how the principle is to be interpreted is not as clear as it might be. One interpretation is that a teacher can encourage a child to become aware of a particular item or way of proceeding. However, awareness is unavoidably the child's own business, and the teacher at most can be sensitive to those items that the child might become aware of in the near future. A characteristic of these items is that they be in the child's zone of proximal development where there is indication that the child is momentarily aware of these novel items of experience.

There are other issues that a close reading of the monograph will reveal. It is an interesting monograph and presents several points of view not found in the literature in North America. The readers should enjoy debating these issues, and I hope that some of them are moved to write detailed reactions for journals in mathematics education.

References

Bauersfeld, H., Krummheuer, G., & Voigt, J. (1985). Interactional theory of learning and teaching mathematics and related 'micro-ethnographical studies.' In *Foundation and methodology of the discipline mathematics education (Didactics of mathematics)*. Bielefeld: Universität Bielefeld, Institute für Didatik der Mathematik.

D'Ambrosio, U. (1986). Socio-cultural bases for mathematical education. In M. Carss (Ed.), *Proceedings of the fifth international congress on mathematical education*. Boston: Birkhäuser.

Piaget, J. (1964). Learning and development. In R. E. Ripple & V. N. Rockcastle (Eds.), *Piaget rediscovered: A report of the conference on cognitive studies and curriculum development*. Ithaca: Cornell University.

Sinclair, H. (1988). Foreword. In L. P. Steffe, P. Cobb, & E. von Glasersfeld, *Construction of arithmetical meanings and strategies*. New York: Springer Verlag.

Steffe, L. P. (1988). Learning mathematics of children. In M. J. Behr & J. Hiebert (Eds.), *Research agenda in mathematics education: Number concepts and operations in the middle grades*. Reston: NCTM.

Steffe, L. P. & Cobb, P. (1988). *Construction of arithmetical meanings and strategies*. New York: Springer Verlag.

Steffe, L. P., & von Glasersfeld, E. (1988). On the construction of the counting scheme. In L. P. Steffe, P. Cobb, & E. von Glasersfeld, *Construction of arithmetical meanings and strategies*. New York: Springer Verlag.

Steffe, L. P., von Glasersfeld, E., Richards, J., & Cobb, P. (1983). *Children's counting types: Philosophy, theory, and application*. New York: Praeger Scientific.

Treffers, A. (1987). *Three dimensions: A model of goal and theory description in mathematics instruction—The Wiskobas project*. Boston: D. Reidel.

von Glasersfeld, E. (1981). An attentional model for the conceptual construction of units and number. *Journal for Research in Mathematics Education, 12*, 33-96.

Preface to the Soviet Edition

The 24th Congress of the Communist Party of the Soviet Union has set a crucial task for the science and practice of education and the entire Soviet community: to provide for the comprehensive development of the upcoming generation. The efforts of all Soviet educators, beginning with preschool teachers, should be directed toward this task.[1]

Presently, all children complete the eight-year school. In the next several years, all young people will also receive a complete secondary education. Naturally, the requirements of a school graduate have been changing as well as the goals of instruction. The objective of providing well-rounded personality development is now a feasible and concrete goal.

Mathematics teaching in the elementary school previously amounted to training in computational skills and memorizing the rules for performing arithmetic operations, without mastering the theoretical underpinnings. This method of teaching mathematics did not provide children with the necessary development in mathematics and logic. For example, the curricula for the upper grades did not treat such essential topics for modern education as probability theory, mathematical statistics, and linear programming.

Important elements in comprehensive personality development include mental development, mastery of techniques and methods of mental activity, improvement of cognitive abilities, a certain store of knowledge, and the ability to use this knowledge to solve problems. The immense scientific and technological changes that have occurred over the last few decades have necessitated mental development, improvement of cognitive abilities, and training in rational thinking (accuracy, exactness, clarity, etc.).

Problems of automated production and in computer modeling require of workers in many different fields rigorous and consistent analysis of the processes they are studying. Thus, the habit of logical argumentation is a practical necessity. The study of mathematics is responsible for developing logical thought to the highest degree. The mathematical style of thinking is characterized by laconism, accurate parsing of a line of reasoning, logical consistency, precision of thought, and the ability to use symbols.

A new approach to the content and methods of mathematics education is needed—especially for the coming generation. It is no accident that scholars and teachers today are concerned with reforming the school mathematics curriculum.

Two points have received particular attention in restructuring the curriculum. The first is elimination of the partitions between the individual mathematics disciplines, "constructing a unified mathematics course, instilling it with new content, choosing function and transformation as the central ideas, and including elements of analytic geometry and mathematical analysis" [6:4]. The second is emphasis on applying mathematics to physics and other sciences, since applied mathematics has taken on increased importance lately in fields such as technology, economics, defense, linguistics, biology, psychology, education, and medicine.

Modern science regards mathematics as the study of various structures. The idea of "identifying a restricted set of classes of structures that pertain in all areas of mathematics, establishing their hierarchy, and describing and representing them concisely and expressively by models (or patterns) that are simple and accessible to perception" [6:5] has taken root.

The study of the various structures of mathematics (e.g., algebraic structure—above all the group, and the structure of an ordered or partially ordered set) has attracted particular attention from psychologists and educators. Educators have found that the thought mechanisms are quite similar in children and adults, as has been convincingly shown by Jean

Piaget and Bärbel Inhelder [8]. It turns out that children can learn mathematical concepts at an earlier age than was previously believed.

Fundamental questions concerning the teaching of mathematics have been the topic of discussion at many international seminars in England, Belgium, Switzerland, France, Luxembourg,and other countries; participants have included scholars, mathematics teachers, engineers, logicians, psychologists, historians, and other specialists from socialist and capitalist countries.

In 1962, an International Symposium on Teaching Mathematics in the School was held in Hungary on the initiative of the Hungarian government and with UNESCO assistance. The conclusions and recommendations of this symposium deserve serious attention. It was demonstrated that studies in various countries have shown that elementary set operations and the concepts of relation and function can be used in the school curriculum, beginning with children twelve years of age (and sometimes with younger children).

The International Symposium has stimulated further experimental work on curriculum development for schools in various countries. In the Soviet Union, on the basis of experimental work done over a number of years, such a curriculum for teaching mathematics in schools for all children, beginning in grade one, has already been created by the Academy of Pedagogical Sciences of the USSR. Prominent research mathematicians participated in the development of the curriculum. It was introduced as the mandatory curriculum for the elementary grades as of September 1, 1969.

In order to understand the features of the new curriculum and the significance of seeking new ways of teaching, we must first briefly describe with the nature of the old curriculum and its deficiencies.

Arithmetic Teaching in Grade One of Elementary School Prior to the New Curricula

In the first years after the Russian Revolution, teachers began to reconsider teaching methods as they sought ways to create a new school system. Unfortunately, many elements were introduced hastily into the schools at that time, and much was borrowed uncritically from foreign literature.

A new textbook was published for levels I and II of vocational schools, *Lively Numbers, Lively Thoughts and Hands at Work*. The authors E. Gorbunov-Posadov and I. Tsunzer wrote that they were attempting to construct teaching according to the development and the inclinations of beginning students:

> The investigative spirit is alive in the child; he has an intrinsic organic need to independently find, create, experiment, think, advance, apply the knowledge he has acquired to what he is doing, and work with his hands. The child tries to what is relevant to his life at a given moment into his work or his play. Accordingly, an introduction to the rudiments of mathematics should be based on the child's actual activity—he should be an active contributor during instruction, not a passive spectator [4:3].

Since play is the child's basic activity, the authors proposed using play techniques to teach children in school.

> The child lives by playing; play is his occupation, his work. We provide him with a whole series of games requiring calculation and mental acuity. We believe that a child will learn to count better by playing, that in this way he will best learn about numbers and operations on them. We would like to translate the greater part of elementary mathematics instruction into this kind of self-instruction through lively assignments and play [4:4].

The problem of developing children's mathematical concepts was posed, but the authors still understood the development itself to be self-development.

In the 1930's, along with industrialization of the nation, it became necessary to raise the general educational level of the people. The Central Committee of the Communist Party of the Soviet Union on July 25, 1939 adopted a resolution entitled "On Universal Compulsory Elementary Schooling." This compelled educators and methodologists to develop systematic manuals for teaching children in school. The Central Committee of the CPSU addressed two resolutions to teachers: "On Elementary and Secondary School" (September 5, 1931) and "On School Curricula and Conditions in Elementary and Secondary School" (August 25, 1932). A number of arithmetic courses were created to implement the goals set by the Party in the 1930's.

Soviet methodologists continued developing the progressive line in arithmetic teaching established by the classic figures in Russian education. Rather than simply counting, children were taught arithmetic operations and calculations, since they come to school with the ability to count and with elementary concepts of number. Therefore, the school's task was to systematize the elementary concepts of number on the basis of the abilities the children had already acquired. The process of developing concepts of number was regarded as protracted and highly complex.

The Development of Numerical Concepts in Early Childhood, by K. F. Lebedintsev, had a considerable influence at the time. By observing his own children, Lebedintsev concluded that young children develop the concept of numbers up to five on the basis of distinguishing groups of objects and not at all in the order of the natural numbers. Thus, recognizing a group of two objects and labeling it with the number *two* precedes the naming of *one*. Children distinguish a group consisting of two pairs of objects earlier than a group of three objects. "By virtue of these circumstances, we can conclude that the first numerical concepts emerge in the child chiefly through the perception of small groups of homogeneous objects that occur in the child's environment (eyes, hands, feet, the legs of a table, etc.)" [5:33].

Some methodologists have adopted Lebedintsev's point of view. But most have believed that to develop numerical concepts in children, it is important not only to provide for the perception of groups, but also to teach children to count.

In addition to counting objects, many authors have recommended introducing measurement from the very beginning. They have developed the idea of D. Galanin, a pre-Revolutionary Russian methodologist who stressed the value of measurement for mastering the concept of quantity, which is not present when the child counts individual objects. If we take five glassfuls of water and pour the water into one vessel, a new whole is formed—a pitcher containing five glassfuls. This whole cannot be separated into individual counting units in the way that five pencils can. The comparison of quantities serves as a visual picture when numbers are compared. By comparing the lengths of two segments, we can see at once that one segment is one marking longer than the other, and consequently five is one unit greater than four.

Without dwelling in detail in the differences in teaching methodologies for arithmetic among the different authors, we can make certain generalizations.

1. Most Soviet authors take the view that first-graders must be instructed in two basic areas: first counting, then computation techniques (in studying addition and subtraction).

2. Many authors have regarded it as essential to teach children about numbers and their composition with the children, as preparation for the transition from counting to computation. Some authors have recommended restricting the study of number composition to the first five numbers, and then moving on to the study of operations (I. N. Kavun, N. S. Popova, and to some extent G. B. Polyak). Others have proposed prefacing the study of operations with the composition of the first ten numbers (A. S. Pchelko and V. L. Emenov, among others).

But the authors never explained how and why the composition of numbers should be studied, and they have not always argued along the same lines. For instance, some have indicated that a number can be decomposed in various ways into two, three, or four terms (Emenov), while others have confined themselves to two terms (Polyak). Why a number needed to be decomposed and what limits should be set in the study of its composition remained unclear—theoretical arguments were not adduced. The theoretical and practical value of this preliminary study of number composition (prior to the study of operations) was also unclear.

Some authors have regarded the study of number as a preparation for learning addition and subtraction. Others have seen it as a prerequisite for developing computation techniques. Still others have found in it a means of forming a clear notion of number. A fourth group has maintained that the study of number composition has value in reviewing and systematizing of the rudimentary concepts of the first five numbers, which the children know when they start school.

Thus, a number of issues are unresolved. The decomposition and the composition of a number are distinct operations. Even a small child can decompose a set of objects into smaller groups, but that does not mean that he can compose the number (see Ya. I. Petrov, E. I. Korzakova, and others.).

3. Many methodologists have connected the study of number composition with numerical figures (geometrical figures with a particular number of sides), although there has been considerable discussion about the value of such figures since the beginning of the 20th century.

It has been asked why such importance is ascribed to numerical figures, while from an early age children are surrounded by a multitude of various sets of objects arranged in different forms. Many opponents of simultaneous (integral) perception of numerical figures have pointed out that the perception of quantity is replaced by the perception of the shape of a figure. The authors of methodological handbooks have side-stepped all of these debatable points in silence.

4. A number of authors have ignored the development of the concepts of the set, the first concepts of number, and younger children's learning to count before school. Thus, the methodology of teaching arithmetic in school has lacked a foundation, since there was no continuity with the children's earlier life, and the idea of developing counting skills and the rudimentary concept of number was not pursued. Therefore, it remained obscure what was good or bad in the level of children's preparation as they entered school. The authors accepted how children were trained

without making demands on either the preschool institutions or the parents. They assumed that teaching the children to count and studying numbers and their composition for two or three weeks in school would liquidate the profound defects developed prior to school, and that children could move on successfully to systematic coursework.

5. All authors have stressed the value of teaching children to count. But none of the methodological handbooks has demonstrated the essence of this instruction. Certain authors, such as A. S. Pchelko, have attempted to present certain criteria. Pchelko recommended beginning to teach children with counting off, rather than with ordinary counting, asking the children to make up sets by gradually adding one object to another. His basic idea consisted in helping the children to understand the significance of the total number in counting—in showing that a new element is added. For these purposes Pchelko, G. B. Polyak, and others proposed counting off in the following form: 1 cube, 2 cubes, 3 cubes, etc.—that is, naming the objects in order to subsequently move on to counting without naming the objects. The question arises as to how justified this method of teaching is in a school where the entering pupils have (for the most part) already learned to count. Moreover, the method does not match how young children understand. Studies have shown that for children, the total number does not correspond to the number of objects counted.

6. Considerably greater unanimity has been observed in methodologists' views on methods of teaching the arithmetic operations of addition and subtraction and, most importantly, on teaching computation techniques.

The overwhelming majority of methodologists have considered it essential to study addition and subtraction simultaneously (I. N. Kavun, N. S. Popova, A. S. Pchelko). But even here there have been some differences. The methodological handbook edited by V. L. Emenov recommends covering addition and subtraction separately, while G. B. Polyak's handbook urges separate study of addition and subtraction only for numbers through five, with simultaneous study for the numbers between five and ten.

7. There have also been different points of view on whether to begin the study of operations with arithmetic problems or with numerical examples. Some authors have suggested beginning the study of operations and computation techniques with arithmetic problems on the grounds that the point of the arithmetic operation itself can be understood and mastered only through problems. Others have maintained that the techniques of computation are more easily learned through numerical examples, recommending that the study of operations and computation techniques start with examples and that computation techniques should be applied to problem-solving only when they have been learned.

Thus, we see that instruction for children in grade one, as well as in the entire elementary school, has been reduced to training in computation skills. The curricula themselves have pointed out that instruction in elementary arithmetic "is characterized by its practical orientation and by its concrete content."

The arithmetic course in the preparatory period was constructed concentrically, just as the methodologists in the late 19th and early 20th centuries did. This concentric organization was prompted by the acknowledgment that the realm of numbers should be expanded according to children's mental development and age-group potential. It was unnecessarily rigid to insist on the mastery of a particular skill within the confines of a narrow concentric circle. Inadequate mastery of the skills in one concentric circle impeded learning appropriate computation techniques in subsequent concentric circles.

The considerable atomizing effect of concentric circles impeded understanding of the essence of the decimal number system. Even third-graders had not mastered decimal places, since it is impossible to learn the decimal system when limited to just two places. As a rule, the children made many mistakes in the decimal subtraction of large numbers. These methodologists themselves have written about these mistakes.

Thus, it should be acknowledged that curricula have been too practical in their orientation, too concentric; they have consisted of too many levels and have applied an inadequate scientific standard to the material studied by the students. Moreover, traditional methodologies, which are oriented toward monotonous training in skills and memorization of tables, have not made arithmetic instruction interesting for children.

It has been suggested that the number of concentric circles should be reduced, or that they should be eliminated altogether, and that the theoretical level of arithmetic teaching in the elementary school should be improved. Thus, it is entirely natural that we must again review the curriculum and methods of teaching mathematics, starting with grade one, in view of the great progress in science and technology and the heavy demands made on the student's mental development.

Some Trends in the Reform of Mathematics Education in the Elementary Grades

Several trends have taken shape in the effort to reform mathematics education and create a new curriculum. One school has maintained that reform should be based on a fundamental change in the content of knowledge; another has insisted that revision and improvement of teaching methods is paramount. Among the debatable issues was the question of whether to begin instruction in grade one with pre-numerical studies, with various set operations, or with numbers and counting, as in the past.

Some investigators believed that grade one should include a *pre-numerical period of instruction*, to which considerable attention should be given. In this period, without resorting to numbers, first-graders would be introduced to such mathematical concepts as the *set, relations among the elements of a set, equality and inequality of sets*, and *operations with sets* (union, intersection, complement). Children would become acquainted with the concept of a *quantity*, with methods of comparing continuous and discrete quantities by measuring them with various "yardsticks," with notations for equality and inequality among quantities, and with letter and sign symbols. They would also be introduced to elementary algebraic operations, which generalize arithmetic operations. These investigators also attached considerable importance to teaching children about geometry. It was recommended that the number and counting in numbers be introduced only on the basis of the material in the pre-numerical period.

Other investigators and methodologists considered it impossible to ignore counting and number at the initial stage of instruction, since counting and numbers pervade our society. Beginning instruction with sets and ignoring numbers inevitably means setting up an artificial situation, since the children coming to school all count very well, as a rule. But teaching counting and numbers does not mean refusing to introduce algebraic concepts into the grade one curriculum.

These investigators have said that school must not only teach, but also develop the child's personality. Fundamental attention should be given to this point in the reform of school education, including grade one. Thus, for example, N. S. Popova has written that as the appearance of the concept of number in phylogeny led to reorganization of the approach to such concepts as *quantity* and *order*. The concepts have lost their independence, they have been "removed" by number, and they can no longer serve as a basis for forming mathematical concepts. Popova believes that there is no need to familiarize children with pre-arithmetical operations, since number itself contains quantitative and ordinal relations (the cardinal and ordinal value of numbers). It follows that instruction should begin with numbers and counting, with particular attention given to the development of conscious counting and full-fledged numerical concepts.

A group of scholars led by L. V. Zankov has principally worked on to developing the most efficient methods of promoting the development of active, precise, business-like thinking in students. This group sees the principal task of school instruction reform in reorganizing teachers' and students' attitudes and creating conditions for joyful study.

The various directions taken in the reform of mathematics education have been manifested in a number of books. Professor A. I. Markushevich, a member of the USSR Academy of Pedagogical Sciences, has developed a draft of a grade one curriculum. K. I. Neshkov and A. M. Pyshkalo, associate members of the USSR Academy of Pedagogical Sciences, have published a textbook based on their experimental work [7]. In the experimental curriculum included in this book, work in grade one is envisaged as starting with operations on sets. This section includes various exercises dealing with the operations of the union, intersection, and difference of two parts of a single set, as well as an introduction to the commutative and associative properties of the operations of union and intersection. Then students move on to counting sets and their subsets. They study written and printed digits, and practice determining and recording the numerical quantity of the union, intersection, and difference of two parts of a single set; they study the operations of addition and subtraction for numbers up to twenty. They learn about geometric figures and simple measurements; they study arithmetic operations on numbers up to 100.

Another direction is reflected in the book *What is New in First-Grade Arithmetic Instruction*, by L. V. Zankov [10]. Zankov lays out the basic principles in the design of a mathematics course and in the methods of teaching arithmetic. In his opinion, these principles will further students' general mental development and will provide for high-quality theoretical knowledge and practical skills.

Especially noteworthy is the work by a group of research psychologists at Moscow State University, which is reported in the book *The Formation of Knowledge and Abilities on the Basis of the Theory of Step-by-Step Mastery of Mental Operations* [2]. Other fine work by a group of research psychologists at the USSR Academy of Pedagogical Sciences Scientific Research Institute of Psychology is summarized in the book *Age Potential in the Mastery of Knowledge* [1].

The authors of these books have concentrated on reorganizing the very content of mathematics education in the elementary grades, on the most rational design for it, and on its psychological foundations. Experimental curricula for the regular mathematics course were based on this research, differing significantly from existing curricula "both in the breadth of the material and in the depth with which guiding principles are demonstrated" [3:71].

Proceeding from the need to improve the theoretical level of elementary school teaching, they propose a fundamentally different course design, starting with the initial stages of instruction, in which the theoretical assumptions would "provide the students with orientation in the new mathematical phenomena encountered in the course."

Advancing the principle of step-by-step development of mental operations and of basic types of orientation (a theory asserting that mental activity results from transferring external material actions onto the plane of reflection, and that reflection passes through a series of stages), the authors consider the creation of an orientation base for action to be exceedingly important. Above all, the specific aspect of the subject being studied should be revealed for the students, so that in their study of arithmetic they might confront "a new way of assessing things"—so that they might adopt a mediated approach to the everyday, empirical notions that they acquired before starting school. In the arithmetic course, basic concepts should be singled out which would characterize the object being studied in a new and scientific way and which would lead in students to new evaluations of quantitative phenomena. The authors regard measure as such a constructive concept for elementary arithmetic. Measure allows the development of a mediated evaluation of quantitative relations. The concept of the unit is introduced on the basis of measure. "The unit is what is measured off and is equal to its measure" [9:83]. In these conditions a unit begins to be perceived through its relation to measure, rather than by juxtaposing one object and a series of objects. Measuring becomes the fundamental form of activity, and every number functions as a result of measuring, rather than simply counting separate entities. The concept of measure is learned through measuring, and the concept of the unit is learned on the basis of it. "The empirical approach to evaluating quantitative relations is thereby supplanted by a theoretical one" [9:83]. The concept of measure also fosters the concept of the decimal number system, in which each new decimal place is a new measure in counting. *Ten* functions as a new measure that the previous measure goes into ten times. The correlation among the places is regarded as a correlation among measures. The students understand the correlation of the various measures—the transitions from one measure to another.

Mastery of the concept of measure permits the student to comprehend the concepts of number and operations on numbers.

The next principle advanced by the authors is the deductive principle of instruction. "The best orientation in a subject can be achieved by studying general rules—the basic principles of phenomena." However, mastery of these principles is possible at the elementary stages of instruction only if they are presented in a materialized form that provides for action. For example, the rule for forming the natural sequence of numbers by means of $n + 1$, where n is a given natural number, can be represented as a staircase where the relations at each level produce the relations between the numbers. Using this model of the natural number sequence, the students learn the composition of numbers, numeration, and the principle of the decimal system.

Since children best learn the principles of the decimal system with large numbers, a linear, rather than a concentric curriculum design is required. This design makes it possible to immediately proceed to the *general principle of the operations of addition and subtraction* without singling out techniques that depend on the size and structure of a number. This general principle of operation functions for material of various types. Thus, children can learn complex concepts by modeling.

With the inductive design, however, an operation is connected with inessential attributes of the same phenomena, and partial generalizations occur. This inevitably gives rise to the need for constant re-learning.

All operations on models must be accompanied by verbal commentary—by explanation of what the student is doing and why. As the model is mastered, the verbal commentary is removed, and only the "verbal scheme of the operation" remains. Verbal formulation of an operation should occur during the operation, not after the operation is finished. Reasoning aloud promotes an awareness of the operation itself. At first the reasoning is detailed, but as the operation is mastered it should be shortened by curtailing less essential operations, which can be rapidly restored if necessary.

The authors believe it is possible to introduce terminology and various conventional symbols at once. Proceeding from the principles outlined above, these authors have developed an experimental curriculum for teaching arithmetic.

These are the typical features of the old curriculum and the basic trends in the search for new methods of teaching mathematics to children. Research in this area is continuing; many of these questions require further and deeper study and testing in schools and kindergartens for all children.

The New First-Grade Mathematics Curriculum (Approved by the USSR Ministry of Education)

A new mathematics curriculum for grade one was introduced on September 1, 1969. The curriculum was the result of a great deal of scrupulous work by the Elementary Instruction Sector of the Scientific Research Institute for Teaching Methods of the USSR Academy of Pedagogical Sciences, under the direction of S. M. Yazykov. Research associates of the Sector, N. A. Menchinskaya, and members of the Department of Pedagogy at Leningrad's A. I. Herzen Pedagogical Institute, under the direction of A. A. Lyublinskaya, were involved in its development and testing and in the writing of textbooks and manuals. A special role was played by N. A. Menchinskaya in providing psychological foundation for the curriculum.

The new curriculum is based on numerous studies conducted in rural and urban schools in various provinces and regions of the country. Collectives made up of teachers, psychologists, and methodologists took part in extensive testing of the preliminary draft of the curriculum. During this experimental work, there were systematic observations of the work done by students (good and poor ones) and of their performance on homework assignment. Mistakes, difficulties, and success in the work done by teachers and pupils were analyzed.

What are the requirements and principles by which the new curriculum has been designed? What should preschool children know? The curriculum reflects the immense task set by the 24th Congress of the Communist Party of the Soviet Union (CPSU) for the entire Soviet community: provide the nation with young people well-trained and versed in theory. For this task to be accomplished we must:

1. Reorganize the elementary school-for-skills into an elementary school-for-development.

2. Develop in the students, beginning with grade one, an interest in cognitive activity and cognitive abilities; equip the students with a system of mental and practical operations; develop a conscious attitude toward reality. The student should be trained as a thinking citizen and an active member of society.

3. Strive for students to internalize what they know. The student should know how to obtain new knowledge on his own and use it in real life. For this, he must be taught techniques and methods of mental activity both in schoolwork and in extracurricular work.

4. Teach students to substantiate their knowledge in theory and to apply proofs. To do so, they must master various mental operations (analysis, synthesis, comparison, generalization, classification, seriation).

Techniques of mental activity do not become automatic like skills; they are developed over a long period of time in exercises of varying content and degree of difficulty. They are demonstrated by the ability to use previously acquired abilities to solve problems of greater complexity and under different conditions. These are the principles in the design of the new curriculum.

What is the content of the new curriculum? Children are to achieve a high theoretical level in mathematical knowledge. Mathematical knowledge (quantitative, spatial, and temporal) must be mastered in its interrelationships and in functional dependencies (the number of units of measure depends on the size of the units when a certain quantity is measured; distance depends on time; and so forth). Thus, the former arithmetic course is replaced by a composite course called "Mathematics," consisting of arithmetic, algebra, and geometry.

Let us consider the basic content of the grade one curriculum from the standpoint of continuity with the preschool curriculum. The basic line of continuity is that the grade one curriculum at present combines teaching and instructing children with development of their cognitive abilities, which is also typical of the preschool curriculum. In the grade one curriculum the theoretical level of education is raised. Teachers set about developing students' ability to apply their knowledge in practice and, accordingly, to drill the corresponding abilities and skills. All of this requires mental preparation for children in preschool.

In the area of elementary mathematical knowledge, children must be prepared to perform observations and identify the essential part of a task, to generalize and systematize their accumulated knowledge, to use it in their everyday activity and play, and to master very simple concepts.

The school curriculum begins with the study of the first ten numbers and simple geometric figures. The concept of a natural number is developed on the basis of practical operations with sets of objects. At the same time, children develop some important generalizations (e.g., the principle for forming each successive natural number, the relation between any natural number and all the preceding and following numbers, etc.). The study of addition and subtraction up to ten is based on the children's knowledge of the properties of the natural number sequence $n + 1$. Then, methods of adding (or subtracting) a number by means of its parts or by transposing terms are studied. Thus, children are immediately provided with various methods of adding and subtracting numbers up to ten on the basis of their knowledge of number composition and their ability to find one of two addends, given the sum and the other addend: $9 - 6 = 3$ because $9 = 6 + 3$, and if one of the addends is taken away from the sum, we are left with the other addend.

As they study methods of computation, children learn the various mathematical expressions. For example, they learn to write and read such simple expressions as "the sum (or difference) of two numbers" ($5 + 4$ and $6 + 4$; $7 + 2$ and $7 - 2$). Comparing these notations, the students perceive basic principles of computations, and thereby learn what sign to place between them—greater than, less than, or equal to:

$$5 + 4 < 6 + 4; 7 + 2 > 7 - 2.$$

As they gain practice in comparing various types of expressions, such as 6 + 1 and 6 - 1 or 4 + 6 and 6 + 4, children become more profoundly aware of the meaning of the arithmetical operations. This increases their interest in mathematics and develops their powers of observation, their need to validate judgments, and their habit of checking their work.

During this period, students become familiar with arithmetic word problems. As they solve problems on finding sums and remainders, they analyze the numeric relations contained in the text of a problem and choose the necessary operations. Problems on increasing (or decreasing) a number by several units are also encountered at this stage, with the problems expressed in both direct and indirect form. Problems on finding an unknown term are also studied, with the letter x introduced for the first time ($x + 3 = 8$). This form of notation makes it possible for the connection between the quantities that are given in a problem and the unknown quantity (for instance, between the sum and one of the addends) to be represented in an abstract form to the students. In this way, children learn to write any problem as an equation. For example, consider the following direct problem. There were 7 glassfuls of water in a pitcher, and 5 glassfuls were poured out. How many glassfuls were left in the pitcher? Or the inverse problem: several glassfuls of water were in a pitcher; 5 glassfuls were poured out, and 1 glassful remained. How many glassfuls of water were left in the pitcher?

During the period when they are studying the first ten numbers, students also become familiar with geometric material, which is considered in close connection with the arithmetic material. Even in the first lessons, various types of triangles and circles are used as visual aids to counting. Then polygons are introduced and the students count the sides, angles, and vertices and learn some of the properties of geometric figures. During this period, students learn to measure segments in centimeters; they measure and compare segments. This is one of the visual foundations for the comparison of numbers. Seventy hours are allotted for the topics "Numeration" and "Addition and Subtraction up to 10"; 30 of these hours are for "Numeration and Simple Figures" and 40 for "Addition and Subtraction."

The restructuring of mathematics teaching in school has necessitated a review of the preparation provided before students start and a restructuring of the preschool mathematics curriculum. This required, on the one hand, a thorough study of the mental potential of preschool children and, on the other, investigation of whether they could gain a deeper mastery of mathematical material, with a view toward the overall development that is needed for success in school work.

These studies began to be conducted in the 1950's at the Scientific Research Institute for Preschool Education of the RSFSR Academy of Pedagogical Sciences (later in the USSR Academy of Pedagogical Sciences), at the Scientific Research Institute of Psychology of the Ukrainian SSR, and in various departments of preschool education, including the one at the A. I. Herzen Pedagogical Institute in Leningrad. The "Preschool Education Curriculum" is based on these studies and on the experience of the best teachers.

A student at a pedagogical institute—a future organizer of preschool education—should not only understand the requirements of the existing "Education Curriculum"; he should also have a clear picture of the prospects for its future development. Two or three years will pass before the student in a preschool education department will himself begin to teach the methodology of imparting elementary mathematical knowledge to students in a pedagogical secondary school; they, in turn, will begin working as preschool teachers only after another two years, and their first students will go on to school four years later. This means that the student needs to see prospects for the development of the discipline eight to ten years ahead. Therefore the curriculum and the textbook for the methodology of developing elementary mathematical concepts in preschool children cannot be oriented merely toward today's practices.

This is why the student will find in this volume not only what and how to teach children when instructing them in mathematics on the basis of the existing "Education Curriculum," but also indications of its subsequent improvement according to scientific research and the achievements of practical experience.

Since the discipline is constantly developing and society's requirements are moving ahead, the "Education Curriculum" cannot be hard and
fast; it will be improved even further. The duty of preschool workers who
have a higher education is not only to understand the principles governing
the development of the discipline, but also to participate in every possible
way in devising solutions to new problems and introducing scientific data
into practical work.

1

Aspects of Teaching Preschool Children the Elements of Mathematics

Instruction and Development of Children

A child's personality is formed and his mental development takes place in the process of various activities. From the very beginning of his life the child is surrounded by people who influence his development and with whom he establishes emotional contact. The child is also surrounded by a multitude of things that possess various properties and qualities. Studies show that even infants have great potential to learn about their environment and analyze the objects they perceive. This enables them to adapt to the constantly changing components of their activity (feeding, for example).

Children start at an early age to develop notions of the world around them during the process of perceptual and productive activity: various attributes and properties of the world of objects—color, shape, quantity; the spatial arrangement and the number of objects; and relations among people (to the child himself, to one another, to the things around them). They gradually build up the stock of sensory experience that will be the basis for forming elementary mathematical notions and the first concepts.

The question arises whether children should be given an opportunity to develop spontaneously, or whether they should be guided in the process of getting to know the world around them. The problem of instruction and development is still unresolved in many countries. It is no accident that highly animated discussions of this problem arose at the 18th International Congress of Psychologists (1966).

Until recently, bourgeois pedagogy has taken the position that children are to develop spontaneously. As a rule, the age-group potential of children has been rigidly defined, and school curricula have been set up in strict conformity with that potential. But the burgeoning of science and technology has disclosed the limitations and the incompleteness of these curricula. It is necessary to raise the level of school education, and this means reviewing children's potential at various age levels.

The development of preschool children has always been regarded in bourgeois pedagogy as a spontaneous process, and the need for strict curricula for this age has been denied. But these views conflict with society's requirements, and in many countries broad experimentation was begun, primarily involving the content of education. As a result of these experiments, the experts unanimously concluded that the cognitive potential of children, including those of preschool age, is considerably more extensive than had been previously supposed. Thus arose a new question: "How could this potential be used most efficiently?" The problem of instruction and development had to be considered in a new way.

Soviet psychology and pedagogy, which is based on Marxist-Leninist doctrine, regards development as *the process of mastering the social and historical experience of mankind.* Mastery of the knowledge developed by mankind promotes a restructuring of all of the mental functions, raising the child to a new developmental level. The conclusion follows that *instruction should precede in advance of development.* In teaching, one must always be oriented toward what children can do with the aid of adults, under their supervision, rather than toward what they are capable of doing by themselves.

The well-known Soviet psychologist L. S. Vygotskii has stressed that the orientation must always be "toward the zone of proximal development." He wrote: "... we can take account not only of the developmental process that is finished today, not only of its already completed cycles, not only of the maturation processes that have already been undergone, but also of the processes that are now arising—the ones that are just maturing or just developing" [5:448].

Instruction thus *guides development, acts as a source of development.* This view is held by Soviet psychologists and educators and is in opposition to the views held by representatives of other schools of thought, such as the American psychologist Edward Thorndike, for whom instruction and development were identical, and the Swiss psychologist Jean Piaget who separated the two processes, believing that instruction does not influence the spontaneous course of development.

Instruction should not be identified with development because each of these interrelated processes has its own basic principles. L. S. Vygotskii writes: "It would be a great error to suppose that these external laws governing the structure of the educational process coincide completely with the internal laws governing the developmental processes that are engendered by instruction" [5:270]. A comparatively long time passes between the first exposure to knowledge and mastery of it. "The child masters certain skills in a given subject before he learns to apply them consciously and voluntarily" [5:269]. An internal mental process occurs in the period between ignorance and knowledge—that is, development occurs.

The rapid growth of science and technology has confronted education with yet another problem. The school curricula cannot be reorganized as rapidly as science develops, and will inevitably lag behind. Therefore, students must learn to acquire knowledge on their own, both during their studies and after finishing school. They must be trained to follow the development of science and technology. Consequently, it is important that instruction from the early years onward not only communicate preexisting knowledge but also develop children's mental abilities. Hence we conclude that we must use developmental methods of instruction, which promote the formation of such mental operations as analysis, synthesis, comparison, abstraction, generalization, classification, and seriation (to name a few) and the development of cognitive interests, observation, and discourse.

It should not be forgotten that thought can develop fruitfully only on the basis of learning. P. P. Blonshii, one of the most prominent Soviet psychologists, has written "... And if there is no [learning], then there is no basis for the development of thought, and the learning cannot mature to the proper extent" [1:250].

We know that arbitrary information can be learned by a child through memorization, without thorough comprehension. This is why Soviet pedagogy and psychology emphasize the necessity of *conscious* learned. The knowledge that is acquired merely by memory is superficial and is not used in life. Students who have acquired their knowledge only by memory are always ready to respond since they never subject it to any doubt. Such students are usually quite surprised when gaps are found in their responses. But if students have acquired their knowledge consciously, they subject it to self-verification before responding. On this case P. P. Blonshii writes: "Learning without verification is mere memory work, occurring arbitrarily; learning that is controlled by self-verification is memory working under the control of thought" [1:23]. Therefore, in supervising development during instruction, we must try to see that students' attention is directed not only to the content of the material to be mastered, but also to the methods of execution.

The teacher's task is to organize the children's activity, for it is only in activity that the child's development occurs. When children encounter a certain problem, they have a need to solve it. But they can do so only after mastering new methods of action, behavior, and thought. A conflict arises between their need and their potential, between the known and the unknown. This conflict is the motivating force in development. Thus, *instruction influences the child's mental development, through activity directed by the teacher.*

Many studies have been devoted to the problem of children's mental development in the past decade. Of particular interest for the methodology of teaching the elements of mathematics to children are studies conducted at the Ukrainian SSR Scientific Research Institute of Psychology under the direction of G. S. Kostyuk. These studies show that preschool children achieve higher levels in distinguishing attributes of objects (color, shape, size) if they are instructed than they otherwise achieve. Children also successfully master the operation of seriation, learning the relative size of each element in a series (larger than the preceding one and smaller than the subsequent one). This relativity principle is transferred to other modes (quantity, sounds, etc.).

Through instruction, children five or six years of age successfully develop the concept of number; quantity is abstracted from all of the other spatial-qualitative attributes of objects. They develop the ability to see and establish relations between sets and subsets, and classes and subclasses, as well as the ability to prove their judgments and conclusions. Children pass more rapidly from concrete to abstract conceptual thought; they develop the thought operations essential for mastering scientific concepts.

All of the psychological studies done in the Soviet Union provide persuasive evidence that qualitative changes in the child's mental development occur during instruction. G. S. Kostyuk writes:

> Instruction not only accelerates children's passage from lower to higher structures of intellectual activity. It is a necessary condition for their formation. New structures are thus not merely introduced from without—they are created during instruction from previously formed structures according to patterns embodied in the social experience learned by the students. In this process, external stimulation always operates through the students' internal activity [4:79].

Thus, studies by Soviet psychologists offer convincing proof that instruction plays a decisive role in children's development. It is important, then, that teaching methodology be carefully developed so that it provides not only for the communication of knowledge, but also for the improvement of thought operations.

Unique Aspects of Teaching the Elements of Mathematical Knowledge to Young Children

Even in early childhood, children become familiar with collections of objects, with a set of sounds and movements, perceiving them with different analyzers (visual, auditory, etc.). They compare these collections and distinguish them according to quantity. During the process of instruction, children learn methods of establishing the equality and inequality of sets and learn to name quantities with numbers. At first they develop a notion of an indefinite quantity of elements, and then a notion of a set as an integral unity. This gives rise to interest in comparing sets and in determining more precisely the quantity of elements in them; with time, children acquire counting skills and the concept of number. All of this occurs in practical activity directed by adults that has the distinctive character of educational play.

Children also begin early to distinguish objects by size, color, and shape, by spatial arrangement, and by other attributes. By imitating adults, they try to measure objects in a primitive fashion, first placing some objects on others, then by sight or with the aid of ordinary measuring devices.

Thus, all of the prerequisites are met so that children, by relying on sense-effective perception, can learn not only to recognize various quantities, but also to represent their perceptions and ideas properly in words, using appropriate designations, such as *larger-smaller* (for quantity), *wider-narrower*, *taller-shorter*, *thicker-thinner*, distinguishing these linear changes from changes in total volume (*more-less*, *large-small*). This sort of differentiation is entirely accessible to preschool children when there is suitable adult supervision, as shown by R. L. Berezina, V. K. Kotyrlo, T. V. Lavrent'eva, Z. E. Lebedeva, E. V. Proskur, and others.

As soon as children begin to move about by themselves, they become actively involved with space and spatial relations among objects: first they approach (not without some difficulty) objects that interest them, and then they move away from them. It turns out that some objects are in front of them, while others are behind them or to the left or right.

Training allows the toddler to gain an early understanding of such words as *nearer* and *farther*. Children also orient themselves in a practical way in the spatial arrangement of objects, and adult assistance helps them to determine their position verbally, first in relation to themselves and then in relation to other objects (the teddy bear is to the right of the doll, but the bunny rabbit is to her left).

In time children develop an elementary notion of near and far space, although still a very concrete one (the garden where they go for walks is near, but Daddy's work is very far away). Relying on concrete notions such as these, as a result of personal experience and training by adults, children gradually arrive at broader generalizations; in the older preschool period time becomes a measure of space ("The Black Sea is so far away that you have to go by train or fly in a plane").

As they operate with objects, children soon begin to understand their spatial correlations as well: they put handkerchiefs in their pockets, they seat dolls at the table, they put teddy bears on the sofa, they sit down between Mommy and Daddy, they take coats down from hangers. Children borrow prepositions and adverbs to reflect the spatial relations between things from the speech of those around them, but the generalized significance of these prepositions and adverbs receives special attention and comprehension only as a result of instruction.

The entire everyday routine of children and adults is the precondition for children to develop a sense of time and the ability to use the corresponding terminology: [it is] *time*, [it is] *early, now, later*. This vocabulary of temporal terminology undergoes intensive development during children's interaction and activity throughout their early and preschool years. The toddler begins to be interested in the meaning of the words *yesterday, today,* and *tomorrow*, which enables the adult to introduce the toddler to the *fluidity, duration,* and *periodicity* of time—that is, to develop a *sense of time*.

Learning the meanings of words promotes children's ability to generalize the properties of objects (for any word is a generalization, to some extent). Moreover, children do not perceive objects and their properties and relations passively; rather, they influence them actively, transform them, and deal with them in time and space.

Thus, the source of elementary mathematical notions is the actual surrounding reality, which children come to know during their diversified activity, in their associations with adults and under their instructive supervision.

Without teaching, many facts and phenomena or properties of objects would remain outside the child's field of vision and perception. But instruction in daily life is episodic and cannot encompass all children simultaneously. Furthermore, it cannot provide for systematizing the knowledge that is acquired. For children's mathematical development, however, it is very important that all of their notions and concepts about quantity and number, notions of magnitude, shape, time, and space, be given in a definite system and sequence.

N. K. Krupskaya stated that: "mathematics is a chain of concepts: if one tiny link drops out, what follows will be unclear" [3:697]. Regardless of how little knowledge of mathematics children acquire before starting school, it should become gradually more complex, with a view toward what can and should be presented at any given stage in the children's development. This is why instruction through lessons is the fundamental and principal means of developing children's mathematical notions. Ordered notions and properly-formed elementary concepts, like thinking ability developed at the proper time, serve as a guarantee of successful future schoolwork.

Sensory Development—The Sensory Basis for Children's Mental and Mathematical Development

Sensory processes underlie small children's cognition of the qualitative and quantitative attributes of objects and phenomena. Toddlers come to know the qualities and properties of an object through their practical activities: they seem to trace its shape and size with their eye movements;

they feel and inspect a shape or material with their hands. These operations of investigating or studying an object are called perceptual operations. They are functionally connected with children's practical activity—their play, work, or studies.

"The dresser is behind you," the child is told. "But where is it *behind*—where my back is?" The child attempts to define this more precisely, backing up against the dresser in order to feel concretely and get to know the object's spatial position in relation to behind.

"Find the toys that are shaped like this triangle." Children outline the triangle with their fingers, investigating its shape, and then they look for an object that is analogous to this shape, carefully "studying" it with eye and hand movements.

"Place one mushroom on top of each of the pictures on the card that shows mushrooms." And the child inspects them on the card, first poking a finger at each of the pictures, as if to show himself where these pictures are. "You have to lay out the mushrooms from left to right with your right hand—this way," and the teacher shows him how. The child moves his right finger along the card, from left to right, investigating the suggested route.

Numerous facts about similar perceptual operations testify that sensory processes underlie the development of the first mathematical notions. A comparison (by shape, size, quantity) occurs in perceptual operations—a contrasting with what has already occurred in the child's past experience. Therefore, it is highly important to organize the accumulation of experience to teach the child to make comparisons using socially significant standards and the most efficient methods of operation.

The operation of establishing a one-to-one correspondence is the basis of comparison in mathematics. It is also the sensory basis for the development of children's counting activity. Studies and teachers' observations have shown that it is only in the actual activity of comparing different concrete quantities—both continuous and discontinuous—by contrasting the elements of one quantity with the elements of another, that the child comes to recognize that the qualities are equal or unequal. For example, in comparing a row of red circles with a row of blue ones and contrasting the elements of one set with the elements of the other, the child arrives at a conclusion: there are more red circles and fewer blue ones.

Comparing two line segments in length by placing one segment on the other or measuring the length in some arbitrary units, the child determines that they are equal or unequal. And if divisions have been marked off on the segments, the child indicates how many more (or fewer) divisions one segment has than the other segment when comparing the two.

Since the experience and knowledge of preschool children is still extremely limited, instruction proceeds primarily in an inductive manner: first concrete knowledge is acquired, with the aid of an adult, and then it is generalized into rules and principles. However, this method, although essential and important for the mental development of young children, also has certain drawbacks: children do not know how to go beyond the limits of the isolated facts and examples which form the basis of the generalizations to which they have been led. They cannot subject a broader range of knowledge to analysis, and thus their development of independent thought and striving is limited. Therefore, in addition to the inductive method, instruction must also make use of another method— the deductive method, where thought and learning proceed from the general to the particular. This is substantially promoted by mathematics instruction, since the deductive method is characteristic of mathematics. Children should learn to concretize a rule once they learn it, by analyzing their previous knowledge and experience.

A combination of the inductive and deductive methods promotes the highest mental development in children. Children should not always be placed in the position of a "pioneer," nor should instruction always lead them from the accumulation of isolated, concrete knowledge to conclusions and generalizations. Children must also learn to master the previous knowledge accumulated by mankind, to appreciate it, to be able to use it to analyze their own experience and to analyze facts and phenomena in the world around them. For example, at a certain stage, we familiarize children with the quadrilateral and its basic properties (four sides, four vertices, and four angles). Since children already know about the square and the rectangle, it is important for them to perceive a quadrilateral as a broader, more general concept.

Turning to children's experience, on the one hand, we ask them to independently find and name the familiar figures that have analogous properties (four sides, four vertices, and four angles) and that might be classified as quadrilaterals, and on the other hand, we ask them to look for objects or parts of objects that have the shape of a quadrilateral; this sort of concretization deepens children's knowledge of a quadrilateral.

Familiarizing children with the polygon and its general properties proceeds analogously. To make their knowledge of a polygon more concrete, the children indicate and name triangles, squares, rectangles, trapezoids, and rhombuses of various dimensions. Thus, all these figures are included in the concept of a polygon. The polygon is superimposed, as it were, on the whole variety of closed figures bounded by line segments (both regular and irregular figures, and large and small ones).

Consequently, it is necessary to use varied methods to develop children's thinking in order to teach them to apply the inductive and deductive methods, to help them understand the unity of the general and the specific, the abstract and the concrete.

As they master the accumulated experience of society, children come to know a system of standards: the colors of the spectrum, the musical scale, measures of weight and so forth. Knowing the standards enables them to see the richness and diversity of the world around them, and assists them in actively perceiving and investigating the properties and qualities of the objects in their environment. The world appears before the child in a wealth of shapes and colors, and in a diversity of sizes and quantities.

Kindergarten training should provide not only for imparting knowledge to children, but also for developing their mental abilities, the mechanisms of mental activity, which facilitates the transition from empirical to conceptual knowledge. These principles form the basis for the "Kindergarten Education Curriculum."

In recent years the kindergarten curriculum has become considerably more diversified in the realm of mathematics. There are now sections on introducing children to space and time relations; methods of measuring discrete and continuous quantities, various kinds of extension, weight, and the capacity of vessels; the relation between parts and the whole; and so forth. All of these promote children's mental development and successful preparation for school.

The value of preparation consists not so much in a perfect correspondence between the knowledge presupposed by the grade one curriculum and the kindergarten curriculum (as is often improperly assumed), but rather in children's mental development. While teaching children the elements of mathematics, the teacher should teach them to think logically and develop their speaking ability. But most important, he should know the subject of the discipline that he is teaching to the children. N. K. Krupskaya has written: "A teacher in any particular discipline must be aware that in order to be a good teacher, one must above all have a thorough knowledge of the discipline. Of course, this condition is far from sufficient, but it is a *necessary* condition. In the study of *every* discipline...what is essential is a *comprehensive* study..." [2:616].

The preschool teacher should be well oriented in a number of elementary mathematical concepts (the set, the number, the natural numbers), know the basic mathematical propositions, be familiar with the historical origin of numbers and counting and of number systems, and so forth. He must know the psychological aspects of the development of mathematical concepts in children in order to understand children's difficulties as they arise and find ways of eliminating them. Knowing how counting and measuring developed in human society, the teacher will have a more profound understanding of the difficulties that mankind has surmounted, and will have a clearer conception of the significance of the knowledge that he imparts to children and that they must master.

2

Teaching Methods in School and Kindergarten in the 19th and 20th Centuries

Methods of Teaching Children Arithmetic in Elementary School in the 18th and 19th Centuries

We do not know exactly what teaching methods were used in antiquity, but there are grounds for assuming that the methods were dogmatic and unsubstantiated. For example, Egyptian manuscripts give the following instructions: "Do this in this way..." or "Do this as is customary..." Similar recommendations are given in the manuscripts of ancient India: "See how this was done earlier." But in certain Greek documents one sometimes finds a conclusion: "Which is what we were to prove," signifying that the authors are attempting to substantiate a certain rule.

In ancient times there were no textbooks in modern sense and the arithmetic collections which did exist were lists of practical instructions on how to do certain arithmetical computations—that is, they were made to suit purely practical needs (colonial trade, calculations of various kinds, and the like).

How were children taught mathematics in Russia in the 18th and 19th centuries? We obtain an idea of the methods of teaching mathematics from the first printed Russian textbook *Arithmetic* by Leontii Filippovich Magnitskii (1669-1739), written in 1703. This book was epoch-making in the evolution of our native mathematics.

L. F. Magnitskii was one of the most prominent men in Russia during the time of Peter the Great, both in his general education and mathematical knowledge. Magnitskii received his initial education at the Moscow Slavo- Graeco-Latin Academy. There he studied Greek and Latin, and then he independently studied Dutch, German, Italian, and mathematics, thus becoming familiar with the mathematics literature available in other countries. His *Arithmetic* thus reflected the state of mathematics not so much in Russia as in Europe.

Of course this textbook seems unusual today. For example, it often presents the arguments in verse form, and the text is accompanied by symbolic pictures. Here is Magnetskii's definition of arithmetic: "Arithmetic, or the art of numbers, is a worthy and unstinting art, intelligible to all, having a multitude of uses, and most highly praised; invented and presented by the finest arithmeticians who have lived at various times, from the most ancient to the most modern" [6:56-57]. Magnitskii defines arithmetic as an "art," having in mind the art of problem-solving.

Other features of this book should also be noted. The printed text and the page numbers were Slavonic, but the computations were written in Arabic numerals. Magnitskii points out the advantages of the Arabic numeral system and only briefly mentions the Latin and Slavonic systems.

Magnitskii called numerals *designations*, in contrast to zero, which he calls a *cipher*. He divides numbers into groups: the numbers from one to ten are *persty* (in Slavonic this means *fingers*); the numbers which are multiples of ten or hundred are *sustavy* (meaning *joints*); and all of the other numbers such as 12, 304, or 468, Magnitskii calls *compositions*. Magnitskii borrowed this terminology from the ancient Roman authors, where digital counting was used extensively.

Magnitskii's definition of *numeration*: "Numeration is counting which teaches us to name all of the numbers designated by ten by signs such as 1, 2, 3, 4... " Magnitskii finishes his number table up to 1024 in verse form: "Number is infinite, to our minds... And the end is known to none but God the Creator alone" [6:57].

Russian mathematical terminology had not yet been developed, and therefore Magnitskii gave all of the names of operations in Latin and in Russian translation. His book first introduced the concepts of decimal fractions, progressions, and the quadratic equations, which hitherto had not occurred in Russian mathematical literature. Thus, Magnitskii's *Arithmetic* played an enormous progressive role as a general education book in which the recommended practical methods were founded theoretically. However, despite all of the merits of this book for its day, it also manifested a characteristic dogmatism—learning rules without proofs.

Mathematics was taught from Magnitskii's *Arithmetic* for over 50 years. The basic teaching method in school was memorization of numeration, definitions of operations, and results of solving examples or problems, with no explanation. For example, with respect to the study of the multiplication table it is stated: "The student must have the following table fixed so firmly in his memory that he can respond or write down without delay how much two times two is, or three times three, or whatever."

Indicative of the time are the poet G. R. Derzhavin's recollections of how he was taught geometry in the gymnasium "without rules or proofs." Dogmatic teaching methods were retained in the schools even in the 19th century.

In the first half of the 19th century there appeared educators who understood that the reason for poor performance in mathematics, and in other areas of knowledge as well, was to be found in the teaching method itself, rather than in the lack of abilities in the children. Thus, the mathematician and methodologist P. S. Gur'ev (1807-1884), author of the books *A Manual for Teaching Arithmetic to Young Children* (1839) and *Practical Arithmetic*, wrote:

> Children study arithmetic in school for 4 or 5 years in a row, incessantly repeating the same thing, and yet the greater part of the pupils, upon finishing such a lengthy course, not only fail to learn it as they should, but even develop an aversion to it and to all of mathematics. On the other hand, with a different presentation and with a timely stimulation of the pupils' independence, there is no doubt that the same discipline would by no means seem so burdensome and boring, for they would soon realize that everything included in it is merely the further development of what they have been doing already and are doing all by themselves [9:VIII].

However, Gur'ev's books, methodologically advanced though they were, nevertheless failed to exert the needed influence for reorganization of instructional methods, and teaching continued to be dogmatic.

The Monographic Method and Its Critics

Improvement in arithmetic teaching in Russian elementary schools began in the second half of the 19th century. A book by V. A. Evtushevskii (1831-1888) appeared in 1872, entitled *Methods of Arithmetic*—an aid for teachers' institutes, teachers' seminaries, secondary school instructors, and parents.

Evtushevskii took the basic position of the German methodologist A. V. Grube and the Swiss educator J. Pestalozzi (1746-1828) as the basis for his method. In Switzerland, Pestalozzi had effected a revolution in the teaching of arithmetic. He stressed the significance of the use of visual aids as the single foundation for all cognition, including arithmetic. "Children's exercises in elementary computation should be carried out using *real objects* or at least representations of them; the children must gain a firm mastery of the fundamentals of arithmetic, since that will prevent errors and confusion in the future" [13:243]. Pestalozzi developed an entire system for teaching counting to children. Number, shape, and the word are the triad that formed the basis of Pestalozzi's teaching method.

The German educator Grube used Pestalozzi's ideas, publishing the book *A Manual for Calculation in Elementary School, Based on the Heuristic Method* (1842). In the 1860's this guide became known in Russia through a book by W. Paulson entitled *Arithmetic by Grube's Method*. Grube's method was becoming widely prevalent in Europe and America at the time.

Grube believed that all numbers between 1 and 100 were accessible "to direct contemplation; therefore one must have a clear conception of those numbers with all of their constituent parts" [8:30-31]. Since all computations involving numbers over 100 proceed by analogy with the numbers up to 100, Grube considered it especially important to have a clear conception of the composition of all these numbers. Therefore, he proposed studying the numbers in sequence from 1 to 100, comparing each new number with all of its predecessors in terms of their difference and their respective factors—that is, "measuring" a number by the previous numbers, as Grube put it. This method of studying number was called monographic—that is, it was a method of describing a number.

During the study of each number, the materials for calculation were the fingers on the hands, lines drawn on the blackboard or in notebooks, and sticks. For instance, in studying the number six, the student was first asked to lay out the sticks one by one. Then the following questions were asked: "How many sticks make up our number? Count them. Count off one stick at a time until you reach six. How many times greater is six than one? What part of six is one stick? How many times does one stick go into six?" and so on.

Then the number being studied was compared in precisely the same way with the number two, and the students were asked to lay out the six sticks two at a time and to answer such questions as: "How many twos are there in six? How many times is two contained in six?" Similarly, the given number was compared with all the preceding numbers (three, four, five).

After every group of these exercises, the operations were written in the form illustrated in Table 1. Then the results of the table were memorized so that the student was able to produce all of the arithmetic operations immediately without resorting to computations. According to Grube's method, no computation techniques were taught to the students. Operations as such and computation techniques that depend on arithmetical laws were not studied. In Grube's method the material to be covered was arranged by numbers rather than by operations. All four operations were immediately applied to every number studied. Reciprocal operations (subtraction and division) were learned at once by comparing differences and factors (what part of one number another number represents).

Table 1.   Comparison of the Number Six with the Preceding Numbers

The Number Six Compared with:				
One	Two	Three	Four	Five
$1 + 1 + 1 + 1 +$ $1 + 1 = 6$	$2 + 2 + 2 = 6$	$3 + 3 = 6$	$4 + 2 = 6$	$5 + 1 = 6$
$1 \times 6 = 6$	$2 \times 3 = 6$	$3 \times 2 = 6$	$4 \times 1 + 2 = 6$	$5 \times 1 + 1 = 6$
$6 - 1 - 1 - 1 -$ $1 - 1 - 1 = 0$	$6 - 2 - 2 - 2 = 0$	$6 - 3 - 3 = 0$	$6 - 4 = 2$	$6 - 5 = 1$
$6 \div 1 = 6$	$6 \div 2 = 3$	$6 \div 3 = 2$	$6 \div 4 = 1 \ (2)$	$6 \div 5 = 1(1)$

Grube's monographic method acquired popularity as a result of V. A. Evtushevskii's book *Methods of Arithmetic,* in which this method was given in a somewhat modified form. Evtushevskii recommended beginning by decomposing the number to be studied—e.g., the number six—into equal terms, and then he asked the students to divide up six cubes in any way they chose; only afterwards were the various decompositions arranged in order and written on the blackboard: 5 and 1 = 6; 4 and 2 = 6; 3 and 3 = 6; 2 and 4 = 6; 1 and 5 = 6. Evtushevskii proposed studying every number from 1 to 20 in this way, and for the numbers between 20 and 100 he advised going into detail only on those that have many factors, such as 24, 32, 36, 40, 45, and 48. Evtushevskii did not recommend studying every number past 100. Under Grube's method, however, all the numbers up to 1000 were studied in detail.

But the basic distinction between Evtushevskii's method and Grube's lies elsewhere. Grube believed that the idea of number is innate, and one need only assist the development of what has been primordially given. But Evtushevskii proceeded from the position that the concept of number can be developed only on the basis of repeated observations of specific quantities:

> A child cannot have innate notions and concepts of real objects—
> they need to be developed... What kind of impression can be made
> on a child's mind by preformed concepts of number, addition, or a
> fraction when these concepts are communicated to him for the very
> first time, if he has not built them up himself from a multitude of
> individual notions? For such an abstract concept as number, it is
> insufficient to tell the beginner to learn that it is a collection of units
> [5:7-8].

In contrast to Grube, Evtushevskii takes a materialist approach to the
development of concept of number in children:

> The concept of number in general is formed, like any other abstract
> concept, by generalizing specific concepts—and only gradually;
> only by actually counting objects many times can the child realize
> that number is not something intrinsic to any objects of a particular
> kind, but that it can pertain to all objects and, finally, can exist as a
> concept... in abstract form... First less general concepts are formed
> in the child's mind—for example, 20 nuts, 20 people, or 20
> archins[1]—followed by a more general concept—20 units [5:14].

Why does Evtushevskii recommend the monographic method for
elementary school? He believes that before school a child acquires a mass
of concrete knowledge, but that it is random, unorganized, and incoherent. This must be put into a system, but every system is logical. The
student must, therefore, be taught the elements of this logic. In the
author's words, mathematics is accessible to everyone; he objects strenuously to the notion that mathematics is accessible to only a select few
or that it requires a particular cast of mind. It is not a matter of children's
minds, Evtushevskii stated, but of teaching methods, for it is the teacher
who "casts" the pupil's mind. "But he is free to pile up educational
material in that mind, instead of actually forming it properly" [5:22].

Mathematics possesses extraordinary potential for teaching students
to think logically, Evtushevskii maintained, for "every truth in mathematics rests on the preceding ones and itself becomes the logical foundation
for further truths" [5:24], and this teaches the mind attentiveness and
concentration, flexibility, and the ability to compare ideas and truths.

Evtushevskii sees the system for training students' thought in the study of numbers and relations.

As we see, Grube and Evtushevskii have diametrically opposed view of the same monographic method in its initial theses and the interpretation of its aims and fundamentals. It is no accident that Evtushevskii's methodology was adopted by Russian teachers, and his book went through 15 editions (the last appeared in 1912).

However, as early as the 1870's opponents of the monographic method already began to appear. In 1874 even Leo Tolstoy criticized it: "These German methods had another considerable advantage for teachers... that the teacher need not... work on himself or his teaching methods. With this method the teacher spends a large part of his time teaching what the children know, and moreover, teaching right from the textbook and it is easy for him" [18].

Here is what teacher S. A. Rachinskii, had to say on this score:

> Perhaps this method is necessary when you start to deal with five-year-old children (or with idiots); but it smacks of exceptional artificiality when you are dealing with children twice that age... One must avoid spending too long on what the students already know: it engenders boredom, teaching them not to expend the requisite mental energy.

Dissatisfaction with the Grube-Evtushevskii method increased continuously. In the 1880's and 1890's, a whole galaxy of Russian mathematicians sharply criticized it, preferring either the method of studying operations or else the computation method.

What shortcomings did Russian mathematicians see in the monographic method? In the first place, the initial thesis of the method was criticized. The method presupposed that numbers up to 100 (according to Grube) or up to 20 or higher (according to Evtushevskii) can be conceived of visually as a group of units. However, the critics stated that there is no such ability. We can visualize a group of two or three, or at most four objects. But for a larger number we must always resort to counting. Therefore, it is pointless to study numbers and their structure by decomposing them. There are over 5000 decompositions for the first

100 numbers, and memory alone is unable to digest them. It is also psychologically impossible, since there is no visual representation of these numbers (K. P. Arzhenikov).

Second, the monographic method was criticized for being tiresomely boring and for the extreme monotony of its techniques. On this point Leo Tolstoy wrote:

> These gentlemen (Grube and Evtushevskii) command us to study merely the numbers 1, 2, 3, 4, forgetting that every child has learned these numbers and their relations without school. It would be impossible to understand or to feel the complete criminality of a book like Grube's arithmetic text without having oneself experienced the great boredom that this sort of thing produces. And it is already in its second edition! Therefore, how many children's souls have been tormented and spoiled, how many naive teachers have been ruined... Formerly, we learned the definitions of operations in mathematics; now we do not even perform the operations themselves, since, according to Evtushevskii, it is only in the third year that students begin numeration, and it is presumed that it takes an entire year to teach children to count up to 10 [18].

Since operations as such were not singled out for special instruction under the monographic method, but were subordinated to the study of number by means of the difference between a number and the preceding number children did not comprehend the significance of each arithmetical operation, nor did they differentiate them: teaching was reduced to training children's memory and skills. Children were compelled to produce the difference and compare factors, starting with the very first numbers, and this confused them and failed to ensure learning. The failure to understand and the mechanical mastery of the rudiments of arithmetic that arise form the monotony and boredom of the methodological techniques took away the students' desire to do arithmetic.

It should be noted that criticism of the monographic method developed not only here, in Russia, but also in its native land—Germany (Grass, Falk, Knilling, Tank, Knoppe, Hartman, Reuther, and others).

However, individual methodologists remained true to the method. In the 1890's it was somewhat modified in Germany by the German didactician and psychologist, W. A. Lay (1862-1926). Lay's book, *A Manual for Beginning Instruction in Arithmetic, Based on the Results of Didactic Experiments*, was translated into Russian by D. L. Volkovskii. Lay proceeded from an assumption that man has an innate ability to perceive a group of objects integrally (simultaneously). "Two or three things can be clearly and distinctly perceived and conceived of simultaneously" [10:6]. Then he writes: "The essential element in the concept of number is postulation, the recognition of being—that is, a logical, rather than merely a sensed process" [10:80]. Thus, according to Lay, number is not a reflection of real aggregates in the consciousness and the result of comparing them with one another, but an innate ability to assert (postulate) quantity in a group without resorting to counting, that is, to perceive a group simultaneously, and label it with a number.

Considering that children in modern society learn about groups of two or three objects at an early age, Lay sought means of further developing the ability to perceive an aggregate immediately, simultaneously, without resorting to counting one by one. Lay used various numerical figures in an attempt to clarify what shape, size, color, brightness, and distance (grouping and arrangement) counting devices should have in order to yield the best results in number perception [10:83]. Lay conducted experiments such as the following.

He showed the children a numerical figures with circles 0.5 cm in diameter; the distance between the circles was equal to the diameter of the circles, and the intervals between the squares was 1.5 diameters. The numerical figures was displayed to the children for 0.5-1.0 second and then covered up. The children were to represent what they had seen and answer the question "How many?"

Lay, too, gives some of the resulting data.

a) A girl of six who had spent three years in preschool, depicted the numerical figures flawlessly—three, four, five, six, seven, and ten, but could not say how many circles there were in figure 7. Lay concludes that the girl had a distinct notion of the number even though she did not know its name. She was unable to draw the figure 12 even after it was shown to her five times, with each demonstration lasting more than one second.

b) A boy of five or six (of indifferent aptitude) was able to count only to four. He could not properly depict numerical figures 3 and 4 even after he was shown them five times, and he determined the figure 4 without looking at the figure. He drew figure 5 correctly, but was unable to find the number by counting.

c) A boy of three or four who had been in preschool about one year knew how to count to 10. He represented the numerical figure 3 by one point; upon the second showing, he arranged three points in a row, but was unable to name the number. He represented the numerical figures for 4 and 5 accurately. But he drew figure 6 only after he was shown it five times and had opportunity to examine it.

What conclusions does Lay draw from these examples?

1. Without preliminary exercises, children can perceive and remember numbers, imagine them, and represent them from memory.

2. Numerical notions encompass not only the first ten, but larger numbers as well, while the notion of objects in a series cannot exceed three.

3. Distinct numerical notions can emerge and exist without counting, and counting likewise plays no part in their representation.

Thus, Lay does not agree with the generally accepted opinion that the concept of number emerges only as a result of counting. Relying on Pestalozzi, Lay asserts that number and shape are akin to one another and that the former can be deduced from the latter, and vice versa. Thus, Lay came to the conclusion that a distinct notion of number must be developed through shape. He believed the square to be the most suitable shape. The number configurations he recommends are even called "Square Numerical Figures" or "Lay's Numerical Figures."

The task of instruction, according to Lay, is to develop a clear, distinct image of every number up to 20. "Picturing a number means to revive the sensory and motor elements which enter into the observation of the number" [10:80].

How does instruction proceed, according to Lay? Children are shown a numerical figure. They examine it, then close their eyes and describe the arrangement of the points. For example, the figure for four has one circle in the upper left-hand corner, one circle in the lower left-hand corner, one circle in the upper right-hand corner, and one circle in the lower right-hand corner (Figure 1). Lay believed that "the more distinct, clear, and vivid the observation of things, the more distinct, clear, and vivid will be the numerical concepts reflected in that observation [10:85].

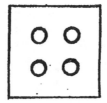

Figure 1.

The description is followed by a sketch of the given numerical figure and by composition on Lay's counting frame. After working on the image of a number, the children move on to the study of its composition. Three of the four circles are covered (temporarily), and the children perceive only the upper left circle; then it is covered, and the other three are exposed, and all of this is described: one and three makes four. Then it is also explained that two and two makes four, as does three and one.

Finally, the students solve problems on the composition of the number four, based on what they have just learned. The response is given at once, without calculations, on the basis of their recollection of the number's composition.

As we can see, Lay is using the same monographic method, but further equipped with numerical figures. Russian teachers did not use this method. But his admirer D. L. Volkovskii—an instructor in Moscow gymnasiums—developed his own book on the monographic method (1914). Volkovskii intended it not only for elementary school, but also for the preparatory classes in women's gymnasiums, for kindergartens, and for home instruction.

Thus, the monographic method found its way into the kindergarten. Children were taught counting basically according to this method for many years even in Soviet kindergartens.

The drawbacks that had already been pointed out by the critics of the monographic method in the 19th century were typical of Lay's method as well, but, like Grube's method, Lay's approach was an especially vivid manifestation of the idealistic philosophy. Number, in Lay's opinion, is inherent in the human consciousness as the postulation of being. Number orders being; it is none other than an innate logical category with which human consciousness is endowed. Therefore, children should be taught number rather than the activity of counting. This initial thesis leads Lay to search for stimuli that can promote the development of what is incorporated in human consciousness. He sees the answer in giving a number as the most easily remembered shape—a square in the case of four. Thus, Lay replaced the perception of quantity (number) by the perception of form. The children in Lay's experiments correctly reproduced the general shape of the drawing without counting the circles. But Lay asserted that they had a distinct notion of number. The mistakes that the children made both in representing and naming the numbers are clear. Naming number words in order is not in itself the activity of counting, although Lay took it to be. The child had no numerical concepts for the number words he named. Naturally, he could not count three points on the numerical figure either, and he reproduced only the shape of the drawing that had been shown to him.

Thus, the criticism of the monographic method was just. It also retained its force with respect to Lay's method. It was rejected for the schools, for it did not develop the student's thinking, but amounted to merely training their memories, and it was boring.

This method was uncritically adopted by workers in Soviet preschool establishments, since Volkovskii's book was directly addressed to kindergartens. This why it is so important to know the history of the monographic method and its criticism in the 19th century.[2]

The Method of Studying Operations

The method of studying operations replaced the monographic method in the schools. Arithmetic instruction was based on study of the methods for performing the four arithmetic operations. In this case numbers were merely the material by means of which the arithmetical operations and computation techniques were studied. The method of studying operations arose almost simultaneously in Russia (P. S. Gurev, 1807-1884) and Germany (A. Disterweg, 1790-1866). However, the method did not make much headway in the Russian schools at that time, and it was only in 1885, when the criticism of the monographic method had developed and *Methods of Elementary Arithmetic* by the Russian mathematician A. I. Goldenberg (1837-1902) had appeared, that the method of studying operations became prevalent. "Teaching children calculation is intended to teach them to perform operations on numbers consciously and develop children's skill at applying these operations to solve problems with general, everyday content" [7:III].

Children should be able to calculate and understand calculations—this is the essence of the method; that is, they should understand the meaning and specific features of the operations, along with the basis of the decimal system. Instruction in the computation method is built around concentric circles involving decimal places. Counting and operations, rather than individual numbers, are studied within each concentric circle.

Goldenberg recommended beginning instruction with numerical examples. He reasoned in the following way:

> Before solving a problem, students must know how and be able to perform the necessary operation on the numbers, as well as remember the table results; children learn this by examples. Solving problems, regardless of how simple they are, requires some mental activity on the youngster's part; he has to identify the arithmetic content of the problem—that is, the numeric question presented in the form of a very simple story.

Such an approach, in Goldenberg's opinion, creates too heavy a load for children; therefore, they must first be acquainted with the mechanism of computations through examples, and then proceed to problems. But there were other representatives of the operations method who demonstrated the need to start with problems. Thus, S. I. Shokhor-Trotskii (1853-1923) writes in his *Methods of Arithmetic*: "To develop proper notions in students, and subsequent concepts of the four operations, these sections of an elementary arithmetic course can be based on simple problems"[15:8]. He cites the French educator Jean Masset who said that just as humanity has learned to do computations by proceeding from the practical necessities, so too children should begin to learn "not by an abstract rule," but by solving specific problems. This point of view was shared by another methodologist, F. I. Egorov (1846-1913), who believed that arithmetic instruction in school should begin with solving simple problems, which would help children understand the meaning of operations on numbers. Thus, the method of studying operations using problem material was vital in the pre-Revolutionary school.

The Conflict Between Materialist and Idealist Views in the Methodology of Teaching Arithmetic

A study of the pedagogical and methodological literature in the last half of the 19th century and the early 20th century indicates two trends in school arithmetic teaching: the monographic and the computational. These approaches also influenced the development of methods of teaching children before they begin school. The conflict in issues concerning methods of teaching arithmetic often concealed a deeper conflict between the materialist and the idealist world-views. This emerged in the views of certain authors on the source and the process of developing the first numerical concepts, notions, and counting abilities in children.

A number of authors maintained that the concept of number is innately inherent in human consciousness. Therefore, instruction must proceed "from number to number." Understanding of arithmetical operations also develops on the basis of the concept of number. This interpretation was also the foundation for the monographic method. At the elementary stage, the authors indicated, a set is first perceived simultaneously without counting and is named with a number, and then the number can be studied comprehensively—that is in all of its possible combinations (the composition of the number). Once a number composition has been mastered, suggest the proponents of this method, it provides for learning the arithmetical operations itself; therefore, there is no need to study computation techniques. This influenced the sequence of instruction in the monographic method as well: (a) exercises in perceiving a set without counting it, and naming it with a number (association); (b) study and memorization of a number's composition; (c) exercises in arithmetical operations based on this number composition.

Other authors asserted that the concept of number develops in our consciousness only through reflections of quantitative relations involving real world objects and phenomena during a person's interaction with sets, and certainly not through contemplation and animation of what is supposedly innate to the person. In teaching methods, these authors assigned first place to activity with sets—that is, to practical work with them, to comparison of sets even before the children had learned to count using number words. For example, the children find a one-to-one correspondence between a quantity of notebooks and a quantity of students. This comparison enables them to establish that two equal sets are equal or unequal. On the basis of activity that involves juxtaposing the elements one to one, the concept of number should also gradually develop. The educators belonging to this group defended the computation method of instruction in school—also known as the operations method. They taught students to count sets, to master numeration, and then transferred the children to the study of arithmetical operations and computation techniques—that is, they went from practical manipulations with sets and their comparison to a mastery of the operations of counting and an understanding of number, and then to a mastery of the concept of the natural number sequence.

Various authors substantiate their methods in different ways as they present them. These differences are conditioned by their views on the origin of number—whether a number is, in the author's opinion, an innate property in the thinking of someone who aspires to order the chaos of the world, or whether it is a reflection of actual reality in the consciousness. For instance, Shokhor-Trotskii, Egorov, and others, in defending the computation method of teaching arithmetic in the school, did believe that the concept of number is innate; therefore, they recommended using the monographic method of teaching number to children in the preschool years in order to activate this innate property. On the other hand, Evtushevskii, who defended the monographic teaching method, substantiated it by maintaining that practical activity with sets (in play or in life) had already developed children's ability to count and their elementary concept of number prior to school; but the numeric notions that children have formed are still highly chaotic, and the school needs to set these notions in order. This is promoted by the monographic method, in the author's opinion.

Thus, the views on children's mathematical development have been determined not only by the method adopted by various authors, but even more by their point of view on the origin of number. This is particularly evident when it comes to the issue of teaching preschool children.

The representatives of bourgeois psychology were not able to resolve the dispute either. Two theories—the theory of the perception of groups of objects and the theory of counting—were advanced with respect to the two trends in methodology. Each of these theories attempted to determine what was innate: counting or number. Proponents of the theory of group perception maintained that the child is born with an ability to grasp a set as a single, spatially-organized whole, without counting it— i.e., simultaneously; they therefore supported the monographic method of teaching. Representatives of the other theory maintained that it is not number itself that is innate, but rather the idea that the members form a sequence in time—that is, mastery of the natural number sequence, as a result of which the child can name the numbers in order as he counts, but cannot identify the total quantity (how many in all). Therefore, ordinal rather than cardinal counting should be taught first. At first glance this theory corresponded to the computation method, but its adherents claimed that the ability for ordinal counting was innate. As we can see, the representatives of the two psychological theories were taking idealistic positions and disagreed only about what is innate—number or the sequential nature of the numbers. Thus, confined by the philosophies of idealism or metaphysical materialism, neither the educators nor psychologists of the late 19th and early 20th centuries were able to understand the highly complex transitions in the development of consciousness from concrete activity and perception of concrete sets in space and time to the activity of counting with number words—to the synthesis of the elements of a set into the concept of number.

Soviet pedagogy and methodology of mathematics teaching are based on a Marxist interpretation of the origin of all mathematical concepts. The set, number, counting, and many other concepts arise and develop during a person's diversified activity and his interaction with the material environment. Someone who perceives his environment through his senses and activity gradually comes to know and abstract out the essential aspects of objects and phenomena, and by this means he develops concepts, including those of mathematics.

F. Engels convincingly demonstrated the materialistic basis of mathematical concepts. In *Anti-Düring* he repeatedly emphasizes: "Both the concept of number and the concept of a figure are borrowed exclusively from the external world, and did not spring up in the mind as a result of pure thought" [12:31].

Basically the same process of cognition of surrounding reality occurs in the small child, although many concepts have already been developed so that he absorbs them ready-made from adult speech. But he learns the meaning of these concepts in proportion to the sensory experience he himself acquires through his activity. In an early work Karl Marx wrote: "It is known that the first theoretical activity of the reason, which is still vacillating between sensation and thought, is *counting*. Counting is the first free theoretical act of reason *in the child*" [11:37].

Thus, the concepts of counting, number, and the natural number sequence are not innate, but are developed during a child's diversified activity with sets of objects and phenomena, through the comparison of certain objects and phenomena with others, and through their counting and measurement—that is, by means of cognition of quantitative, spatial, and temporal relationships.

Issues in the Methodology of Teaching Number and Counting to Children in Preschool Pedagogical Literature

Before the Russian Revolution there were no special methodological manuals on teaching young children to count, although the need for them had already been recognized. Therefore, many books written for the schools were at the same time designed for the family and the kindergarten. In the 20th century the monographic method, which had been supplanted in the schools, migrated to the kindergartens and was uncritically adopted by Soviet preschool establishments, prevailing there until the 1950's.

The broad development of the nationwide network of kindergartens after the Revolution required an entirely new system of public preschool education. Soviet preschool education was created in conflict with the various bourgeois systems and theories: the theory of free upbringing, the theory of self-development, the method of plans, and others.

In the preschool literature published in the 1920's and even in the 1930's we still encounter patently idealistic views on the interrelations between development and education. L. K. Shleger (1853-1923) wrote, for example, in his book, *Working with Seven-Year-Old Children*: "Without attempting to provide ready-made knowledge to the child, the kindergarten has to develop his ability to extract this knowledge himself from the life around him" [14:5].

Similar views were expressed to deny the need for kindergarten curricula or the need to teach children. The teacher's role was limited to the creation of conditions conducive to self-education and self-instruction by children. It was believed that children should be free to select their pursuits according to their own inclinations. Shleger wrote:

> Everyone can do what he himself has decided to do, select appropriate material, set goals for himself and attain them. We should speak of a life curriculum rather than of a curriculum of studies. This curriculum should be based on natural inclinations and strivings that are common according to observations of children... [14:17].

Therefore, the educator's task consisted only in promoting the organization of the child's life, providing an impetus, evoking his desire to extend his experience, and in making his knowledge deeper.

This general trend also settled the issue of how children acquire the ability to count. Counting

> should be related to all the children's activities, and not be an abstract study. In life the child encounters number, measurement, computation, simple counting, the order of numbers, and all of their operations, at every step... The instructor should use every convenient occasion to give the children practice in counting [14:18].

Thus, even for the seven-year-old there is no curriculum for counting nor are there directions on teaching methods; the development of numerical concepts, according to L. K. Shleger, should be accomplished via children's daily life and play. The well-known educator, E. I. Tikheeva (1865-1941), held similar views at this time:

> Children of preschool age must not be taught calculation, but the normal child should comprehend the first ten numbers by the age of seven. All of the numerical concepts that are accessible at this age should emerge from the life he lives and in which he takes an active part. By playing, working, and living, he will certainly learn to count by himself if we adults will be his inconspicuous accomplices and guides in the matter [17:95].

But Tikheeva recommends special play lessons with didactic material, in order to reinforce the knowledge or the quantitative concepts that children acquire in their lives. "These games should be brought into play when the child has already extracted a certain numerical concepts from life itself; they serve to make this concept comprehensive and to reinforce it, to strengthen the necessary counting skills" [17:95]. But Tikheeva regards it as inadmissable to force ar compel a child to play with this special material.

Tikheeva developed special didactic material for play lessons, which she describes in her book *Counting in the Life of Small Children*. In this book, as in her book *The Modern Kindergarten*, she reflects the extensive experience of her own pre-Revolutionary practical work in the "kindergarten for all social classes" which was organized by the Society to Assist Preschool Education.

The entire course of child development, in Tikheeva's opinion, should be natural, without constraint or pressure. This course is naturally correct, leading "to the normal development of a child's numerical concepts." Mastery will be accomplished easily and naturally if the material corresponds to "the needs of each child at each point in his development."

Tikheeva indicated that everyone can acquire numerical concepts— "never and under no conditions can a person be shut off from numeric perceptions"; thus it is impossible to imagine a person, even an illiterate one, who had never been taught anything, who would not know how to count or have any notions of number. "Under normal conditions, the child's mathematical development is accomplished easily and naturally" [16:4-5].

Tikheeva considers it normal that the school must begin arithmetic instruction by teaching counting, since some firstgraders are unprepared. This phenomenon will be eliminated when children learn reading, writing, and counting independently and in due course. Therefore, Tikheeva expresses indignation about a proposal by one author (E. I. Ignatev) for teaching children: "Urged on by his idea and ceasing to consider children and life, on the very first pages of his pamphlet he shifts to regular instruction, promoting techniques and complexities that cannot be considered at the preschool age" [16:6]. In her opinion, "the child, in playing, working, living, and using every convenient occasion in life on his own, learns all by himself everything that he needs to learn in his first years..., mastering it in precisely the form in which life itself presents the knowledge to him" [16:7].

Thus, in her theoretical statements Tikheeva is an enemy of any systematic instruction for small children, believing that up to the age of seven they should learn to count by themselves, during their daily life and play, and at the same time she objects to complete spontaneity in upbringing. She emphasizes the value of proper mastery of the first ten numbers:

> If the child masters the first ten numbers properly, without any disruption in the basic course along which his *innate mathematical thinking* (italics ours—A. L.) is to be directed, all of his subsequent mathematical development will rest on a durable and firm foundation. And this foundation should be laid in the preschool years [16:8].

Tikheeva objects to group lessons because that which is not the inclination of some children is "foisted" upon everyone. In her opinion, children learn reading, writing, and counting easily and inconspicuously without systematic training, while teaching one another.

For these purposes Tikheeva set up a series of aids such as paired pictures, and lotteries etc. She worked up 60 problems for play lessons to reinforce quantitative and spatial notions, explaining that they are needed because mathematics, as an exact science, requires a systematization of learned numerical concepts. She advised choosing natural materials for counting material—pebbles, beans, leaves, seeds, as well as small toys, buttons, or ribbons. Tikheeva uses the same method—life itself—to introduce children to the concepts of *greater—less, taller—shorter, wider—narrower, more expensive—cheaper, shorter—longer, heavier— lighter, thicker—thinner,* and *deeper—shallower.*

She considers it necessary to teach children numerals, for which she introduces games employing paired cards, where a numeral is written on one and a numerical figure on the other. She recommends using counting boxes in which small objects are placed, according to a numeral or numerical figure, and she proposes adding the digits to groups of toys in various places in the room. On the basis of all this knowledge, Tikheeva introduces children to the operations of addition and subtraction and with their "notation" using cards on which the digits and signs are written.

Problems are introduced along with examples. Here she recommends using every suitable occasion. "A boy had two pieces of candy. He ate one. The problem we've got," she says, "is how much candy was left?" In games the children encounter a number of various combinations of arithmetical operations, and the teacher should also be sure to employ a wide variety of operations.

On the basis of making up and solving problems in practical life and based on pictures, Tikheeva intends for children to move on to solving oral problems without such visual aids. The child is offered a card on which the text of a problem is printed. After reading the text, the child produces the sequence of the operations and, aided by manipulable numerals and signs, writes down the problem. Tikheeva also recommends training the children to compose and invent problems on their own, using small toys and objects for this purpose.

Tikheeva also ascribes considerable attention to measurement. She would familiarize children with objects of different size at a very early age, equipping them with the terms *large—small, wide— narrow, long— short,* etc. She is striving to develop a chromatic sense in the children, a feeling for proportion, by creating aids for progressively increasing and decreasing an object's size and matching some objects to others according to their dimensions—for example, matching buckets of the appropriate size to peasant dolls carrying yokes on their shoulders. Using such games that involve distinguishing between sizes, she considers it possible to present measurement with the commonly used measures to five- or six-year-olds. For this purpose she introduces children to the arshin and teaches them to use it. The children also acquire a notion of volume by measuring the capacity of a vessel with a glass. She introduces scales in order to demonstrate weight and volume for various materials, and brings out the functional relation between weight and volume for the same material and for various materials. Tikheeva indicates that all of these forms of measurement should not be aimless; instead, they should be educational: they are to be included in games so that the knowledge acquired is connected to practical tasks (such as playing store). While familiarizing preschool children with number as an expression of quantity and measure, she believes it possible to give them fractions, too, since in their play children divide an apple, a piece of paper, a string, a circle, or a square into halves or quarters, and they divide dry and liquid substances into equal parts. "The children do all these operations themselves and acquire a quite distinct graphic notion of the half and the quarter" [16:52].

For familiarity with fractions, she developed a special aid called a "Circle Divided into Ten Parts." It is made up of ten pairs of cardboard circles (25- 30 cm in diameter) painted in bright colors; one circle in each pair has been divided into sectors, while the other remains whole. In each pair the circle was divided, first into two, then three, then four... and finally ten sectors. At the same time, all this material was used for spreading out brightly colored mats, which greatly interested the children.

These are the basic features for developing numerical concepts in children elaborated by E. I. Tikheeva. It directly reflects the ideas that characterized pre-Revolutionary preschool education and pedagogy as a whole—denial of instruction, curriculum, and collective forms of work.

Tikheeva's requirement that everything be taken from life and that teaching be based purely on practical experience is a sign of the times. Practically speaking, however, she felt a need for systematic instruction in counting; but, because of limitations in her theoretical views conditioned by the times, she made countless qualifications in defending her didactic aids, explaining her projected sequence of work exclusively by the need to systematize the knowledge that children acquire in their everyday life.

While theoretically standing up for nonintervention in the child development process, Tikheeva was in fact actively guiding that development, teaching the children by organizing individual and group play lessons under the teacher's supervision. She directly stated that the time would come when all children would come to school prepared, but she regarded it as possible to implement this "training" only individually. In practice, however, she included in all her aids directions for group play lessons (every possible type of lottery, dominoes, paired pictures, etc). Tikheeva insisted that teachers refrain from interfering with children's development, while at the same time indicating that her methodology must be used in working with each child.

In the methodology she directed all of her attention to developing aids—that is, to creating purely external conditions—rather than to the particulars of children's mathematical development and how to improve it.

The range of knowledge actually outlined by Tikheeva for preschool children, despite all of her assertions about the uselessness of a curriculum, is very considerable. Whether it is within every child's power to learn it is unclear, for those who fail to learn should apparently be classed with the group of children who are not gifted in mathematical thinking. Tikheeva does not disclose the difficulties that confront children as they learn mathematics, nor does she indicate how a child makes the transition from perceiving a collection of objects to number, or from counting to arithmetical operations and to solving examples and problems. The theoretical views of the time limited the potential of such a talented educator as E. I. Tikheeva. Believing it unacceptable to teach children systematically, she did not work out the essentials of a methodology for teaching children to count, nor did she substantiate it in theory: she did not show how or why children must be taught to count; she did not indicate ways to furnish children with rationally substantiated computation techniques for solving numerical examples and problems. She ascribed a teaching role to the didactic aids themselves. In her opinion, the teacher should organize a process of self-teaching and merely exercise control over how children follow the rules of the game. This showed the direct influence of bourgeois preschool pedagogy, which overestimates the significance of didactic play and toys—the so-called principle of autodidacticism (Froebel, Montessori, and others). But Tikheeva manifestly denied the role of direct instruction and the teacher's influence on the child.

These are the contradictions in Tikheeva's general pedagogical views and specific methods. A remarkable expert practitioner, with a profound knowledge of the child, she realized the necessity and the value of teaching, and of a gradual increase in the complexity of educational material, but in substantiating her recommendations she did not manage to overcome the influence of idealistic theories. Despite the fallaciousness of certain opinions, a number of Tikheeva's statements on pedagogy in general and her aids for counting retain their value to this day. They have been absorbed into the common body of Soviet preschool education.

A considerable role in developing methods of imparting mathematical knowledge to children in kindergarten was played by F. N. Blekher. Her book *Mathematics in Kindergarten and the Null Group* (1934) was the first educational aid and curriculum for counting for the Soviet kindergarten. Her methodological letters (1938, 1943, 1945) served as a guiding document for kindergartens at that time.

In the preface to *Mathematics in Kindergarten and the Null Group*, Blekher writes that this aid was based on the scientific works of foreign and Soviet authors and on a generalization of the best experience in children's institutions. However, the author says, there is still a great deal of work to be done on studying the process of children's mathematical development in kindergarten and on refining age-group methodology. Therefore, the author regards this book as a step toward creating a genuinely scientific methodology.

Referring to foreign authors (Descoeudres, Beckman, Filbig, and others), Blekher points out that children perceive different numbers at different ages. Thus, children distinguish and recognize the number *two* at the age of 3 or 4, the number *three* at 4 or 4 1/2, and the number *four* at 5 or 5 1/2.

With this as a starting point, Blekher developed a curriculum for teaching counting in kindergarten. Thus, in the younger group (ages 3 and 4), she indicated that the children should have formed a clear notion of quantity up to four and learned to name these groups with number-words (that is, to recognize and name the number). In the intermediate group (ages 5 and 6) the children determine quantity up to ten and master the concept of a *pair* (a pair of gloves, a pair of galoshes). She also proposes introducing the numerals from one to five in the intermediate group. In their everyday life children also use ordinal numbers. In the older group (ages 6 and 7) the children should have a firm mastery of the first 10 numbers and of the numerals up to 10. They should learn to carry out the operations of addition and subtraction and move on to the second ten numbers, the concept of the quantity zero, and solving arithmetic problems in one operation.

What methodological devices does Blekher recommend for implementing the goals she outlines? In her opinion, all the work should occur in daily life, and the instructor should make the most of every common event. The knowledge thus acquired can be reinforced in individual play lessons with didactic material [4].

In everyday life, children perform various errands for their teacher—bringing or removing a quantity of objects, remembering the number of sleds or shovels taken on a walk, and many others. What is most important is that the children learn to grasp a group of objects as a whole or as parts of the whole, without counting: "Here there are two shovels and three shovels—that means five."

For practice in "grasping numbers" without counting, the author recommends using numerical figures, and also arranging objects in the form of a numerical figure, first covering them with a napkin, and then removing it and asking the children to determine the number of objects rapidly, without counting. "We have often stressed that children must become skilled at grasping number in groups," F. N. Blekher writes, "they must be able to consider a number not just as a collection of individual units, but as something consisting of individual groups" [3:67].

Blekher considers counting the lowest stage. In her opinion, if children have already learned to count, they must get rid of the habit. Simultaneous perception of an entire group is the goal of the exercises. Thus, all of the methodological techniques recommended by Blekher are geared toward that goal. Children gradually begin to learn what smaller groups constitute a certain numerical figure and to remember number composition. All of this enables them to learn to solve arithmetic problems without resorting to computations. Thus, in playing and practicing with the aid of didactic material, the children easily identify not only the first ten numbers, but even numbers up to 20.

How does Blekher propose to conduct lessons with children? The author has decided objections to conducting frontal lessons, which she tolerates only for children in the older group (seven-year-olds). But even here Blekher insists on a stipulation: a simultaneous lesson with a group should in no way mean that all of the children are occupied in the same way or are working, as the author says, "at the teacher's command"; the children are to work individually, each using his own educational aids. Therefore, lessons with the children are unthinkable without aids and didactic material. For these purposes Blekher introduces in the kindergarten a booklet on mathematics for every child and instructions for working with it [1, 2].

What are the drawbacks of Blekher's methodology? One problem is that she underestimates the significance of counting all of the elements in a specific collection and replacing this activity by the perception of an integral group and identification of its quantity. The reason for this problem is the influence in those years of structural (Gestalt) psychological theory, on the one hand, and of Lay's didactics on the other. At the time Blekher had no opportunity to subject the Gestalt theory to critical analysis or to conduct a theoretical analysis of the methodological foundations of the monographic method. Soviet child psychology had just begun to develop, and Blekher had nothing to rely upon in developing her methods. For instance, she asserted that a prerequisite for mathematical development is mental development, and that it is useless to teach a child to count if he has not yet achieved a certain level of mental development. However, because she does not link the level of mental development with age, but only with the knowledge acquired independently in life, Blekher contradicts herself somewhat, by denying the significance of teaching a child to count.

Another of the author's mistakes is that she has not perceived the distinctions between a specific set of objects and number as an abstract concept. Every concept, including the concept of number, is formed via activity, in this case the activity of counting. Therefore instruction should begin with the actual activity of counting, where the first step is to establish a one-to-one correspondence between the sets themselves. But Blekher, while giving the children practice in recognizing groups of objects and naming them with a number word, merely promoted an association between the number and the quantity in the group, supposing that this was the way to develop the concept of number. Thus, Blekher, like many other authors of arithmetic methodologies at that time, did not clearly understand the activity of counting and the relations between set and number. All of this resulted in Blekher's actually taking the position of the monographic method in teaching methods: recognition of a number, recollection of its composition, and on that basis, recollection of the operations of addition and subtraction (three and two are equal to five because I remember the composition of the number five). Therefore, Blekher taught children no computation techniques for problem solving.

A third source of flaws in Blekher's methodology is that, in her opinion, the teacher should assist the child's self-development, but should not intervene actively in his development. This led the author to the idea of auto-didacticism—that it is necessary merely to create external conditions for the child's self-development in arithmetic. Therefore, Blekher assigned first place to children's everyday life, in which they acquire the necessary knowledge of number, and to reinforce that knowledge she created a series of didactic games that the children were free to use. She strenuously objects to any attempt by adults to impose them. As we see, F. N. Blekher is also characterized by the same views on spontaneous development and autodidacticism which were taken in the 1920's and 1930's by L. K. Shleger, and in part by E. I. Tikheeva, and many others.

The merit of the methodology developed by Blekher is that she, like Tikheeva, devoted considerable attention not just to number but also to the development of the notions of size, shape, space, and time. It is to her credit that she produced a series of didactic games for children's independent lessons. Many of her didactic games for these sections of the curriculum retain their value even today.

Thus, in search of a new system of education, workers in preschool institutions first borrowed certain views and methodological techniques from bourgeois pedagogy. This is because there was still no research on children's mathematical development based on Marxist methodology. The influence of bourgeois views on a number of pedagogical issues (spontaneity of development, the theory of free education, and auto-didacticism, among others) led educators not to intervene actively in children's development. Only the need to create favorable external conditions for children's self-development was suggested, and so didactic games were developed which the children were to use according to their own wishes.

Frontal lessons, which were described as mandatory, were held simultaneously with all of the children, but each child could choose an aid according to his own inclination and occupy himself with whatever he pleased. Thus these lessons were not instructive in nature, did not exert a purposeful influence on all the children, and failed to provide for their proper development.

In teaching children to count, the indicator of success was the ability to grasp a certain group of objects immediately, without counting. The details of children's mathematical development—how stable the children's knowledge was with this teaching method, or how much that knowledge promoted their preparation for school—had not yet been studied. The origin of the very method of teaching children to move from number to number was not subjected to critical analysis at that time. The question of the relations between number and counting was not even asked and consequently it remained insufficiently studied.

In the 1930's the need to study how children develop abilities and skills in the area of number and counting became even more pressing. The first investigators of this problem were the psychologist I. A. Frenkel in Leningrad and L. A. Yablokov and E. I. Korzakova in Moscow; then, in the 1940's, G. S. Kostyuk and others in Kiev, and N. Lezhava in Georgia; and in the 1950's, A. M. Leushina.

In the 1960's and 1970's the study of preschool children's development of mathematics expanded considerably; large scientific teams began to work on these problems. Aspects of how children develop notions of size and shape, of the measurement of length, weight, and volume, and of spatial and temporal relations were studied, and an appropriate teaching methodology was produced. Other objects of investigation were how children understand elementary functional relationships and transitive relations, how they assimilate the mental operations of classification and seriation using mathematical material, and their notion of a set.

A significant contribution to the study of children's formation of elementary mathematical concepts in the preschool years has been made by studies on sensory development conducted at the Scientific Research Institute for Preschool Education of the USSR Academy of Pedagogical Sciences and at the Scientific Research Institute for Schools of the Ukrainian SSR Academy of Sciences, among other institutions. Studies in teaching mathematics to the preschoolers which have been conducted in other Socialist countries [19]. All of these studies, based on Marxist methodology, have made it possible to develop a methodology for forming rudimentary mathematical notions in preschool.

3

The Development of Children's First Mathematical Knowledge of Sets, Number, and Counting

The task of teaching children rudimentary mathematical knowledge and abilities consists in isolating the most essential items which can ensure general development of their capacity for independently finding connections in their knowledge and abilities. In order to disclose the essential characteristics of objects and phenomena, to show them in different interdependencies, the teacher must lead children to general guiding principles. How can children be brought to an understanding of mathematical interrelationships and interdependencies, and to the development of simple mathematical concepts? When and at what stage in the children's development can these concepts be assimilated?

Our brief historical survey has recounted various educators' views on how children perceive number and learn to count in the initial stages of development. The formerly prevalent view that simultaneous perception of a group is an innate ability has not stood up. A child can indeed perceive a group without counting if it lies in a single field of vision and is a standard group (two eyes, two hand, two feet, five fingers). But children do not identify the group when there is a different arrangement of the same items—for example, five dolls standing in a row on a table, two teaspoons that have fallen on the floor, or two windows in different walls of a room.

Proponents of the theory of perception of a group of objects, as we have seen, attempted to assign a certain standard shape to a group to assist in its identification (numerical figures). But in such instances the shape was identified, but not the quantity. It was necessary to determine whether this psychological theory, the basis for the monographic method, was valid.

Another psychological theory, called the counting theory, proceeded from different facts. According to observations by the proponents of this theory, children, even though they had no notion of numbers, soon recalled and named the number-words in order, sometimes very many of them. But although they "counted" fluently aloud, they could not determine the number of objects. Thus it was concluded that children first master the order of number-words, but not quantity. Therefore, children must first be taught to name the numerals in order, and then to correlate numerals and objects. This point of view, as indicated in Chapter 2, was adopted by many 19th century methodologists who shared the theory of the operations method. Since these authors worked only with school-age children and did not study the development of children before the age of 8, they speculated that the preschoolers could also perceive groups of objects and label a group with a number-word typified.

Therefore, a number of issues that were very important for developing methods of teaching counting and number to children in school remained unclear in Soviet preschool pedagogy.

1. What is counting—an activity or an operation? What is its structure and how do small children learn to count? Does counting consist of naming number-words in order?

2. What is number—a notion or a concept? If number is a concept, what is its sensory basis, and how do children make the transition from the notion to the concept of number?

3. It is known that children learn number by counting objects over and over. What is the role of the spatial factor in determining number in this instance?

4. How are number and counting interrelated—what precedes what? If there is a unity rather than an identity, what is the structure of that unity?

We can provide an answer to some of these questions. We know from the history of the origin of number and counting that people counted even when they had no number-words. At that time counting meant establishing a purely practical correspondence between various specific sets (see "Manual Counting," "Counting with Knots on a String," "Trading Goods One-to-One," "Counting by Notches," etc.). Paramount in counting at this time was the ability to see each separate part in an aggregate, without leaving anything out. A uniformly repeated word was often of assistance in effecting this separation (for example, among the Papuans, *be-be-be-be-be* = *ibon-be*—i.e., *hand*).

Reflected in a person's consciousness during a comparison of two aggregates was the equality or inequality of the numbers in the aggregates being compared, based upon a one-to-one correspondence between them.

It follows that for primitive man the practical activity of comparing two aggregates and an understanding of equality or inequality of them were primary. Number, which appeared significantly later, was the product of man's practical activity with sets. These stages in the development of number bear witness to man's developing need to determine with increasing accuracy the numbers in aggregates by means of an element-by-element comparison.

In this way the natural number sequence gradually developed as a collection of various classes of sets, labeled by different numbers, each of which is an index of its individual class of sets (five land masses of the world, five fingers on a hand, five measures in a given length, five measures in calculating time, and many others). What is common to the entire range of sets here is the class that is labeled by the number five. Consequently, number is an index of a class of sets, or the concept of the class. Notions of specific sets and of operations with them, and understanding that sets can be equal or unequal in number all contribute to this concept.

Some can now offer some conclusions:

1. Counting is an activity with the attributes involved in any activity: a purpose, means (the operation of counting), and a result in the form of the total as an index of a certain class of sets.

2. The essence of the counting activity is to establish a one-to-one correspondence between the elements in a specific aggregate and

the terms in the natural number sequence as the standard set of numbers (each of which is an index of a certain class of sets).

3. The specific nature of the counting activity consists in operations with specific aggregates—that is, with finite sets as perceived in various ways (visually, aurally, tactilely, etc.). Thus uttering number-words in order is by no means the activity of counting, since the purpose—the object of counting (specific sets)—is missing, and there is no result.

For many years the following questions have remained unclear: How are the first notions of sets developed? What is the role of the spatial arrangement of a set in its perception? What is the role of the various means of perception in developing a notion? How is the transition made from the notion of set to the concept of number as an index of class of sets? What is unique about children's mastery of the counting activity at different age levels? How do children develop a notion of the natural number sequence? Psychological research conducted in the Soviet Union has helped provide answers to these questions.

The Development of Children's Notions of a Set[1]

At an early age children accumulate notions of aggregates consisting of homogeneous objects: "many dolls," "three blocks," "five fingers on a hand." They begin generalizing these first notions, as reflected at first in their passive discourse. Thus, studies show that the 15-month-old child can perform the task of building a "little house" or "little houses," a "big house" or "big houses," of bringing a "car" or "cars," and of planting a "flower" or "flowers" (see L. G. Kalinina, V. V. Danilova, and others).

The 18-month-old toddler, having begun to speak actively, names individual objects or collections of them, using singular and plural noun forms: "this is a block, these are blocks"; "house—houses"; "doll—dolls"; "uncle—uncles"; and so on. Children of this age are attracted by groups of homogeneous objects (beads, buttons, rings). They sort them,

Research Library
AIMS Education Foundation
Fresno CA 93747-8120

move them around, scatter them, then collect them again, spread them out in a straight or curved line on a table. Children love to pick up a number of objects such as buttons and watch them scatter when they open their fingers. The perception of a group of objects or phenomena is promoted by the child's entire surroundings—the set of familiar and unfamiliar persons, the set of objects (houses, trees, vehicles) that move about before the child's eyes, and uniformly repeating sounds—that is, homogeneous noises and sounds (a clock's ticking or striking). Children perceive the groups of objects and phenomena by various perceptual means—auditory, visual, kinesthetic, etc. They have themselves performed homogeneous movements many times: they have thrown the same toy from the playpen, they beat their spoon on the table. All of these forms of homogeneous operations and impressions leave their mark upon the cerebral cortex; they are summarized. I. M. Sechenov has written on this subject: "... Frequent repetition of so-called homogeneous effects should entail an isolation of the sum of the paths which correspond to the constant elements in the impressions" [3:303].

The initial development of the notion of a group of objects and their individuality also creates a basis for children to distinguish between singular and plural number in nouns and adjectives and early mastery of this grammatical form in speech development.

The following description of a set is given in mathematics: "A set is a collection of objects considered as a single whole" [1:80]. Sets are regarded as either finite or infinite. Small children deal only with finite sets.

A child's notion of a set is still highly diffuse in the first developmental stages: it has no distinct boundaries and is not perceived element by element. This sort of perception characterizes an indefinite group, rather than a set as a structurally integral unity; its quantitative aspect is not yet realized in a precise way. For instance, children are happy to see many identical little dolls or different-colored buttons in a box. But once they take out a few, they immediately forget about the rest. Small children likewise do not notice if the number of elements in a set is diminished and some of them disappear. The notion of plurality at this level corresponds to using singular and plural word endings in speech: they do not yet reflect precise quantitative composition.

The notion of indefinite plurality is typical of children up to the age of two years. Everyday examples demonstrate this clearly: the child is asked to put all the blocks in a box or to collect all the spoons on the table and take them to his mother. But the child puts away only a few blocks or takes a few spoons to his mother and considers the task done ("Have you put away all the blocks?" "Yes, all of them," the child answers). For an adult, the word "all" means the aggregate of a set as a structurally integral unit, but for a child "all" means some vague plurality. Three-year-olds often perceive a set within its limits, but distinct perception of all the element in a set is still impossible; they are unable to keep track of every element in a set.

A preliminary conclusion ensues: the notion of a set as a structurally integral unit must be developed in small children, and they must be taught to see and distinctly perceive every element in a set. Instructive lessons involving groups of two- and three-year-old children must be devoted to this training.

However, the transition from perceiving an indefinite group to perceiving a set as a structurally closed whole is a lengthy process consisting of several stages. One of the first is the stage of forming the notion of a finite set. At this stage the child's attention is focused primarily on the "boundaries of a set." For example, the child may be asked to pass out plates to all five of the dolls standing in a row, or to feed all of them. The child will feed only the first and fifth, paying no attention to the ones in between, firmly convinced that all have been fed. He will do the same thing when asked to place mushrooms on a card showing four mushrooms in a row. The child covers only the end pictures with his mushrooms, the first and the fourth, and considers the task done. Such facts indicate that perceiving and designating the boundaries of a set are becoming paramount for children at this stage.

What is the cause of the difficulty that has now arisen for the child? The problem is that in perceiving plurality the child has always counted from a single point—for example, starting from the middle and spreading objects out to both sides. Now, in the perception of a structurally integral set, there are two points to count from, and the child's actions move from the endpoints to the center, as observations of hand and eye movements show. The changed character of the child's movements is evidence that his perception of a set has been reorganized. The perception of the two "endpoints" in a set has become paramount and essential for the child.

Children's concentration on the boundaries of a set naturally weakens their perception of the entire composition of the elements: those elements in a set not at the ends seem to go unnoticed. The conclusion follows that *an adult must provide a new stimulus for the children to perceive all the intermediate elements in a set between the extremes.* But the child does not arrive at this all at once. In an assignment involving placing objects on pictures in a row, the child usually starts by filling up the entire part of the card that lies between the extreme elements, without putting every object on a picture, but instead squeezing the objects close together—that is, the child merely fills up the area between the extreme elements and does not yet reproduce the number of elements. Even demonstration does not always bring about accuracy in reproducing the elements in a set. This is evidence that the perception of the quantitative composition of a set is still quite diffuse.

As for imitating the demonstration, we know that developing motor skills through imitation presents even greater difficulties for the small child. Inadequate motor experience and the lack of the necessary visual and kinesthetic signals mean that visual impressions still cannot evoke the necessary motor associations in children (see A. V. Zaporozhets, G. A. Kislyuk, and others).

It is also very important to bear in mind the following facts that research has uncovered. When perceiving plurality, children begin their movements from one point, most frequently located in the center of the plural quantity. This perception procedure is promoted by body structure—particularly the sagittal arrangement of the hands (right and left). Children usually arrange objects in this way: to the right with the right hand, and to the left with the left hand. In the perception of a set as a structurally integral unit, two counting points appear in hand and eye movements: from the boundaries of the set to its center. As children master these two points, their need to fix both of them disappears. The child starts counting from one of the points, but the other is no longer designated, although the child does not go beyond the boundaries of the area between the two points. If the initial point is the right boundary of the set, the operation is done by moving the right hand from right to left and, conversely, if the initial point is the left boundary of the set, the child moves his left hand from left to right for the whole sequence. This kind of movement stereotype develops at the age of two or three years and is retained for quite a long time. But since the right hand becomes increasingly active with age, the right-to-left movement of the right hand and the eyes becomes increasingly stable. It is often still present even at school age, as can be judged from the many typical errors in arranging the letters in the word *mama* (*am-am*), or in the written arithmetic examples such as $7 - 9 = 2$; there are also errors in problem solving as cited by A. S. Pchelko: $83 - 67 = 24$; $52 - 28 = 36$; $12 - 8 = 16$; and many others. "Wherever the working hand goes, the connected visual axes of the eyes go," writes I. M. Sechenov [4:395].

The conclusion follows that *we need to ensure timely development of the left-to-right movement of the right hand and eyes in order to match the spatial arrangement of our written language.*

Children's Unique Perception of a Set Arranged in the Form of a Numerical Figure

The issue of the role of numerical figures in the development of number emerged long ago in the methodology of arithmetic instruction.[2] The defenders of numerical figures, as a rule, have been proponents of the simultaneous perception of a set by young children. They argued that integral perception of a group is more accessible if the circles are given a certain shape rather than arranged in a row (W. A. Lay, Folkel, D. L. Volkovskii, L. V. Glagoleva, F. N. Blekher, and others).

What are the distinguishing features of a young child's perception of a set arranged in a row or in the form of a numerical figure, and what is the difference? Investigation of this question has shown that the spatial closure of a set in a numerical figure really does more to promote its perception as a structurally integral unit than does its linear arrangement. Even very young children who see three, four, or five buttons pictured on a card and arranged in the form of a numerical figure usually take a handful of buttons from the box and pour them out onto the card. Older children try to put the buttons on their pictures, but by no means always in the same quantity; they fill in even the spaces between the individual pictures. It should be noted that children's hand and eye movements are different than when they reproduce a linearly-arranged set. As a rule, children use just one hand to put buttons on the pictures. If a child lays down buttons with his right hand, he usually starts from the bottom right drawing and proceeds counterclockwise. But if he distributes buttons with the left hand, he usually begins with the bottom left button and proceeds clockwise.

These features of movement lead us to believe that a set represented in the form of a numerical figure is actually perceived by children as a single closed whole, even though, just as in a linear arrangement, it is not reproduced in the proper quantity. But a comparison of data on the reproduction of a quantity of elements when a set has a linear arrangement and when it is in the form of a numerical figure bears witness to the advantage of the linear arrangement. The smaller the children, the greater the value for the perception of quantity that the linear arrangement of a set takes on. Using the technique of laying buttons on pictures, children ranging in age from 18 months to 2 years reproduce a set that is arranged in a row more accurately (75%, as opposed to 50% for an arrangement in a numerical figure). By three years these figures have equalized, since children learn the technique of laying on buttons.

Thus, arranging elements in the form of a square or a triangle actually does promote the simultaneous perception of a set as a single, spatially closed whole, but this more complex form of arrangement significantly complicates the identification of individual elements. For teaching the operation of counting, however, distinct identification of all the elements in a set is most important.

The pedagogical conclusion follows that at the elementary stages of teaching children to count by means of establishing a one-to-one correspondence between the elements of sets it is advisable to place a collection of objects in a linear arrangement.

Role of the Color of Elements in Perceiving a Set Arranged as a Numerical Figure

At the early stages of development children do not notice the color of the elements of a set: they take buttons of any color and arrange them in both directions from the middle. But as soon as they begin to perceive a set within its boundaries, they become more meticulous about using homogeneous elements. This also bears witness to changes in the nature of their perception. Whenever the children accidentally take a button of another color, they correct their error by glancing at the set as a whole. On their own initiative they exchange some buttons so that everything in the set will be of the same color. Children are this meticulous about the uniformity of the set for any arrangement, but they strive to make up sets with homogeneous-colored elements earlier for the numerical figure than for a linear arrangement, although they continue to distinguish the number of elements poorly.

The tendency to create sets consisting of qualitatively identical elements increases with age and becomes independent of the form of arrangement. Thus, for children of five years or over a set is always finite and always consists of qualitatively identical elements. Thus, whenever the first three elements in a linearly arranged set are red, and the next three are blue, children perceive it as two distinct sets. The attribute of uniformity in a finite set at this stage of development is most often color—that is, the attribute of quality in the elements. But uniformity in the elements of a set can be expressed by generic attributes of type, as well as by various qualitative attributes (color, size, shape).

Hence, one of the tasks in subsequent instruction should be to expand the children's notion of the uniform composition of elements, without violating the basic attribute of the set, and remembering that a set is a collection of homogeneous elements. This can be done by introducing generic concepts, such as a *set of toys*, whose elements would be a doll, a teddy bear, a toy pyramid, a block, a car, and so on.

When introducing sets of varied objects, children must be taught to group the elements in a set according to various attributes, thus developing their independence. For example, the different elements that make up a set of toys can be included in another set whose elements are grouped according to color: a red circle, a red block, a red flag, a red square, a red pyramid, and so forth.

Exercises of this kind, involving grouping of sets according to a certain criterion, help children to master classification as a mental operation, on the one hand, and promote the development of an understanding of the interrelationships among various sets and of a certain coordination among them, on the other. The roots of the operation of classification and seriation[3] "should be sought, not in the concepts and statements with which speech operates, but in the basic operations of connecting or ordering which are applicable both to integral (continuous) objects and discrete aggregates" [2:409].

Methods of Comparing Sets Adopted by Children of Different Ages

The Influence of Spatial Factors on Preschool Children's Perception of a Set

Small children begin comparing the numerical value of sets very early, determining the larger and the smaller when they have a practical need to do so. For example, a mother gave her older son three pieces of candy and her younger son (18 months) only two pieces of the same kind of candy. The toddler, looking watchfully at his brother's candy, reaches out for it and expresses his dissatisfaction. How did he find out that his brother had more candy—what influenced him as he compared the sets? Three pieces of candy occupy more area than two pieces, if they are identical in size—that is one criterion. Or the toddler could have compared the pieces element by element and found that he was short one—that is another method of comparison. But try to put two pieces into a greater area and three into a smaller area, and the child is no longer in a strong position; he is inclined to think that he was wrong in his claims. Studies by N. A. Menchinskaya, A. M. Leushina, and others persuade us that various qualitative spatial factors exert an influence on the perception of sets.

When children are delayed in developing the ability to differentiate the elements in a set, they often form the habit of estimating the "size" of a set not by the number of elements that make it up, but by different qualitative spatial attributes—for example, according to the sizes of its elements, or the area occupied by the set. For some children this tendency is retained even into the primary school. However, with age the urge to determine the size of a set according to its qualitative spatial features diminishes, but it can be retained for a rather long time because the quantitative aspect remains poorly differentiated for a long time if it is not the focus of attention.

Therefore, it is crucial to develop children's ability to differentiate the elements in a set at the right time, so that they do not restrict themselves to perceiving it as a structurally integral unit; and even in the pre-number period children should be taught to compare the numbers in sets by actually establishing a correspondence between their elements.

Methods of Teaching Element-by-Element Comparison of Sets and the Ability to See All the Elements in a Set

It was indicated above that in reproducing a linearly arranged set, children arrange buttons to fill in the space between its extreme elements, but not in the same quantity. In order to teach children to properly reproduce a set shown on a card, they must see every element in the set and reproduce it by placing objects on it. Studies and extensive experience have shown convincingly that even children of two or three years can be taught the technique of placing objects in one collection on pictures of objects in another collection.

Children were given a card with 3-5 buttons drawn in a row, and the technique of moving the right hand from left to right was suggested. The children repeated this movement on their own cards, as if investigating the given direction. Then they were told that all the pictures were to be covered with buttons, without leaving any out. This technique proved to be altogether accessible to children over two, and in certain instances even younger (18 months). The sequence of hand movements and movements of the children's eyes as they follow the hand and the pictures plays a particularly important role. Both promote the development of children's ability to see the elements of a set. As a result of such exercises, by the age of three all children have mastered the technique of superposition and can reproduce a set from a model shown them (cf. Chapter 9).

The next technique, which is even more significant for developing the ability to perceive the quantitative aspect of elements in a set, is the technique of association. But preliminary study of children's potential for mastering this technique has revealed a number of special features.

The association technique is more complicated than the superposition technique since it requires a clearer differentiation of elements within a set and greater independence. Children who have thoroughly mastered the superposition technique experience considerable difficulties when they are asked to place the same number of buttons as in the model onto the lower strip under the buttons depicted on the card. Toddlers up to 2 years 6 months place the buttons and squeeze them together without paying attention to the quantity represented on the card (Figure 2).

Even among three-year-old children who have thoroughly mastered the superposition technique, approximately only one-third can use the association technique. Even five-year-old children have difficulty in acquiring this skill.

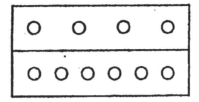

Figure 2.

How do children behave if a set is arranged in the form of a numerical figure rather than linearly? Up to the age of three years, children almost invariably cannot fulfill this assignment, even if the instructions are accompanied by a demonstration of what they are to do. Some three-year-olds do attempt to arrange buttons, but they do so in a unique way: they lay buttons around the entire card, squeezing them close together (Figure 3). Yet, almost all of the children could work with the technique of superposition.

It should be noted that it is not just the technique itself that presents difficulties for the toddler; it is also the meaning of the words "put beneath" and "associate" (some children slid their buttons under the card). It follows that children in their second and third years should be

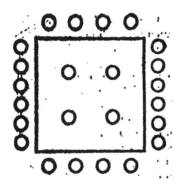

Figure 3.

given a practical explanation of the distinctions between the words "place on," "associate," and "put beneath."

Even older children (five years of age), when arranging on a strip as many buttons as there are in a numerical figure, distribute the buttons either around the four sides of the square; around three sides; along two sides; or they construct the shape of the numerical figure directly on the table, though not in equal quantity (Figures 4 and 5). Their attention is focused on the method of the new operation of associating, thus supplanting their perception of quantity.

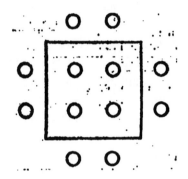

Figure 4.

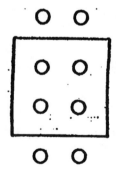

Figure 5.

What is the cause of difficulty in learning to associate the elements in one set with the another, and why is this method the most significant in developing quantitative perception of sets? To place one button under another in a collection of buttons, one must differentiate the spatial relations among all the elements in the set, perceiving their quantity precisely, both in a linear arrangement and in the form of a numerical figure.

Why do children learn the superposition technique comparatively easily when perceiving the same sets? In solving a problem by the superposition technique, the child places a button on a picture of the button, covering it, and the pictures themselves are guides; but the spatial relations among the buttons as drawn do not play a substantial role in the operation, and the child does not notice them. What is important for the child is covering all of the pictures in the collection in sequence. Thus, the superposition technique promotes, on the one hand, development of the notion of a set as a structurally closed whole, and, on the other hand, reinforces the child's awareness that a set consists of individual elements. But the total number of elements is still of little interest to the child.

What is the cause of difficulty in associating elements—what new problems arise for the child as he learns this technique? The child must reproduce precisely the number of elements that form the given set. To do so, he must perceive not only the representations of buttons, but also the spatial relations among them. Only then can the child establish the quantity of the set. However, the child has not yet learned to take account of the distances between the pictures. While he is guided by the picture itself during superpositions, the child must rise to a new level in the perception of a set in order to use the technique of association. He must learn to see the spatial relations among the drawings—that is, among the elements within the set—which will lead to an accurate quantitative perception of them.

Without yet learning to analyze the spatial relations among elements either in a linear arrangement or in a numerical figure, the child fills up the area within the boundaries of the set, squeezing the buttons close together, and thereby reproduces an inadequate model of the quantity. And if instruction does not devote sufficient attention to the spatial differentiation of the elements within a set, there will be significant errors in the child's perception of the quantity of an aggregate even at the stage where he has apparently learned to count using number-words. Let us cite one example of this kind of behavior.

> Yura P., 5 years and 1 month of age. Yura can freely count up to 13. He counts seven buttons in a row on a card, and then he counts out the actual buttons one by one, placing them down in a row on the lower strip, but without seeing to it that the buttons are lying precisely under their pictures in a one-to-one correspondence. After placing six buttons, Yura stops, believing his task to be finished, since he seems to have filled up the entire area within the boundaries of the set. When he counts both sets again, at the teacher's request, he detects the mistake. While counting, Yura moves the buttons slightly, by accident. Spotting a vacant space under the last button in his model, he moves his buttons even closer together and adds another two buttons. On his own initiative, Yura counts the two collections again, and again realizes that he has done something wrong. "That's not right," Yura says. He moves the buttons closer together again, adding one. There are seven buttons in the model, and he now has nine. Counting again, he says: "I have it wrong. For some reason it isn't working out; I'll have to move them again." Moving them still closer together, he adds another button—a tenth—and again realizes that he has done it wrong. "It's not working out again. Now you've made the work harder. But it will work out somehow." An attempt at helping is decisively rejected: "I'll do it myself. You've made the work harder to guess at. But how does it go?" Yura ponders. "Why don't you try putting the buttons on the circles," the teacher advises, nevertheless. Yura takes the advice. "Seven!" he exclaims happily. "See how many extra I took. It wouldn't work out. There were extra buttons."

Thus, only after a hint was Yura able to juxtapose the elements in one set one to one with the elements in another. When doing the assignment involving taking a set arranged in the form of a numerical figure and reproducing it in a linear arrangement, Yura counted five buttons on the card, and then took some buttons one by one, without counting, and laid two buttons on each of three sides of the square: the top, right, and bottom.

Yura looked carefully at the buttons he laid out, comparing them with one another, and reasoned aloud:

> "This one goes with that one—this one doesn't go with that one, but with this one," and so on. He then removes one button and counts both sets. But, as he counts, he does not hear a correspondence in the last two number-words. "How can I do this right?" Again, he compares the elements with one another: "This one with that one, this one with that one (pause), and so this one doesn't go with that one, but with this one." He counts everything again and joyfully declares: "Here there are five and here there are five. Now it's right."

Thus, Yura has not yet mastered the genuine significance of counting. He knows only one thing—there will be equal sets when the last numerals correspond as he counts them off. When he does not hear that correspondence, he thinks he has made some mistake, but what he has done wrong remains unclear. This can be demonstrated with one more example.

> Yura counts the seven circles on a card as shown in Figure 6 but mistakenly says "six." "You've counted wrong." "No, everything's right," Yura objects, but he counts them again "Oh no, it's not all right. Seven." Yura starts to place buttons around the shape, but the teacher reminds him that they are to be placed in a row. Yura lays down buttons one after another, counting off the numbers, but he counts his movements rather than the buttons. For instance, putting down the fourth button in the row, he says "five" because he said "four" as he took it from the box. Laying down another button and calling it number six, Yura says, "That's all," considering the job done; he has already forgotten the number of buttons on the card. "Count to see if you have put them down right." Yura counts the circles on the card but leaves one out, saying that there are six circles. Counting again, he finds that there are seven: "Seven, but I forgot that one. Oh, I just keep forgetting about it!" He counts the pictures of the buttons again and decides that there are seven. "Seven," he asserts, and begins counting the buttons he laid out. "Six," he says. "Wrong again." After thinking about it, he adds one button and, satisfied, declares: "Now there are seven. See what a hard problem you gave me."

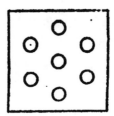

Figure 6.

What should receive particular attention as we analyze children's behavior? Children do not use counting as a means of determining the number of elements in a set. As they name the numerals in order, they wait until they reach the number-word that corresponds in sound to the numeral named in counting the other collection. Thus, for these children number is not yet an index to the quantity of elements in a set. The children ascertain by counting that two sets do not correspond only because the last two number-words sound different. These children are still unable to use the counting activity in a genuine sense as an activity to establish a one-to-one correspondence between objects and the numbers in the natural number sequence. They easily lose their place as they count, making careless correlations between the number-words and the objects in a collection. Sometimes they leave out number-words, sometimes they omit objects as they count, and sometimes they name two numbers at once while correlating a single object with them. The children seem to manifest active behavior in counting, but they have not yet risen to the level of understanding its significance.

The example we have cited indicates that the children have prematurely begun to count using number-words. They have not yet developed distinct perception of all the elements in a set. They have not learned to compare sets practically, by comparing their elements one-by-one. Not having this knowledge means that they cannot have a clear-cut mastery of the counting operation and cannot achieve a deeper understanding of the significance of number as an index of set equivalence. Naturally, for these children the significance of the number sequence also remains unclear; they find it easy to violate the sequence since their recollection of the order of the number-words has developed only on the basis of vocal-motor associations.

These facts show that it is extremely important to develop notions of sets and the various operations with sets as early as the pre-number period of instruction. The conclusion should follow that from an early age children must be taught not only to distinguish between "many" and "one" but also to develop a notion of a set as a structurally integral unity and a distinct perception of the individual elements that make up a set. All of this will enable the child to become skillful in counting the elements of a set using number-words. Preliminary work with sets will enable the children to understand the concept of number and to learn counting sooner and more thoroughly in the future.

The Significance of Operations Involving Sets in the Pre-Number Period

Various operations involving sets can even be done in the pre-number period. We have already pointed out children's tendency to perceive a set as a unified whole if all its elements are qualitatively alike. While this tendency is fully justified in the period of transition from the perception of plurality to the perception of a set as a structurally integral unit (at the age of 2-4 years), later it interferes with further development. For example, suppose that four fish are lying on a table and there are six fish in a box. A six-year-old child perceives them only separately. When asked how many fish there are in all, he answers that if the fish are taken out of the box and spread out on the table, there will be ten. Or, as another example, a little girl draws two houses on each side of a river. When asked how many houses there are in all on both sides of the river, she answered: "if these two houses are moved to the other side, there will be four." The different spatial arrangement of the elements in a set interferes with perceiving them as a unit.

Therefore, children must be asked to perform various operations involving sets: to compose a single set from two groups, each possessing its own qualitative features which are not distinctive for the set as a whole. For instance, they might have to put several red flags and blue ones together into a single set of flags or, on the other hand, to partition a single set (of circles) into subsets using a certain criterion (color, size, shape, appearance, etc.). Thus, a single set formed according to a generic attribute can be ordered into subsets according to different attributes. All these new subsets can be compared or contrasted with one another, thus demonstrating the quantitative relations among them—equality or inequality—without yet expressing them in terms of number.

Research among first-graders has shown that not children who have gone on from kindergarten to school are able to order sets according to different criteria or to understand the various relations among them.

It follows that children need to work with sets throughout their preschool years. The development of the notion of a set as a structurally integral unit deserves particular attention, and at the same time children must be taught to see each individual element in a set. There is no need to rush children into counting with number-words. It is considerably more important to teach children how to make an element-by-element comparison of two sets and establish a correspondence between their elements. In the intermediate and older preschool years it is advisable to teach various operations with sets, to teach children to compare sets with different qualitative attributes, and to see the equality or inequality of sets, both practically (without counting) and while teaching counting with number-words.

The Role of Various Perceptual Analyzers in Developing Counting Skills and Notions of Sets

The child is surrounded by various sets, which find their expression not only in objects but also in sounds, movements, and the like. The child perceives these sets by means of various perceptual analyzers—visual, auditory, tactile, and kinesthetic, to name a few. Through the internal reception of sensations the child perceives the motor actions of its heart, breathing, and so on. All these sensations transmitted to the cerebral cortex, serve as a basis for forming the notion of the indefinite plurality of different phenomena, as emphasized by I. M. Sechenov. The child begins to accompany recurring homogeneous objects and phenomena with the identically repeated words, "Here... here... here" or with others of the sort.

Perceptual analyzers play various roles at different stages in the perception of a set and its elements. The *kinesthetic analyzer* plays a leading role in developing the activity of counting itself, and the notions of plurality and set. Counting without motion is impossible. For instance, we may seem to be counting the students in a lecture room silently, without resorting to hand movements, but we are counting with our eyes, transferring our gaze from one person to another.

Moreover, we pronounce the number-words mentally. No one hears these words, but physiological studies using special equipment testify to the movement of our vocal-motor apparatus. The same also occurs during the perception of a set by other perceptual analyzers.

In counting sounds, not only do we often name the numbers mentally, but we even nod our heads slightly or make other rhythmic movements (with our hands or feet), seeming to separate out each sound, and thus we perceive it more distinctly. It is no accident that I. M. Sechenov called the motor analyzer the "fractional" analyzer of time and space. Thus, counting is impossible without the participation of the motor analyzer in some form or other. And the less developed counting is in children, the greater the role movement plays. Thus, at the very earliest stages in the development of counting, the child, in comparing sets, actively juxtaposes the elements of one set with the elements of the other one-by-one because he is establishing a one-to-one correspondence between them. As he learns to count with number-words, the child pronounces them aloud while pointing to objects and actively correlating each number-word with one of the elements in the set. Even when adults have difficulty counting silently, using their eyes, they invariably resort to hand movements (when counting the votes in a large auditorium, for example). A pointing hand helps count the voters' raised hands more accurately. Nor is it accidental that the first number-words in almost every language are monosyllabic. In Russian the number *odin* 'one' is often replaced by the monosyllabic *raz* ('*one*'—or more literally, 'once'). The number-words *one, two, three, four, five, six, seven*, etc., enable us to mark the rhythm of movement. Therefore, they are widely used where rhythm must be reproduced distinctly—in physical education classes, in teaching music, singing, and dance, and in rhythmic gymnastics.

Popular pedagogy has observed the connection between the first number-words and movement, and has created so-called counting rhymes. All this shows the motor analyzer is fundamentally important in counting the elements of sets and in forming the first notions of sets.

Other perceptual analyzers play various roles at different stages in development. Let us consider the role of the *visual analyzer*. In early childhood, when the child's attention is drawn to the boundaries of a set, when these boundaries are primary, the role of the visual analyzer is significantly intensified. Children perceive a set visually as a single spatially closed whole. Later, interaction between visual and motor analyzers increases; proper pedagogical supervision can substantially aid this process. The techniques of superposition and association force the child to perceive not only a set in its boundaries, but also to trace every element in the set visually and reproduce it. As already stated, this reshapes the nature of children's hand movement. The visual perception of the whole in combination with its elements becomes increasingly more complete.

A linear arrangement of the elements in sets assists in developing children's ability to delineate with their hands and trace with their eyes the sequence of all the elements from left to right. This in turn gives rise to a stereotype in eye and hand movements taking in the objects in a collection and prepares children for the operation of counting using number-words.

In the pre-numerical comparison of sets, one-to-one comparison of the elements of two sets, the child is brought to visual perception through movement. As he compares two collections, the child sees that they are equal or unequal. Thus, while actively and visually perceiving a set in combination with its elements, the child begins to distinguish sets according to their size and to reflect this distinction in words. Children gradually develop a need not only to distinguish but also to count the number of elements with number-words. The vocal-motor analyzer links up hand and eye movements and the visual perception of aggregates. These connections develop when the child is exposed to properly organized pedagogical work.

All of this again confirms the conclusion that instruction for small children should begin not with counting using number-words but by having children actively create sets themselves and compare them by the techniques of superposition and association, so that the children gradually become familiar with equal and unequal aggregates. ("There are more mushrooms in the top strip, and there are fewer circles on the bottom one; there are more rabbits, and fewer carrots; there is an equal number of dolls and cups, there are just as many cups as dolls.") Linear arrangements promote the most distinct visual perception of a set as a whole and of its elements.

What role is played by the children's naming of numerals using the *vocal-motor perceptual analyzer*? Children are inclined to repeat number-words after adults very early. What causes this, and what function do they perform?

Sasha (2 years and 3 months), watching the lights in buildings, moves his hand as if pointing to them, and accompanies his movement with the words "one, three, five, eight"—that is, he is imitating adults' movements in counting.

Children of four or five accompany their motion on a swing by reciting numbers: "one, two, three, four, five, six, seven, eight, fourteen," and then repeat the same words after a pause. The number-words give rhythm to the movement.

N. A. Menchinskaya has quite rightly observed that the first number-words serve as a distinctive accompaniment to children's general movements. Children even remember the order of the number-words relatively easily if adults teach it to them. However, whether the naming of numbers is chaotic or whether it is done in order, children form purely auditory and vocal-motor connections, which gradually correlate with general movements of the hands, torso, head, and other parts of the body.

The number-words are pronounced in rhythm with general movements just as adults regulate the rhythm of calisthenics. The number-words uttered do not designate counting and do not serve to generalize quantity.

If this unilateral correlation is repeated many times, it gradually takes on a particular meaning for the child—it becomes a distinctive signal to stop, like the word *stop*. When a child who seems to have learned to count reproduces a set based on a specified number, he sorts out the objects and names the numbers, waiting until the given number-word occurs. If he skips it, he continues naming all the numbers he knows, while continuing to lay out objects. This signaling function of numerals can be observed in children of five, six, or seven years, but it is especially vividly marked in five-year-olds. Thus, many five-year-old children, while counting out a given number of buttons, name the numbers as they select buttons. But this is not counting with a view to determining the quantity. In naming the numbers, the children wait for the number-word that was indicated, and they stop selecting buttons once it turns up. But the children cannot tell how many buttons they have taken even after counting them again, pointing with their fingers. The total number does not serve as an index of the set's size for them; it is only a conventional signal to stop, as was shown in Yura P.'s behavior. Thus, only learning the number-words by heart merely gives rise to a vocal-motor stereotype, and the particular numbers perform the function of a stop signal.

The conclusion follows that number-words, even when uttered in order, are nothing more than a vocal-motor stereotype; they do not reflect comprehension of the meaning of number. Therefore, early training in naming the number-words, even if the numbers are recited in order, in no way assists in developing counting or the understanding the meaning of number.

What is the role of the *auditory perceptual analyzer* in teaching children to count and in developing the concept of number? It has already been pointed out that repetition of uniform movements creates a notion of a set bounded by time. The same occurs in the perception of sounds by the ear—that is, in a temporal sequence. The perception of sounds and movements one after another promotes a more distinct differentiation of the elements of a set, which are synthesized in the mind into a unified whole bounded by time (with a beginning and an end).

A small child who does not know counting or number-words is asked by the teacher to knock as many times as the teacher knocks. The child hears the sounds and sees the teacher's hand movements. But how does he perceive and reproduce them?

Before the age of two children do not yet reproduce the quantity they perceive by ear: instead of the two or three sounds they have heard, they knock many times. Somewhat later, in proportion to the amount of practice they have had, they begin to listen attentively to the number of sounds and to watch the teacher's motions, and then they start to reproduce three to five knocks. So, again the perception of a set by ear develops from an indefinite plurality to a set when a small number of sounds, three or five, that are perceived in succession begin to be synthesized within temporal boundaries and perceived by children as a structurally closed whole. Research shows that this revision occurs at the stage as the visual perception of a set.

But if the sounds that the child perceives are accompanied by spoken numbers or even by the meaningless words of a counting rhyme, the child reproduces them in a greater then usual quantity. A word accompanying a sound promotes a sharper differentiation of every sound and movement.

The conclusion follows that the rhythmic recitation of words in a counting rhyme or number-words helps children to differentiate more distinctly the individual elements in a set that are perceived by ear and reproduced in movement, just as the words "*another, another, another...*"

or "*here's... here's...,*" uttered by the children at an early age, helped them to differentiate the elements in a set of objects.

And while the visual analyzer promotes the synthesis of individual elements into a single structurally closed whole, the auditory, motor, and vocal-motor analyzers promote the identification of particular elements within that whole.

This interaction among the analyzers is extremely important for developing the perception of a set as a whole and of the elements that make it up. We arrive at the pedagogical conclusion that all the analyzers must be used in developing counting and the notion of a set in children. A one-to-one correspondence is established between sets perceived by different analyzers.

The Development of Counting in Children

As we study and observe children's operations with sets, we can note their great interest in the plurality of identical objects. Children set out collections of objects on a table or on the floor, most frequently in a horizontal line, a curved line, or a ring. They often squeeze the objects close together—for example buttons, plates, or cups. Two-year-olds are greatly attracted by the plurality of homogeneous objects, but they are indifferent to whether all of the elements in a set are identical in color and size. As they lay down one object after another, they seem to be dividing up a plurality into elements, and this is what attracts their attention. For example, in taking apart the rings on a ring pyramid, they set them out in a row, or they pull apart the wooden dolls of a series that fit one inside of another, one by one, and place them in a very inaccurate row. Homogeneity in sounds or movements is also attractive to children at this age. They willingly repeat the same motion: they rap with a spoon or some other object; they repeatedly open and close the top to a box or the sugar bowl, or they open and close the door to a room many times; they throw objects one after another, while watching them fall; they love for grownups to swing them from side to side or toss them up in the air. Thus we see that various kinds of plurality attract children's attention between the ages of 18 months and 2 years: objects, sounds, movements. The manipulations with plurality serve as a propaedeutic of the children's future activity in counting; this becomes particularly evident when all movements with objects are accompanied by a repetition of one word: "*Here's... here's... here's...*," or "*Another... another... another...*," or "*Here... here... here....*" It is important that every word that the child repeats be correlated with one object or one movement. The word helps to single out elements from a plurality of homogeneous objects or movements—to isolate one element from another more distinctly. Here a one-to-one correspondence (still unrealized by the child) is being set up between the quantity of objects or movements and the number of homogeneous words that are uttered. Of course, this technique is still used spontaneously by the child, but it serves as a certain preparation for the child's future counting activity. This sort of manipulation with sets can be regarded as the *first stage* in the development of counting. An interest in comparing quantities and sets appears later on. Such behavior is typical mainly of children in their third year and can be regarded as the *second stage* in the development of counting. The tendency to compare shows up in children in various ways. For example, toddlers try to compare the sizes of the cookies they have received and so they hold the cookies next to one another, but of course this is imprecise. In other instances children argue among themselves about who has the bigger ball at home and stretch their arms out wide to show the size. These are the first and still quite diffuse methods of measuring and demonstrating the dimensions of an object. Children watch carefully to see that everyone gets an equal number of nuts or pieces of candy when each one is given several pieces. They begin comparing every piece of candy in one group with the candy in another group, thus determining the numbers in the sets. All of these facts are evidence of children's attempts to determine the number in a certain collection or the size of objects—more, fewer, an equal number through comparison. Of course, these are only first attempts at coming to know number through comparison, but their origin is obvious. This tendency arises by virtue of imitating the actions of adults, but principally by virtue of the children's having long ago formed a notion of vague plurality; at this stage a notion of a finite set as a structurally integral unity begins to develop. It is this that enables children to make an element-by-element comparison of one group of pieces of candy with another, establishing a one-to-one correspondence between them: A, B, C, D, is equivalent to a, b, c, d. At the *third stage* in the development of counting, the sequential naming of number-words begins to be included when the elements of the sets to be compared are being contrasted. Development of this stage is largely conditioned by teaching. In the absence of such, or with improper teaching, the children do not learn the techniques of correlating numbers with the entities in sets (elements in sets are omitted, or else they correlate one number with several objects), and, as a rule, they are unable to generalize the entire set which they have counted. When asked "how many?" they start counting the set again, and again they do not generalize the total quantity—they do not answer the question. This is often encountered when adults are in a hurry to teach counting with number-words and do not teach the element-by-element comparison of specific sets and the determination of their equality or inequality based on the comparison—that is, they do not provide for sufficient practice with sets in the pre-number period. But if they have learned in the pre-number period that sets are equal or unequal, children begin showing an interest in counting and they start naming sets with numbers. Children are quicker at understanding the significance of the total number in counting. They differentiate between the total in counting and the counting process—a distinction that is highly important for this stage. Children also learn with comparative ease that sets of equal number are always called by the same number-word. Children do not learn skill in counting objects in large quantity right away. As before, when comparing two aggregates consisting of an equal number of elements, or two aggregates one of which contains one more element, four-year-olds learn to count using number-words, first up to five, and later (at the age of 5 or 6) they learn counting up to 10. At the *fourth stage* in the development of counting, preschool children (of

5 or 6 years) already have a clear mastery of the sequence in naming the numerals, and correlate a number-word with each element in a set with increasing precision, independently of the way in which the set is arranged and the quality of its elements. They not only learn the significance of the last number as the total, but they also begin to understand that a number shows the equivalence of sets independently of their spatial and qualitative features—that it can always serve as an index of quantity alone. The strict sequence of numbers is affected by the interrelationship among all of the numbers of the natural sequence; every succeeding number is one unit greater than its predecessor, and every preceding number is one unit less than its successor.

Thus, at this stage the children posses an understanding of the quantitative significance of number (its relations to a unit) and an understanding of reciprocal relations between contiguous numbers in the natural sequence. At the *fifth stage*, depending on the children's knowledge and abilities, children of 6 or 7 can be taught to count sets of various unit bases, where groups consisting of several objects (three, five, ten) are counted, instead of individual objects. The children learn that the counting unit can be an entire group, not just a particular object. This counting of groups deepens the comprehension of the significance of a unit. Counting rises to a new and higher level. The *sixth stage* in the development of counting coincides basically with the first grade in school. While practicing counting sets with various unit bases (counting groups of ten objects, for instance), children learn to count by tens (one ten, two tens, three tens, etc.)— that is, they approach an elementary understanding of the fundamentals of the decimal system. Then, as they master the names of the tens (ten, twenty, thirty, etc.), the children understand their significance and are able to prove it through the use of concrete materials. As counting evolves, children form a whole series of concepts, and a new type of activity—measurement—develops. First using the counting of particular objects, then groups; measuring a certain length with various everyday measuring devices, then with the commonly accepted units of measure (the meter or the centimeter); measuring solids and liquids first with everyday devices (a glass or a spoon, for instance), then with standard units (the liter, the kilogram, etc.); measuring air and water temperature in degrees; measuring the duration and passage of time in hours, minutes, etc.—through these activities the children learn the concept of number, which develops, expands, and rises to an increasing level of abstraction. While the knowledge and estimates of the quantities in certain sets were empirical and practical in the younger pre-school years, relying on sensory perception, the gradual mastery of elementary mathematical knowledge brings the children's development up to the level of mediated evaluations. This in turn serves as a basis for developing a new activity in the children—computation. Computation deals with numbers as abstract concepts, while counting always deals with specific sets (objects, sounds, movements, lengths, volumes, among others), which are perceived by various analyzers.

Supervising the Development of Counting

Learning counting and, during the process, developing a whole series of concepts is not accomplished all by itself, but as a result of adult-organized instruction. The toddler's visual notions are still quite diffuse. Thus it is very important to create a clear image of the operation of counting from the outset—for instance, directing the right hand's left-to-right movement when using the techniques of superposing or associating objects in a collection to a linearly arranged pattern or the techniques of operation in reproducing a set that is represented in the form of a numerical figure. Detailed instructions on the nature of an operation are equally essential at subsequent stages of instruction as well—for example, in counting objects according to a specified number, or in counting sounds or different movements. It is important that all movements in counting be done properly from the outset. Here it must be remembered that counting is, in its structure, a complex system of intercoordinated, individual operations. It consists of a number of particular operations that are still unknown to the child. Without knowing them, the child, often imitating adults, grasps only some of the external operations in counting—for example, he might pronounce the numbers chaotically and move his hand while doing so, as if "counting" objects. Naturally, he makes numerous errors, since his image of counting as an activity is still highly diffuse. A. V. Zaporozhets' studies on the development of voluntary movements is convincing evidence that an appropriate organization for the child's orientation in the terms of the assignment and in the nature of its performance ensures a more rapid mastery of the operation and the development of a skill (gross errors disappear, the skill becomes clear-cut and is easily transferred to new conditions); here the mastery of the operation becomes accessible to the toddler as well [5:177,228]. Studies also show that counting with number-words proceeds along a high complicated route. The counting process consists of a number of components, each of which the child is to learn (the isolation of each object in a set, its demonstration, the correlation between it and the number-word, which is named in order), while at the same time mastering their interrelationship. The motor component (indicating objects in counting) takes its own developmental course. At first the child moves the objects around, then touches them, then points to objects at a distance, and finally singles out each object with his eyes only—that is, without depending on a manual operation. This reconstruction is accomplished gradually from the younger to the preparatory groups. The development of the *vocal component* is also achieved. From naming number-words aloud during counting, the child passes to naming them in a whisper, and then he merely moves his lips, and finally pronounces them to himself, without moving his lips. The conclusion follows that the vocal and manual operations undergo a common developmental course: from an external, detailed operation to an internal, abbreviated one. An eye movement and an uttered word perform the function of dividing up the set; the word and the eye movement gradually begin to replace the hand operation, becoming the basic medium of the act of counting. Therefore, it is important to disclose every component in counting to the child, to create a distinct image of this complex operation, so that he will use it in different life situations. What is central is that counting with number-words must be taught on the basis of the comparison of two sets that are expressed by contiguous numbers. In a visually represented inequality in the numbers in sets, the number of elements is named by different contiguous numbers, and this fact discloses the essence of counting and the meaning of the order of the number-words to the children in a graphic way.

Developing Children's Notion of Certain Segments in the Natural Number Sequence

Children begin using number-words early, as they listen to adult speech. But only the external aspect of adult counting is adopted. The order of the number-words that are named is often a copy of a certain telephone number that the child has heard from adults, or a house or apartment number. The order in which number-words are named is not stable and sometimes changes for a single child. Professor I. A. Frenkel' has called this random naming of number-words *chaotic counting*.

But the naming of numbers is gradually ordered. Children learn the number order for particular parts of the natural number sequence—up to five, say—and then go on to say the next numbers chaotically. Individual numbers from the ordered segment turn up again among the chaotically named numbers—1, 2, 3, 4, 5, 8, 12, 2, 5, 40. The subsequent ordering of the names occurs on two levels: on the one hand, the segments of numbers that are remembered in sequence grow, and on the other, the children start to realize that each of the number-words always occupies a certain place, although they still do not understand why three always comes after two, or six after five. The children are merely forming audio-vocal-motor connections between the numbers that are named, in the same way that any meaningless ditty is remembered, such as *ai-ni-ki-be-ni-ki-si-ko-le-sa, ai-ni-ki-be-ni-ki-knap*. Even adults are unable to start this ditty from an intermediate syllable—from the syllable *ko*, say—because only the audio-vocal-motor connections between the syllables are formed in the memorization here, and the single syllable that was named does not evoke a whole chain of words.

Young children memorize number-words in the same way, since the meaning of these words remains unknown to them. When the word chain *raz, dva, tri*, etc. (one, two, three) has been learned, it is utterly impossible to replace the word *raz* with the word *odin* (one). The connections that have been formed are disrupted, and the child is silent, not knowing what should follow the word *odin*. Sometimes, to please the adult, a child—between the ages of 2 1/2 and 3 years—will name the word *odin* to precede the entire chain that has been memorized: *odin, raz, dva, tri*....

Cases are also encountered in which a child perceives the first two or three number-words as one word, putting the stress on the first two or three number-words as one word, putting the stress on the first syllable—*razdvatri* (*one*twothree) or *razdva* (*one*two). Here the child is correlating this complex of syllables with one movement or object as a distinctive adjectival word. "That's *yazdvat' i* [un-two-tree]," Lenochka says while putting a toy on the pine tree in the doll corner. Apparently she has heard how people were counting, and the unfamiliar word *razdvatri* was associated with the pine tree. It also happens that a child will, instead of slurring the numbers into one word, accompany them with a hand movement that does not correlate the number-words and the objects. Therefore, it is interesting to observe how children begin to conceive of a segment of the numbers in the natural number sequence that they have learned. Do they create a concrete image of the series, or is it lacking? There is apparently no specific notion of the natural number sequence for children at the level of mastering number-words as a vocal-motor chain. The children do not yet know the sequence, much less the place of the number-word in the system of the other numbers. In such instances we can hardly speak of a visual image; rather it is an auditory image of the word "onetwothree."

The number-words are lined up in a row, as it were, and named in order later on, but this occurs gradually. At first only a certain set of numbers is ordered, and afterwards the numbers are named, although with gaps, but always in ascending order: 1, 2, 3, 4, 5, 6, 8, 10, 12, 15, 18, etc. After learning that the numerals in the first ten are combined with the names for the tens to make 20, 21, 22, 23, 24, 25, 26, 27, 28, and 29, the children go on to name them in this way: "twenty ten, twenty eleven," and so on. But it is worth while to correct them and name 30 after 20, as the stereotype is restored and continued: 31, 32, ..., 39, thirty ten, etc. Some children now begin to understand that after 29, 39, or 49 there are particular words whose names they do not yet know. In these instances the children pause, waiting for help from and adult.

However, as we have stated above, even naming a large range of numbers is not evidence of mastery of counting or of the formation of a clear notion of the natural number sequence.

Nevertheless, a certain image of the natural number sequence is emerging in the children. In the absence of special instruction this process occurs in a very protracted and distinctive way. In such instances the child is in the position of a "pioneer," as it were, rather than a heir in mastering the knowledge of his contemporary society. Therefore, children of the same age can turn out to be at different levels of knowledge. Those who do not know the relations between contiguous numbers cannot answer when asked what number comes before three or what comes after three. They simply start naming the numbers in order from one, two, etc. They are unable to solve a problem such as the following one right away: "I have 6 pieces of candy. If I am given one more piece, how many pieces of candy will I have?" They begin counting the imagined pieces of candy. It is even more complicated for these children to give the correct answer if the number of pieces of candy is being decreased by one. Thus they will count out six pieces of candy on their fingers, put down one finger, and count the rest again. This behavior is most typical of children of 5 or 6.

Other children, when responding to a question of what number comes "before" a specified one or "after" it, replace the terms *before* and *after* with the terms *in front of* and *behind* and name the next number, regarding it as the one standing in front. Many children who name the next number still cannot name the preceding one. For these children the natural number sequence seems as if it is moving forward. We have tentatively called this notion a *spatial image* of the natural number sequence. In performing and assignment of finding a number that is greater by one unit, these children begin naming the number-words mentally or out loud, starting with "one," as if to go through the whole sequence.

Thus, although these children have formed a spatial image of the natural number sequence on the basis of the understanding that every successive number is greater than its predecessor, they have not yet mastered a precise notion of the difference relations between the preceding and the succeeding numbers, and thus they are deprived of the potential for immediately naming a number that is a unit greater or less than an indicated number. Thus, the characteristics of the formation of a notion of the natural number sequence consist in the fact that it only gradually becomes a concept as it develops. The empirical notion of the natural number sequence as a purely "spatial" image, in proportion as the children learn the reciprocal relations between contiguous numbers during instruction, is reconstructed into the concept of the natural number sequence, whose basis is an awareness of the essential attribute of number—of its difference relations between the contiguous numbers $n \pm 1$, where n is a given natural number. The children begin to learn the basic principle of construction of the natural number sequence: each successive number is one unit more than its predecessor, and every preceding number is one unit less than its successor.

Accumulated experience persuades us of the possibility and the necessity of disclosing reciprocal and difference relations to children during instruction. It is advisable to demonstrate these relations to the children in comparing two sets by establishing a one-to-one correspondence between them. We can conclude from what has been presented that it is essential to familiarize children with the reciprocal relations between contiguous numbers while teaching counting, relying on the comparison of specific sets in this instruction.

In the work by J. Piaget and B. Inhelder on the study of the features of children's spontaneous development of the operations of ordering (seriation) of sets and their understanding of ordinal relations, it is pointed out that reciprocal relations in the ordered sequence of a set are inaccessible to preschool children. The authors indicate that this understanding becomes possible only at the level of "operator" operations—that is, at the level of mature mental activity, which is accessible only to children of 8 or 9. But research by Soviet authors (L. A. Venger, E. V. Proskura, A. M. Leushina, and many others) disproves the conclusions drawn by Piaget and Inhelder. In conditions of organized instruction, children of 6 or 7 possess an understanding reciprocity.

Teaching counting and numeration should by no means be reduced to a one-sided understanding that the farther a number is from the start of the counting, the larger it is. A number reflects dual relations: a relation to one (its quantitative value) and a relation to its "neighbors," that is, to the contiguous numbers (ordinal relations). These dual relations of a number should be revealed in combination to the children. Still, even when numeration is studied in school, teachers forget to show the number's relation to one, supposing that the children have already learned the number's quantitative relation. If that were the case, students would not solve this example as follows: $12 - 8 = 16$. The following reasons are usually discovered for this error: the child's failure to understand the principle of digit order, or the child's unregulated eye movements (the juvenile stereotype of movement from right to left).

But the most essential reason consists in the following: the pupil does not see that when he decreases the number 12, he obtains a larger number, 16. He does not notice the absurdity of his result, although he may speak of decreasing the number 12. He has not mastered the quantitative significance of number, for he is accustomed to determining a larger or a smaller number only on the basis of its distance from the beginning of the counting.

Therefore, in the study of numeration through the first 10 numbers, both the concept of a number's relation to one (its quantitative significance) and the concept of the reciprocal and difference relations between continuous numbers must be developed simultaneously in children. As practical experience shows, this is entirely possible to show and explain to children if one relies on a visual comparison of sets expressed by contiguous numbers and on the establishment of a one-to-one correspondence between the elements in these sets.

4

Aspects of Children's Development of Notions of Size, Shape, and Mass (On the Basis of Sensory Perception)

The Physiological Mechanism for Perceiving the Size of an Object

Perceiving an object's size, shape, and weight is a sensory problem. Sensory development is one of the primary problems in the training of preschool children. V. I. Lenin assigned a considerable role to sensation in the process of cognition: "... sensation is a truly direct connection between consciousness and the external world; it is a conversion of energy from an external stimulus into a fact of consciousness" [2:46]. Therefore, it is important to observe how children develop notions about properties of objects such as size, shape, and mass, and what perceptual operations give rise to them. Until recently, perception was regarded as a passive process rather than as an activity performed by the individual. But studies have shown that perceptual operations crucially depend upon determining the properties of objects by inspecting them.

An object's size, shape, and weight are perceived by various perceptual analyzers—visual, tactile, and muscular. I. M. Sechenov has said that space, time, and displacement are reproduced during the motion of the receptor apparatuses. If an object is in our immediate vicinity, we perceive its size and shape by tactile-motor or visual analyzers. Visual perception of the size or shape of remote objects depends on the distance between the object and the onlooker and on the object's position (whether it is in either a horizontal or vertical position at the same angle of vision). The perception and comparison of the size of two objects depends on whether they are at the same distance from the onlooker. The visual perception of an object at a distance involves both vision and movement of eye muscles. These various conditions ensure that the development of the perception of object size and shape is a complex and protracted process.

It has been shown in the works of I. M. Sechenov "The Physiology of the Sense Organs" and "Brain Reflexes" that the regular interaction between the size of the image on the retina and eye muscle contractions is a peripheral mechanism in perceiving the size of an object. An object's size perceived when there is an appropriate degree of contraction of the visual axes at a certain visual angle, and this axial contraction is measured by the muscular sensation. A change in the visual angle is an index of a certain object size on the retina. We cannot judge an object's size exclusively from the retinal image, since the image on the retina depends on the object's distance from us. It is possible to ascertain an object's size is visually only by establishing a cortical connection between the components of the visual analyzer—the retina and its motor component (the eye muscles)—which adjust the eyes to perceive an object at a certain distance.

Sechenov cites the following fact as proof. If we take three objects of different sizes and place each of them at a distance from the eye such that all three are perceived at the same visual angle, the perception of magnitude will vary despite the equal visual angles. In analyzing this fact, Sechenov writes:

> This occurs because, in the act of seeing each of the three objects, a varying degree of contraction of the visual axes accompanies the common visual angle for the three objects—a greater degree of contraction for the nearest object, a weaker one for the farthest one. This pattern is repeated millions of times in a person's life, and the following series of visual-muscular associations becomes consolidated in his mind: a given visual angle + increasing contraction of

the visual axes = diminution in the objects; the same visual angle + decreasing contraction of the visual axes = enlargement of objects... [3:273].

Therefore, the notion of the size of objects seen by an adult is determined by the visual angle + the degree of contraction of the visual axes and the magnitude of the accommodative movements [3:276].

Thus, the perception of the magnitude of objects (like other spatial attributes) is accomplished by the moving eye. Therefore, Sechenov ascribes a special role to muscular sensation.

Through muscular sensation the eye, like the hand, "feels" an object. It functions as a measuring device. The sensations that arise on the basis of movement serve as the "gauges." They help to introduce individuation and delineation, which perception by an immobile eye could not achieve. On this subject Sechenov writes: "Spatial vision is measuring vision from the very beginning of its development" [5:509]. The direction of the eye movement changes, depending on what object is being perceived; a long or tall object, a broad or thick one, a large or small one.

The sensations that arise when an object is touched with the hands also play an important part in the development of the perception of size. However, with practice, a temporal connection is set up between the retinal image and the proprioceptors of the eye muscle, on the one hand, and the objects' size as verified by touch, on the other—a connection that subsequently makes it possible for objects to be compared visually by size, without resorting to tactile verification.

The word also promotes consolidation of the temporal connection. An object's size is evaluated, on the one hand, by means of sense perception and, on the other hand, by means of a word that generalizes this perception.

Thus, according to the teachings of the founders of Russian and Soviet physiology, the perception of size (just like other apparent properties of objects) is accomplished by establishing complex systems of intra-analyzer and inter-analyzer connections; it has the nature of a reflector.

The Development of the Perception of Object Size in Young Children

Adults and children share a common mechanism for perceiving size. This mechanism, however, has not yet taken shape in the child. How are the complex systems of intra- and inter-analyzer connections formed in the child? It is well known that the retina of a newborn child has the same structure as that of an adult. Therefore, objects yield the same image for the infant as for the adult. But, as has already been noted, the size of perceived objects cannot be assessed from only one retinal image. At first the infant does not possess the ability to watch—that is, to bring the visual axes of the eyes together at a single point and transfer them from one point to another. In other words, the infant has not yet learned to control the motor component of the visual analyzer. This ability is acquired and developed as experience is accumulated. Without sufficient experience, small children often make false conclusions about the size of objects, since they judge them solely from the size of a retinal image.

Sechenov has also pointed out the role of the word included in the perception process in developing children's ability to distinguish objects by size and to make appropriate statements about them. By repeatedly perceiving objects of different sizes and their component parts, located at varying distances, and by connecting these perceptions with the names of objects and the designations of their sizes, the child learns to compare and name them and to determine which is larger or smaller. These notions about the different sizes of objects and about the whole and its parts are refined by tactile sensations, which are combined with visual sensations during perception. Sechenov writes:

> The child has learned to find the difference between the number of visual spheres covered by the image of an entire object on the retina and by a part of it. Then the child can finally distinguish the size of two separate objects pictured on his retina; the one whose image occupies more space will be the larger object, and the one whose image occupies less space will be the smaller [4:134].

Thus, Sechenov shows that the complex conditioned reflex underlying the visual perception of dimensions is cultivated gradually, through lengthy experience. This experience starts accumulating at an early age, when the perception of size involves establishing connections among the visual, tactile, and muscular-tactile sensations triggered by toys and objects of various sizes with which the small child operates. The child gradually builds up sensory experience at perceiving and estimating size.

Numerous psychological studies have shown that to develop the most elementary knowledge of size, the child must accumulate a host of specific notions about the objects and phenomena in his environment. Studies in this area have been conducted under the direction of B. G. Anan'ev at Leningrad State University, as well as at the Scientific Research Institute for Preschool Education under the direction of A. V. Zaporozhets and L. A. Venger, and at the A. I. Herzen State Pedagogical Institute in Leningrad under the supervision of A. M. Leushina, A. A. Lyublinskaya, and others. The notion of size, like other types of spatial distinctions (relations among objects, etc.), is a considerably more complex process than distinguishing the other qualities of an object. As with shape, children accumulate notions of size during their everyday activity.

The ability to perceive object sizes at different distances and in different positions is called perceptual constancy in psychology. Constancy in perceiving object sizes is developed with experience. Numerous studies on the emergence and development of constancy in children demonstrate that it is developed only at the end of the first year, in proportion to accumulated experience, and it is built up by means of operations with objects.

As a result of these operations with objects, reactions not only to objects of various sizes, but even to relationships among objects of different sizes can be cultivated in children in their second year of life, even before they have learned active speech. But their experience in distinguishing sizes remains local for a long time. A size attribute that has been learned is reinforced in the child for a specific object as absolute rather than relative: "Only our dog is big."—"No, my Marinka is big," two-year-old children will argue. Regardless of a doll's position and size, even small children recognize it. Constancy in perceiving objects that are repeatedly encountered gradually becomes comparatively stable.

Preschool Children's Perception of Object Size

Preschool children between the ages of three and seven can already distinguish the sizes of many familiar objects. At three or four, children can be sent to fetch the large ball or the long stick. These words and notions about the differences in the parameters of dimension are already found in their passive speech. Children also correctly identify the figures of an adult and a child at a distance. All this indicates constancy in perceiving the sizes of objects that occur in their experience over a long period of time. Taking into consideration the local character of small children's notion of size, it is essential that they encounter like objects of differing sizes.

As I. M. Sechenov indicated, the word that designates a certain attribute of an object plays a considerable role in the perception of object size. The words *big* and *little* serve as a universal definition of perceived size for preschool children. Whether an object changes in length or width, in height or thickness, or in several ways at once, children describe all these changes as *more* or *less* and *big* or *little*. Comprehension of the meaning of the word *size* is absent even from the passive discourse of four-year olds. Most four-year-olds are unable to answer when asked the size of a ribbon, a tower, or a book. They might ask in surprise: "What do you mean, size? I don't understand." And when answering the question, they might name the color of objects given to them, or the quantity, but not the size.

But, although they do not have a precise word to designate a certain dimension of an object (*long* or *short*, *wide* or *narrow*, *high* or *low*, etc.), preschool children actually do distinguish them. At the same time, as psychological research shows (B. G. Anan'ev, L. A. Venger, A. A. Lyublinskaya, and others), speech and precise words have an immense influence on the perception process. The word leads to identifications of the general features of an individual object. The word is the bearer of a specific concept. Therefore, "in the development of perception, speech functions to include in perception the logical components represented by the word," L. A. Venger writes, "enabling mental operations and categories to influence perceptual activity and its results" [6:13].

In introducing children to various kinds of dimension, teachers fail to consider the significance of designating them precisely with a word and themselves often say *big* or *little* instead of giving a precise name to the parameters of the dimension (*big tree* instead of *tall, big pencil* instead of *long* or *thick, big chair* instead of *high*).

Even in comparing the sizes of objects, the task itself is often formulated improperly. Instead of saying, "Find an object of the same length (or width)," the teacher says, "Find one that is just like this." And since an object possesses many attributes, the child carries out this assignment according to the most familiar attribute (color, the object's function, etc.). The word *same* has many meanings and does not reveal what the teacher had in mind. The perceptual operation should include a precise word that will help develop the concept of a certain type of dimension. When there is no precise word, children usually remain even longer at the level of a first- signal task.

There is another very important factor in the recognition of size that is not taken into consideration—the relative character of the given concept. *Long* and *short, wide* and *narrow*, and other parameters are relative concepts; therefore, they can be comprehended only on the basis of comparison—contrasting two objects in size. In order to familiarize children with the words *long* and *short*, the teacher must first bring out the meaning of the concepts *longer—shorter*. And, as many studies show (L. A. Venger, E. V. Proskura, R. L. Berezina, etc.), only a selection on the basis of comparison provides for the differentiation of the various parameters of dimension. This selection should gradually grow more complex: selection between two objects is replaced by selection among three or more, and the children are ultimately led to understand the sequence in decreasing (or increasing) a certain dimension and to gain sense for the relativity of size. When properly instructed, children begin putting objects in correct order according to size.

While placing objects in increasing (or decreasing) order according to a certain parameter, children learn ordinal relations by analogy with the reciprocal relations between consecutive numbers in counting. However, both the perception of simple relations between two entities and mastery of the relations in a sequence require instruction, as has been persuasively shown in a number of studies.

Thus, the perception of object size always amounts to contrastive measurement of objects according to various dimensions and determination of which is wider or narrower, longer or shorter, higher or lower, thicker or thinner, larger or smaller (using all parameters or a number of them).

Children's Isolation of Three Dimensions in an Object

Many objects can be characterized by three dimensions (length, width, and height). In estimating the size of three dimensional objects, we compose a description of the size of the object (*a deep but short cabinet, a bookcase narrower than the buffet, all tables of the same height*). We refer to many objects as *thick* or *thin*, with their diameter in mind.

But in order to make up such a description, we must be able to analyze the objects—to identify the corresponding dimensions in each object and establish size relations among them. How do preschool children conceive of three-dimensionality in objects?

There is a widely held opinion that children have no understanding of three- dimensionality even at the end of their preschool years. But many recent studies have shown that, given instruction, children in the older and preparatory preschool groups can properly carry out a task that requires them to identify length, width, and height in objects (R. L. Berezina).

For instance, Serezha K. (6 years and 11 months of age) was told to: "Look carefully at the box and show where its height is." He inspected the box from all sides and, showing the height with his spread fingers, said: "It is short." "Now show the length." The boy moved his finger from left to right along the front face of the box, accompanying this action with the words: "Here, this is the length." When asked to show the width, Serezha showed the width across the top face of the box.

Thus, this boy subjected the box to a fully conscious analysis for the three dimensions. Singling them out caused him no noticeable difficulty. Such operations can be observed in a number of children in the older and preparatory preschool groups, although showing the height in different objects gives them trouble. Thus, for example, children often deny that a short box has height: "This box has no height," six-year-olds say. Some show the top surface of the object instead of the height, passing their hands along the top.

How do three- and four-year-olds perceive three dimensions? When asked to find the tallest or longest object among a number of given objects, three-year-olds usually select the largest object, based on its total size; children of three perceive the words *long* and *tall* as synonyms for *big*.

Four-year-olds begin to differentiate in selecting objects according to greater length or width, but only if the object's length exceeds its width. It is considerably harder for children to find an object's height. For instance, children will find a high tower, but when it is a matter of different-sized boxes, where the heights are not immediately evident, children rarely find the tallest one, declaring: "There's no tall one here." It should be noted that even children in the older preschool group experience considerable difficulty in performing this task.

However all these difficulties are merely the result of deficiencies in the teacher's work on comparing, distinguishing between the different dimensions, and demonstrating the meanings of measurement terms to children (*longer—shorter, long—short, wider—narrower, wide—narrow, taller—shorter, tall—short, thicker—thinner, thick—thin*).

Experience shows that children in the older and preparatory preschool groups require an insignificant period of time to learn to find all three dimensions in objects shaped like a rectangular parallelepiped. Instruction makes children begin to be interested in seeking out various parameters in objects or toys in different positions in space. Children find the length and width of objects especially rapidly and accurately, and only height continues to cause them trouble. The hand's movement along the length, width, or height of an object plays a considerable part in finding an object's dimensions; it helps the children to differentiate an object's length, width, or height more accurately. Children love to "experiment," assigning different positions to objects and determining the parameters of dimension. Thus, children will find the height, length, and width of a pencil case standing on a table. Then they will lay it down horizontally and again seek its length, height, and width, which have changed in the new position. Such investigations become an interesting game. Their interest in this activity prompts children to contrast and compare objects by sight (which one is taller or shorter, which is thicker or thinner).

Development of the Ability to Gauge Comparative Size by Sight

At first, small children measure objects in a practical way by superimposing or associating one with another. In gauging comparative size by sight this technique becomes useless. To measure, for example, a tree's height or the length of a fence by sight, sight estimation must be developed. This ability is promoted by the act of comparing objects. The eye seems to absorb or generalize the methods of the actual operations performed by the hand. The development of sight estimation is therefore highly important and should also be taught explicitly. Even Rousseau found it necessary to teach Emile to compare the sizes of objects by sight, comparing the height of a building with that of a person, or the height of a tree with that of a steeple.

We know from previous studies that the threshold potential of sight estimation increases with age. Indicative of this is the solution to an elementary problem such as picking the larger object of two objects of different size. Is a correct solution of the problem always determined by the threshold potential? For example, it turns out to be more complicated for children to choose an object of a certain dimension according to a model; they are only half as good at solving this problem as at finding the size of two objects by placing them back-to-back. A new intellectual task confronts the children—finding a method of comparison. This task becomes increasingly complex in proportion as the magnitude of the difference between the objects to choose between diminishes.

An even more complex problem for children involves picking a stick equal to a model made up of two smaller sticks. Children of three or four years cannot do this problem at all, and children of five to seven years by no means always solve it, although they show an interest in it. Apparently, the reason is not that they cannot solve the problem, since a many children do manage to solve it, but rather their inadequate training in techniques and methods of sight-estimate operations.

In comparing three objects, one of which is the model, the child should learn to compare each object with the model and decide whether they are equal in size; that is, he must master the operation of successive comparison, the most efficient method of solving the problem. This must be taught to children.

Thus, the model presented to the child should play the role of a standard to which other objects are to be compared—it should be a measure of linear quantities. Therefore, it is quite important that the child also perceive this standard as a measure. Children should be asked to make such a "measuring stick" (model) themselves, so that it could serve as an intermediate link for comparison.

The next task consists in teaching children methods of measuring with using a measuring stick (showing them that the end of the measure must be aligned with the end of the segment to be measured) and, by comparing the measuring stick with the object, determining whether they are equal or unequal. As research and experience have shown, when a measuring stick is introduced, accuracy in determining size increase significantly even when the objects to be compared are only minimally different. A measuring stick plays exactly the same role in giving two segments a length equal to that of a model.

Consequently, solving sight-estimate problems depends not so much on the sight-estimate threshold as on the mastery of certain methods of making sight-estimates. Several conclusions for methodology necessarily follow: children must be consistently taught practical methods of contrastive measurement such that sight-estimate operations gradually increase in complexity. The more complex the sight-estimate problem, the more important it is to outline a sequence of instruction (at first on a practical level).

Our analysis of how children perceive the size of objects, suggest four conclusions.

1. Children begin to make sensory distinctions in the sizes of objects at an early age. However, toddlers often reinforce the size attribute for specific objects and thus do not always immediately recognize relativity in size estimation.

2. Children of preschool age often experience considerable difficulty in distinguishing the different dimensions and in estimating size, since, on the one hand, they do not always have precise command of the word that defines a dimension, and, on the other hand, they do not pay proper attention to developing sensory perceptions of object size.

3. Children in the older and the preparatory preschool groups have shown potential not only for differentiating various dimensions when they are perceived and compared in isolation (length, width, height, thickness), but also for recognizing three-dimensionality in objects regardless of their position in space.

4. Research data also show diverse ways in which sight-estimation of object size is developed by the use of conventional measuring sticks.

All of these conclusions should have an impact on teaching methods.

Children's Perception of Geometric Figures

Geometric figures are standards that a person uses to determine an object's shape. Shape, like size, delineates one object from another in space. The shape of objects has acquired a generalized reflection in geometric figures. How can preschool children learn the shape of an object, and how does their perception of geometric figures become more exact? The development of a notion of shape is one of the problems of sensory training.

A notion of an object's shape as the boundary between the object and the space around it emerges very early in children. Experiments have shown that an infant identifies what he drinks milk from according to the shape of the bottle. At an early age children identify familiar objects independent of their position in space (for instance, a doll or a table upside down). But a preschool child does not recognize a square if it is not facing him in the customary position but is, for example, rotated 45 degrees. In such instances the immediate similarity of shape vanishes. In order to recognize the square, one has to turn it mentally, and the preschooler cannot do, since his practical experience with this object is extremely limited. It follows that the child does not yet see an identity in the shape of various objects that are less familiar to him; therefore, he cannot generalize them on the basis of shape.

A considerable role in the identification of objects is played by geometric figures, with which everyday objects are compared. It is therefore extremely important to familiarize children with the basic geometric figures and teach them to distinguish and name them regardless of their size. Studies show that at first children of three or four perceive geometric figures as ordinary toys and by analogy with familiar everyday objects, giving them the names of these objects: a cylinder is a glass or a post, a trihedral prism is a roof, a cone is a tower, two circles in a row are eyeglasses, a rectangle is a little window, and an oval is a little egg (S. N. Shabalin).

Under instruction by adults, children's perception of geometric figures is gradually restructured. Children soon stop identifying them with objects and begin merely comparing them, as reflected in their speech: a cylinder is like a glass, a triangle is like a Young Pioneer's necktie. And finally, children begin to perceive geometric figures as standards with which they can compare everyday domestic objects (a ball or an apple is a sphere; a carrot is a cone; a plate, saucer, or wheel is a circle, etc.). A geometric figure functions as a model for sorting out objects. Children can also sort out geometric figures according to the model. What is the role of the model for the child's selection in the perception of a geometric figure? Studies have shown that as early as the second year, children freely select a figure according to a model, but only if the two figures that they have to choose between are contrasting in shape (e.g., a square and a semicircle). Distinguishing between a rectangle and a square, or between a square and a triangle is considerably more complicated for children of two or three, since they must identify subtler features of shape.

But what goes into the selection itself? Here two processes are combined: (1) acquaintance with the model, that is, a careful analysis of its structure; and (2) identification of the model from among the other figures by comparison, that is, finding and identifying the same essential characteristics in the objects. This, of course, is a complicated task for young children, and instruction is required to enable them to cope with it.

Identification of a geometric figure does not imply the existence of a concept. An elementary concept of geometric figures becomes completely accessible to children only at the age of six or seven years. Defining a concept means accurately identifying the corresponding class of objects and enumerating their essential attributes. Older preschoolers gradually learn (as a result of instruction) this definition of a concept with an indication of the general class of an object and the distinguishing features of this class. Moreover, knowledge of the simple properties of geometric figures, and understanding of the relations between certain types of geometric figures become accessible to children of six or seven years. In geometry one concept is often defined in terms of another broader one. For instance, we say: "A square is a special case of a rectangle." However not every rectangle is a square, since in a square all sides are equal, but in a rectangle only the opposite sides are equal.

A square and a rectangle, in turn, can be defined by the even broader concepts of a parallelogram and a quadrilateral, and, even more broadly, by the concept of a polygon. An entire system of increasingly complex coordinated concepts can be represented in this way, and studies show that children evince considerable interest in this representation. Establishing these connections and coordinations develops and intensifies children's powers of thought, teaches them to perceive the surrounding world in a new way, and cultivates systematic and logical thinking.

The conclusion for teaching methodology is that in introducing children to various geometric figures, the teacher must gradually direct their attention to elementary properties (the number of vertices, angles, and sides in a figure, equal and unequal sides, their relative position, etc.), and teach children to group geometric figures according to attributes, thus emphasizing the invariance of shape.

What are the methods of introducing children to geometric shapes, and what is the role of the word? It has been demonstrated in numerous works on psychology and education that cognition of the structure of objects, their shape and size, is realized not only as a shape is perceived visually, but also through actively touching it, feeling it under the control of vision, and naming it with a word. The combined work of these perceptual analyzers promotes a more accurate perception of the shape of objects.

A single visual perception of an object does not satisfy the small child. In order to get to know it better, both younger and older children try to touch the object, take it in their hands, finger it, and sometimes turn it around. The visual and tactile examination can be different, depending on the object's shape and construction. Therefore, investigation by the visual and motor-tactile analyzers with a subsequent verbal explanation is extremely important or even essential for perceiving an object and determining its shape.

However, many authors note that preschool children manifest a very low level of investigating the shape of objects. They most frequently confine themselves to a cursory visual perception and thus determine the shape imprecisely, without distinguishing completely between the shapes of the oval and the circle, or the rectangle and the square (even when the objects have clear shapes).

When an object with a more complex shape is being perceived, however, only certain of its properties are grasped—its dimension, angles, depressions, or circumference, for instance—and the figure as a whole is not identified. Studies have shown that children are unable to discern an object's characteristics or identify its component features on their own. The way children draw is especially persuasive on this point. Thus, the hand and the eyes interact in identifying shape, helping each other, and this information is fixed in the word.

Studying the genesis of the movements of children's inquiring hands shows that a three-year-old's movements are more like grasping than feeling motions. But the hand movements of four-year-olds begin to show active feeling motions in the palm and the front surface of the fingers. Feeling is done by one hand, and the fingertips do not take part in touching.

Children of five or six years feel an object with both hands. Their hands move towards each other or diverge. The children still do not systematically observe the entire contour of an object. And finally, six-year-old children begin tracing the entire contour of a figure with their fingertips. The feeling motions seem to simulate the object's shape.

The genesis of eye movement is also persuasive evidence that eye movement along the outline of a figure seems to simulate its shape and promotes precise discernment. But this movement is typical only of six- or seven-year-old children. At an earlier stage (between the ages of three and five) the eye movements encompass only the internal areas of a figure. At first its size is apparently inspected, and only around the age of five does the eye start to encompass the most characteristic part of the form, thus promoting recognition of the perceived object to a certain extent. As a result of the improved method of inspecting a figure with the hand and eye and simulating its shape, not only is precision in recognition ensured, but the child also develops the ability to solve more complex sensory problems, to correctly reproduce a figure perceived while drawing, modeling, or building.[1]

We conclude that children must be taught methods of investigating the shape of a geometric figure or object according to contours as early as possible. The necessity for this actual simulation of a shape gradually disappears, to be replaced by the mere visual inspection of a figure, by the creation of an "ideal model and a perceptual image."

The methodology of teaching the perception of shape should also take into consideration another feature conditioned by the individual peculiarities of children's development. Some children show a particular interest in the entity with which they are concerned (an object or geometric figure), ask questions about what they are seeing, and try to name it and define its properties. Others prefer not to examine the entity themselves but only to hear what adults say: the word becomes most important for them. The varying quality of perception determines how complete and clear their notions are. Studies show persuasively that the more meager the child's sensory experience, the more superficial will be its notions of the entity, and the sketchier its specific image. Such differences in perception in young children most often result from their previous training. Therefore, children must be trained to make observations from an early age, without rushing to verbal conclusions and generalizations.

If the spoken word is included in the direct perception correctly and at the proper time, it deepens perception, promoting the retention of what is observed. Words do not reduce sensory knowledge of the properties of an object, but rather raise it to the level of a generalization. Words outside of sense perception do not evoke specific images; they merely awaken a recollection of what the child has been told by adults. The specific image itself will remain indistinct and schematic, as before.

The conclusion for teaching methodology is that the word must always retain a sensory image rich in specific content. Thus, for small children geometric figures take their place beside ordinary toys; the children manipulate them like other toys, and their shape is not yet differentiated from the manipulations of play. Later on the child's cognitive activity gradually begins to be differentiated; there appear techniques for tactile-motor and visual inspection of the shape of geometric figures, and comparison of them, first with everyday objects, and then with everyday objects that have the shape of geometric figures (feeling individual objects, inspecting them from different sides, and so on). Finally, the child's investigation becomes systematic and regular, and is based on the contours of the figure: the correlations of the figure's sides are carefully examined, the sides are counted, and various distances and sides of the figure are measured.

As studies have shown, the development of children's cognitive activity is considerably accelerated and improved under an adult's instructive guidance. It follows that it is essential to teach children proper techniques of investigating the shape of geometric figures at an early age; to develop their ability to ascertain their elementary properties; to teach the selection of figures of different colors and sizes according to words and models; to teach them to group geometric figures according to different attributes (shape, size, color); to teach them how to find the similarity between the objects around them and certain geometric figures; and to teach them how to modify figures and make new models of objects.

The Distinctive Development of Children's "Sense of Weight"

Children's sensory development is multifaceted. Also quite important is the development of a "sense of weight," also known as the baric sense, which is a necessary basis for the later concept of the weight of objects and methods of measuring it.

Even small children distinguish all objects by their mass, reflecting their perceptions in the words *heavy or light*. The toddler tries to lift a chair and, realizing that he cannot, turns to adults for help. The word *heavy* appears comparatively early in children's speech. Children perceive differences between heavy and light objects when they bring muscle groups into play, and at first only when they encounter sharp contrasts in weight (e.g., a child's chair and a doll chair). But, as certain studies have shown, the perception of differences in the weight of objects grows increasingly profound.

M. Montessori, E. I. Tikheeva, and Yu. I. Fausek have devoted considerable attention to the development of the baric sense. To cultivate subtle differentiations in preschool children's baric sense, Fausek, for example, offered a box with several compartments, in which were placed 6 x 8 x 0.5 cm wooden panels made from various kinds of wood: walnut, whitewood, alder, ash, mahogany, etc. The difference in weight of 12 paired panels of each kind varied from six to eight grams. The polished panels preserved the natural appearance and color of the wood. The exercises with the panels amounted to making subtle distinctions in their weight by weighing them in the palms of both hands. The children caught on to these distinctions with comparative ease, according to Fausek [1].

The development of the baric sense deepens the children's cognitive activity. While at first children's notion of heaviness is always connected with an object's large volume, as the baric sense is developed the children realize that small objects can be heavier than huge ones (a large balloon is lighter than a small rubber ball), and spheres of the same size can vary in weight, depending on the material of which they are made. Gradually children come to a practical understanding of why a small metal ball will sink in water while a large ball floats; as he weighs both objects on his palms, the child grasps their difference in weight. This sort of practical experience brings children to an understanding of new, different connections between weight and volume, not only direct, but also indirect connections.

The pedagogical conclusion is that it is important to devise methodological techniques for developing the baric sense in children as a sensory basis for subsequently measuring weight.

5

Developing Techniques of Measuring Length, Mass, and Vessel Capacity for Older Preschool Years

Measurement in terms of commonly accepted units of length, mass, and vessel capacity is a part of mathematical knowledge. Counting objects and making elementary measurements are two types of activity which are closely connected with man's elementary needs. F. Engels points out: "Like all of the other sciences, mathematics arose from the *practical needs* of people: measuring the area of plots of land and vessel capacity, reckoning time, and mechanics" [2:37-38].

A characteristic property of size is that it can be measured—that is, compared in one way or another with a certain definite quantity of the same kind which is taken as the unit of measurement. The very comparison process depends on the property of the quantity to be measured and is called measurement. As a result of measurement we obtain an abstract number that expresses the relation between the quantity being measured and the quantity taken as the unit of measurement.

Measurement broadens our representation of objects and phenomena in the surrounding reality. The practical measurement of time and other quantities, such as mass and vessel capacity, deepens our temporal and spatial representations, promoting the development of logical thinking in conjunction with sensory faculties.

Measurement whereby a short unit is marked off a certain number of times along the quantity that is to be measured includes (as Piaget points out) two logical operations. The first is the division process, which enables the child to understand that a whole consists of a number of parts put together. The second is the operation of displacement or substitution, which enables the child to connect one part to another, thus creating a system of units [3:125]. On the basis of this description, Piaget arrives at the conclusion that "measurement is developed later than the concept of number, because it is harder to divide a continuous whole into interchangeable units than to count up elements that are already divided" [3:126].

In recent years the study of notions and concepts in older preschool children and first-graders has yielded persuasive evidence that measurement skills and abilities are very significant. Measurement of continuous quantities, as many studies have shown, helps give students a deeper understanding of the concept of the unit. Actually, children often form connections that are not entirely correct when they count discrete objects: the unit is perceived as an individual object, as a separate element in a collection. Therefore, it is important and essential to train children to count not only individual elements, but also entire groups (the subsets that make up a set).

Including the measurement of quantities along with counting discrete sets makes it possible to deepen children's mathematical concept of number to an even greater degree. Counting and measuring should not be contrasted to one another. Each of these activities is directed at its own problems and mutually enhances the concept of number. In order to measure, a child must have learned to count—for instance, he must be able to count up the number of units in measuring length, mass, or vessel capacity. Thus, Piaget is correct in emphasizing that the development of counting and of the concept of number precede measurement to a certain extent.

The role of measurement in developing early mathematical notions was considered long ago in works by the great didacticians J. J. Rousseau, H. Pestalozzi, and K. D. Ushinskii, and in works by major methodologists of mathematics, D. I. Galanin, A. I. Gol'denberg, V. A. Latyshev, and others.

A number of Soviet educators, E. I. Tikheeva, L. V. Glagoleva, F. N. Blekher, etc., have also pointed out that preschool children of preschool age must require practical experience with methods of measuring different quantities. E. I. Tikheeva believed that children of five or six should be involved in measurements of various types: "It is very easy to give them practical experience with the meter and teach them to use it" [5:49].

L. V. Glagoleva shared the same opinion:

> Seven-year-olds should be taught to measure lines and the sides of a square or rectangle with a centimeter ruler and a decimeter, and to measure the length and width of the classroom, the length of a garden path or vegetable garden rows with a meter. The children should be able to draw a line of a certain length in their notebooks, and to measure the blackboard or a strip of paper of a given size. They should be able to measure a liter and a bottle in cups, and should have a notion of a kilogram of bread, potatoes, granulated sugar, etc. [1:45-46].

Glagoleva introduced children to the following units: the meter, decimeter, and centimeter; she recommended teaching them to measure with their hands and paces, by sight, using cups, glasses, spoons, and other units. She introduced them to 1-, 2-, 3-, 5-, 10-, 15-, and 20-kopek coins. Later studies also confirm that children can be taught to employ various units of measurement (the meter, the liter, the kilogram).

Measuring provides for the formation of new associative series of connections between counting and measuring. The quantity represented by a certain number is linked with the notions of dimensions and with children's development of a baric sense (weight).

In practical life children often have to measure (selecting the parts for building something, measuring off planks for work working, measuring their height, among other things). These types of measurement are still empirical—they are still not "real" measurements—but they clearly show that the children are attempting to penetrate to the essence of quantities and to use quantitative indices in their activity.

In the first semester of grade one the school curriculum calls for the development of measuring skills, together with skills in counting the elements of discrete sets. Counting and measurement promote an understanding of the quantitative relations in both discrete and continuous quantities. A "measure" becomes a criterion for the quantitative expression of magnitudes. Considering that as early as the first semester in school children are expected to be able to draw segments and shapes according to given centimeter measurements and to carry out various measurements with a meterstick, in the preparatory group they must understand the meaning and significance of the words used—the names for the units of linear measurement (meter, centimeter).

It is the job of the preschool establishments to prepare children for their school instruction. For this purpose, in particular, children of six and seven must be taught to measure with standard units so that they will have a deeper understanding of the conventional measurements in school (measurements of length, mass, and volume).

Six- and Seven-Year-Olds' Knowledge of Methods of Measuring Length

Most children of six or seven know that they must measure objects in order to determine their length. Some children correctly point out that the length and height of tables, cabinets, and similar objects, are measured in meters. Children who do not know the conventional units say that measurements are made with a ruler, a stick, a meter stick, or a tape measure. These answers show that the children are naming only the objects with which measurements are done rather than naming the units, and are describing their external attributes ("There are 20, or 30, or 70, or a lot of numbers drawn on it"; "In the store they measure with a meter, but it is a wooden one"). When asked what is measured with a meter, the children name various objects (bed sheets, furniture, a painting, paper, a person's height).

Children's notions of the measurement of dimension reflect their personal experience. Children are aware that they have to measure in order to determine the sizes of objects; they also know that their own height is measured, but they discuss the means of measuring very imprecisely ("With a centimeter," "Measuring by heads," "You have to stand back to back," "You draw a line on the door at home").

In their daily lives, without special training only certain children master the methods of linear measuring. They place an arbitrary measuring device on a ribbon, start at one end, mark the end of the measure with a finger, and continue measuring from exactly that point, while counting the number of measures that are laid off. Some children try to measure a ribbon in this way, and after marking the end of the measure, later fail to orient themselves from that point: they lay off the second measure either beyond the end of the first or on a part of the tape that has already been partially measured. Thus, marking off the end of the first measure does not provide them with a precise point for further measurement. Therefore, the number of measures they arrive at is imprecise. Finally, a considerable number of children use a measuring device absolutely at random. They move or shift it, or they start measuring somewhere other than the end of the ribbon, and so on. Their actions cannot be called measuring. These children are merely trying to copy the external actions of adults, without penetrating to their significance and content. But in as much as some children grasp the general meaning of linear measuring all on their own, investigators conclude that this type of activity is quite accessible to five- and six-year-olds when there is instruction, and that it is very interesting for them (L. Georgiev, R. L. Berezina, Z. E. Lebedeva, and others).

How do children conceive of the measurement of mass? Studying children's responses and their weighing techniques shows that children of five or six have a distinct notion that mass is determined with scales. When asked how to find out how much flour or granulated sugar certain sacks contain, children, as a rule, respond: "It must be weighed on the scales," "It has to be measured on the scale." "Put it on the scales and see." There are some responses that reflect everyday experience with dry measures: "It can be measured in cups," and so on. But even these children know that in stores all products "are weighed out on the scales."

Children also know that weighing is done by placing weights on a scale, but many do not know the mass of the weights themselves ("Weights are large and small, heavy and light"). Some indicate variants of the different masses of the products being weighed (4 kg, 12 kg, 15 kg, 20 kg, 40 kg, 100 kg, among others) rather than the mass of the weights themselves; only certain children gave proper names to the weight's masses (1 kg, 2 kg, 5 kg).

If we compare children's responses on measuring mass and length, it becomes evident that they know more about measuring mass. This is because they have richer experience in making observations when various products are weighed in stores. But the children's knowledge and skills need considerable refinement and systematization through regular instruction.

As studies have shown (R. L. Berezina, L. Georgiev, and others), children are weakest at measuring vessel capacity (measuring solid and liquid substances). Most children do not know, for example, how to measure the milk in a pitcher: "In centimeters," "With a ruler," "Measure it on the scales," "Measure it with a thermometer." Their answers indicate that they are a long way from actual measurement of liquid volumes, and the very word *measure* evokes only familiar associations from them. As a rule, children do not know the names of the measures of liquid volume, either. Some name only the measuring devices that adults use in their daily life (dipper, ladle, mug, glass, etc.). However, in giving accounts of purchases children say that they went with their parents to but a liter of milk or kvass, but they usually do not know that a liter is a measure. Children also lack distinct notions of different vessel capacities, and they do not know the techniques for comparing their volumes.

The ability to measure various objects has considerable value for children's general mental development. Therefore, the curriculum for older preschool children calls for instruction in the measurement of length, mass, and vessel capacity with standard measuring devices.

During instruction children learn that measurement enables us to give a more accurate quantitative description of the object being measured. They learn that there exists a functional relation between the number of measures and their size and that the numbers of measures stands in an inverse relation to the size (the smaller the measure, the greater the number of them when a single length, mass, or vessel capacity is being measured).

Experience in measuring with arbitrary measuring devices brings children to understand the significance of conventional measures and appreciate measurement as a mathematical operation by which a numerical relation is established between the quantity to be measured and the unit of measure, the scale, or the standard that has been chosen.

Thus, instruction in methods of measuring length, mass, and vessel capacity has shown that it is quite possible to teach preschool children to compare the masses of objects or various types of dimensions, not merely on the basis of sensory perception and distinction, but also by understanding the mathematical significance of a quantity as its numerical index.

The empirical knowledge that children acquire in their lives is gradually systematized during instruction, and their mental activity developed. " Effective mental activity," as Yu. A. Samarin writes, "depends not only on knowledge as such, but also on the degree of systematization" [4:482].

Scientific research and generalized practical experience have made it possible to develop a curriculum and methodology for working with children in every preschool age group.

6

Developing Children's Spatial Orientation

The problem of a person's spatial orientation is broad and multifaceted. It includes his notion of magnitude and shape, spatial distinctions, the perception of space, and an understanding of various spatial relations (that is, determination of an object's position in space among other objects, depth perception, etc.).

Studies in educational psychology have shown that spatial distinctions emerge very early, but that they are a more complicated process than distinctions based on the qualities of an object. Various perceptual analyzers (kinesthetic, tactile, visual, auditory, and olfactory) participate in developing spatial notions and methods of orientation in space. However, in small children the kinesthetic and visual analyzers play a special role.

Spatial orientation is accomplished on the basis of direct perception of space and verbal designation of spatial categories (location, distance, and the spatial relations among objects). The concept of *spatial orientation* includes an estimate of the distances, dimensions, shape, and mutual position of objects and their position with respect to the body of the onlooker.

In a narrower sense the expression *spatial orientation* means orientation in a locality. In this sense, orientation in space means the determination of a "standing point"—that is, the subject's location with respect to the surrounding objects—for example: "I am to the right of the house." Orientation in space also means the localization of the surrounding objects with respect to a person orienting himself in space—for example: "The cupboard is on my right, but the door is on my left." It also means determination of the spatial arrangement of objects with respect to one another—that is, the spatial relations among them—for example: "The teddy bear is sitting to the right of the doll, and the ball is lying to its left." When there is movement, spatial orientation is essential. A person cannot successfully move from one point in a locality to another without spatial orientation. This orientation always requires solving three problems: statement of the goal and selection of a route for the motion (a choice of direction), preservation of the direction during the movement, and achievement of the goal [2:81].

Perception of Space by Young Children

Many studies have been devoted to studying the development of spatial perception in young children. They show that the perception of space emerges when an infant of four or five weeks begins to focus his eyes on an object at a distance of 1-1.5 m. Eye movement to follow moving objects is observed in infants of two to four months. In the initial stage, the gaze-shifting is made up of jerky movements. Then a second phase sets in, involving continuous sliding movements to follow an object moving in space, as observed in various infants at three to five months of age.

Along with the development of a gaze-fixing mechanism, differentiated movements of the head and the trunk develop; the infant's own position in space changes. "At this age movement of an object elicits eye movements," D. B. El'konin writes [1:79]. However, the child still does not examine or search for objects. Looking for objects appears later, on the basis of following an object's movement in space with the eyes. Therefore, it is sometimes almost impossible to draw a clear line between following and searching. As the child amasses sensory-motor experience, his ability to distinguish entities in space grows, along with differentiation between distances. Thus, the three-month-old infant learns to follow an object at a distance of 4-7 meters, and at 10 months the infant can follow an object moving in a circle. This process of seeing a moving object at various distances indicates that even before one year of age the infant begins to master spatial depth. Thus, the movement of an object becomes a source for sensory development and reorganization of the sensory functions before the child himself begins to move toward objects.

Apparently, the infant first perceives space as an unbroken continuity. Movement separates an object from the mass of surrounding space. At first the focusing of the glance, then the turning of the head, the movement of the hands, and other actions show that things that move are becoming objects of the infant's attention, even stimulating his own intermittent movements.

The ability to follow an object's movement in space develops steadily. At first the infant perceives an object perceived in a horizontal direction; then, after lengthy practice, the infant learns to follow an object's movement in a vertical direction, which expands his field of vision and stimulates his movements toward the object. The movements of the object and the infant gradually begin to develop sensory mechanisms jointly.

The infant's actual mastery of space expands considerably as he adopts a vertical position and begins to move (walk) on his own. As the infant moves, he learns the distance between one object and another and performs operations somewhat reminiscent of measuring distance. For example, if a child is holding on to the back of the crib with one hand and wants to move to the sofa, he will repeatedly reach out his hand toward the sofa at various points in his movement, as if measuring the distance. Once he figures out the shortest way, he lets go of the crib and starts to move, leaning on the sofa seat. With walking there emerge new sensations of overcoming space—a sensation of balance and acceleration or slowing of movement—which combine with visual sensations.

This practical mastery of space by the child functionally transforms the entire structure of his spatial orientation. A new period begins in the development of spatial perception, the spatial attributes and relations of objects in the external world.

Gaining practical experience in dealing with space permits the child to gradually learn words to generalize the experience. Immediate, everyday experience still plays the leading role in the cognition of spatial relations and in the development of notions during the early and younger preschool years. The preschool child accumulates experience during diversified types of activity (outdoor play and building games, drawing activity, observations during walks, etc.). As experience is accumulated, words become more important in developing a systemic mechanism for perceiving space.

Some Features of Preschool Children's Spatial Orientation

Spatial orientation requires the ability to use some *system of reference*. In early childhood, the child orients himself in space on the basis of what is called a sensory reference system—that is, according to the sides of his own body.

In the preschool years the child learns a verbal reference system based on the basic spatial directions: *forward—back, up—down, right—left*. Instruction in school helps children learn a new reference system of reference based on the directions of the compass: north, south, east, and west.

It has been established that learning each successive system of reference is based on a firm knowledge of the previous system. Thus, studies have demonstrated convincingly that in order for third- and fourth-graders to learn the directions of the compass, they must be able to differentiate the basic spatial directions on a map. For instance, children at first associate *north* with the spatial direction *up*, *south* with *down*, *east* with *right*, and *west* with *left*. But for the small child, the differentiation of the basic spatial directions is affected by the level of his orientation with respect to "himself," the extent of the mastery of the "scheme of his own body," which is, in essence, a "sensory reference system" (T. A. Museiibova).

Another system of reference, the verbal system, is later superimposed upon it. This occurs as a result of reinforcing the directions distinguished by the child's senses, represented by the corresponding words: *up, down, forward, back, right, left.* Thus, the preschool age is the period when children acquire the verbal reference system based on the basic spatial directions.

Studies have shown that the child first correlates directions with certain parts of his own body. In this way he establishes regular associations such as: "*up* is where the head is, and *down* is where the feet are," "*forward* is where the face is, and *back* is where the back is," "*right* is where the right hand is, and *left* is where the left hand is." Orientation to his own body serves as a starting point for the child to master spatial directions.

Of the three paired groups of basic directions that correspond to the various axes of the human body (frontal, vertical, and sagittal), the first direction a child identifies is the *up*, apparently because of the primarily vertical position of the child's body. *Down*, the opposite direction along the vertical axis, as well as the paired groups of directions characteristic of the horizontal plane (*forward—back* and *right— left*), is differentiated only later. Evidently, precise orientation in the horizontal plane based on these characteristic pairs of directions is a more complex problem for the preschool child than differentiation of the different planes (vertical and horizontal) composing three-dimensional space.

Even after basically mastering the pairs of opposite directions, the young child still makes mistakes in distinguishing the directions in each pair. Persuasive evidence of this is the way children confuse right and left, top and bottom, and forward and back. The distinction between right and left, founded upon the differentiation of the right and left sides of the body, presents particular difficulties for preschoolers. Consequently, children only gradually come to understand the pairing of spatial directions well enough to name them and make practical distinctions.

In each pair of spatial designations, first one direction is identified—e.g., *under, to the right, up, back*—and then the opposites appear through comparison with the primary directions—*over, to the left, down, or toward.* Thus, differentiation of one of a pair of interrelated, opposite spatial relations depends on knowledge of the other, and so teaching methods must develop reciprocal spatial notions simultaneously. All of these facts indicate that preschoolers' learning of the verbal reference system for the basic spatial directions is a lengthy and unique process.

How does a child acquire the ability to *apply* or use this reference system for orientation in surrounding space?

Stage I begins with actually trying out directions, expressed in a real correlation between the surrounding objects and the original reference point.

Stage II is marked by visual estimation of the arrangement of objects at a certain distance from the initial point. An exceptionally significant role is played by the motor analyzer; its participation in making spatial distinctions gradually changes.

At first the entire complex of spatial-motor connections is represented in a highly detailed way. For example, a child backs up against an object and only then says that this object is located behind him. The child touches an object to one side with his hand, and only then does he say which side the object is on—the right or the left. In other words, the child actually correlates objects with the sensory reference system based on the various sides of his own body.

Direct movement toward an object to establish contact with it is later replaced by turning the trunk, and then by a motion of the hand in the appropriate direction. Subsequently, the broad indicative gesture is replaced by a less noticeable hand movement. Then this hand movement is replaced by a slight movement of the head and, finally, by a mere glance directed toward the object that is being located. Thus, the child passes from an active method of spatial orientation to another method, based on visual estimation of the spatial arrangement of objects with respect to one another and to the subject who perceives them. This perception of space, as I. P. Pavlov wrote, is founded upon experience of direct movement within space. Only through motor stimuli do the related visual stimuli acquire their vital, or signal meaning. Thus, as children acquire experience in spatial orientation, externally expressed motor reactions become intellectualized. The process of their gradual reduction and the transition to the level of mental operations is a manifestation of the general tendency away from the materialized and practical in the development of mental activity.

Children's Orientation in a Locality

As spatial orientation develops, the nature of the reflection of perceived space changes and improves. The perception of the external world, as I. M. Sechenov has indicated, is broken up spatially. This partitioning is "imposed" on our perception by an objective property of space—its three-dimensionality. By correlating objects in space with the various sides of his own body, a person effectively partitions space according to the basic directions. One perceives the space around oneself as a locality divided into different zones: the front, the right, the left, and the back, or just the right and the left. But how does the child arrive at this perception and understanding? What is the potential of preschool children?

At first, the only objects that children take to be situated in front of, behind, to the right or to the left of them are those that directly border on the corresponding sides of their bodies or are as close as possible to them. Consequently, children at first orient themselves in an extremely limited area. Orientation itself is accomplished via contact proximity in this instance—that is, literally onto and away from oneself.

At three years of age, children show a potential for making visual estimates of the arrangement of objects with respect to the initial reference point. It is as if the boundaries of the reflected space are moving away from the child, but locating objects situated in front, behind, to the right, or to the left involves representing extremely narrow sectors of space directly adjacent to the sagittal and frontal lines. These seem to be straight lines in the locality which are perpendicular to each of side of the subject where the reference point is established. The position of an object at an angle of 30-45° in the front-right zone, for example, is not defined by the child as being either in front or on the right. "It's not in front, but more to the side," the child usually says in these cases, or: "It's not on the right, but a little to the front." Space, which was at first perceived diffusely, now seems to be divided into segments.

When the child is five, the area of the segments he picks out—front, back, right, and left—gradually increases. The extent of their remoteness along one line or the other (frontal or sagittal) increases. Now the child defines even remote objects as situated in front or behind, to the left or to the right. The area of the segments of the sagittal and frontal lines also increases gradually; they seem to move closer to each other. The child gradually begins to be aware of the locality as a whole in its indivisible unity. Each segment or zone is still considered absolute and is defined only as *front*, *back*, *right* or *left*, which are at first kept strictly separate from each other. The possibility of reversing them is still excluded.

Later the child picks out two primary zones: either the right and left, or the front and back. Two more sectors (or two sides) are then identified in each of these: in the front zone, for instance, the front right and front left sectors; in the back zone, the back right and back left sectors. If the right and left zones are primary, they will contain front right and back right sectors as well as front left and back left sectors. The child now clearly designates intermediate points in space: front right, front left, and so forth. The child at this age interprets the partitioned nature of the unified space that he perceives according to the basic directions. He identifies various zones and sectors within each zone, while allowing for reversals and for mobile borders. Study of the development of children in their preschool years, before any instruction, has shown that only certain children of six or seven achieve the highest level. But instruction makes that level accessible to all six-year-old children.

Features of Preschool Children's Perception of the Spatial Arrangement of Objects

The stages of spatial orientation toward oneself, away from oneself, and away from objects do not replace one another, but coexist, entering into complex dialectal interrelationships. It was indicated above that orientation toward oneself is not only a definite level but also an indispensable condition in orientation in the arrangement of objects both away from oneself and away from other entities. In determining the situation of objects people constantly correlate the surrounding objects with their own coordinates. Children do this particularly vividly when they determine the given sides in relation to themselves, then do a mental rotation of 180° and, while standing in the position opposite the standing person, determine that person's left and right sides. Only then can children determine the spatial situation on the other person's right or left. Consequently, the orientation in relation to themselves is the initial one. Orientation away from oneself presupposes an ability to use a system where the origin of reference is the subject, but orientation away from objects requires that the origin of reference be the object with respect to which the spatial situation of other objects is determined. Here one must be able to dismember various sides of the object: the front, back, right, left, top, and bottom. The development of spatial orientation toward oneself, away from oneself, and away from another object in the situation of objects also occurs during the preschool period. An index of its development in children might be the gradual transition from the child's use of a system with a fixed point of reference (toward the child) to a system with a freely transferable reference point (toward other objects).

Features of Preschool Children's Perception of the Spatial Relations Among Objects

How does the development of the perception and reflection of spatial relations among objects proceed in preschool children? At *Stage 1* the child perceives surrounding objects as "detached entities," without being aware of the spatial interconnections that exist among them. While children of an early age have an amorphous and undismembered notion of space, in the preschool period the reflected space is discrete. Thus, many children between the ages of three and five define various spatial groups of objects as adequate merely because the objects included have something in common. For example, three identical objects that are variously situated with respect to one another are shown on two cards. "The cards are the same," the child says. "Here there's a teddy bear, and here there's a teddy bear, too; here there's a bunny, and here; a *matryoshka*, and here's a *matryoshka*..." The child sees the identical objects, but seems not to notice the spatial relations in the arrangement of these objects, and therefore does not see the differences between the cards. This same feature of perception was indicated above, when the children were guided merely by the representation of objects in reproducing them by the method of superimposing, without noticing the spatial relations among them. Therefore, the technique of associating the elements of one group with those of another proved to be highly complicated for them. *Stage II* is characterized by the first attempt at perceiving spatial relationships. A distinctive transition is made from the discrete character of spatial perception to the reflection of spatial relationships. But the precision in evaluating these relationships is still relative. For example, the distance at which an object is situated from the adopted reference point is still very difficult for the children. They perceive the spatial relations of objects situated comparatively close to one another as a continuity. For instance, when arranging toys in a straight line or a circle, they press them close together. This shows their striving to establish contact in arranging the objects in a row, one after another, or opposite one another. This is why, when a set is being reproduced by the technique of association children try to reproduce not so much the quantity as the proximity of the elements to one another. Their evaluation of spatial relations is still highly diffuse, although they are not a matter of indifference to the children, in themselves. *Stage III* is characterized by further improvement in the perception of the spatial arrangement of objects. Determining spatial relations by the contact technique is replaced by a distant, visual appraisal of these relations. A considerable role in the proper evaluation of the relations among object belongs to language, which promotes a more precise differentiation of them. The children's mastery of the significance of spatial prepositions and adverbs enables them to give a more accurate interpretation and evaluation of the arrangement of objects and of the relation among them. Research and practical experience have shown great possibilities for children's recognition of spatial relations and for the development of abilities for independently designating the location of concealed objects among other objects, using spatial prepositions and adverbs. Abstracting the spatial relations among objects is a lengthy and complex process, which is not completed at the end of the preschool period, but continues to be perfected during school instruction. A general conclusion is that the child's cognition of the "scheme of his own body" is the basis for mastery of the verbal system of reference according to the basic spatial directions. This also affects the proximity of the disposition and direct contact between subject and object when their spatial relations are being determined, at the initial stages. The child transfers the "scheme of his own body" to the object that is serving as a fixed reference point. Therefore, it is highly important to teach the child to distinguish the sides of objects (front, back, lateral, and so on). The motor analyzer has an immense role in developing children's spatial orientations. Reliance on a complex of actual motor connections gradually diminishes. The children begin developing a distant, visual evaluation of the spatial situation of objects, which enables them to determine the location of an object and its relation to themselves and to other objects at any point in the locality with increasing precision. The general course of development of the process of orientation in space and the reflection of it is the following: first, diffuse, unbroken perception, against a background of which only particular objects are singled out without the spatial relations among them; then, on the basis of notions about the basic spatial directions, space begins to be divided up, as it were, according to these basic lines—vertical, frontal, and sagittal, with the points on these lines singled out as situated in front or in back, to the right or left, gradually moving farther and farther away from the child. As the isolated segments increase in length and width, they are gradually closed up, forming a general notion of a locality as a single continuous but differentiated space. Every point in this locality is now precisely localized and is define as situated in front, or in front to the right, or in front to the left, or whatever the case may be. The child is approaching the perception of space a whole in combination with its continuity and discreteness (T. A. Museiibova). As we see, children's cognition of space and their orientation in it are a complex and protracted process, and children's development of spatial notions requires special training, which is envisaged in the methodology. The basis of such training should be primarily the accumulation of sensory knowledge about the objects in the environment in their spatial relations. Vocabulary work and the perception of effective speech, both in various lessons (in mathematics, speech development, pictorial activity, and physical fitness) and in the children's games and daily lives, have considerable significance for the formation of a mechanism for second-signal regulation of spatial distinctions.

7

Perception of Time by Preschool Children

Time and Its Properties

Time exists objectively, outside and independent of our consciousness. The perception and cognition of time are merely the reflection of truly existing time in our consciousness. The characteristics of time are: 1) its fluidity—time is related to motion; 2) its irreversibility; and 3) the absence of obvious form—"it is unseen and unheard."

The very word *vremya* ("time") is derived from the Old Russian *veremya*, which means "rotation." The past, present, and future are interrelated in such a way that they cannot change places. The property of time's irreversibility, the passage of time in one direction, expresses the perpetual evolution of nature and society along an ascending line, from old to new. The basis for the perception of time is sensory perception. A complex of various perceptual analyzers promotes the sensory perception of the malleability of time, but I. M. Sechenov ascribed particular significance to auditory and muscular sensations. "Only sound and muscular sensation give a person a notion of time; not by their entire substance, but only in one respect—the malleability of sound and the malleability of muscular sensation" [2:77-78]. Therefore, Sechenov referred to sound and muscular sensation as the fractional analyzer of time and space.

I. P. Pavlov pointed out that timekeeping is characteristic of every component of the nervous system, to each of its cells, and he proved experimentally that any perceptual analyzer can "tell time." Pavlov stated that the physiological basis for time perception is an alternation between stimulation and inhibition, which makes it possible to "tell time." This idea has been confirmed by a number of studies: time is underestimated when the stimulatory process in the second signal system is relatively predominant, and it is overestimated when the inhibitory process is relatively predominant. Thus, precision in estimating time intervals is ultimately determined by the dynamics of the process of stimulation and inhibition. Differentiation of time intervals is nothing other than a result of conditioned reflexes for time.

The Psychology of Time Perception

Man's perception of time is conditioned by the whole course of evolution within the animal world. However, the perception of time even by animals high on the biological ladder is a purely biological phenomenon, qualitatively different from man's perception of time. Man's conscious perception of time has developed as a result of his social and productive activity. Animals completely lack man's various tools for measuring time, emotions, temporal concepts, and sense of purpose.

Man's time orientation reflects time in two distinct but complementary ways. One is the immediate sensation of duration, conditioned by visceral sensitivity, which forms the basis for conditioned reflexes. The other is actual time perception, the most complicated and complete form of reflection, which develops on a general organic basis and is closely related to the generalizing function of the second signal system. Direct perception of temporal duration is expressed in our ability to feel it, to appraise it directly, and to orient ourselves in time without auxiliary means. This ability is referred to as the "sense of time." In different types of activity the "sense of time" functions as a sense of tempo, as a sense of rhythm, or as a sense of velocity. The experience gained in differentiating time based on the activity of many perceptual analyzers plays a certain role in developing this sense. Thus, the "sense of time," along with sensory perception, includes logical components as well: knowledge of time measurements. Thus, the "sense of time" depends on an interaction between the first and second signal systems.

The "sense of time" can exhibit various degrees of development. In the early years it develops on the basis of a wealth of sensory experience without knowledge of the standards of time. A baby cries because it is feeding time. Once the infant is satisfied, he lies quietly, smiles, and goes to sleep. The infant does not yet have a generalization of the "sense of time"; it remains connected only with the specific activity on which it based—that is, it has a relatively narrow sphere of application. But learning the units of time and how to apply them will provide an opportunity to use the "sense or time" more broadly.

The "sense of time" is developed and perfected during practical activity, as a result of specially organized exercises, and learning the methods of evaluating time. In these instances it begins to function by regulating activity.

Thus, on the one hand, the developing perception of time has a sensory basis, and on the other hand, it rests on a mastery of the commonly accepted standards for evaluating time. The sensory perception of time is promoted by all the strictly periodic basic processes of our organic life (the rhythm of breathing, the heartbeat, etc.). In precisely the same way the entire rhythm of daily life promotes the cultivation of conditioned reflexes for time.

Psychological studies confirm the major role of the second signal system in developing notions of time and in assessing time intervals. Language makes it possible to determine various time segments in accepted units of measure and to determine the tempo, rhythm, and sequence of processes, as well as their alternations and periodicity.

The basis for time perception, as with any other form of perception, is the system of long-range actions that make up an image (B. G. Ananev). Time functions as a particular characteristic of the course of these processes in rhythm and tempo, in sequence, etc., which is measured by conventional standards.

What is involved in assessing, measuring, and reproducing a time interval? Studies have shown that verbal assessment of a time interval is the least precise, and that the most precise perception of time is observed when a time interval is reproduced. This is conditioned by the fact that while evaluating and measuring require merely that the time interval be mentally compared to a certain standard retained in the memory, reproduction of a demonstrated time interval requires not only that it be compared mentally with a standard, but that the interval actually be compared with the demonstrated standard. Difficulties in measuring a specified time interval are conditioned by the need to evaluate the interval and then measure it, which involves a number of perceptual analyzers—a combination of the vocal-motor, motor, and visual analyzers, for there is no single time analyzer which could take charge. The various properties of time are reflected by a complex of analyzers.

Thus, all psychological studies stress the special role of language and socially-established standards in the perception and evaluation of various aspects of time.

Problems in the Development of Time Orientation in Preschool Children

Physiological studies have shown that children of various ages develop conditioned reflexes for time at different speeds, and that preschool children acquire them unsteadily and with considerable difficulty.

Children's perception of the malleability and fluidity of time, along with its irreversibility and periodicity, is hindered considerably by the absence of visual forms. It is also complicated for children to understand the meaning of the words designating temporal relations because they are relative rather than absolute. For example, what is the difference between the words *now* and *right now*, or *today*, *yesterday*, and *tomorrow*? S. L. Rubinshtein writes [1:275]: "When these time designations have identical meaning, the specific moment in reality that they refer to is continuously moving. This is a complication that the child cannot immediately control." Therefore, we know that preschool children often ask adults: "Today it's tomorrow, but is it today now?" "Does the year go around in a circle? It was summer, but now it has passed, and it will come back again."

In the early stages of development the child orients himself in time on the basis of extra-temporal, qualitative attributes. Let us consider an example.

> Preparing to go to bed, *Sana N.*, aged 2 1/2, washes up and says to her mother, "Now I'll say, 'Good morning!'" Her mother responds, "No, you'll say that in the morning, but now it's nighttime." Sana asks, "What's the difference?" The mother laughs. Sana says, "We've just washed up, so now we should say 'Good morning!'" Her mother answers, "The difference is that in the morning it is daylight and people are starting to work, but at night it is dark and people are going to bed. At night we say 'Good night.'" Sana replies, "No, you say 'Good night' when you put on your nightgown. But I have just washed up now, and so I should say 'Good morning.'"

As we see, children's interest in time relations emerges very early. Although toddlers have trouble learning the special terms for time, they begin to correctly use the temporal inflections of verbs for the present, past, and future tense depending on their general speech development.[1]

Young preschoolers can provide more distinct time localization for events that have distinctive qualitative attributes. They begin to distinguish between the parts of the day by connecting them with the characteristic activity for those periods. They correlate certain familiar and emotionally attractive events with a definite time: "We have a Christmas tree when it's winter," "We'll go to the country when it's summer."

Children of four and five determine with relative accuracy brief time intervals that are familiar from personal experience. For example, they may know that they have a music lesson or a counting lesson after a day off from school, they expect it, and they get ready for it, asking their teacher about it. However, their notions of the duration of these lessons are imprecise. Although the teacher often cautions the children that there is only one minute left until the end of a lesson and that they should hurry, the warning does not organize their activity because they cannot imagine the duration of a minute. They do not connect the word *minute* with a sensory perception.

Notions about longer time intervals are imprecise even for older children. Their notions of the distant past are even dimmer. But children are interested in the past, although it is localized in time differently for different children, largely depending on whether adults bother to familiarize the children with temporal relations and whether they discuss the localization in time of various events known to the child. It turns out that children can learn a great deal given suitable guidance. Let us cite an example.

> Adults are talking about a trip to the Pushkin mountains. Sana N. (5 years and 9 months) expresses delight about the subject. Her mother says, "We'll be going to the Pushkin mountains, to the village of Mikhailovskoe, where Pushkin lived and worked. You will see it all there yourself." "Oh, how funny you are, Mama. Pushkin is dead." "Did he die a long time ago?" "Very long ago—100 years ago." "And how long ago is that? When you were little?" "Why, what are you talking about, Mama (laughs)! Even you and Papa weren't around when Pushkin died. But you know, Mama, if he hadn't been killed, he would have died of old age anyway. He probably would have died when I was very, very little."

Such examples as these testify that it is at least somewhat possible for older preschoolers to understand the remote time of certain historic events. Since the "Kindergarten Education Curriculum" specifies that older preschoolers learn about certain historic events, it must be ensured that children of this age develop more distinct time orientation.

The ability for more precise localization and understanding of the sequence of events in time can be promoted by awareness of the causal relations of the events, and above all by the development of the ability to use various time standards, thus making it possible to express temporal relations quantitatively. S. L. Rubinshtein writes: "Although temporal notions are usually developed relatively late in children (particularly when insufficient attention is devoted to cultivating them), their inaccessibility should not be exaggerated" [1:276].

Language plays a considerable role in developing a notion of time: it helps abstract and generalize various time segments according to their duration—second, minute, hour, day, week, month, year, etc. Children's accuracy in using these special designations depends on the specific content ascribed to each temporal standard—the basic attributes that characterize it. But the specific attributes characterizing certain time segments are quite local, since they are determined by differing conditions of geography, economy, and everyday life. Day will not always be characterized everywhere by light and by work, nor night by darkness and sleep. Therefore, it is extremely important to find other visual means to point out the regular changes in days, times of the year, etc. General attributes must be found which are characteristic of a certain standard. Thus, to understand the words *yesterday*, *today*, *tomorrow*, etc., it is first essential to understand the fluidity and cyclicity of days. The Moscow chimes often serve to notify young children how one day gives way to the next. "The day is turning," say children of four or five. Children of three or four can be aware of the standard of a "day," its structure (morning, afternoon, evening, night), and its duration and cyclicity if they receive proper adult guidance. Understanding the repetition of days helps familiarize children with the meaning of other time standards (days of the week, months, seasons, years), each of which the children enhance with distinctive specific attributes.

Thus, time begins to function actively for children as a characteristic of actual life processes: it characterizes duration, speed, sequence, tempo, and rhythm in these processes.

How are time categories actually reflected in the speech of children in their preschool and primary school years? Studies indicate that children of six or seven use temporal adverbs properly, but that not all time categories are realized at the same time or are properly reflected in the children's speech. Adverbs designating the velocity and localization of events in time are learned better, while adverbs expressing duration and sequence are not learned as well. However, a few lessons devoted to the meaning of the most difficult time adverbs help children comprehend them more precisely. We conclude that the process of giving vocal expression to temporal concepts in children between the ages of six and eight is in a stage of continuous growth. This development occurs with particular intensity between the child's sixth and seventh years if the process is directed. However, subtle differentiation of temporal relations still proceeds slowly in the preschool years, and depends largely upon the child's general mental and speech development. Training and educating the child is one powerful means of directing this process.

Some teachers complain that children have no conception of the approximate duration of an hour or a minute, and cannot say which is greater—an hour or a minute, a day or a week, even though they know the terms. Even older children cannot explain the significance of a clock or a calendar. Most children cannot interpret the movement of the hands of a clock, and they take wristwatches to be ornaments that adults wear on their wrists. Many children of six or seven cannot name the days in the week or the months in order, nor can they correlate the dates of familiar holidays with them. Similarly, they cannot correlate the months with the seasons of the year, nor do they know the casual relationship of the seasons. Children are unaware of the continuity of certain moments in their routines, the duration of lessons, and so forth.

This happens because the episodic lessons (done with children primarily by the verbal method) during which they learn about the attributes of the parts of the day (morning, afternoon, evening, night) and the seasons and memorize the order of the days of the week and the months frequently involve only rote learning. They do not develop basic concepts of time in the children—its fluidity and irreversibility, its rhythm and tempo, or its cyclic and periodic nature. The information children acquire about particular temporal designations remains on the surface of the juvenile consciousness, without revealing temporal relationships.

Psychology and physiology stress the need to develop children's "sense of time" (N. I. Krasnogorskii and others). It has been pointed out that three factors affect the assessment of time duration: the content of the activity, the degree of interest, and age. Time that is filled with varied events is rich in content and usually passes unnoticed, so that an estimate of its duration will be too short. On the other hand, the more monotonous the passage of time and the poorer its content, the more "drawn out" it seems, and it is estimated as lasting longer than it really does (S. L. Rubinshtein).

It follows that the second factor, the degree of personal interest in the given activity, undoubtedly affects the time estimate. An activity that is interesting to the child passes faster, its duration seems not unnoticed, and the estimate of its objective duration decreases. On the other hand, an activity that does not elicit positive emotions is perceived as more protracted than it actually is; the child wants to be rid of it as soon as possible. The study of children's notions of a one-minute duration shows that they do not understand the constantly repeated instructions: "Sit quietly just one minute," "Wait a minute," and so forth. The children do not know what can be done in this extremely small time interval; they have no sensory experience corresponding to the words *one minute*. Nevertheless, it is obviously essential to be able to estimate the duration of one's work. The teacher's warning, "Children, finish playing with your clay; there is only one minute left," is often heard in class. But the words "one (or two) minutes" have no sensory content for the children, and thus remain obscure. Some children of six or seven try to estimate the duration of their activity by themselves, but, as indicated above, their estimate is subjective and depends on their personal interest in the work and on the richness and diversity of its content. It is interesting that children of different ages (five, six, and seven years) estimate the duration of a minute with no perceptible differences. We can conclude that this sort of stagnation is conditioned by deficiencies in their education.

It should be recalled that some systems of preschool education, including that of Yu. I. Fausek, included special "lessons in silence" to promote the development of a sense of time (the children were asked to sit quietly, closing their eyes for one minute, which the teacher timed by the clock).

Pedagogical experimentation and the experience of many kindergarten educators provide convincing evidence that when children learn various methods of determining duration to employ along with sensory experience, they develop an objective estimate of the duration of time segments of 1, 5, 10, or 15 minutes using an hourglass. Children start putting this time estimate to good use in their activity and behavior. They develop a "sense of time", and gradually learn to respond to instructions pertaining to time ("don't be late," "finish at such-and-such a time," etc.). Time instructions mobilize children's attention and provide for rhythmic performance of tasks. They quickly select what they need and get to work without the usual brouhaha (T. D. Rikhterman).

Thus, since it is quite possible to impart to older preschool children certain abilities for regulating their own activity in time, their "sense of time" must be developed; the sensory experience of the duration of certain time segments should be connected with telling time by means of both words and special devices (hourglasses, followed by clocks and wristwatches).

Along with the development of a "sense of time," children need to form a notion of the fluidity, irreversibility, and periodicity of time, which leads to a grasp of the segments of the 24-hour day (morning, afternoon, evening, night), the days of the week as reflections of the repetition of days, seasons of the year, their sequence and cyclicity, and so forth.

The research of a number of authors shows that children have considerable potential to master the various temporal notions and concepts and the ways to develop them. This is taken into consideration in the methodology (see Chapter 12) and makes it possible to elevate teaching to a new and higher level.

8

General Didactic Principles in Teaching Children Elementary Mathematics

Teaching preschool children involves not only communicating knowledge and fostering abilities and skills, but also developing mental abilities and cognitive interests (the desire to learn and constantly find out new things)—that is, developing the child's personality.

The methodology of teaching mathematics at this stage is based on general educational principles: developmental instruction; the scientific approach and its connection with life; accessible instruction; systematic, logically consistent, and stable learning; the individual approach; conscious and active learning. But how are these principles to be applied in teaching elementary mathematics?

The Principle of Developmental Instruction

During instruction a child acquires certain knowledge, but teaching should by no means be reduced to shifting knowledge from an adult's mind to a child's mind. It is important for learning to ensure the development of children's powers of thought, that they develop an interest in knowledge and become mentally active, and that certain interrelationships form. Developmental instruction is aimed at developing the child's personality as a whole.

The principle of developmental instruction in elementary mathematics for young children envisages primarily introducing the children to the cognition of quantitative, spatial, and temporal relationships. The world is revealed to the children in new connections and relationships. The new way of looking at familiar objects also gives the children a new attitude toward them, stimulating their cognitive interest and developing their curiosity.

For example, looking at a long-familiar tree, they are struck by its tall, thick trunk and the abundance of branches of various sizes and shapes (thick, thin, long, short, straight, curved, and broken ones). Comparing trees, the children establish which is taller and which is shorter. As they examine the leaves on these trees, they find differences in their shape or size. This new way of seeing sharpens their perception of the objects around them.

However, in kindergarten, just as in school, the principle of developmental instruction is often violated. First, insufficient attention is paid to activating the children's thought in class. Teaching is often based merely on imitation and memorization. Of course, small children need to be taught practical operations with sets, methods of comparing their number, and the counting operation. They need to be taught to carry out the arithmetic operations, learn about the properties of geometric figures, and begin to measure magnitudes. If they do no master generally accepted techniques their thinking cannot be activated. Teachers must provide instructions and demonstrations when new material is being studied. But, depending on how well the children have learned a technique, they should be given an opportunity to think and act independently (even at the earliest stages). Even three-year-olds, for example, can act on the basis of purely verbal instructions, without the teacher showing them what to do. This causes them to recall techniques they have already learned.

Another error frequently made in teaching is not to ensure that children reflect their knowledge through diverse solution methods and statements. This often leads to stereotyped responses, which the children memorize but do not comprehend. It is important for children to think about the best way to answer a given question, or how an answer can be formulated differently, as well as how to prove that their answers are right.

Children must also be taught not only to prepare themselves to respond, but also to listen to their classmates' answers, inserting the necessary additions and corrections. "Who noticed a mistake in so-and-so's answer? How should it be corrected?" or "Who will add to so-and-so's answer?" "How can this be said (proved) in another way?" or "Who did it in a different way than so-and-so?" These questions stimulate the children's thinking.

During developmental work it is very important to teach children to use knowledge they have acquired in other circumstances, outside of class. The goal of developmental instruction is to train children in flexible thinking. The young child's thinking above all reflects what is first done in actual operations with specific objects, representations of them, or conventional symbols. Therefore, it is very important that instructional lessons work on children's performance of external practical and materialized operations, which subsequently, according to Professor P. Ya. Gal'perin's theory, are transferred to an internal level (as they are reflected in audible speech), as they think "to themselves." The development of thought passes through a number of stages. Each stage reflects at a different depth the materialized operation that is actually performed.

P. Ya. Gal'perin has called the various levels of depth of reflection the parameters of human activity, and has identified four basic parameters. At the first level operations are performed in complete detail. At the second level they are generalized to a certain degree, and he referred to this level as the measure of generalization. At the third level children become conscious that they must perform certain operations, and not others, and that these operations must be complete. At the fourth level children master all the operations and make them somewhat automatic; and he referred to this level as the measure of mastery.

The levels of depth of reflection are formed during the children's own activities. Five stages of various operations have been observed in research.

At the first stage, when an operation is performed with objects or with representations of objects, the child learns all the operations that the teacher shows him through practice, and it is highly important for the child's subsequent development that he achieve practical mastery at this stage. At the second stage, while each operation remains the same, some operations are abridged because they become somewhat generalized. The third and highly important stage is marked by audible discussion without relying on visual material, while at the fourth stage children begin talking to themselves. These two stages demonstrate that children are aware that certain planned operations are necessary and must occur in a particular sequence, and must be complete. Therefore, at the fifth stage the child is already capable of carrying out an entire set of operations silently, with no external reminders; many operations become automatic.

Thus, a mental operation, as it develops, begins with a material or materialized operation (detailed operations with objects or their conventional representations) and only gradually evolves into a representation of those operations in the mind. The child then makes the transition to mental operation with abstract scientific concepts.

Let us consider these stages in more detail through examples of teaching children to count.

Stage One. Operations are always taught to young children using objects or conventional representations of them (dolls, pictures of dolls, or an equivalent number of circles). The representations can vary from pictures to charts and diagrams. At this stage an operation consists of a number of specific acts carried out in a strict sequence, usually specified by the teacher's instructions. The child should perform them in the indicated sequence. For example, small children may be given the following assignment: put buttons on cards depicting the same buttons; lay them down with your right hand, working from left to right. As we can see, this operation consists of three acts: (1) differentiate the right hand from the left; (2) show the direction from left to right; (3) place the buttons accurately on their pictures.

Let us give another example of an assignment given to a group of four-year-olds: count the number of circles on two cards and determine how many circles there are on each strip. This operation also consists of a number of sequential operations acts: name the numbers, correlate each of them with exactly one circle, point at it, correlate the number named last with the total number of circles on one card, and remember the total number. The same procedure is followed with the circles on the second card, and the answer is given: there are five circles on one card, and four on the other. There are more circles on the card with five, and there are fewer circles on the card with four. The number five is greater and the number four is smaller.

At this stage every operation should be anticipated by the teacher's instructions and realized by the children, and gradually mastered by them as well. These detailed strings of acts train children in the methods of operation.

Stage Two. The level of materialized operation remains the same, but the number of steps can be reduced because some will have become automatic. This accelerates the operation to some extent, but the acceleration is accomplished consciously rather than spontaneously. Therefore, in case of error or doubt the child can always return to the earlier complete, detailed operation and check. Reduction of the number of steps shows that they have been generalized and thus learned. Conditions are created for divorcing the operation from external supports, and it becomes possible to move on to the third stage.

Let us give an example. Children are given a new assignment—to place buttons on one strip of construction paper so that their quantity is equal to the number of buttons shown on another strip above it (the technique of association). The children themselves have to remember that they should work from left to right with the right hand.

The children do this assignment rapidly. The teacher asks them to check themselves. The children silently and rapidly do what they were taught at the first stage—place the buttons on the pictures. All the pictures are covered, the sequence of steps is preserved, but some steps have become automatic (for example, placing the buttons accurately on the pictures from left to right with the right hand). Some have been eliminated (for example, the need to first demonstrate the direction of movement from left to right). The children announce the completed assignment aloud: "I've put as many buttons on the lower strip as were drawn on the upper one." "And how did you do it?" the teacher asks. "I looked at the buttons on the top strip and put my own under each picture." "Which hand did you use?" "My right hand, going from left to right," the child answers.

Another example. Children in the five-year-old group are asked to count the Christmas trees standing on the teacher's shelf and the mushrooms on her desk, to indicate how many objects there are in each place, and to say which number is greater and which is smaller.

The children count the trees in a whisper, nodding their heads slightly, and some make movements with their fingers at a distance, after which they raise their hands to answer: "There are four trees and five mushrooms. Five mushrooms are more than four trees." "But mushrooms are little. Why do you think that there are more of them?" asks the teacher. "We can make it real clear," a child says. "Put one mushroom under every tree. Then we are short one tree—one mushroom is left without a tree." "Go put them that way yourself." The child rapidly puts the mushrooms under the trees, confirming that five mushrooms are more than four trees. But one boy makes a mistake and counts five trees at a distance. When the children observed that he had made a mistake, the boy began pointing his hand at each tree, counting aloud—that is, he returned to the detailed operation, including the hand gestures and audible counting of the trees. "I counted to myself and I made a mistake," is how he explains his error.

Stage Three. The third stage is the stage of audible speech without relying on objects. The rapid transition from operating with objects to silent operation in the head, to oneself, is fraught with a considerable number of errors. Therefore, it is important that the children speak aloud as they do the actual operations. The teacher should not confine himself to stating that everyone has done the assignment correctly. It is important for the children themselves to explain how they have acted. A spoken explanation of the method of performing an assignment permits a gradual transition to first giving a preliminary description, which develops the children's planning activity.

Let us give the same examples, but at the next level of performance by three-year-olds. "Tell how you will put the mushrooms on the lower strip," the teacher says beforehand. "I will put down the mushrooms with my right hand, this way" (indicates the left-to-right direction). "Correct, from left to right," the teacher says, to make it explicit. "And what else must you be sure to do?" "I'll put a mushroom below, under each mushroom on the top strip. Then I'll have as many mushrooms on the bottom as are on the top strip." "Right, but how can you say it another way?" "The mushrooms on the top and the bottom will be equal." "Now do the assignment," the teacher says.

This spoken elaboration of the material operation is extremely important: language generalizes the operation, detaches it from the object, transforming the physical operation into a mental one, or into a mental representation of it. This makes it possible to give a mental answer to the question: "Of two numbers—four and three—which is greater (or smaller) than which? How much greater (or smaller) is that number than the other?"

By asking children to explain about what they are going to do, the teacher confronts them with the need to express the physical content of the operation in words. Verbal speech is communication for another person—that is, it has a social function. At the same time it is controlled by the listeners, not merely by the children alone; a material operation with which the listeners are familiar unfolds step by step, and the listeners can correct and supplement the explanation. This combined spoken operation becomes significant for everyone, and the children begin to understand the significance of their own responses as they try to give a maximally complete description of the practical operation at hand. This increases the children's awareness and sense of responsibility. The characteristic situational speech of the young child becomes consciously contextual.

The teacher must not allow a child to learn his verbal instructions mechanically, by rote, because then the child often does not use the instructions, but acts in his own way. He acquires "mechanical" knowledge. This occurs because the teacher fails to understand the significance of speaking aloud and rushes to repeat the instructions before the child has actually mastered the material operation. This is why it is important that the teacher not confine himself at the second stage to stating the results of the assignment that has been done, but rather ask the children to relate their work methods afterwards, preparing them for the transition to the third stage.

It can also happen that the children actually know how to perform the assignment, but their operations are not properly reflected in speech: the first-signal stimulus is not connected to the second-signal stimulus, and the actual operation or the method of operation is not generalized in words.

Thus, verbal speech is not only communication about an operation but is also the operation itself, though executed in spoken form: the operation is conceived but not produced at the given moment; it is merely planned. It is quite important to teach the children this.

Stage Four. The fourth stage sees an increasing transference of verbal speech to the internal level. Children seem to repeat the instructions to themselves, but in a more abbreviated form. This is the first form of mental operation in the proper sense of the word. The children create their own plans of operation, as it were. For example, they count objects shown to them silently, to themselves, but if they doubt that their results are correct, they resort to going through the actual operation verbally and point to the elements in the set as they count—that is, they return to the third or even the second stage.

Stage Five. The fifth stage is internal, silent speech, and the internal speech is terser than before. As we talk to ourselves, we do not pronounce all the words that we would say in addressing another person. Internal speech is stenographic speech, as L. S. Vygotskii has observed; it retains only certain vestiges of external speech that are crucial for the individual. Responses are rapid at this stage. But at the slightest mistake the child may himself return to the fourth stage, or even to the third or second, since he knows how he can correct his error. Therefore, it is very important not to rush, but still to pass from one stage to the next at the right time.

By retaining the stages in the development of mental operations when children are taught elementary mathematics, and by observing the level of the reflection of actual operations, the teacher provides for the development of the children's minds, and not merely for memorization of the knowledge communicated to them—that is, the teacher implements the principle of developmental instruction.

In planning teaching assignments or in implementing a certain curricular task, the teacher should have a clear conception of the system of lessons, outline the stages in instruction, select material that will attract the children, develop instructions (hints and questions for the children), attempt to foresee the children's reactions and how to guide them, and devise methods of activating the children's thought and collective attitudes, and of manifesting their independence.

Not only children's thought and speech, but also the tenor of their entire personality (attitude toward themselves and classmates, toward their activity, and toward the teacher, among other things) evolves under the influence of developmental instruction. The instructional influence engenders growth in children's cognitive interests and powers (memory, thought, observation, imagination, purposefulness, will to overcome difficulties, and so forth) and develops group attitudes (children's shared joy during one another's triumphs or upon achieving a goal).

The Principle of the Scientific Approach in Instruction and Its Connection to Life

The scientific approach means selecting educational material and teaching methods according to the purposes and goals of development and instruction, as well as considering the children's age. Above all, the teacher must reveal the world to preschool children in its richness of forms and colors and in its diversity of relations.

The goal of mathematics education for small children is to provide not so much a system of scientific knowledge as to teach them to see surrounding reality in quantitative, spatial, and temporal relations. This knowledge must be systematic, revealing the interconnections of the different aspects (quantity, shape, size, etc.), and it should be provided via concrete, everyday material. At the same time, it should rest on the scientific foundations of mathematics and of educational and child psychology. Thus, for example, the study of number and sets lays the foundation for teaching children about quantitative relations. Various operations with specific sets (union, inclusion, complement, intersection, comparison, and so forth) depend on a set-theory approach; introduction to quantities is based on the methods of measuring various magnitudes (length, mass, volume, and others); learning about the diversity of shapes of everyday objects depends on a knowledge of geometric forms and their elementary properties.

Educational and child psychology shed light on the ways children think—visual-effective and visual-figurative thought, which require teaching methods that provide for gradual transition from concrete to abstract knowledge. Logical thinking and the form of abstraction and generalization should develop gradually and naturally on the basis of the visual-effective and visual-figurative thought. These processes must not be forced artificially.

Observing the scientific approach in teaching provides for a natural transition to subsequent learning in school. The scientific approach in teaching means implementation of a combination of operations, knowledge, abilities, and attitudes. The child's thinking and consciousness are developed through activity. Therefore, it is essential to provide multifaceted activity for children so that they do not merely perceive the material repeatedly, but also learn rational methods of working with it: they must acquire the proper attitude toward their activity (toward difficulties or success). For example, it is important that in the instruction process the children themselves realize first-hand in practical terms that number exists independently of the spatial-qualitative features of a set. When working with geometric figures, children must realize that a figure's shape does not depend on its dimensions and varying positions in space. As students learn how to measure various quantities (length, mass, volume), they should be led to conclusions about the functional relationship between the number of units of measurement and the size of the measure.

The children should gradually learn to recognize essential connections and relations, disregarding the nonessential ones; they should learn methods of generalization. All this must be taught to small children.

The scientific approach allows for no popularization or oversimplification. During instruction the children's vocabulary should be enriched, their speech improved, and their ability to construct arguments developed. The children should gradually master precise scientific terminology. For example, they should not be allowed to confuse the words *number* and *numeral*, or call geometric figures by their everyday names ("block" instead of "rectangular prism," "rooftop" instead of "trapezoid" or "triangle," "column" or "roller" instead of "cylinder," "little pyramid" instead of "cone").

The scientific approach and its connection with life require that children apply their knowledge to various conditions. Setting knowledge in various situations makes it quite stable. What matters most is that children grasp the significance of knowledge in practical life and develop an interest in it. The scientific approach in teaching elementary mathematics to children necessitates mathematical training for teachers, in addition to knowledge of the general principles of child development and the individual characteristics of each child.

The Principle of Accessible Instruction

Knowledge accessible to children and accessible teaching methods depend on the level and characteristics of the children's mental development. Until quite recently it was supposed that only empirical knowledge was accessible to preschool children, just as with elementary school children, since their thinking is concrete and operates only with general notions. But modern research into educational psychology shows that elementary concepts and rudimentary types of abstract thought are accessible to preschoolers. First-graders successfully handle a systematic course in mathematics with elements of algebra, displaying intensive mental activity.

However, the problem of the accessibility and feasibility of knowledge for a given age level is far from being completely solved. Some psychologists abroad maintain that it is as if "any subject can be taught effectively in some intellectually honest form to any child at any stage of development" [1:34]. The crucial task is to perfect the teaching methods, they say. Certain American scholars and educators are introducing complex abstract concepts from set theory in play form when teaching mathematics to very young children.

Without denying the indisputable potential for preschool children to learn elementary concepts and to operate with them successfully, Soviet preschool pedagogy believes that the accessibility of knowledge should be confined to a suitable combination of sensory and logical components (see the principle of consciousness and activity).

The accessibility principle depends on a number of rules developed long ago in pedagogy: instruction must be conducted by proceeding from the easy to the difficult, from the known to the unknown, from the simple to the complex, from the near to the remote. But for a child, easy and difficult or near and remote do not correspond to what an adult means by them. Not everything that is close to children is comprehensible to them: e.g., age or kinship differences in persons near to them, or spatial relations between the rooms in which the child lives. Nor is the child aware of the role of a clock sounding the hour in telling time, although the sounds of clocks have attracted his attention from an early age.

The rule of proceeding from the easy to the difficult is likewise flexible. What seemed hard to the child at the initial stage in the study of a curriculum section becomes easy as he masters it, and he takes pride in overcoming this level of difficulty. Let us give an example of a child's conversation as recorded by his teacher.

"I can already count to ten," a four-year-old declares to his friends. "You wouldn't believe the problems I can solve. I think them up myself," answers a five-year-old boy. But his striving to stress the difficulties he seems to have overcome is criticized by older children. "Well, now, you're not really solving problems; you just know the numbers," objects a six-year-old girl. "You don't solve problems until you get to the preparatory group: they write down an example for us, and we make up a problem using the example. Anyone can make something up about anything. Only it has to be the way things really are." Interrupting her, the next child continues: "We even measure a table, its length and width. We get to find out how much greater the length is than the width!" "We're getting ready for school, you know," one of the children clarifies, "and you know what hard problems we'll have to solve then!"

As we can see, in this conversation the children stress the difficulties that they have already overcome and those that are still in store for them in school. But the difficulties do not intimidate them; they take pride in their triumphs. This shows how the easy and the difficult can change.

A very important rule should be observed in working with preschoolers: new knowledge should be given to the children in small doses, with reinforcement through diversified exercises and application in various activities.

Every new task set by the curriculum should be modest, and fall within the children's grasp so that they can master it. Therefore, a general curriculum section is usually divided into a series of smaller tasks, or "steps," and a sequence for their study is outlined. For example, the section that acquaints children with dimension (length, width, height, thickness) is divided into different parameters. When the parameter of length is studied, the children are first asked to distinguish between a long and a short strip of paper by comparing them with the association and superimposition techniques, and then they must select the strip that corresponds to the model from among a number of strips of varying length. Later the longest (or the shortest) strip must be chosen by sight, and one strip after another is laid out in a row. Thus, a strip that is long to the child's eyes becomes the shortest when it is compared with its predecessor, and this demonstrates the relativity of the concepts of *long* and *short*. Such exercises gradually develop the children's ability to estimate by sight, train them to see the relations among the sizes of the strips, and equip them with the seriation technique (arranging strips according to increasing or decreasing length).

The gradually increasing complexity of the curriculum material and the methodological techniques geared toward teaching knowledge and skills makes it possible for children to have a feeling of success in their work and be aware of their own growth, and this in turn promotes increasing interest in mathematics lessons on their part.

The need to divide up sections of the curriculum into lessons finds scientific substantiation in I. P. Pavlov's physiological doctrine of the mechanisms for developing knowledge and skills, which are "long series of conditioned reflexes." The analyzing activity of a small child's cerebral cortex is only capable of insignificant composite stimuli. The first series of temporal connections formed makes possible the formation of subsequent series of conditioned reflexes.

To a certain extent, children's attitudes can be a criterion for assessing their abilities—their liking or dislike for the material. Ordinarily, children love surmounting a difficulty within their grasp, often refusing help from the teacher. Therefore, accessibility does not mean easiness. Moreover, it has been proved in theory and practice that easy instruction can do more harm than good. Thus, V. Latyshev, a 19th-century methodologist, wrote that children should love mathematics, and "can love it if it is presented to them. Let the work always be within the student's powers. But assuredly require work, and require effort. Otherwise the student will not learn to work and will not be interested in it" [3].

Anything children can learn consciously under a teacher's supervision is accessible, straining their minds to the limits of their ability. Since children's mental powers grow, the difficulty must gradually be increased.

Various methodological techniques of presenting material to children make its mastery accessible. The rule that instruction should proceed *from the known to the unknown* indubitably promotes accessibility. In teaching new material to children, the teacher should bear in mind what they already know and study the child's experience. Success in learning new material increases significantly if it is included in the system of the previous knowledge, supplementing and reconstructing the existing information and giving it greater depth.

The rule about proceeding *from the simple to the complex* in instruction means that one must always begin with something that does not cause special difficulties and is somewhat familiar to the children. After all, simple things are perceived without particular strain and evoke a positive response. Simple things are clear. Therefore, the teacher must make sure that everything difficult is made clear or immediate for the children. For example, 3-year-olds may already distinguish between *many* and *one*, but they have an unclear notion that a set is formed from individual objects and that it is very important to see each particular object in that set. As they learn to compare the numbers in sets by juxtaposing their elements (by the superimposition or association techniques), they begin to perceive each element and gradually master the rule for establishing a one-to-one correspondence between them, which is the basis for the counting operation. The children's range of knowledge thus gradually expands from the simple to the complex.

The feasibility of the difficulties placed before children is the basis for developing the internal stimuli of their cognitive activity. Therefore, for instruction to be developmental, the teacher must be guided by the prospects for the children to learn new material, which are realized in reality, under the teacher's supervision—that is, be guided by the "zone of the children's proximate development," as L. S. Vygotskii has indicated.

The Visual Principle in Teaching

The visual principle has long been widely used in practice. Ya.A. Komenskii laid the foundation for this principle when he called it "the golden rule of didactics": "...everything that can be perceived by the senses, namely: the visible—for perception by vision, the audible—for hearing, odors—for smell, that which can be tasted—for taste, and that which can be touched—for touch. If any objects can be perceived by several senses at once, let them be immediately sensed in different ways" [2: 302-303].

The visual principle was first used primarily in the early stages of instruction, since it was believed that small children's thinking is concrete and that they should deal first with things or objects, then with words. Without denying this, modern researchers believe that the visual principle does not lose it significance for students in the upper grades, or even for adults, for the basis of the principle is an understanding of the unity of the sensory and the logical. It is another matter that the character of visual perception changes and becomes more complex with the development of thought. While for small children visuality is expressed in objects and in the immediate perception of everyday phenomena (during outings) or in representations of objects (in pictures), visuality subsequently becomes more complicated, taking the form of a model, a mock-up, a chart, a diagram, or a graph.

Various authors classify visual aids in different ways, but most frequently according to how the surrounding reality is reflected (Sh. I. Ganelin, B. P. Esipov, M. A. Danilov, and others). With respect to mathematics, visual aids can be classified as natural, representational, and graphic.

Natural visual aids include objects, sounds, and movements for which it is possible to count and compare one aggregate with another. This group of visual aids also contains objects in various positions in space of various shapes, sizes, etc.

Representational visual aids include cards with objects drawn on them in various quantities, of various sizes and shapes, and with various spatial arrangements. It also includes cards with geometric figures of various dimensions, colors, and quantities; paired cards with various arrangements of objects; various types of lotteries; tables depicting the composition of a number or a numeral; conventional signs; and many other things.

Graphic visual aids include tables, models (such as a number ladder), and technical drawings (for selecting material according to quantity, dimensions, and shape in constructing objects, etc.).

Natural and representational visual aids are most widely used in teaching preschool children. However, studies by Soviet psychologists and educators disprove the assertion that elementary concepts are inaccessible to children at this age. Therefore, visual aids that model mathematical concepts are increasingly being used in working with older preschoolers.[1]

The use of visual aids in instruction is quite significant if they are united with language. Any visual aid is demonstrated by means of words, which direct the children's attention to the main point, teaching them to separate out the most essential.

Visual aids are used in different ways depending on the instructional goals. In some instances, the children themselves extract knowledge, and the teacher directs their observations and actions. For example, when examining an object, the children can be asked to outline the geometric shape with their fingers in order to become more familiar with its form. ("A sphere is round, and it rolls, but a cube has corners—they keep it from rolling," says the toddler).

The teacher's words play a different role in children's cognition of relationships, e.g., quantitative relations. The teacher directs the children's attention to comprehending not the quality of groups of objects, but rather the relations among them. For example, there are four red circles lying on one strip of construction paper, and there are five blue circles on the strip below it. The children must immediately reflect their observations in words. Therefore, the teacher asks questions such as: "Which strip—lower or upper—has fewer circles? How many circles are there on each of the strips? Which number is less than which, and which number is greater than which?"

Visuality is not an end in itself, but rather a means of gaining a deeper knowledge of the world. Children learn to count by comparing sets: five dolls, four plates, and so forth. They count and compare the sets not to deepen their knowledge about dolls and plates, but to learn to abstract the numbers five and four from specific objects, to become aware of the size of these sets and of the reciprocal relations (four is one unit less than five, and five is one unit greater than four).

Consequently, the visual principle provides for greater depth in sensory perception, and sensory and logical thought are interrelated at all age levels. Therefore, we should speak not merely of visual aids, but of appropriate combinations of visual resources and language.

However, teachers sometimes fail to consider the role of language when using visuality in mathematics lessons. For example, when comparing the number of elements in two sets teachers often confine themselves to a question such as: "Which strip has more circles—the upper or lower?" They are content with the children's response that there are more circles on the upper strip, without asking how many there are. Yet the instructional goal is to show which of two consecutive numbers is greater and which is smaller. Aside from the number-word, children are aware only of sets not expressed by numbers, and their thought stays at the level of isolated perception of specific sets, without rising to the abstract concept of the significance of number as an indicator of the general size of various sets (four mushrooms, four circles, four sides of a square, four sounds, etc.).

Ya. A. Komenskii has said that the external senses should be governed by reason. If the governing maxim is not "the highest observer is reason,", the external senses may supply "chaff, straw, sand, and sawdust instead of grain and flour" [2:302].

The unity of words and visual aids brings about a close connection and proper correlation of the visual and the abstract, the specific and the generalized; it leads to a connection between the object (image), the word, and the action.

Visual aids are not the only teaching aids used in preschool education. All sensations are related to visuality: sounds are perceived by the auditory perceptual analyzer, shape by the tactile-motor analyzer, and spatial relations by the visual-motor analyzer. All types of perception have their place among teaching aids, but the principle one is visual perception, for all types of perception (hearing, movement, touch) are linked with the visual. A quantity of sounds can be represented by means of objects, and pitch by means of a ladder; collections of objects or pictures whose shape is similar to geometric figures can be designed for various geometric figures (for instance, a balalaika or a Pioneer's necktie for a triangle, a coin or plate for a circle, a tabletop or rooftop for a rectangle, an oblong dish for an oval, and so forth). In order to develop spatial notions, the teacher can create cards on which the same object is arranged in various ways (dolls at a table, under the table, on the table, and so on). Both narrative toys and various types of non-narrative material (circles, squares, and triangles) can be used for counting.

Since children develop mathematical notions during their activity and by means of the participation of various perceptual analyzers, they must be exposed to diversified visual didactic material that provides activity for all the children and vividly demonstrates the quantitative and spatial relations of objects. Operating with these models promotes abstraction of the essential aspect from the non-essential, variable features—for example, abstracting the geometric shape of an object without respect to its color or dimensions.

Visual didactic material is usually divided into **demonstration material** and **distribution material**.

Demonstration material is designed for demonstration and working with children called up to the teacher's desk; therefore, it is large in size. Distribution material is smaller; children use it seated at their desks while carrying out an assignment given to everyone at once. Both sorts of materials should be artistically designed: attractiveness is very significant in instruction: it is more interesting for children to deal with attractive aids. The more vivid and profound the children's emotions, the more complete the interaction between sensory and logical thinking, the more intensively the lesson proceeds, and the more successful the children learn.

Visual aids should be used in teaching preschool children by gradually increasing their complexity: proceeding from specific, narrative objects to non-narrative objects; from material visual aids to materialized aids, e.g., to conventional tables (such as a "number ladder"), models (e.g., a string of ten beads), diagrams, etc. Visual aids should change not only from one age group to another, but also based on the correlation between the concrete and the abstract at different stages in the children's mastery of the curriculum material. For example, at a certain stage specific sets can be replaced by number tables or by numerals.

The visual principle is very important, but the use of visual aids should not be unlimited. Visual aids can not only help, but sometimes can even hinder or inhibit mental development. For example, during the study of new curriculum material on counting, the teacher's model or demonstration of the method of operation plays an enormous role. Once a small child has mastered the method of operation, subsequent demonstrations will impede his developing independence. Therefore, the demonstration of a model can be harmful, even in working with 3-year-olds, once the youngsters can perform a task themselves based on verbal instructions. A model can be used in other ways at this stage. For instance, it can be shown after an assignment has been carried out so that the children can themselves check whether they have placed the circles as indicated in the instructions or as represented in the model.

Thus, as he exploits the visual principle in teaching children elementary mathematics, the teacher should think carefully about the visual presentation and the method and place for using it in a particular lesson. It should always be born in mind that while concrete thinking is a foundation for abstract thinking, it is itself developed and reorganized under the influence of abstract thought. Visual aids should also change—for example, narrative toys should be replaced by non-narrative toys (even in the younger kindergarten group).

In implementing the visual principle in teaching, it is important to teach the children to use visual aids themselves, to find and apply them for checking and for proving their own responses. For example, a six-year-old says, "Seven is one greater than six, and six is one less than seven." "Prove to us that what you say is correct," suggests the teacher. The child puts seven Pioneers on a feltboard at the front of the class, counts out six flags, and puts one flag in front of each Pioneer. "See, I took seven Pioneers and six flags, distributed the flags to the Pioneers, and one Pioneer did not have a flag. That means I'm right—six is one less than seven." Thus it is important that words and visual aids be intertwined during instruction.

The Principle of Systematic and Logically Consistent Instruction, and the Principle of Stable Learning

The principle of systematic and sequential teaching means that knowledge must be taught in a strictly logical order and that children's actions and operations with mathematical material should be guided sequentially in order to develop a system of knowledge, abilities, and skills. This principle is particularly important in teaching mathematics. N. K. Krupskaya's stated that mathematics is a chain of knowledge, and when one link is missing, the entire chain is broken. A person acquires knowledge freely when it is ordered. "A head filled with fragmentary, incoherent knowledge is like a storeroom where everything is in disorder and even the owner cannot find anything...," K. D. Ushinskii has written [6:355].

Systematic presentation of material ensures the sequential development of cognitive powers and abilities, teaches logical thinking, and creates an opportunity for learning more complicated material. For example, after learning to distinguish parameters of dimension in an object (length, width, height), children master techniques for measuring them, first using arbitrary measures, followed by the conventional units of measure.

Educational planning and curricula are usually based on the principle of systematic instruction. Systematization of curriculum content requires a systematization of knowledge, abilities, and skills as well. Children acquire systematic knowledge only during instruction if the information is communicated sequentially. Systematization, as noted by I. P. Pavlov, is a very important property of man's higher nervous activity: it introduces clarity and precision, and aids in understanding and retaining the material being studied.

A necessary condition for systematic presentation is sequential arrangement of the material. Therefore, it is recommended that the teacher move on to new material only after the children have mastered the previous material. This rule of sequence and continuity between previous and new material applies both within a single age group, over the course of a school year, and between age groups, from one year to the next. This bond ensures that students' knowledge, abilities, and skills are deep and solid.

An important aspect of developing children's elementary mathematical thought is understanding the internal interrelationships among the different branches of mathematical knowledge, among the quantitative, spatial, and temporal relations which on the one hand should be differentiated, and on the other should represent a mathematical synthesis resting on general theoretical foundations. For example, children learn to count not just individual objects but groups as well; the sides, vertices, and angles of a given geometric figure; arbitrary measures as a result of measuring dimension, mass, and volume; and time segments of various duration (minutes, hours, days, weeks, etc.). All branches of mathematical knowledge are interrelated, even within the scope of the kindergarten curriculum. An understanding of these internal interrelationships promotes children's mental development and a structured system of knowledge.

Intellectual training is not only implemented by means of instructional assignments, it is also furthered during play situations and work, in everyday life, and as a result of interaction with adults. The child acquires knowledge and abilities and develops his mind during all these forms of activity. But the child obtains knowledge episodically, or randomly, during play, work, and everyday life; knowledge is not presented in a structured system and sequence, but is communicated in individual fragments, as it were, thus forming "islets" of knowledge in the child's consciousness. Although the child's knowledge is expanding, and sometimes even becoming more precise, one circle of knowledge is not coordinated with another; they are local.

Moreover, instructional lessons in mathematics develop specific cognitive activity in children, which is not a goal of work or play, where mathematical information is of secondary importance. In play and work no specific knowledge or abilities can be specified as mandatory for everyone, but instructional lessons center around the development of a specific cognitive interest. Therefore, lessons provide a structured set of knowledge and abilities—in a sequence and system.

It is this route from the simple to the complex, from the concrete to the abstract, and from the sensory to the logical that is important in teaching children to count. This sequence in the presentation of information not only develops the children's thinking, but also promotes their understanding of the value of the knowledge they have acquired and reinforces their faith in their own ability. What seemed new and difficult yesterday has been learned today and is now simple. The children begin to be aware of their own growth, and learning becomes interesting. Lessons incorporate material of gradually increasing complexity, which, although accessible, still requires that the children think it over, mobilize their previous knowledge, and bring it to bear on solving the new problem. The process develops their attention, concentration, and alertness.

Therefore it is very important, in coordinating the children's potential and previous material, to offer scope for initiative to their minds. But teachers often provide all information in a predigested form, depriving the children of the opportunity to think and guess for themselves. For example, in an older group the teacher asks that a specified number of objects be represented on one strip of construction paper and one fewer on another strip. After doing the assignment, the children report how many circles they have on each strip. The teacher confines himself to this sort of response and does not ask the children to think for themselves about which number is smaller or greater than the other, and by how much. Another example: the teacher listens to a child's answer giving the difference between two numbers, but does not ask him to prove that his answer is correct (by confirming it by means of a one-to-one comparison of two sets).

The teacher should frequently challenge children to "think" or to "guess," or to answer the question "why." Of course, these tasks must be based on methods of operation that the children know, that they have learned in class. Otherwise the entire process of instruction will be built on mere memorization of predigested material and mechanical imitation.

An indication that instruction is organized to be clear, systematic, and logically consistent is when children are interested, not so much in what they have done (that is, the actual result) as in acquiring new knowledge and abilities. In that case they begin to understand the significance of the teacher's instructions and easily uncover the reasons for errors, regarding them as a consequence of failing to follow the instructions. "I didn't notice that we were supposed to put one fewer circle on the top strip, and I put one fewer on the bottom strip," explains a boy of five years and seven months. "I was hurrying and counted the number of sides and vertices in this polygon wrong—I didn't listen to how I was supposed to count and draw this polygon," says another.

Systematic and logically consistent instruction teaches children to organize their behavior and thinking, encourages self-control, and eliminates blind imitation. If the teacher imparts to the children not only knowledge and abilities, but also the habit of giving clear and logical oral accounts of what they do ("Tell everything in order so that it will be clear to everyone"), they do not simply learn certain operations—they reflect the sequence of their operations in words. The coherence of the exposition becomes prominent along with the content of the lesson. Thus, the children's attitude toward the learning process gradually changes, and a new ability develops—**teachability**.

When properly implemented by the teacher, the principle of systematic and logically consistent instruction helps the child develop his mind and acquire systematic knowledge. Therefore, this principle must be taken into account in planning lessons that vary in form. At one point all of the children may focus their attention on one child who has been called to the front of the room to do a problem. Later all of the children are given the same assignment and do it at their desks using distribution material—for example, they might group sets of geometric shapes according to a certain attribute (shape, size, color), count the number of subsets, compare the groups (subsets) to see which of them has more individual figures, and then say: "I have divided all the figures according to color: one group of different red figures, another group of green ones. The red group contains more figures— eight—while there are fewer in the green group—seven. Eight is always one greater than seven, and seven is one less than eight."

These two types of classwork have different significance. When the topic is new and the children must be shown how to do the assignment, with explanations and supervised practice, it is best to work at the front of the class. The same activity is useful when evaluating the children's knowledge and abilities, and when everyone has thoroughly mastered the curriculum material and wants to be called upon to answer before the group. Responding under such conditions promotes self-assertiveness and the development of a sense of self. Observations of children's behavior during class show that in either case they carefully watch how the child at the front of the class carries out the assignment. Sometimes individual children can be heard prompting him softly (the more complicated the task and the more actively they are thinking, the harder it is for children to think to themselves).

The second form of classwork has different significance. It is intended for practice and reinforcing the knowledge and skills of all the children simultaneously. If the children do a common assignment with a clear idea of the techniques they need, the assignment will proceed successfully and in a well-organized fashion. But if they have not yet learned the method, disruptions occur: the children start talking to each other and are distracted by any outside stimulus.

How can we explain the fact that classwork dealing with new curriculum material, just like work after students have learned material well, are more organized if the children are called upon to respond before the entire group? First, positive assessment of one's knowledge by the other children is pleasant, but what is particularly important is the desire to translate information into language. Only through language can children express their understanding of the relations between numbers or quantities as a result of measurement (dimension, mass, and volume), and these words must be spoken. What is essential for the response is not what the children have done, but how they have done it and what they have obtained as a result of the action (quantitative relations in comparing sets; the number of sides, vertices, or angles in a certain geometric figure). Only through the use of language does the sensory perception of various discrete and continuous quantities become distinct and differentiated. A given operation with sets acquires mathematical meaning only by means of the second signal system. Action without words loses its attraction for the child because the actual performance of the task (e.g., measuring, comparing the numbers in sets) becomes monotonous and undifferentiated, devoid of meaning and uninteresting; enthusiasm for doing the assignment is reduced. Relating the process of the operation and the answer is another matter—that means communicating not just with the teacher but with the other children as well. This reconstructs the children's attitudes toward their own actions, and is reflected in words.

When working in class with distribution material it is very important to end each assignment by quizzing three or four children. By asking the children who has done the problem in what way and what answer each one obtained prepares all the children to translate their action into spoken language and promotes the development of a "mental operation" (thinking to oneself). **The decisive role in teaching children elementary mathematics is played by the second signal system** (word-number). Only by means of language can the entire diversity of quantitative, spatial, and temporal relations in actual reality be represented. Therefore, the children should be asked a few questions after they perform a practical task.

The principle of logical consistency requires that various age groups be given instructions with varying degrees of detail. The logical sequence of operations should be treated in particular detail with younger preschool groups, where both demonstrating and explaining a model play a considerable role. The children should be given all the techniques and shown the entire sequence of operations when reproducing an example. If this is neglected, they make mistakes. For instance, when showing and explaining to three-year-olds how to arrange many blue circles on the left and one red circle on the right on the same strip, based on a demonstration, the teacher did not call the children's attention to the space between the blue and red circles in the example. As a result, many children places all the circles in a row without an interval.

In another class, the teacher was asking the children to find a group of toys and align them with a card on which there were many circles, but he did not show them how to do the assignment. The children walked helplessly around the room between the tables containing the toys, not knowing what to do or what was required of them.

The lack of carefully thought-out instructions often causes breaches in discipline or order in class, giving rise to conflicts among the children. Thus, it is important for young children not only to understand the assignment, but to master the methods of doing it as well. It is therefore essential that the teacher's instructions provide a model by clearly explaining and demonstrating the logical sequence and character of the operations.

Children do not immediately generalize abilities and skills or methods of operation, and therefore do not transfer them to new situations. For example, a teacher taught a group of four-year-olds to count out a specific quantity from a set of toys. But in the next class, when the children were given some cubes from which they were to count out five, the teacher did not remind them of the technique for extracting a quantity of objects from a set; the children converted the assignment into straightforward counting of the cubes, which they had thoroughly learned how to do. The mechanism in this phenomenon is clear: an unconsolidated conditioned reflex has a generalized, spill-over character; encompassing contiguous sections of the cerebral cortex, it elicits earlier responses that have previously been formed. As children learn the generalized meaning of the methods of operation (that is, as the conditional connections are lost), they need not be reminded of the details.

The role of the model also varies at different stages of instruction. In providing a model, the teacher at first virtually does everything that is required, and the model is left before the children's eyes. After doing an assignment, the children check their work by comparing it with the model. The teacher teaches them to check their work, developing their powers of analytical observation and ability to listen attentively to instructions and follow the sequence of operations as they are explained.

When the children understand the role and significance of the model and the instructions, the teacher confines herself to verbal directions, showing them the model only after the work has been done. The role and the place of the model change; now it serves as a means of self-checking. Children who have made mistakes but have not noticed them are asked by the teacher to tell what they have done while comparing their work with the model. As a rule, this helps the youngsters find their mistakes by themselves. They learn to scrutinize and analyze their own work in greater depth.

Heavy demands are also made on the teacher's language. She must precisely formulate the questions she puts to the children and her explanations and answers to students' inquiries. Language plays a particularly large role in mathematics classes. Without language, no mathematical concept, no matter how elementary, can be communicated.

Nevertheless, teachers occasionally make mistakes, confusing the concept of the number and the number-word, the concept of a number and a numeral, or the like. For example, the teacher might ask a group of four-year-olds: "Which is greater—four or five?" The children have not yet developed quantitative notions for these number-words, and they cannot answer this question without comparing specific sets. If they do give an answer, they do so based on how far the given numeral is from where they start counting the numbers aloud, rather than on quantitative notions: "Five is greater, and four is less, since five comes later, and four comes first."

In these instances the number-word does not reflect the essence, the concept of number—it is not yet a second signal, since the concept of number incorporates the images of actual sets perceived by the first signal system (a set of objects that are seen, sounds perceived through hearing, movements perceived by the kinesthetic perceptual analyzer, etc.). It is important that the essential quantitative connections be interpreted in these sensory images and gradually generalized into a concept of number through the number-word, rather than simply establishing external associative connections in the order in which one numeral is named after another. "A word is a pane of glass," said the linguist A. A. Potebnya. The physical content of a word should always be visible through it. The teacher's language must therefore always be clear and precise.

The principle of systematic and logically consistent instruction requires that various perceptual analyzers be brought into play in teaching children elementary mathematics: the visual, auditory, tactile, and motor analyzers. This is mandated above all by the need to create a first-signal basis for the perception of quantity, shape, size, and spatial representations.

There are various different types of sets, and the child should be taught to determine their size by counting (by counting the sounds when a clock strikes, counting a beating pulse or the movements in physical education or music class, for example). By drilling children in counting using vision, hearing, and the kinesthetic analyzer, we enable the analyzers themselves to practice, as well as providing for the development of inter-analyzer connections in the cerebral cortex. The activity of counting is generalized—it becomes applicable in any context: the children count the sounds made by a cuckoo clock, falling drops, thunderclaps, the petals and stamens of flowers, and their own movements. The children form a dynamic stereotype of the counting operation which enables them to respond to highly varied complex stimuli with adequate reactions.

I.P. Pavlov has pointed out that countless stimuli of varying quality and intensity continuously bombard the cerebral hemispheres, and that "all this meets, interacts, reacts, and should ultimately be systematized— equalized, so to speak—and should culminate in dynamic stereotypes [5:240]. In giving children repeated practice in counting using various analyzers, the teacher gradually hones their counting activity; the definition of the quantitative aspect of a set becomes increasingly precise. Using the same number-words in counting sets perceived by various analyzers promotes generalization of their significance and develops the concept of number in children. Thus, on the basis of repeatedly counting the elements in various sets and determining their capacity, the children effect a transition from perceiving a specific set to the abstract concept of number, which is evidence of a qualitatively new level of knowledge and a higher level of mental development.

The principle of logical consistency requires that children employ various perceptual analyzers to master the concepts of shape, size, and spatial relations. The tactile-motor analyzer, in contrast to the visual analyzers, promotes an immediate contact-stimulated perception of the shape, dimensions, and spatial relations of objects. The child outlines the shape of an object with a finger, feeling its size, and this refines his visual perception of the object at a distance, making his cognition of it more profound.

In order for knowledge to be more stable, various analyzers must take part in its perception, children must perceive knowledge and skills consciously, and their thought must operate actively as they isolate what is most essential and discard the secondary. All this knowledge and skill must be provided to children in a logically consistent system, and their instructional-cognitive activity must be properly designed.

Research and practical experience demonstrate that small children grasp new curriculum material very rapidly if it is divided into small parts and presented in a logical sequence. But their knowledge and skills are still unstable, and without reinforcement they rapidly die out, although they can quickly be restored.

Therefore, for the purpose of reinforcement and consolidation, it is very important to review old curriculum material regularly. For example, after devoting three to five lessons to a new curriculum task (a different number of lessons is required for various groups and in the study of various problems), it is advisable to come back and review of this material in two weeks, then in another three weeks, and so on, gradually increasing the interval. The teacher should retain all the problems in view; they must be reviewed from time to time. Previous and current curriculum material should be properly combined in the lesson structure.

It is best to start a lesson with new curriculum material, setting aside a certain amount of time for it, but giving the greater part of the lesson to a review of material that the children have already learned. Mastering something new requires considerable effort, but repeating what is known makes children confident of their knowledge and abilities and gives a positive tint to the entire lesson. The next time more time can be given to this new material, but it is still advisable to return to earlier material at the end of the lesson. This lesson structure is explained from the physiological standpoint by the fact that positively perceived stimuli which occur in passing promote the concentration of stimulation in those sections of the cortex that are connected with a difficult but crucial stimulus (I. P. Pavlov). Reviewing gives a positive emotional coloring to the entire lesson and fosters interest in the new material.

What number of lessons should be devoted to a single topic to ensure firm mastery of the knowledge and skills in various age groups? We know that "repetition is the mother of learning," that repeated lessons, like exercises, are necessary for stable learning; therefore, some teachers specially set aside one lesson every two or three months for reinforcing previous material. However, the specific approach to this problem depends on all the conditions in a given group.

Repetition does not mean that a review should be identical to the previous treatment in content, methods, and form. Pavlov has repeatedly pointed out that success in forming temporal connections (conditioned reflexes) lies not only in numerous repetitions of the same thing, but chiefly in comparing the new and old. Therefore, it is very important for reviews to employ varied instructional materials and procedures and to mix in techniques that have been applied in other topics. For example, when measuring the mass of dry materials with everyday measures, the children must recall how they measured length with other everyday measures (the functional relationship between the nature of the measure—larger or smaller—and the number of measures that go into a given length).

It is also advisable to use knowledge acquired in other types of activity, e.g., in daily life. For example, a knowledge of mathematics is used extensively in drawing. Drawing objects requires quite accurate representation of the object's shape. A knowledge of geometric shapes serves as a standard for learning the shapes of everyday objects and representing them in drawings or with modeling clay. A knowledge of mathematics is required for building in just the same way, so that children can construct an object based on a diagram (a truck, crane, etc.). In analyzing the drawing, the children select the required material based on quantity and shape, and arrange the individual parts in the spatial and quantitative relationships indicated in the drawing. Using their knowledge in different situations ensures even greater consolidation; the knowledge enters into new connections, forming a dynamic stereotype.

Thus, the principle of systematic and logically consistent instruction, in combination with the stability principle, provides for proper and effective organization of lessons and makes it possible to transfer knowledge to other types of activity. The children acquire systematic knowledge, abilities, and skills, and their thinking and speech develop.

The Principle of the Individual Approach

The starting point in the principle of the individual approach is personality development within the collective and by means of the collective. A.S. Makarenko has pointed out the beneficial influence of the collective on the personalities of individual children: "To work with an individual personality, one must know and cultivate it. If I must deal with individual personalities like so many individual peas, not on a collective scale, if I approach them without this collective basis, then I cannot deal with them" [4:173-174].

However, in working with a group of children, the teacher should study and know every child: the development of each child's memory and attention span, the rapidity of each child's perception of visual and verbal material, the nature of each child's interests and thinking, the degree of independence in practical activity and thought, the quality of each child's knowledge and level of general development, as well as mathematical concepts and speech, imagination, creativity, emotional-volitional manifestations, social orientation, and so forth. Conversations with the parents and other family members, together with observations of the child's private life and activity in the kindergarten and at home, bring out the basic outlines of the child's character.

The teacher needs to know all this in order to help the child enter into the children's collective and occupy an appropriate place, and at the same time to provide for a proper pedagogical approach to the child: praising the timid one, instilling confidence in his powers and potential; or, on the other hand, anticipating and avoiding over-confidence; encouraging more active approach from the shy ones and regulating the hyperactivity of excitable children. In working with young children the teacher should have particular regard for their impressionability and emotionality, their easy excitability, variability, and rapid onset of fatigue, and should modify her techniques and instructional procedures accordingly.

The proper individual approach requires psychological awareness on the teacher's part, including the ability to observe the children, interpret perceptively every child's behavior and the reasons for mistakes in assignments, and critically review her own opinions and evaluations.

In training children, the teacher's attention should be directed toward developing their attention and their interest in one another, pride in their classmates' success, and readiness to help others. For this purpose, the teacher should plan carefully for collective forms and methods of teaching and training, where all of the children work on a single curriculum task at the same time and interact actively. However, differentiated instruction in group activity is also possible and necessary; each subgroup of a single collective can be given an problem of a different degree of difficulty within the framework of a single task. For example, one group may be asked to measure the length of a room with standard measures, and another is to measure the length of a table. The tempo of work, the level of ability, and the like are taken into account when apportioning these assignments. Or, for example, the children sitting at one table may be given individual assignments to place varying quantities of objects on three feltboards so that they obtain a "stepladder": one child must deal with two, three, and four objects, another child has six, five, and four objects, and so forth. Again, the teacher should take into account the knowledge and skills of the children in assigning these tasks.

Observations have shown that the rate at which children learn, as well as the tempo of their work, varies from child to child. For example, a one-week break in classes is too much for some; in that time they forget what they have been taught. These children, characterized by a slight variability in the nerve processes, do not regain the lost knowledge as rapidly as others do. As a rule, there are not many such children. But the teacher should work with them in the middle of the week, repeating what was covered by the whole class. During ordinary classes the teacher should also pay particular attention to these children, instilling confidence in them, and the lag will be overcome.

It follows that the need to know and take into account children's psychophysiological traits is most important in the youngest group, where the first abilities and skills at collective work are developed.

As a rule, lagging behind is caused by extended gaps between lessons (i.e., three or four weeks). But the forgotten material is rapidly regained, since problems are assigned in controlled doses and are repeated many times. Therefore, as experience shows, when two or three lessons are missed, the children rapidly catch up on their knowledge without supplementary lessons, but the teacher should show particular attention to the children involved. When there are longer gaps, however, it is advisable to work individually with the affected children so that their knowledge will match that of the other children.

It should be noted that group instruction also has a very favorable influence on each child's individual learning. As they work in a collective, children learn both from the teacher and from each other. They hear their classmates' responses, analyze their own work, and hear evaluations of their work. With group instruction everyone hears the same answer many times. For example, suppose the children are counting sounds, objects, and movements up to five. Fifteen persons are called upon to repeat this counting once or twice, and each child will hear it as many as 30 times. Such repetition would be impossible with individual instruction.

The teacher must explain to the children that their responses are heard not just by the teacher, but by all of the children—they will evaluate, supplement, and improve the responses. In the younger preschool group the children must be taught to answer so that "everyone can hear." This cooperation between teacher and children prevents "teacher-student pairing" and increases children's interest in group lessons and in one another's responses. When the teacher gives individual attention to every child, excitable children learn to control themselves, and relatively inert children start to take an interest in their classmates' answers and develop a desire to inject additions and refinements.

Thus, group lessons encourage learning and the development of abilities and skills by repeating curriculum material in different forms and eliciting responses from the children, who address themselves not only to the teacher but also to the other children present. Therefore, it is very important not only to teach children to respond loud and clear, but also make explicit the significance of doing so. The principle of the individual approach by no means contradicts group instruction; on the contrary, it is successfully combined with collective forms of work.

The Principle of Conscious and Active Learning

All didactic principles are interrelated, but the principle of conscious and active learning is especially connected to the principle of developmental instruction. Its characteristic feature is that it applies less to instruction and more to learning—the child's conscious mastery of knowledge and skills during instruction.

The principle of conscious learning requires that the pedagogical process take into account the unity of the sensory and the logical, as well as the concrete and the general and the concrete and the abstract. **Consciousness presupposes the ability to perceive and separate the essential from the nonessential and the ability to examine a given phenomenon (or fact) in its multitude of connections.** All this develops the personality and systematic thinking and teaches children to substantiate their judgments. Consciousness is especially clearly manifested and enhanced when the situation is relatively complex—when some difficulty or contradiction must be overcome. The learning process is just such a complex situation for small children, for it requires special external and internal behavior and considerable volitional effort. Children must not only be taught to learn, but also to recognize the meaning and significance of learning. As pointed out above, children learn consciously when they first acquire knowledge—that is, as they operate actively with the material they are studying. Children's first mathematical notions take shape on the basis of their activity with sets; they learn the counting operation using number-words on the basis of establishing a one-to-one correspondence between actual sets. They realize that the number of elements in one set and the number of elements in another set can be equal or unequal. If two sets do not have the same number of elements, they are assigned different number-words; if two sets do have the same number of elements, they are assigned the same number-words.

As they perform the operations of adding and subtracting and master the computation techniques of adding and taking away one, children can learn them if by virtue of practical activities they have already grasped that the composition of numbers from units and the reciprocal relations between consecutive natural numbers.

The principle of conscious learning also presupposes that analysis and synthesis should be developed in children, for they underlie any mental process. Successfully solving mental problems depends on the depth of analysis and synthesis and the interrelationship between these two operations. But at different stages in learning material it is sometimes possible to observe a combination of analysis and synthesis, while one part of this combination sometimes predominates. For example, when children's notion of plurality is vague, their attention is principally concentrated on distinguishing individual elements from one another. Children love to sort out the elements in a collection of objects, accompanying them with the words "another," "another," "another," or "here's...," "here's...," "here's...." At this stage analysis predominates over synthesis. But at the next stage, when the children's interest is concentrated on the set as a structural unit, they are often content to note the "boundaries" of this set, while seeming to ignore the elements "inside" it. For example, a boy sees a group of dolls facing him in a row. He feeds only the dolls on the far left and right, but says that he has fed all of them. At this moment it is important for the child to note the boundaries of the set he has perceived: he is collecting the elements into a single whole, as it were. This is evidence that synthesis predominates over analysis at that point.

The task of instruction at every stage consists in overcoming this gap, in teaching analysis in combination with synthesis, because if the analysis is incomplete, the synthesis will be erroneous. The perception of a set as an integral unity still does not provided for an awareness of its quantitative structure. The child must be taught to see the whole in combination with its component elements. "But you have really fed all of the dolls?" the teacher remarks. "Where are the plate and spoon for this doll? All of the dolls have to be fed. Each one of them."

Consequently, at every stage in instruction it is important to teach children to produce a deeper analysis, and a deeper synthesis based upon it. This leads the children to generalization and teaches to single out what is essential. For example, a group of children are each given a square divided into 16 smaller squares (Figure 7); they are asked to shade in the squares in the second and third (horizontal) rows and then in the second and third columns; then they are to count the common squares in the two columns and the two rows and outline them in colored pencil. The children count the squares they have shaded (12) and the number of common squares in this set that intersect each other (4). They determine many belong only to the second and third rows (4) and how many to the second and third columns (4). This operation gives the children a practical understanding of the set operation called intersection, although they do not yet know that term.

By counting various objects over and over again, four- and five-year-old children arrive at the conclusion that number does not depend on an object's spatial and qualitative attributes. The number five can be represented in the form of five pencils, five different-colored flags, five dolls, five squares, five balls, five small circles, or by five parts of a single object—five sides, five vertices, five angles in a pentagon—each represents the same number, five. The children learn to isolate the essential property, in this case the general quantity five, and to ignore all the other attributes—the color, size, and qualities of an object. The children make these generalizations on their own. The teacher brings them gradually to this point, varying the nonessential attributes while retaining the essential ones.

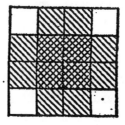

Figure 7.

For example, a three-year-old has already learned the concept of equal and unequal quantities in sets through various concrete examples. When giving carrots to bunnies, the child finds that there are fewer carrots than bunnies; passing out flags to Young Pioneers, the child notices that there are more flags than Pioneers; or there were just as many plates and spoons as there were dolls—that is, there were equal numbers; and so forth. Later, at the age of four, in comparing and counting similar sets, the child realizes that the number four is less than the number five, and the number five is greater than the number four; he understands that number does not depend on the color or size of the object or its position in space. By means of practical comparisons, the child begins to pick out the essential property of number as an indicator of the size of any set. The child learns to see what is common in different things (five fingers on the hand, five flags, five sides of a pentagon) and what is different in things that seem identical (the flags are all red, but there are four in one container and five in another).

It is also very important to develop children's conscious understanding of pairs of opposite concepts: the *right* and *left* hands (or side), *on the right—on the left, in front of—behind, above—below, from above—from below*, *over*—*under*, *more*—*less*, and so on; reciprocal relations between consecutive natural numbers; the arithmetic operations of *addition* and *subtraction* and their signs (+, -); and temporal expressions such as *before* and *after* or *today* and *yesterday*. Setting up opposites in a unified system of knowledge assists children better understanding these paired concepts.

In speaking of the principle of conscious and active learning, we should also note that children's concrete and abstract mathematical knowledge always interact. If children master the set as a concrete notion in the initial stage of instruction, then, as they accumulate knowledge, comparing various sets by establishing a correspondence between their elements leads them to understand number, which is learned as an abstract concept—the indicator of the size of a set. Their knowledge of number subsequently gives them a concrete basis for understanding the strict sequence of connections and relations between consecutive numbers, which gives them an initial notion of the natural number sequence (in the form of a spatial image). Then understanding reciprocal relations leads to the concept of the natural number sequence as a definite system in which each number is one greater than the preceding number and one less than the following number. As the children accumulate information about the numbers up to 10 and start to count groups consisting of 10 objects, they develop a new notion only of the natural number sequence and an elementary concept of the decimal system.

The same process governs the understanding of sets. For the child a set is at first concrete and tangible, but gradually he begins to perceive it not only through vision but through hearing and motion as well, increasingly getting away from the specific isolated set. Different sets can be compared by quantity (sets of sounds and objects, sets of sounds, objects, and movements, etc.). The elements in one set can be combined with the elements in another, forming a new set (for instance, three teddy bears and three dolls together make six toys).

Finally, the conventional symbols and signs (<, >, =, +, -, and so forth) designating the relations between set quantities free the child's thinking from concreteness and material concerns. The words *add* and *take away* become the designations of arithmetic operations instead of representing everyday practical operations, indicators that these practical operations have reached a higher level of generalization.

Thus, the same material at one stage of instruction functions as a concrete image, while at a subsequent stage it loses its concreteness and becomes an abstract concept. But then this abstract concept serves as a concrete basis for the children as they move to a new, more abstract concept.

Thought ascends in a spiral. This means that as teachers implement the consciousness principle in instruction, they should lead children from ignorance to knowledge, ensuring that the children engage in active operations and thoughts during this ascent. The principle of conscious instruction means instilling in children the need to think, the need to confront increasingly new problems, developing an interest in overcoming difficulties and the ability to overcome them (in searching for the most rational means of solving problems), training children to express their thoughts and opinions in speech. All this gives children a conscious attitude toward learning, a persistent interest in mathematical knowledge and an understanding of its significance. Directing children's interests furthers the development of their entire personality. The consciousness principle is very closely related to active learning. Developmental instruction secures this connection.

The principle of conscious and active learning is important both to children's knowledge and skills. Thus, at first they learn simple operations with sets based on a demonstration and explanation from the teacher and they act by the teacher's example or model. After learning the rule and the sequence of operations, they check themselves. A child must sometimes be reminded of the rule, but it need not be repeated explicitly ("Which hand do you put down the circles with, Lesha?" or "You have put the mushrooms under the pictures in the wrong way").

The children gradually learn a whole series of rules, laying the foundation for the development of skills. This creates highly favorable conditions for working and promotes successful performance of assignments. The children also learn to put away aids during and after class. They learn not to be distracted or play with the aids before or during class, but to listen carefully to the teacher's directions. They are taught to carry their work through to the end, striving for precision and accuracy. They acquire skills and the capacity for following their classmates' responses, supplementing or correcting them. They learn to do assignments all by themselves by making a preliminary plan of work, and they learn to study without being distracted. Thus, they develop a new interest in working and learn to make the most of their time.

An important consideration in keeping children active is to keep lessons busy, diversified, and not too long. Lessons should match the children's powers, capacity for work, and attention span. What is most important is not the formal length of a lesson, but whether it has been well thought out and organized.

Let us give an example of what would seem to be a short lesson (12 minutes) in the second youngest group, with 16 students present. The objective of the lesson was to compare the number of elements in sets by matching the elements in one set to the elements in another.

> A child was summoned to the teacher's desk and asked to select and place a collection of certain objects under a collection of others (taking three plates for the same number of dolls, two chicks for two hens, etc.). The other children were asked to watch this child's movements carefully. The teacher worked only with the first child and did not activate the other children's thinking, only saying: "Listen and watch, children." In the seventh minute the children's attention began to weaken and began to concentrate on the behavior of another girl new to the class, who wanted to get up and go up to the teacher's desk without being called upon. An increasing number of children were distracted and attempted to restrain the girl, who did not yet know how to behave in a class. The lesson had to be stopped in the twelfth minute, since no one was listening either to the teacher or to the boy who was working. All the children were occupied with the new girl. What caused such a rapid decline in the children's attention and activity? First, the teacher had built the lesson on the principle of "teacher-student pairing." The teacher was working with just one child without involving the other children in the work; what she said to the other children was merely disciplin-

ary. Second, the teacher had not thought about how the new girl would participate in the lesson. Naturally, the girl turned out to be the children's concern, and they were trying to organized her behavior in their own way.

Thus, the fact that a lesson is brief does not in itself ensure that the children will be active and ready to work. Moreover, experience has shown that even a 30-minute lesson in the intermediate group, if properly organized, does not tire the children. Success is guaranteed by appropriate doses of curricular material, varied assignments and didactic material, and changing methodological procedures designed to make children lively.

Let us give another example of a lesson that took place at the teacher's desk.

The children were counting objects in two sets and determining whether the numbers were equal or unequal by establishing a correspondence between their elements. When the children's attention began to lag, the teacher changed the procedure: summoning four children, she handed them cards with a row of circles drawn on them, and asked them to count the circles aloud and find a group of toys corresponding in number in various parts of the room. The other children were to see that the assignment was done correctly. This injected some animation at once: everyone actively observed the actions of the children who had been called upon, whispering and trying to help: "Not there, not there—there are four over there." Then the teacher asked everyone to check whether the assignment had been done properly and to think about how to prove that the sets found by the children contained equal numbers of elements. Some children suggested counting the elements in both sets, while other suggested putting the objects that had been found on the circles drawn on the cards.

What contributed to making the children active here? The change in methodological procedure: it evoked an orientation reflex and ensured a new upsurge in the children's active thought. It is very important that sedentary lessons alternate with livelier ones, where several people simultaneously take part in carrying out the tasks (finding, bringing, distributing, spreading, measuring, checking others, etc).

From two to four methods can be used in a single lesson with the younger and intermediate groups, and from four to six with the older and preparatory groups. Changing procedures should by no means be an end in itself; it is merely an auxiliary means of teaching children to work without being distracted and to think intensely without unnecessary tension—a means of anticipating "local fatigue" (M. N. Shardakov).

The teacher should also bear in mind that changing material and procedures is not simply a way to make class more "entertaining." Too much "entertainment" can result in a passive perception of what is entertaining; it can be a distraction, leading children away from consciously learning the basic curricular problem. In such cases "entertainment" clearly contradicts the principle of conscious and active learning in achieving the objectives of the curriculum.

For inexperienced teachers, entertainment—children's interest in play techniques—serves as the principle index for positive evaluation of a lesson. Therefore, they try to devise various surprises, methods and techniques to divert the children, which, of course, fascinate the youngsters, but the curriculum task is obscured, remaining unlearned, and the cognitive significance of the lesson is diminished. Let us cite an example.

> In one lesson in the younger group a teacher was to introduce the children to forming a set from individual objects. For this purpose she brought the group a tray on which there stood a hen surrounded by a number of chicks. Her demonstration of the didactic material was accompanied by a story about the hen, who went walking with the chicks, about how she taught them to look for kernels and peck at them, and how the chicks ran around (the teacher moves the chicks around on the table). But then a cat appeared, and the frightened hen called her chicks (they again cluster around the hen on the tray). The children listened with much attention to the relatively long story about the hen and the chickens. In the teacher's opinion, the children showed great interest.

This is true, but where was their interest directed in the lesson? Subsequent discussion with the children showed that the principle source of interest was the content of the story itself—the hen's fear when the cat appeared, her anxiety for her chicks. The curricular objective, creating a set from individual objects, was set aside. The story about the hen was a stronger stimulus than the curricular goal, and although a weak stimulus will contribute to forming temporary connections in concealed form, it does not provoke a response if taken separately. I.P. Pavlov writes that obscuring one form of stimulation by another is determined by the power of the stimulus. Therefore, the lesson objective was not attained.

V. Latyshev, an important elementary school methodologist, has written that the principal element in successful teaching is an awareness of what the teacher wants to teach the pupils when selecting a certain method or technique—an awareness of which aspects of an object need to be pointed out in order to activate the children's thinking.

Beginning teachers often make the mistake of striving to make lessons highly attractive and to provide as much information as possible, which makes the information superficial. "Still," Latyshev writes, "it often happens that one teacher's lessons, which are not all brilliant in appearance and not even particularly lively, ultimately yield much better results than the animated and interesting lessons of another teacher, because the former is able to follow the general idea of the course thoroughly and can elicit work" [3:6].

Thus, the educator's principal task is to evoke active thought and cognitive interest, instilling in children a love for their mathematics studies, and to do so it is essential that the methodological techniques promote the conscious mastery of each curricular task. Application of the principle of conscious and active learning promotes the development of the activity of learning.

The Everyday Life Principle

This principle follows from the dialectal-materialist law on the unity of theory and practice. The developmental value of instruction increases significantly if the information acquired by the children in their lessons, on the one hand, is based on their everyday experience and, on the other hand, can be applied in their lives. Of course, for small children the bond with everyday life is limited by their opportunities—play, lessons, work, living. It is important that children's knowledge of mathematics be used in various types of activity, for then it becomes more meaningful and permanent for them. For example, in preparing material for narrative play, children can apply their ability to count; they can use their knowledge of counting and measuring as they play store, whether as cashier, salesman, or store manager; children can employ quantitative and spatial notions, as well as their knowledge of geometric shapes and the various parameters of dimension, in drawing or building activities. Naturally, situations where knowledge of mathematics can be applied arise constantly in everyday life. For instance, in setting the table a child must count the necessary number of plates and spoons and consider the spatial distribution of the objects on the table (to the right, to the left, in the middle, from the edge); in preparing for an outing, toys and equipment must be counted; during outdoor games, children measure the distance to the goal or between the "home bases" for two playing teams. Finally, knowledge is also applied in didactic games, which the teacher chooses in accordance with the curricular material. The potential for transferring knowledge and abilities to new situations bears witness to development in children's thinking and their awareness of the significance of what they have learned; practical application of knowledge deepens it.

It is also useful to call the children's attention to how adults use their mathematical knowledge in life—why one needs to be able to count or to measure. All this increases children's interest in acquiring more and more mathematical knowledge and develops their desire to learn. It is therefore very important that teachers think carefully about situations in which the children's mathematical knowledge can be applied.

9

Curriculum and Methods for Teaching the Elements of Mathematics in the Second Kindergarten Group (Three-Year-Olds)[1]

Organizing Instruction for Children in the Second Group

Work with three-year-old children should be geared toward developing their notions of a set, toward the perception of differences between sets by comparing the number of elements, and toward the ability to determine whether sets have an equal or unequal number of elements. Children can perform this comparison even if they do not yet know number. It is important for them to learn through observation that sets can differ in their quantitative structure. This stimulates interest in comparison and teaches them to determine differences by number-words by means of counting. But instruction in counting and assigning number-words to sets will be done with children of four or older.

Studies in child development from the age of one and a half years show that the first notions of sets begin to emerge in early childhood, when the child is learning to speak, but the process of developing children's notions of sets and number must be guided.

Two-and three-year-old children must first be taught to make practical comparisons of the elements in two sets, comparing small sets with one another and determining which is greater or smaller or whether they have an equal number of elements. The concept of a set is the basis of all mathematical concepts. It must therefore be given particular attention in every kindergarten group. A set can be perceived by various perceptual analyzers: sounds are perceived by hearing, unseen sets of objects by touch,and movements by the muscular sense—the kinesthetic analyzer. Small children perceive a set as a unified whole when it is made up of identical elements, but they must be taught to perceive a set as a unit if its elements are not identical.

The sameness of set elements can be determined by various attributes. For example, the common attribute for cubes of different colors is shape. But a set of cubes can also be specified according to the attribute of color—e.g., red cubes or green cubes. Thus, children must be taught to perceive a set as a whole, while picking out its most essential feature, such as the shape of a cube. At the same time, they should be able to group its elements according to another attribute, such as color; that is, they should know how to separate the parts of the set.

Teaching children to see and compare two sets by contrasting their elements means creating a first-signal basis for the future activity of counting. The process of teaching young children to count requires logically consistent and carefully considered methods. The mastery of number is something of an indicator of abstract thought, which the child does not develop all at once, but rather during many operations with sets. Therefore, children must first be taught to compare sets element by element, without counting them. This makes possible a transition from perceiving and comparing specific sets to the activity of counting and the development of the abstract concept of number.

The study of counting in children also shows that children cannot be taught counting and number solely through everyday life and play. Play and the everyday environment are attractive to children not because of quantity, but because of a wealth of other aspects. For example, a child sees no need to count the eyes or hands of a doll while playing with it. The children examine the eyes and may even name them with the word "two", but it is not a number reflecting the equal size of any collection of two objects; for them, rather, it is merely one of the doll's attributes. Therefore, the child who points to two eyes, two hands, or two feet on a doll does not see this quantity in his environment: when asked to point out two Christmas trees the child points out three. Studies demonstrate that for children the word "two" does not yet function as an index of a definite class of sets.

"Situational" instruction is not successful because the children are placed in situations where there is a highly complex composite stimulus: in play and in the child's practical living, the quantitative aspect and counting are among the very weak components.

That is why in specific situations, e.g., while watching the fish in an aquarium, the child may distinguish between two fish and three, but in other situations he will be unable to perform the same task; the stronger components of a composite stimulus, by virtue of negative induction, inhibit the weak ones. Watching fish as they swim or setting the table for breakfast or dinner, of course, displace the weak, incidental impressions about quantity which the child has received in these situations. Therefore, there is a need for special lessons where a set and the number of elements in it are the strongest stimuli, and all the other components are weaker and subordinate to them.

Special mathematics lessons can be conducted simultaneously with an entire group of three-year-olds, but they must be thought through clearly. In certain cases, bearing in mind the children's development and conditions in the group, it is possible to conduct lessons with small groups of from four to six children, but only as long as all the subgroups get an opportunity within a period of one or two days. The advantage of collective work is that all the children are pointed in the same direction, and cooperation and mutual instruction can take place.

Lessons should be held once a week, at a regular day and time. This schedule fosters the essential sense of purpose in the children, heightens their interest, and provides optimal opportunity for learning. At first the lessons should not last longer than 10 or 15 minutes, but they should gradually be increased to 20 minutes.

In order to maintain children's attention level, the teacher must make sure that the lessons are diversified, varying the didactic material or methods. In lessons with small children it is advisable to use play techniques, which should not be an end in themselves, however, but merely a resource in the accomplishment of curriculum objectives.

Only individual children who have missed many lessons on account of illness or have poorly mastered material need to have individual lessons when the interval between lessons stays within a week (because of low nervous system mobility).

Curriculum Material for Three-Year-Olds

Work to develop three-year-old children's notions of sets can at first involve games with various aids. As early as the second year, when learning to talk, children easily learn the singular and plural endings. They say: "Give flag" or "Give flags," "This is doll," "These are dolls." As children play with nesting toys (nested dolls called *matryoshki*, sets of small boxes, eggs, or bowls, or a ring cone) at the age of one or two, they take them apart, pulling out one *matryoshka*, then another, and so on, and are delighted to find that there are many of them. They take apart the boxes or the bowls, making groups of many boxes or many bowls. As they take ring after ring from the post, they are pleased to wind up with a large number of rings. As they work actively with these aids, they "create" a set by themselves, as it were, which they then try to collect into a unified whole. It is important for the teacher to stress in words what the child is actually doing: "You have a lot of little rings: this one, this one, this one, and this one...," the teacher says, pointing out every element in the set that has been scattered by the child. "There are many rings in all. Come, let's gather them all together and put them on the post." The child starts putting the rings back on, without yet paying attention to their size. It is important for the child to collect them together, to create a single whole. The child frequently accompanies his actions with the words:

"Another one, another one, another one." "You've collected all of the rings, there are a lot of them on the post, but there is only one post," the teacher sums up.

The child should gradually be taught to collect the rings on the post while taking their size into consideration as well. For this purpose, the child may be asked to find the largest ring, and then, after putting it on the post, again asked to find the largest, and so forth. In focusing attention on the separation of the rings, *matryoshki*, or bowls, the teacher imparts to the child a method of breaking down a set into its elements and a method of combining these elements into a single whole, emphasizing the quantitative aspect—the fact that a set is composed of elements. The child is learning to see "one" and "many," and at the same to perceive the size of the particular elements of the whole: "There's one *matryoshka*, but there are many *matryoshki* in it, and all the *matryoshki* are of a different size."

Three-year-old children must learn that the set is a single whole consisting of homogeneous objects. They should first be taught to represent a whole from homogeneous objects and to pick out the elements—to see them within the whole. Therefore, the first lessons on the set must enable the children to understand the relations between the concepts "one" and "many," and realize that a set consists of elements—that is, of individual objects. The processes of combining the elements into a single whole and separating the whole into elements should occur simultaneously.

The second goal is to teach children to see the component parts in a single set of dolls—dolls with red bows and dolls with white bows—that is, teaching the children to group sets according to different attributes. A third and equally important goal is to show the children, using concrete groups of objects, that sets can be equal or unequal with respect to their elements. For these purposes, the children must be taught practical techniques of establishing a correspondence between the elements of sets: to compare the elements in one set with the elements in another and, using this comparison to determine which set has more or fewer elements or whether the elements are equivalent, without yet naming the given sets with number-words. This also constitutes the first-signal basis for the future operation of counting.

Since small children's quantitative perception of a collection of objects is still closely linked to the spatial arrangement of the elements of the sets, one curriculum goal is differentiation between quantitative and spatial perception. This differentiation is promoted by the development of proper skills in moving the hands and eyes.

Thus, the curriculum for three-year-old children includes the following points.

The children must be taught to form sets by themselves, composing them from individual objects, and to pick out one object from a set. They should understand the relations between "one" and "many."

The children must be taught to group sets according to different attributes.

They should be taught to find "many" objects and "one" object in their surroundings ("What objects are there many of in this group, and what object is there only one of?", "There is one car, but it has many wheels," or "There are many chairs and tables, but there is only one aquarium, although it has many fish in it.").

They must be taught to use the techniques of superimposing and associating elements in one set with elements in another, arranging the elements in order, using the right hand to place them horizontally from left to right. In comparing sets, the children must be taught to correlate the elements in the sets one to one, precisely respecting the intervals between the elements.

The children must be taught to see and establish relations between sets without resorting to number.

Children should practice the ability to reproduce sets by hearing, repeating from one to three claps or knocks without counting or naming the number. For example: "Knock the same number of times as I knock," "Take the same number of toys as the number of times I knock," or "Show the card with the same number of carrots as the number of times I knock."

The children should understand the following expressions and use them actively in their speech: *as many... as, equally, more-less, one apiece, a lot of*; they should learn to make the words *many* and *one* agree grammatically in gender, number, and case with nouns; and they should understand the meaning of the question "How many?". They should be taught to use the following expressions in responding: "Here there are the same number as there" or "Here there is an equal amount."

For making distinctions in size, children should be taught to compare objects according to dimension (using contrasting sizes) and express the results of their comparison with words such as *longer-shorter, the same as* (equal in length), *thicker-thinner, the same* (equal in thickness), *bigger-smaller, the same as* (equal in volume).

As they learn about shape, children should be taught to distinguish certain geometric figures, the circle, square, and triangle, and to find similar shapes around them (for example, balls and plates are round, but books, boxes, blocks, and sheets of paper have corners). Children must learn to identify these forms by tactile-motor and visual investigation and reproduce the shape of objects in a drawing.

The development of spatial notions should begin with an orientation in the parts of the child's own body and the corresponding determination of spatial directions: *in front*—where the face is; *in back* (or behind)—where the back is; *on the right* (or to the right)—where the right hand is (the one with which I hold a spoon or draw); *on the left* (or to the left)—where the left hand is.

The children should know what they do with which hand, when and with which hand they perform certain actions, such as the hand they use to eat, draw, or wave. They must be taught basic orientation in time, naming and distinguishing in practice between morning, afternoon, evening, and night.

Sample Lessons with Sets in the Three-Year-Old Group

As indicated above, lessons with children should promote the development of notions of sets and the ability to group sets according to different attributes and compare sets element by element, as well as the superimposition and association techniques.

In these lessons the basic object of the children's attention is the quantitative aspect; their understanding of the relations between *one* and *many* is refined. The children come to realize that any set consists of individual homogeneous elements, which will later mean in the language of arithmetic that every number consists of units. Familiar objects that are grouped together according to various attributes appear to the children in a different aspect, one that is new to them, and this arouses their interest.

The constant repetition of the same words with different material that accompanies the children's activity and observations promotes the mastery of new terms, which are gradually introduced into their speech. These lessons chiefly emphasize the quantitative aspect, but other aspects, such as color and shape, are also retained when the same objects are grouped according to different attributes. The children begin to understand that sets can be formed in different ways. It is not so much the objects themselves as their qualities that become the stimuli, and when the elements in sets are compared, it is on the basis of their spatial-quantitative relations. The children are happy not so much because they see blocks, ducks, and the like, but rather because there are many of them, because they can themselves separate the blocks into red ones and yellow ones or group the ducks into gray ones and white ones.

It is important for new knowledge to always be built upon knowledge that has already been acquired, and for children to be able to apply their knowledge in other types of activity—that is, in different situations.

Forming Sets from Individual Elements and Separating One Object from a Set

In one of the earliest lessons children find out that every collection is composed of individual objects, and that it can be separated into individual objects. The children become familiar with the expressions *many, one, one apiece,* and *none.*

Let us consider approximately how such a lesson might proceed. The children are asked to point out where there are many toys, and each child is to take one toy, subsequently creating a group of many toys by putting them all together. The teacher brings in a tray on which are arranged blocks of two colors in a quantity equal to the number of children. The children greet the tray with a cry: "Look how many there are!" Each child receives one block. At first the children are attracted by the color of the blocks; they examine their own and each other's. With a view to directing their attention to the quantity of blocks, the teacher asks each child how many blocks he has. As the teacher summarizes their answers, she emphasizes that everyone has one block, and there are no blocks on the tray. Then each child puts just one block on the tray, and the set takes shape before their eyes. The teacher now only points out that there are again many blocks on the tray, and the children have none. "How did this happen?" the teacher asks, explaining: "Everyone has put down just one block: Vasya one block, Zhenya one block, and so on, and together we have many blocks." Then the teacher asks individual children if they have any blocks. "No," they answer. And the teacher emphasizes it: "Nobody has blocks." Next the teacher gives one block apiece to four or five children, asking who has how many, and summarizes their answers: "Lena, Valya, Vova... have one block apiece, and the other children have none, but there are many blocks on the tray." Then all the children again receive one block apiece and observe that the teacher has no blocks left, although each child has one. The teacher shows the children two shelves where there are no blocks and asks them what to do so that there will be many blocks on the shelves.

The children note that they would all have to put their blocks there. The teacher suggests placing all red blocks on one shelf and all blue ones on the other. Each child is to decide which shelf his block should go on. Each child puts one block on a shelf and watches to see how more and more blocks come to be on each shelf. The teacher, calling the children by name, says that each one has put down just one block, but taken together, there turn out to be many blocks.

Ducks are brought out to replace the blocks (gray drakes and white ducks) in accordance with the number of children, and the same exercise is done with them. During the lesson the children should be prompted to use the words *none* and *one apiece*. "How many ducks did each of us take from the tray?" "One apiece." "How many ducks were left on the tray?" "None."

Then the children drop the ducks one after another into two pans of water, after having been asked to put the gray ducks in one pan and the white ones in the other. Their attention is focused on the fact that there were many ducks and that they have been divided according to color: "Now there are many gray ducks in one pan and many white ducks in the other pan." Then the lesson changes into a game. The children's statements that there are many ducks in the pan or that there are none at all usually continue to resound for a long time.

The knowledge acquired by the children must be reinforced. At the next lesson they should be shown that any set is composed of individual objects: one, another one, and so forth. However, in order to make a connection with the previous lesson, it is important to begin the review lesson by utilizing some of the earlier materials. Three or four of these lessons should be conducted with three-year-old children, always varying the material. As a result, the children begin to use the new words relatively freely and relate how they themselves have made up "many."

In these examples the children learn to see that a set consists of different parts, such as red and blue blocks or gray and white ducks. Another variant of the separation of a set on the basis of color can also be used. After distributing blocks to the children, ask how many blocks everyone has and what color they are, and then ask them to put only the red blocks on the tray, then only the blue ones. When generalizing that there are many blocks on the tray, it must be stressed that some of them are red, and some are blue. Thus, the teacher will train the children to see not only the set as a whole, but also its components, each of which differs from the other component in the color of the individual blocks. Here, by comparing both parts element by element, it is possible to determine which blocks there are more of (for instance, the set consisting of red blocks is greater than the set of blue blocks).

Repeated observations of such assignments show that the children approach them with interest. On numerous occasions the youngsters have sorted out sets in their games, but they never focused on forming a set from separate individual objects or a unified set consisting of different parts. This is a new element that builds on the familiar, and it arouses the children's interest in the assignment.

Finding "Many" and "One" in the Child's Environment

In subsequent lessons the children learn to find sets and single objects around them in the singular. At first it is easy for children to single out and name single objects in the room. While they usually have difficulty finding groups of objects, some cannot even find groups of objects in their field of vision on their own. The children name only the groups of objects that the teacher points out to them: "See what we have many of on the rug (on the shelf)." A question can help the children divide the room into individual areas and direct their attention to one area; thereupon, they can see a group of homogeneous objects concentrated in a given area.

There are three-year-olds who manage the assignment better, but at first they pick out only sets of objects which are unified spatially in a group (e.g., fish in an aquarium, pencils standing in a container on a shelf, dolls sitting on the sofa in the doll corner, the wheels of a car, the legs of a toy horse)—that is, they name a collection that falls within their visual field as a unified whole. But almost none of the children begin by naming seemingly obvious objects such as the set of tables or chairs, or the children themselves.

What is the reason for these difficulties? In order to find a set of objects of a certain type in the room, the surroundings must simultaneously be analyzed from several points of view at once, but synthesized only for the quantitative attribute. In such cases one object must be singled out from the complex situation of the room, attention must be concentrated on it, and similar objects must be mentally combined into a single whole, a unified set—neglecting all the other objects—although actually they remain scattered about the room, as before. This means that the quantity must be separated from the spatial arrangement of the objects in the room, their spatial relations overcome, and the objects mentally combined into a single set.

Despite the difficulties, the children are always quite interested in doing these assignments. Their interest is aroused partly because they are approaching familiar surroundings from a new side, one that is still unknown to them, and they are captivated. The objective of instruction is to direct the children's attention to spatial-quantitative analysis and develop their ability to abstract the quantitative aspect of objects and mentally synthesize identical elements into a single set.

Let us give a sample list of tasks by which this objective can be met. First, the children can place objects on different feltboard strips, one to the right and the other to the left. The children are asked to put just one mushroom on the left, on the red strip, and to put many mushrooms on the green strip on the right. Next, the task can be changed: for instance, the red strip can be put on the right and the green one on the left, with the number of objects staying the same as before (one on the left and many on the right); then, without shifting the strips, the teacher can change the number of mushrooms on them (many to the left, one to the right). It is important to teach the children to listen attentively to the instructions pertaining to the number and location of the objects and to connect the quantity either with the color of the strips or with their spatial arrangement.

Another variant of the task might involve a different arrangement of the strips: one on top, and the other below it. The children should again connect the quantity of the objects—circles, for example—with the color of the strips and the arrangement.[2]

After the children have carried out these assignments, the teacher asks them how many circles each one has put down on the strips. It is very important, as shown by experience, to teach the children to coordinate their sensory perceptions with words—not just those they hear, but also those they utter— transforming the practical operation into speech.

A third variant of the assignment would be to ask the children to find one object and a set of objects on specially prepared desks. Here they are to look for a set of objects (many, one).

Let us describe the organization of this activity. On one table there are one cone, one cup, one toy dog, one teddy bear, one car, and so on. On the other tables these toys are arranged in groups: there are many cones on one table, many cups on another, many toy dogs on a third, and so forth. The children are told to find a specified quantity.

The tasks can vary in complexity, depending on the developmental level of individual children. An assignment to "bring many cups" demonstrates all that the child has to do: distinguish between where there is one cup and where there are many. An assignment to "bring many of any one toy" requires an independent choice, which is more complicated for the youngster. Therefore, it is important to call the children's attention to the arrangement of objects on the tables before the lesson begins, have them examine them, and state that the objects on one table have been arranged so that there is one of each and those on the other table are arranged in groups (in large numbers). There are terms the children already know, and they are reinforced in this lesson.

Here is a fourth variant of the task, where the toys are arranged differently: for example, the teacher may put many teddy bears and one toy dog on one table, one teddy bear and many toy dogs on another, and so on—that is, the same object is represented in one instance by a single object and in the other by a group. The task is made more complicated because the children are asked to find "one" and "many" at the same time.

The children do not bring up the toys, as in the previous lesson, but after finding them, they stand by the table and tell the others what they have found. This develops their speech and trains them in using the words *one* and *many,* providing them practice in making the former agree with the noun it modifies.

Usually the children name the toys first and then say the word "many" or the number-word as in: "Cups—many," "Teddy bear—one." In this formulation the number-word acts as the predicate, and, as is well-known, a predicate is more active than a modifier. This sort of sentence construction shows that the child's thinking is oriented toward seeking out and identifying the quantitative aspect. Therefore, this formulation cannot be regarded as erroneous at this stage: it is absolutely natural. Before these lessons, the children were unable to speak in this way. They usually named the objects and their number separately. Seeing many cups, the child resorts to the plural form that he knows and says: "Cups." "How many cups?" the teacher asks him. "Many," the child answers. "Cups—many," the teacher formulates, and the child repeats after the teacher. "What else do you see?" "A teddy bear." "How many teddy bears?" "One." "Cups—many, and teddy bear—one," the teacher says and the child repeats. Thus, the children gradually master the construction of a simple sentence, which they start to say on their own: "Cups—many," or "Teddy bear—one."

The teacher can get the children to combine these two sentences into one: "Cups—many, and teddy bear—one." The children should also be taught another formulation, where the word "many" or the number-word becomes a modifier: "There are many cups and one teddy bear." The children learn these formulations easily if counting lesson is designed not only to develop their perceptions and notions but also to develop their speech.

After such a series of exercises, which enable the children to see and compare many objects and one object, it becomes possible for them to find any sets in their surroundings. But a certain sequence is required—groups of toys and individual toys should first be arranged on various objects (cupboards, shelves, tables, and windowsills). As the teacher asks the children to find many toys and one toy, she lists the parts of the room and the objects where the sets and the individual toys might be located. This expands the children's field of observation.

The complexity of subsequent assignments can be increased by not preparing the sets beforehand: they are always represented in a group and should be found by the children in a natural situation. But first the children's attention can be directed to various parts of the room: they can be asked to look on the floor, the walls, the ceiling, the windowsills: "Look everywhere."

As pointed out above, this task requires that the young child carry out a highly complex mental activity—the ability to subject his environment to analysis. Therefore, it is only as a result of doing these assignments that children start to find sets under any circumstances: first they can find sets located spatially in a single visual field, and then, after repeated practice, they can find sets that are dispersed in space but can be generalized mentally.

In these lessons the children's interest in the quantitative aspect of objects around them develops and grows: they begin to notice on their own what had previously escaped their attention. For example, they notice that there are many small pictures on the different walls in the room, but only one large one.

Consequently, based on the sensory perception of a set consisting of several elements and comparing it to a set consisting of one element, the children form a logical notion of a set as a unity that always consists of individual objects; this set is to a certain extent no longer dependent on the spatial arrangement of its elements. This notion of a set already demonstrates a degree of abstraction, although it still relies on sensory perception.

These new notions also start to be gradually reflected in the children's speech. When a very young child looks at the elements of a concrete group of objects and accompanies his observations by saying *another, another*, and refers to a single, visually perceived group with the word *many*, then the child is beginning to generalize the elements in a set mentally, for the individual objects continue to be disconnected in space in his immediate perception. This is the sequence for developing the general notion of a set as a unified whole.

After the ability to distinguish between "many" and "one" becomes more secure, these terms can be used in other activities, such as forming many balls and one plate out of modeling clay or pasting many small flags and one large flag onto a sheet of paper. Differentiation of the notions of "many" and "one" cannot begin with drawing because the quantitative aspect is not the principal element for the children in that activity. Now, however, they hear and focus their attention on what quantity of which objects is to be molded or pasted. As before, quantitative relations in these lessons remain incidental for the children; nonetheless, since they are developed in special lessons, they do play a role in drawing.

Thus, at a certain stage in development it is very important for children to use their knowledge in other types of activity, which makes the knowledge more active and significant. At the same time, this knowledge enters into increasingly diversified connections, and the establishment of a multitude of inter-associative connections promotes the child's mental development.

Comparing Sets by Establishing a Correspondence

Before children are taught to count, they should be taught techniques of comparing the elements in one set with the elements in another—the techniques of superimposing one set on another and associating one set with another.

The **superimposition method** is the simplest. The elements of the sets must be arranged in a row. Objects are superimposed on drawings with the right hand moving from left to right in order, one object after another. The teacher demonstrates on the blackboard how the objects are to be superimposed—which side to begin on—and then asks the children to show with their fingers the direction of the hand's movement from left to right.

The curriculum tasks in this assignment are to teach children to superimpose toys on the corresponding pictures, maintaining the same quantity, to distinguish between the right and left hands and ascertain the direction of hand movement from left to right, and to teach the use of the expression "as many... as" in describing what has been done.

The children are given cards with objects drawn on them in rows; there are two mushrooms on one card, for example, and three on another. Each child is also given a box of mushrooms (or objects) whose number is greater than the number of mushrooms (objects) drawn on the card. Before starting work, the teacher demonstrates and tells how to superimpose the mushrooms. The number of mushrooms on the cards changes: once they have placed mushrooms on the first card, the children proceed to the next (with three mushrooms), and so on. Later, the number of mushrooms can be increased to five, since the set is not yet expressed by a number. It is important for the children to feel that the sets are different in quantity, but without counting them. They should develop an interest in the method of distinguishing these sets—that is, in counting.

The mushrooms can be replaced by fish, rings, or circles. But regardless of how the objects change, the same number of them must be set down as are given on the card. The children begin to understand that the quantity does not depend on the character of the objects, that it can be equal for different objects that make up a set. Children's notions of equal sets are thus gradually expanded, and they learn the significance of the phrase "just as many... as."

It is very important here to encourage the children's speech. "How many circles did you set down, Valya?" asks the teacher. "Many," the child usually says. "Right—you have put down just as many circles as mushrooms." The teacher suggests repeating this sentence; gradually the children themselves begin to use similar expressions. For the knowledge to become more stable, it is very important that what the child has done and has achieved is spoken aloud.

The superimposition technique means that the children's attention is increasingly diverted from the objects themselves and focused on making the sets equal and ensuring that the individual elements represented in the drawings correspond to the actual objects.

Children should be told at the very start that the mushrooms are to be placed only on their pictures—that mushrooms can be left in the box if all of the pictures are covered. This precaution is necessary because not all children immediately correlate one element in a set with another, even when superimposing them.

In summarizing, the teacher should not restrict herself to silently checking and drawing a general conclusion about whether the assignment has been done properly. She should ask one or two children how they did the assignment ("I put one mushroom on every picture of a mushroom").

As assignments are carried out and the teacher explains the errors, the children's operations gradually become correct. They learn that the elements in sets should correspond and that the spaces between the drawn objects remain empty. Another more prevalent error in early assignments is to attempt to operate with both hands, moving from the middle to the ends, and to disrupt the direction of right-hand movement from left to right. Children must be constantly reminded of this, since the previous stereotype in hand and eye movements is not revised all at once.

A sensory notion of the correspondence between the elements in two sets and the methods of operation in the early assignments can be provided by demonstrating the operation, in combination with spoken annotation. The children can then perform the task based on exclusively verbal instructions. But in the transition to purely verbal instructions, it is important at first to maintain the previous situation—then the words, like a second signal, begin to function "on the spot," as the physiologists say. Later, any objects can be superimposed on any drawings based on a verbal set of instructions: "Set down just as many objects as are drawn in the picture (or on the card)." Even a verbal reminder—"Do the placing with your right hand—from left to right—" becomes clear to children without a demonstration.

The next technique which the children are to learn is the **association technique.** The purpose of the lessons with the children is to teach them to correlate the elements in one set with the elements in another. But the assignment is more complicated: every element must be singled out while at the same time seeing its spatial arrangement and preserving the spaces between the elements.

Let us cite some sample lessons. The children are handed pieces of paper showing two strips. Several red circles (or objects) are pasted or drawn on the top strip, while the bottom strip remains empty; the children are to place circles (or objects) on it, while there are more physical objects than drawings on the card. The teacher, relying on what the children already know, suggests first superimposing blue circles on the red ones in equal quantity, and then shows them how to put the blue circles on the bottom strip under the red ones, removing the blue ones one after another and working from left to right.

Then the assignment becomes more complicated: the teacher gives the children some yellow circles and asks them to place them on the bottom strip under the red ones, one precisely under the other, starting from the left. In order for the children to check whether they have correctly placed the yellow circles on the bottom strip, the teacher proposes superimposing them on the red ones. "Anyone who makes a mistake and takes more yellow circles will have some left—there will be nowhere to put them," the teacher says.

While it is very important in these lessons not to leave the children's mistakes uncorrected, they should also not be emphasized; rather, the teacher should express confidence that next time the children will be more attentive and will be able to place the circles properly. The children's attention should be directed to the reasons for their mistakes, particularly different spaces between the circles in comparison with the model.

Once the children master the superimposition technique, they are usually quick to learn the association technique. As they accumulate practice, the number of errors decreases, even as early as the first lesson. The children begin to show an interest in each other, watch whether the assignments are done correctly, and give advice: "Yours is not right—it should be this way!" But if the children have not been prepared to use the association technique, learning it will cause them trouble.

It is essential to continue developing the children's speech in every lesson. When the teacher asks, "What did you do?", the children should reply that they have put as many circles on the bottom strip as were drawn on the top strip, and tell how they lined them up (circle under circle). The teacher asks the children where there are more (or fewer) circles—in the box or on the card. "There were more circles in the box, and fewer on the card," the children answer after learning to see whether the number of elements in the two sets is equal or not.

Let us point out four mistakes encountered in using the association technique.

1. The children begin to set down the objects from the middle, moving to the right with right hand and to the left with the left hand, returning to an earlier stereotype in their movements.

2. They do not see the spaces between the objects depicted on the card, and begin putting objects close together in a row on the bottom strip, making sure only that the "boundaries" of the set correspond to one another. In such cases the children set down a greater number of objects than shown on the model strip.

3. When verifying the quantitative correspondence between the objects and their representations through the superimposition technique, some children at first do not understand the connections between the superimposition and association techniques. For example, after putting circles on the bottom strip, the children calmly put the extra ones in the box without realizing that the superimposition technique can be used to check their work.

4. Some children (few, as a rule) do not see the spaces between the objects for a long time, even though their attention is called to them. For these children it is advisable to rule the strip into squares, in order to help them to observe that the circle is in its own square; then they begin to follow the spatial-quantitative correspondence among the elements more successfully.

A variant lesson in association involves placing small toys next to other toys that are located on individual tables. For example, a group of

Christmas trees (three or four) might stand on one table, and two or three rabbits on another. The children are given a small box containing mushrooms or carrots, with more of them than needed. They can be asked to put one mushroom under each tree or give one carrot to each bunny. Once they have done the assignment, the children say that they have set down just as many mushrooms as there are trees. "There are the same number of mushrooms and trees," the teacher says, emphasizing the one-to-one correspondence between the elements in two sets with the same number of elements. "Which did you have more of—trees or mushrooms?" she asks. "There were more mushrooms," the child answers, pointing to the mushrooms left in the box.

At this stage, operations such as "Let's dress the doll" or "Let's feed the teddy bear" can be proposed to the children during play (without yet using numbers). But the assignment itself should be confined to preparing clothes for the doll or dishes for feeding the teddy bears, so that the children can then switch to playing. Therefore, it is best to call this assignment "Let's prepare clothes for the doll." The items of clothing should be provided in greater or lesser quantities than the number of dolls in order to develop the children's notions of sets with the same or different numbers of elements and make it necessary to select doll clothing in equal quantities ("just as many... as"). The children are asked to put one dress or one shirt apiece on each doll. They again employ the expression *one apiece*, with which they are already familiar. They note that they have more of one type of clothing than there are dolls, and that there is not enough of another type: there is less.

These assignments can be varied: for instance, the teacher can summon three or four children to her desk and give them a set of balls—one apiece, with the number of balls possibly less than the number of children. The children establish this either independently or under questioning by the teacher. Another variant is for some children to get big balls and some to get small ones. The children put the balls on the floors in pairs (big and small). A child is called upon to determine which balls there are more of, or whether there are the same number of each. This type of lesson gives the children practice in recognizing the size of the balls as well as their quantity. After four or five lessons using different variants of the association technique, the children learn the technique.

It should be noted that as the children's knowledge about sets becomes richer, they become increasingly fascinated by lessons in mathematics and await them with interest. They evince a new point of view in their perception of the objects around them: they begin to pay attention to the various sets in their immediate surroundings—"There are many trees in the garden," "Our house has many windows."

The Perception of Sets by Various Analyzers

The sets in the children's surroundings vary in nature: a set of homogeneous objects, a set of homogeneous sounds, and so forth. These varying sets are perceived by different perceptual analyzers: visual, auditory, muscular, and others. The recurrence of the homogeneous sensations perceived by a certain perceptual analyzer forms a basis for the general notion of a set. Therefore, children must be given practice from early childhood in perceiving sets with different analyzers, and must be taught to compare the elements in one set with the elements in another—for example, reproducing via movements, a set perceived by hearing. This promotes the establishment of inter-analyzer connections.

A number of techniques can be used for this purpose in working with three-year-olds. Calling upon individual children, the teacher can ask them to strike a drum, musical triangle, or table just as many times as the teacher taps. The children do not do the assignment properly right away: at first many tap an indefinite number of times. These assignments often follow the following sequence:

1. The teacher claps once and puts a toy on the table, claps again and again puts down a toy—and so on, three, four, or five times.

2. A child is called upon to look at these objects and clap.

3. All the children put down toys on their own tables, one apiece, to conform with each clap by the teacher.

4. A child is called upon to clap (at his place) just as many times as he or she has toys.

5. The teacher claps, and the child, who perceives the sounds by hearing them, claps the same number of times.

As they practice, the children learn to listen more and more carefully to the number of sounds and to scrutinize the number of movements being made by the teacher.

Unable to represent the number of sounds by a number-word, the children reproduce the sounds quite correctly up to three on the basis of sensory perception, and some do so even up to five. Thus a one-to-one correspondence is established between the number of toys and the number of movements and sounds produced.

By correlating each movement with a visually perceived object, children learn to generalize sets. "You knocked many times—just as many times as there are pictures here." "You knocked just as many times as there are roosters here." "Show the picture where there are just as many objects as the number of times I knocked." These assignments bring the children to understand that sets vary both in their character and in quantitative composition.

On the basis of this—at first purely sensory—perception of various sets consisting of no more than three to five elements, it subsequently becomes possible to introduce four-year-olds to counting in a more complete form, when the numbers in the natural number sequence become one of the sets.

Methods for Developing Spatial and Temporal Notions in Children in the Second Youngest Group

The Size and Shape of Objects

With children in the second youngest group it is important to develop their perception of the size and shape of objects, and to enrich and perfect their sensory experience. This work should be done not only in lessons but also in didactic games and in daily life. An object's size attracts children's attention directly. During their activity, children should gradually develop distinct and correct notions about the properties of the objects around them (color, size, shape).

Children's sensory experience is enriched in operations with objects: as they feel objects, they get to know their size and shape. And if their actions are accompanied by spoken words from an adult designating the qualities of the objects and the operations carried out by the children, their vocabulary is enriched and their thinking developed. Experience in dealing with various objects leads the children to elementary generalizations: different objects can be big, little, long, or short. Objects can also be round (a plate, saucer, or ball) or have corners (a book, table, or notebook).

At the beginning of the year (in September) lessons should be done in the form of didactic games, working with the children in subgroups (four or five persons). For instance, the teacher might introduce a ring pyramid (or cone) consisting of 10 rings and call the children's attention to the fact that it is smooth, and the rings are all of the same color; the children stroke the pyramid, feeling its form. "Are all the rings on the pyramid the same size?" the teacher asks. The rings are removed. As they put one ring on top of another, the children realize that they are of different sizes. The teacher asks the children in turn to choose the largest ring and put it on the spindle. Everyone selects the largest ring from those remaining, but it always proves to be smaller than the preceding one. The teacher points this out to the children, giving them their first introduction to the relative nature of the concepts *big* and *small*. The children outline the rings with their fingers, and the teacher stresses that all of them are round.

Then another pyramid is introduced—again a single color, but consisting of squares gradually decreasing in size. The children's attention is focused on how it is different from the first pyramid (one is smooth and even, the other is angular and uneven). Removing the squares, the children become familiar with their shape, name it, and outline it with their fingers. As they compare the shapes of the ring and the square, the children conclude that the rings in one pyramid are round and the squares in the other pyramid have corners. Placing one square on top of another for comparison, they realize that they are of different sizes. Each pupil in turn is asked to choose the biggest square and to put it on the spindle. The children again see that the biggest remaining square is smaller than the ones already on the spindle.

The children are given both pyramids, along with the scattered rings and squares, and two or three put them together, each time following the rule of choosing the largest ring (or square).

In subsequent lessons the task can be made more complicated: the rings (or squares) for the pyramid can be selected according to a model given to the children. Two identical pyramids are used for this sort of assignment: one belongs to the teacher, and the other is spread out on the table so that the children can choose rings according to the model. Selecting rings according to a model is a more complicated task for the children; therefore, it is most expedient to start instruction in this technique with lessons on distinguishing between *big* and *small*, since this is the property of objects that the children know best. By superimposition the children compare the ring (or square) in the model with the ring they have chosen, first bringing them to the teacher and then doing it independently.

This assignment can have extremely diversified variations, with the models given in decreasing or increasing order, or even helter-skelter; the rings can be placed at random on one table or in different places in the room; the rings in the model can be selected in one color, and the rings for the children in another.

A more complicated assignment requires the children to remember a model that has been shown to them and choose a ring of the appropriate size from memory (this technique helps to develop sight estimation). For developing sight estimation it is advisable to use a popular didactic toy as well (nested cubes, *matryoshki*, small bowls, eggs, or casks) and certain aids recommended in the Montessori system (bars with cylinders, geometry supplements, the long and the short ladders, etc.).

Popular didactic toys can be very broadly applied to studying the size of objects. They enable children to become thoroughly acquainted with the concepts *larger* and *smaller* (*large* and *small*) and with other parameters of dimension: *taller-shorter* (for the *matryoshki*), *fatter-thinner* (for the casks), *deeper-shallower* (for the bowls). By putting together the *matryoshki*, the children learn spatial orientation; when they distribute bowls to the *matryoshki*, they correlate the sizes of certain objects to that of others.

N. K. Krupskaya attached a considerable role to popular toys. On the subject, she wrote: "The child does not yet distinguish magnitudes: he must be given toys that will help him to learn magnitude. Good toys in this respect are those such as eggs that are set one inside another, various nested boxes, small wooden animals of various sizes that the children are familiar with, or people figures. The children might arrange the figures by height or by size..." [1:208-209].

Krupskaya also proposes giving the children a blackboard and colored chalk so that they can "draw lines of various sizes, in different directions, erase them and draw others" [1:208-209]. Then she advises giving the children various toys—hard, soft, solid, large, and small—to develop their sense of touch, "... to teach them to distinguish objects by touch, to distinguish shape by touch, while taking a certain object from a bag" [1:209].

Thus, children's initial familiarity with the size and shape of an object makes it possible to teach them systematically to recognize the various parameters of dimension—length, width, and height.

The children should be taught techniques of comparing magnitudes in the lessons. For this purpose the teacher should have a collection of materials of varying length, width, and height. Cardboard (or wooden) strips of contrasting sizes can be used, such as a long and a short strip of equal width or a broad strip and a narrow one of equal length (see Color Figures 15 and 16).

The teacher demonstrates the technique of comparing the length or width of two strips by placing them side by side or superimposing one strip on the other. To highlight a particular parameter (width or length) in bolder relief, it is advisable to choose strips of different colors, such as a long red strip and a short yellow one. In teaching small children the superimposition technique, they must be made aware that two edges (or a corner) of one strip should be aligned with two edges (or a corner) of the other: it will then be obvious which strip is longer. The comparison should be reinforced orally: "The red strip is longer, and the yellow one is shorter."

After demonstration and explanation, strips of different lengths and different colors are distributed to all the children. By superimposing the strips on one another, the children establish which strip is longer and which is shorter. It is very important to teach the children not only to compare strips to determine their length, but also to recapitulate the comparison process and the relations between the strips orally: "The red strip is longer than the yellow one, and the yellow strip is shorter than the red one." During the assignment the children can exchange different-colored strips two or three times. The teacher leads the children to conclude that the size of the strips does not depend on the color.

Assignments for teaching children the technique of laying one next to another can be similar to the assignment described above. In this instance it is better to use strips of different lengths (or widths) but of the same color. In developing this technique of measuring side by side, the children should be taught that two sides of the strips should be aligned: the shorter sides, as if they continued one another, form a vertical straight line, and the long sides of the long and the short strips should coincide. This technique should be reinforced in action and speech. Using the indicated techniques, the teacher teaches the children to compare the two strips by width as well (wider-narrower, or wide-narrow).

In order to introduce the parameter *taller-shorter* (*tall-short*), the teacher can use a wooden board containing holes whose diameter is equal to the diameter of two round sticks of different colors, one of which is noticeably shorter than the other. The children compare the lengths of the sticks, laying them on the table in a row, and they find that the red stick is longer than the green one, and the green one is shorter than the red one. Then they are each given clay stands with two holes and two sticks of different sizes and colors. The children themselves insert the sticks in the holes and say which color stick is taller and which is shorter (for each individual child).

It is quite possible to impart to children a notion of thickness (*thicker-thinner*) using pencils, choosing them in one size for length but in a different, contrasting size for thickness. The holes into which the children put the sticks of different heights will not do in this case. Only one thin pencil can go into the hole, and a hole of larger size is needed for a thick pencil. If a little slab is made from fresh clay, a hole for a thick pencil can be hollowed out for the children (it should be substantially larger than the one for a thin pencil). Then, after comparing the pencils that they have put in the holes, the children conclude that they are identical in height but that one pencil is thicker than the other.

By ascertaining the differences and relations among different objects (*longer-shorter*, *wider-narrower*, *taller-shorter*, *thicker-thinner*), the children gradually learn that objects can differ in size and be identical in shape.

It is hardly advisable to introduce children to both unequal and equal sizes at the same time. At first unequal sizes should be particularly stressed, and only on the basis of inequality should it be shown that objects can also be the same size. There are longer and shorter strips, and there can be strips of the same length (broader, narrower, and the same length, etc.). Somewhat later the word "same" (in length, width, height, thickness) can be replaced by the word "equal" (in length, width, height, thickness), but there is no need to rush this substitution: it is appropriate only when the children are properly oriented in recognizing the various parameters of dimension and can use such expressions as *longer* (than what?) or *shorter* (than what?).

Newly acquired knowledge must also be used in other lessons—e.g., in drawing a wide and a narrow path, or making a long carrot and a short one from clay. The teacher should watch that as the children examine illustrations or relate objects, they use an expression in their speech such as "The tree is taller than the house," or, on an outing, that they determine that the trees are taller than the shrubs by comparing the trees and the shrubbery, or that the trunk of one tree is thicker than that of another; that a tree's branches are thick or thin; or that a river is wider than a creek.

It is important to remember that very young children can be aware of parameters of dimension, but that above all the words must be accurately differentiated, which depends entirely upon the developmental work done with the children.

Recognition of **shape** begins very early. By the age of three, children have even learned the terms for some shapes: a *round* ball, a *round* plate, or a *round* saucer. But the children still do not know the various properties of geometric figures: the square, the circle, the triangle are perceived as toys. This does not mean, however, that the children do not distinguish their shapes—they do say cube and triangle in order to build a house and its roof; circle, square, and triangle in order to design a pretty picture; and so on.

Geometric shapes should also be included in didactic games: squares, triangles, squares. The children learn the names and characteristics of these shapes by inspecting their contours by both the tactile-motor and the visual analyzers.

The objects surrounding the children are also varied in shape, there are considerably more rectangular objects than round ones. It is very important to teach the children to see the shape of objects and to classify them in an elementary fashion as round or angular. The geometric figures they know should form the basis for this classification. The children themselves say that a ball, sphere, and plate are round, a fish and a cucumber are rounded but lengthened, and a block, book, and box have corners. The children are therefore ready to differentiate objects.

How is such a lesson conducted? Let us assume that the children know how to differentiate and name geometric figures (the square and circle). The teacher first checks their knowledge by exhibiting a large circle and a large square and then asking them to find corresponding shapes in their boxes (the children's objects should be of different colors) and say who has which shape and what color it is. "How do we tell that this is a circle (or a square)?" asks the teacher. The children, outlining the contours with their fingers, say that the square has corners, but the circle does not.

Then the teacher displays a plate (or saucer), and asks the children to outline it with their fingers and think what the plate is like—a circle or a square. The children are called upon to outline the plate with their fingers and say that it is like a circle. In precisely the same way they are asked to determine what the top (or bottom) of a box is more like, and why. The children answer that it has corners like a square.

After giving the necessary instructions about methods of comparison, the teacher moves on to the second part of the lesson. She places a circle on one table and a square on another, and hands three selected children one small item apiece: a plate for one, a saucer (one of the doll dishes) for another, and a piece of paper (from a notebook) or a pocked handkerchief for the third. Then the teacher asks them to outline the shape of the toy with one finger and take it to the table containing the geometric shape that is most like each object. "Here are a circle and all the round things," the teacher says, and the children list them: "A plate, a saucer, a marble, a ball." "Here are a square and all the things with corners," and the children name them: "A piece of paper, a handkerchief." Later the children make similar generalizations themselves.

As the children learn grouping techniques, the practice games can become more complicated: they carry out similar tasks at their own desks, inspecting not one, but two, three, or four objects that are given to them. Or, sitting at a single table, the children place round objects in one box and angular objects in another. In time the objects can be replaced by pictures of objects, and thus the collections can be varied considerably.

Spatial and Temporal Notions

It is appropriate to develop spatial and temporal notions in the group of three-year-old children, using daily life, routines, outdoor play, and morning gymnastics.

Studies of children's spatial orientation have shown that they are based on the children's ability to distinguish the parts of their own bodies. With this in mind, it is extremely important to teach children to make clear distinctions between the parts of their bodies and the corresponding names, and they can be introduced to spatial directions on this basis. Distinguishing the right hand from the left, or the right part of the body from the left, assumes particular significance. The children experience considerable difficulties here, which can be eliminated if they are simultaneously made familiar with the names of their two hands and their different functions: the child holds a spoon with the right hand, and a piece of bread with his left, or the child holds onto the plate with the left; the child holds a pencil and draws with the right hand, but holds onto the sheet of paper with his left hand so that it will not slip.

Bearing this in mind and reminding the children repeatedly, the teacher develops their ability to distinguish the parts of their bodies and determine the spatial arrangement of objects and the spatial direction of movements: *forward-back, in front-behind, from right to left, from left to right.*

Temporal notions (morning, afternoon, evening, night) should also be developed in daily life, while going through routines. These parts of the 24-hour day are also differentiated according to the changing activities of children and adults. But since adult activity in these time segments is not homogeneous, it should be taken into account what activity is typical of a particular location or geographic area. The description of a time segment must be concrete and convincing for every child; in explaining, the teacher must therefore employ a multitude of criteria.

Thus, in the three-year-old group children can acquire a great deal of knowledge in their daily life, and only subsequently can this empirical knowledge become the subject of specialized lessons.

The small child learns in various situations, and there should be no insurmountable obstacle between special instructional lessons and daily life; rather, there should be a natural continuity. For example, on an autumn outing the children might gather many different leaves, and the teacher could mention that they can be grouped according to different features. Some children might begin grouping their leaves by shape, others by size, and still others by color.

Another example is when the children have learned to distinguish the parts of their bodies and know that *in front* means in front of the face and *behind* means behind the back, etc. This information can be reinforced firmly in playing with dolls. It is very important that the knowledge acquired by the children in the specialized lessons be reinforced in their daily lives.

10

Curriculum and Methods for Teaching Elementary Mathematics in the Intermediate Kindergarten Group (Four-Year-Olds)

Organizing Work with Four-Year-Old Children

The intermediate group usually contains children who have come from the preceding group, the second youngest, but there are also often a number of new children who have not previously attended preschool. The teacher must take into account the structure of the group and construct lessons on a differentiated basis at the beginning of the year. The curriculum stipulates that lessons become more complex; therefore, for children who have just entered kindergarten, it is advisable to have a number of lessons based on the three-year-old curriculum. Even with children who have come directly from the three-year-old group, it is often necessary to recall what was studied in the past year, since some knowledge and skills are usually lost over summer vacation. It is advisable to devote September to repeating the previous curricular material and proceed to the study of new material somewhat later.

Further development of the notions about set, size, and shape, and about spatial and temporal relations is scheduled for the intermediate group, but the children will also be taught to count and acquire an elementary concept of number.

In the group of four-year-old children it must be particularly stressed that a set can consist of homogeneous objects, but individual parts often possess different qualitative attributes, such as different colors or sizes. The children must be taught to spot the subsets in a given set. This will lead the children to understand the essential and less essential attributes of a set as a unified whole.

Since the children have learned to compare the number of elements in sets in the previous group by means of the superimposition and association techniques and to determine the capacity of sets, they can be interested in counting with number-words.

In the three-year-old group the children were introduced to various parameters of dimension and taught to compare strips of varying lengths and widths and sticks of varying heights and thicknesses using the superimposition technique, determining which were equal and which unequal. In this group the children must not only be taught techniques of selecting strips and sticks that are equal in length; they must also be brought to the point where they can distribute them according to increasing or decreasing length.

The curriculum for the intermediate group calls for further refinement and sharper differentiation of geometric figures and their names. This is fully accessible to four-year-olds, since they use various geometric shapes (building materials, geometric mosaics, etc.) which they distinguish in practice. In this group they can be introduced to certain properties of these shapes (stability and instability) and encounter them in various sizes (small and large cubes, large and small circles). It is very important to link acquaintance with shape to quantity and counting (counting the vertices, angles, and sides in a figure).

In this group the children should continue learning to compare the shapes of everyday objects with familiar geometric shapes (a page in a book is like a rectangle, a round pencil is like a cylinder).

All this knowledge promotes a new and deeper notion of the surrounding objects. Children are often happy with their discoveries, which they seem to make by themselves ("A piece of paper has corners, and a table has corners, and there are corners in the room, and the cupboard has corners"). What is most important is to provide the children timely knowledge that contributes to the development of curiosity and the power of observation. The curricular objectives have been selected accordingly.

Curricular Material for the Group of Four-Year-Old Children

Teachers of four-year-olds should train the children to distinguish the components of a set as a unified whole and compare them, determining whether or not they have the same number of elements without resorting to counting.

Based on a comparison of two collections arranged in a row, one under the other, the children should be taught to count the elements in each of them, determining whether or not they have the same number of elements. They must use proper counting techniques: naming the numerals in order, correlating the last numeral with the entire set as counted. For example: "one, two, three, there are three geese in all; there are an equal number of roosters and geese, three of each."

The teacher should drill the children practice in counting and comparing two groups of objects represented by consecutive numbers (two and three, three and four, four and five). The objects should be arranged in two rows, one object under another. The children count: "one, two, three, there are three roosters in all." "One, two, there are two mushrooms in all." "There are three roosters and two mushrooms in all." "Three roosters are more, and two mushrooms are less; then three is more, and two is less."

The teacher should make the children understand that quantity does not depend on the size of the objects or their arrangement in space. Children should be taught to see whether two sets contain an equal or unequal number of elements based on counting, when the objects in different groups are situated at various distances from one another (Figure 8).

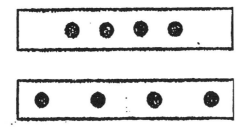

Figure 8.

Children should be taught to see whether two sets contain an equal or unequal number of elements when the objects in each group are of different sizes (Figure 9). The teacher should teach them to count out, lay out, and fetch a number of objects based on a model or a given number, counting out from a larger quantity. For example: count out as many ducks as I have put down; count out and bring here just as many fish as there are circles on your card; count out four roosters and three fish.

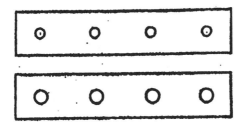

Figure 9.

The teacher should teach how to determine the number of objects in a collection by touch, by counting sounds, and by counting one's own and other people's movements. The children should be taught to produce a number of movements based on a designated number. For example, count how many triangles there are on your card, and tap on the table with a hammer that number of times; clap your hands five times; and so forth. They should learn to do arithmetic up to five by counting: one and two; two and two; two and three; three and three; three and four; four and four; four and five; five and five (based on a comparison of the numbers of elements in two sets).

The teacher should teach the children to make numerals agree grammatically in gender, number, and case, providing fully detailed answers. For instance, "On the top strip I put four red circles, and I put three blue circles on the bottom strip. There are more red circles and fewer blue ones; the number four is greater than three, and the number three is less than four."

Magnitude. The teacher should provide practice in comparing the dimensions of objects, gradually decreasing the degree of contrast in size (giving three objects of various sizes, and then five). The teacher should teach the children to arrange objects in increasing or decreasing order of their length, width, height, and thickness; for example, the longest, a shorter one, an even shorter one, an even shorter one, the shortest.

Techniques of comparing the dimensions of objects should be first taught by direct superimposition or association, and then by sight, developing sight estimation ("Bring a strip of the same length," and so forth).

Shape. The children should learn the names of the geometric figures, which they already know in a practical sense: sphere, cube, cylinder, rectangle, square, circle, triangle. The teacher should drill them in techniques of performing tactile-motor investigations of geometric figures and point out their particular attributes: a cube has many angles or corners, while a sphere and a cylinder have none; a sphere and a cylinder can roll, but a cube is stationary. The teacher should teach them to differentiate angles, vertices, and sides in geometric figures. Rectangles and squares have four angles, four vertices, and four sides apiece, but a triangle has three angles, three vertices, and three sides; a circle has no angles.

The children should realize that all geometric figures can be of different sizes (large and small cubes; large and small spheres; large and small cylinders; large and small circles; large and small squares; large and small triangles; large and small rectangles). The children should practice comparing the shapes of everyday objects to geometric figures: a pencil is like a cylinder; a plate is like a circle; a page or a notebook (or book) is like a rectangle; an inkwell is like a cube; a ball is like a sphere; a Pioneer's necktie is like a triangle; a handkerchief is like a square.

The teacher should drill the children in distinguishing between round, rectangular, and triangular objects. For example, find rectangular, square, and round objects in the room (the tabletop is rectangular, the window is rectangular, the seat of the chair is square, the light bulb is round).

Orientation in Space. The children should be able to indicate the direction of movement with respect themselves (forward, backward, up, down, to the right, to the left) based on knowing the parts of their own bodies. They should be able to describe in words the position of an object with respect to themselves (in front of me is a table, behind me is a cupboard, on my right is the door and on my left is the window, above me is the ceiling and beneath me is the floor).

The children should know the meanings of the words *nearer-farther* and *near-far*, and should be able to use these words ("I put the brushes farther from myself, and the pencil nearer; on the right I have pasted a square and on the left a rectangle, and I put a circle in the middle").

Orientation in Time. The teacher should reinforce and expand the children's notion of the 24-hour day and its components. They should know that morning, afternoon, evening, and night together make up a day. There are four parts to a day: morning, afternoon, evening, night; the children should know their sequence.

The teacher should acquaint the children with the changing days and expressions: *today, yesterday, tomorrow*, as well as the meaning of the words *faster-slower* and *fast-slow*.

Sample Lessons on Sets and Counting in the Four-Year-Old Group

Development of the Notion of a Set

It is advisable to begin working with four-year-old children just as with three-year-olds—by developing the notion of a set. It is important for them to realize that a set can consist of parts and to learn to identify these parts. For example, there are many children in the group, but among them are both boys and girls. Are there more boys or girls, or are there an equal number of each in the group? The children can be asked to divide up into two groups, boys and girls, and stand in two rows opposite one another. A comparison of the rows will show who has no partner: some boys have no girls opposite them. "Then there are more boys," the children conclude. Thus, there are many children in the group, but that "many" includes boys and girls, and it turns out that there are more boys than girls—the parts of this "many" are not equal.

In the classroom there are many different pieces of furniture, such as chairs and tables, but during a comparison it becomes clear that there are more chairs and fewer tables. Consequently, the parts again turn out to be unequal.

One possible assignment is the following. Circles are distributed among the children, who are seated at tables—three colors for each child, in various combinations. For instance, one child gets more red circles than any other color, fewer green, and even fewer blue circles; another child gets the same number of red and green circles, but fewer blue ones, and so forth—that is, all the children will have different parts of the set of circles. "So, everyone has many circles, but what parts do your sets consist of?" "Three parts: red, green, and blue." "Can we find out which of these parts is larger or smaller? Or are all the parts equal?"

The children are asked to think about how to make this clear. They recall what they have already done. They have learned to place objects in a row with the right hand, proceeding from left to right. They know how to arrange circles accurately under one another. The assignment is within their powers, and they try to do it carefully. Circles of the same color are arranged in rows so that every circle in one row is under a circle in the other row. Upon questioning, it turns out that it has come out differently for each child: one has more red circles, fewer blue ones, and very few green ones; another, on the other hand, has more blue circles than anything else, but fewer red and green ones, although they are in equal numbers; and so on. At the end of this assignment the children are asked to mix the circles up again: "Once again there are many circles," the teacher says. "But you know that this set consists of different parts—red, blue and green circles."

Of course, at first this assignment can be simplified by having the children make up a set of circles of two colors, arranging matters so that all the children have more red circles than blue ones, and so forth (simplifying or complicating the assignment depends on the children's level of preparation).

Now we can retreat from our earlier convention that a set should consist only of *homogeneous* objects. The children learn to see, on the one hand, the entire whole, which possesses a common attribute, and, on the other hand, its parts, which in turn possess their own attributes that are nonessential for the set as a whole; these are also sets—they enter into the structure of the larger set as parts. Comparing the elements in two sets creates a firm visual-sensory foundation for the transition to teaching the children to count using number-words.

The idea of a specific set is immediate and accessible to very young children if their attention is directed to it. Indeed, they have many toys, but this "many" is varied in its composition. It is very important and valuable to point out these components and show the children the interrelationship between the parts and the whole—important not only for their mathematical development, but also for their general mental development. It is more valuable than rushing to teach them to count, although we by no means underestimate the value of teaching children to count.

Differentiating and Identifying Sets with Numerals Based on the Teacher's Counting

It is recommended that teaching children to count begin by comparing the numbers of elements in sets and identifying the larger and smaller ones. These sets should differ by one element in their quantitative make-up. The children determine that one set is larger and the other is smaller in quantity. The teacher indicates that these sets can be counted and the number of elements in each ascertained, which the children can learn to do by themselves.

Teaching counting includes two sides: first, ascertaining the larger and smaller sets and determining the quantity of elements using a number-word, which is based on counting the elements; and second, the counting process itself. If the objective is determining sets and naming them with number-words, then counting is a means of achieving an objective—a process. It is advisable for the children to learn the objective of counting first. This objective should be demonstrated to them, and then they should be armed with appropriate means.

Since the objective and the means are interrelated, and simultaneous mastery of them causes certain difficulties (the children do not differentiate them immediately), these aspects of counting can be shared, provisionally, between the teacher and the children. The teacher implements the counting process, and the children name only the total number based on the teacher's counting and ability to distinguish the number of elements in sets: they say how many elements there are in a given set.

The children's attention in this period is focused primarily on **comparing the number of elements in sets** and on the basic objective of counting—**the total number**. Various sets representing consecutive numbers can be used for comparison. Let us give several sample lessons of this kind.

The teacher, as usual, puts objects on two blank strips: three mushrooms on the bottom strip and two radishes on the top one, placing each radish over a mushroom. The teacher explains to the children that now they will not only ascertain where there are more objects and where there are fewer; they will also state where there are how many. But since they are not yet able to count, the teacher will do so, and the children will name where there are how many. The teacher counts the mushrooms, and then the radishes, using the techniques that the children will later learn: "One, two—two radishes in all," emphasizing the total number. "How many radishes in all?" "Two radishes," the children answer. "Now we'll find out how many mushrooms there are: one, two, three—three mushrooms in all," the teacher says, again emphasizing the result of the counting. "How many mushrooms?" "Three... three... three..." the voices ring out. "Three what?" the teacher says, to make it more precise. "Three mushrooms," the children say. "Did you remember how many radishes I counted?" (Not all the children remember at once, although individual voices are heard.) "I'll count again, and you remember how many radishes and how many mushrooms there are." The teacher counts. The children's voices can be heard: "Two radishes... three mushrooms..." "Do you see which there are more of?" "Mushrooms." "And how many of them are there?" "Three mushrooms." "What are there fewer of?" "Radishes." "And how many of them are there?" "Two." "Two what?" "Two radishes." "Right." The teacher herself summarizes: "There are two radishes—fewer of them—and there are three mushrooms—more of them. What are there more of? Think: two radishes or three mushrooms?" "Three mushrooms are more," some children respond.

Adding one more radish, the teacher asks, "Now what can we say about the radishes and mushrooms?" "They are equal," the children say, seeing that the number of elements is equal. "How many radishes and how many mushrooms?" "Three of each." "I'll check to see if it's true that they are equal—three of each." The teacher counts and makes the statement: "Three radishes in all." Then the teacher also counts the mushrooms and summarizes: "There are three mushrooms in all. Some of you were right to say that there are three each of radishes and mushrooms; now there are just as many radishes as mushrooms—three radishes and three mushrooms. But how did this happen? Why have they come to be equal, three each, when there were fewer radishes—two in all?" "You put down another radish, and they became equal." "How many radishes and how many mushrooms are there now?" "Three of each." "Why have the mushrooms stayed as before— three?" "You didn't add anything to them," the children say. This is a very important conclusion, which they arrive at themselves by comparing the two sets. They see that the addition of one object changes the quantity, and therefore the number as well.

Then the teacher takes other groups of objects and puts them on the same two strips. She asks the children to explain which objects there are more of and which there are fewer of, again counting both sets and reminding the children to remember the total number. Then she asks the children to show where there are two objects and where there are three, forming associative connections between the "smaller set" and the number-word two and between the "greater set" and the number-word three. Since the children have previously compared sets many times, without counting the elements, and their eyes have learned to distinguish sets easily, associative connections between sets and number are formed with comparative ease. They do not arise merely by perceiving a set and naming it by means of a number-word, but rather as a result of the counting operation that the teacher is carrying out. Giving a number as an index of a set's capacity becomes an expression of opinion for the children, rather than simple memorization, just as when they learn the name of an object.

Thus, for the children to learn a total number based on the teacher's counting depends, on the one hand, on their ability to discern sets, by comparing the elements, and, on the other hand, on the teacher's new method of counting the elements of a set with number-words. The children acquire this new knowledge by relying on what has previously been learned.

Consequently, when children are taught to count, their attention is focused in the earliest lessons on comparing and distinguishing sets and identifying them with number-words—as total numbers based on the teacher's counting. The children thus learn that not all the number-words named by the teacher are equivalent. Only the last number she names is the total and pertains to the entire set as a whole. This is a very important conclusion for the children to make, and the teacher must ensure that they arrive at it.

For example, the teacher counts two trees and three mushrooms beneath them, and then asks the children whether there are more mushrooms (three) and fewer trees (two). Remembering that there are two trees and three mushrooms, the children can answer such questions from the teacher as: "Why are there fewer trees if they are larger than the mushrooms in size (they are tall and the mushrooms are short)?" The children show that there are more mushrooms because there is one mushroom without a tree—there are not enough trees; there are fewer of them. That means that two is less than three. "Can we say that there are two mushrooms? Listen—I'm going to count the mushrooms again." Counting, the teacher names the numeral *two* among the three numerals. The children say, "No, you can't." But they still cannot give an explanation. The teacher's question compels them to reflect: some say that one mushroom must be taken away, others say that at first there are two, then three, and therefore three mushrooms. Not all the children fully understand why, when counting one, two, three, one cannot say "Two in all." For this, the number-words must evolve into the concept of number. But asking the question does suggest the conclusion to the child that only the number-word that is named last summarizes the entire set; it becomes the total number—the index of the total number of elements. Moreover, on the basis of comparison they see that there are more objects in the set that is called three.

It is not necessary to do a great many assignments where the counting process is carried out by the teacher; the children themselves begin to express the desire to count sets of objects. They echo the teacher in counting, as if to assist her; they declare that they already know how to count: "I'll do it myself!", "I can count by myself." The teacher keeps up their interest and begins to call on those who have already memorized the order of the number-words, but at this stage of instruction the correlation between the total number and the entire set is most important.

There is no need to hurry in teaching children the counting procedure: it is more important to prepare them for this stage. For their counting skills to become more stable and conscious, the children must have well-developed notions about sets and how to compare them element by element and about the quantitative relations between sets expressed by different numbers.

Teaching Children the Operation of Counting

The next task is to teach the children the operation of counting and deepen their notions about counting as a specific human activity. Why do people count—what do they want to find out? Mommy counts the money when she goes to the store; she wants to find out whether she has enough to make her purchases. The teacher counted the pieces of candy and then gave them out equally to the children. Through such everyday examples, based on their own observations, the children can be led to see that there is always a purpose in counting—to find out how many in all—and that counting itself is only a process for achieving that goal. Learning to count means learning to determine the total number of something—for example, how many plates from a large stack a person must count out in order to set the table for dinner, or how many balls were taken on an outing, so they can all be returned to the kindergarten. An awareness of the significance of counting as an activity is very important—it increases the children's interest in learning to count.

Counting can be taught using lessons such as these (based on comparing two sets that have the same number of elements or differ by one element). Where should the children's attention be focused at this stage of instruction? The basic elements in counting are:

1) naming the numerals in order;

2) correlating each numeral with exactly one object in a set;

3) mastering the significance of the total number—that is, understanding that the last number named in counting refers to the last object and at the same time to the entire counted set. It is an index of the total number of elements in the set.

The purpose of counting is to find a total number, and the means of achieving this goal is naming number-words in order and correlating them with each element in the set. Consequently, the children need to continue instruction in differentiating the counting total from the counting process.

What teaching methods promote this? Movements play a special role in teaching children the operation of counting with the aid of number-words. At the earliest stages, the counting operation should certainly be accompanied by pointing at every object with the hand. The pointing gesture or a slight shifting of the object, accompanied by naming of the number-words aloud, helps to break up the set and single out each element more distinctly. Equally significant is the generalizing gesture in the form of a circular movement, showing that the last number-word refers to the entire set as a whole and is the total number.

Of course, the nature of the movements should gradually change—for example, when the counting is finished, the entire group of objects can be given to someone else or moved, while simultaneously naming the total number ("Here are five roosters for you," "Here there are four little trees in all").

Another technique that emphasizes the significance of the total number is to name it along with the objects being counted. For example, some children are counting rabbits, and there is a carrot opposite each rabbit. "One, two, three- -three in all," the children say. The teacher asks, "Three what?" "Three rabbits," the children answer. "And how many carrots?" The children count: "One, two, three—three carrots in all." Naming the objects together with the total number emphasizes its particular significance, making it stand out from the counting process.

As they practice comparing sets, the children observe that when the sets have the same number of elements, regardless of how they are expressed, they always obtain identical total numbers; but if one group contains one more object, they obtain consecutive numbers. Thus, the children gradually begin to understand the differences between the numbers. "Here are two flags, but there are three flags," a child says, pointing to each of the strips. Now, shifting one flag to the strip with two flags on his own initiative, he happily declares: "And now there are two here, and three flags here. I moved it here myself."

Changing the visual material also leads children to the important conclusion that, although sets are composed of different objects (rabbits and carrots, apples and cherries, or whatever) of various sizes (large and small), these sets can contain equal numbers of elements; and equality is always expressed by the same number-word. Thus a number gradually becomes, for the children, an **index of the size of a set.** In this way, the children realize through experience, though not immediately, that the number two is always greater than one, and the number one is always less than two—that is, they begin to understand the interrelations between consecutive numbers—a given number can be greater than one number and at the same time less than another. And this makes it easier to understand the relative nature of the concepts of *more* and *less*, which is very important for their mental development.

The children should be drilled in transforming sets—for example, they can be confronted with the problem of making a set of two objects from a set of three objects, and vice versa.

Through these exercises the children see that when just one element is added to an existing set, its size increases and is referred to by a different number-word, the next one, but if one object is removed from the former set, it becomes smaller and is referred by another number-word—the preceding one. It is essential to emphasize these reciprocal relations in comparing sets and naming them with number-words: two is more than one but less than three; three is more than two but less than four; five is more than four but less than six; and so forth. Visual comparison of the elements in two sets named by different consecutive numbers gradually brings the children to an understanding of **difference relations.**

Counting should be taught using equal and unequal sets expressed by the numbers 1 and 1; 1 and 2; 2 and 2; 2 and 3; 3 and 3; 3 and 4; 4 and 4; 4 and 5; 5 and 5. At first it is advisable to stay within the first three numbers, especially at the earliest stage, before teaching the counting process, and moving on somewhat later to counting with all the first five numbers; here it is particularly important to emphasize the significance of the last number as the total.

Exercises in the Operation of Counting

The lessons can be varied, but at first the teacher should rely on techniques the children know well. Let us give several sample lessons.

The children are given cards containing two blanks strips on which small objects can be placed (circles, squares, triangles, or toys). The teacher puts three trees on her desk, asks the children to count them, and then asks them to lay out on the upper strip just as many red circles as there are trees. After this assignment is accomplished, the children are asked to place on the bottom strip just as many mushrooms as there are circles on the top strip and to say how many mushrooms they have laid down. Calling attention to the trees, circles, and mushrooms, the teacher asks what can be said about their quantity. The children usually respond: "There are the same number of trees, mushrooms, and circles." "How can this be said in a different way—more precisely?" the teacher asks to suggest the idea of equality to the children. "They are all equal," they answer. Or: "There are just as many mushrooms and circles as there are trees."

The children do not arrive at this generalization immediately; after the teacher's question they start counting each of the sets again, and only then do they say: "Three of each everywhere." A one-to-one correspondence is thus established visually.

What is new in this assignment? The children count the trees on the teacher's desk at a distance. But they themselves create an equivalent set out of circles—that is, they must know what "as many as" means. Then they put as many mushrooms on the bottom strip and determine that all three sets have the same number of elements by counting the elements.

Sets consisting of toys can be replaced by sets of geometric figures: triangles, circles, or squares of various colors. The arrangement of the quantities on the strips should also vary—for example, the top strip should contain first more, then fewer circles, now of one color, now of another; it is important for the children to see that quantity or number is unrelated to spatial arrangement or color in the elements of a set. Furthermore, changing the assignments teaches the children to listen carefully to the teacher's instructions and associate numbers with the names of objects, with their quantities and the spatial arrangement of the aggregates. The teacher points out incidentally the geometric figures that make up the counting material; for example, she asks the children to choose triangles from the box and put them on the strips. This alternation in the materials and character of the assignments is, on the one hand, necessary to avoid repetitions in the children's operations and, on the other hand, very useful for developing the children's perception, which is directed simultaneously at the quantity, the shape, and the spatial arrangement of the objects.

In one lesson the children can be asked to place the sets based only on a **specified number**, rather than according to a model. This assignment is more complicated because the children must already have a distinct notion of the quantitative significance of number. "Put three blue triangles on the top strip and four red circles on the bottom one." The teacher watches to see that the quantity is associated with the indicated geometric figures, their color, and their proper arrangement on the strips. It is very important for the circles and triangles to be placed precisely under one another.

Of course, all this cannot be remembered at once: the children do not always precisely associate the quantity with the objects or the objects with their color and arrangement. Therefore, when there are many mistakes the assignment should be simplified—e.g., by giving only circles of two colors, thus introducing fewer attributes; then the children will need to remember only the quantity and the color of the circles, as well as the location of the given set. If no more than two or three children make mistakes, the teacher should not rush to correct them during the assignment. It is better to call upon the child who makes a mistake for an answer after hearing two or three correct answers. "Children, let's hear how Kolya did the assignment. Did he put the circles down correctly?"

Often children notice their own mistake as they are describing aloud how they did the assignment. "You said three blue triangles, and I took four, but three red circles. I made a mistake." If the child does not find the error, the other children can point it out.

Such assignments train the children to listen to one another's responses, to contrast and compare. They gradually learn the connections between a number, the names of objects, their qualities, and the arrangement of sets.

Once they learn to count, the children use their newly acquired skills in every situation when the number of objects must be determined. During instruction they should also learn that **sets of objects expressed by the same number can be arranged in different ways**. For example, the elements in a set are arranged at a considerable distance from one another on one card, and they are comparatively close on another card, although the number of elements is identical for both sets. By counting, the children determine that they are equal. To check this equality, they can be asked to cover up the pictures of circles on one card with triangles and then move these triangles onto the circles on the other card. The children demonstrate in practical terms that the sets have the same number of elements. They become more convinced of the value of counting as a reliable means of determining quantity.

Both the material and the methods can be varied. For example, groups of various numbers of toys are placed in different spots in the room. Some children are given a card with objects or geometric figures drawn in a row. They are asked to count the number of objects on the card, find the group with the same number of objects, take the card to it, and then tell which objects these are and how many are in the given group.

Another variant of this assignment: a child is given a group of small objects instead of a card, which he is to count by himself; then he must find a group of the same number of toys in the room and, taking his toys over to it, tell the other children how many there are. In order to teach the children to defend their right answers, the teacher asks, "And how can you prove that there are the same number of toys on the table as you had?" If the child cannot demonstrate it, one of the other children can help establish a one-to-one correspondence between the groups of toys.

A more complex variant of the assignment would be to find a quantity of toys based on a specified number. This assignment can be done by several children at once: one will look for four, another for three, another for five, and so on—everyone is to find a group corresponding to the given number without relying on a model. This is harder for the children because they must remember the number for a long time and have a notion of the number. For example, a boy is asked to find three toys (the specific name of the objects is not given). In seeking an answer he approaches a group of four objects, counts them, and steps aside, since he remembers that he is to find three objects. Continuing his search, he stops at five objects, counts them, and again withdraws. But it so happens that counting the different groups has supplanted the assignment, and the child forgets how many toys he has to find. Therefore, it is important to caution the children that they must remember the number. But, if necessary, the teacher or the other children can remind the child of the specified number.

What is new about this type of assignment? The children must orient themselves in the quantity of objects that are not directly in front of them. Earlier the children had a model in their hands, which reminded them of the quantity (small toys or a card displaying objects), and now **they must remember a number that has merely been mentioned**. But in searching for the appropriate quantity they encounter various collections which distract their attention, and they do not find what they need right away. This difficulty taxes their will, and they experience a sense of purpose and concentration; moreover, their memories are drilled.

Similar lessons were also conducted in the second youngest group, where the children looked for "one" and "many" in a special situations, but now their content has become more complicated.

Teaching Techniques of Counting Out Objects

One of the important tasks in this group is to teach the children the ability to count out a quantity of objects from a larger quantity. Counting and counting out are not the same for the young child. In counting, the set limits the child, but in counting out the child is to create a set according to an indicated number—that is, to stop further counting voluntarily. It is advisable for counting out to be taught in familiar circumstances, where there are fewer distracting factors. The teacher should show the children the method of counting out, indicating when the number-word should be uttered as the objects are chosen.

There are many blocks in front of the children, and four blocks are to be counted out. The teacher demonstrates the method of counting out: selecting a block and placing it on the other side of the table, the teacher says, "One"; silently choosing another and putting it close to the first, she says, "Two"; and so forth. The teacher utters the number-word when the actual operation of choosing the block has already been completed. It is important for this method to be taught to young children, since many of them name the number-word as they take the object, and then name the next number-word as they set down the same object—that is, they count their own movements instead of the objects.

For practice the children are given a set of small toys and then asked to choose a certain quantity accurately from among them. They choose the toys, pronouncing the number-words softly. Sitting in a row, they check one another's work and, when called upon by the teacher, tell who has how many and what kind of toys. "Lesha chose five roosters, since you said to pick five toys, but I made a mistake: I took six blocks instead of five."

Assignments involving counting out a quantity can subsequently be varied: the children may be asked to count out a specified quantity and bring it to the teacher's desk ("Bring three toy dogs; four little plates from the dolls' pantry"). The following assignment can also be conducted: count out just as many pieces of doll clothing as it takes to dress four dolls from a larger collection of doll clothing. The children count out four blouses, four undershirts, four skirts, four caps, and so forth.

An assignment involving counting out two types of objects at the same time is even more complicated—for example: bring two toy dogs and three fish, or count out four yellow and three blue circles from a box and bring them (there are many different-colored circles in the box). Of course, it is more complicated to count out a number of circles of a certain color than to count out different objects, since the differentiation of quantity in counting out on the basis of color alone should be more subtle. Therefore, in doing this assignment the children at first make more mistakes than when they bring several different objects apiece.

The assignments can be made more complicated and combined with distinguishing between geometric figures. Not just circles, but also triangles, squares, and rectangles can be used as counting material. As the children learn the significance of number and the various geometric figures, the selection of a specified number of figures can also become more complicated. For example, different figures of various sizes are placed in a box. The child is to choose, say, three large red triangles from the set of geometric figures. Taking the children's level of preparation into account, the teacher can vary the geometric figures and individualize the lessons.

The children gradually learn to count and count out objects from large sets— that is, they learn not only to count specified groups, but also to create quantitative groups by themselves. It is advisable to name the consecutive numbers when giving lessons on counting out, thus enabling the children to gain practice in counting and comparing the set elements that they take; they must say not only what there are more of, but also which number is greater (or smaller), and prove it. The need for proof arouses their thinking: "I brought two toys dogs and three fish." "Which are there more—the dogs or the fish?" "There are more fish—there are three of them, but only two dogs." "Which number is greater than which?" "The number three is greater than the number two." "How can we see that—how do we check that three little fish are more than two big dogs?" The child puts the fish in a row and puts a dog under each fish.

"See? This fish goes with this dog, and this fish with this one, but this fish has no dog, and that means that there are fewer dogs and more fish." All the children should learn the method of visual proof.

The children gradually realize that the objects can be of different sizes, but that size does not play a role in determining number. It must be pointed out that quantity does not depend on size, for the children cannot observe this fact by themselves, and the abstraction of a number is difficult without it. Even among first-graders there are children who apparently know how to count but have great difficulty indicating where there are more or less when comparing two sets with different qualitative features; for instance, it seems to them that if the objects are large, there should certainly be more of them.

Generalizing Groups of Objects on the Basis of Number

The children should learn to generalize different groups of objects on the basis of number. For this purpose a number of assignments can be conducted.

First variant. The children are offered cards depicting different geometric figures of various colors. Thus, there are three red squares on one card, three blue circles on another, four green triangles on a third, and so forth. The problem consists in ignoring color and shape and choosing from the set of various cards only those which depict, say, four figures (four small red squares, four large red squares, four blue circles, etc.). This exercise prompts the children to generalize: "Here all the figures are different; they are different sizes and different colors, but there are four of them on each of the cards."

Second variant. Some large toys are arranged on three tables facing the children: three teddy bears on one, five dolls on another, four ring cones on a third. A child is called upon to count out certain objects from the set in a specified quantity and find the table where he should put them so that there will be the same number. There can be different toys on each of the tables, but in equal numbers. The children summarize as they approach the tables: "Here there are various toys, but there are five of each: five dolls, five roosters, five cars, five bunnies, five fish; on this table there are three of each toy: three teddy bears, three blocks, three fish, three squares, three circles. There are equal numbers of toys on each table: here five, here three, and here four."

As the methods and the material vary, the principal element must be kept in mind: neither should distract the children's attention from solving the basic problem: perceiving sets and counting. An insignificant variation in the lessons' material and techniques only reinforces the children's attention, intensifies their thinking, and helps them gain a better mastery of the curricular material.

Literal repetition of lessons is inadvisable: something new must be included in each of them, with regard for the children's interests and achievements. I. P. Pavlov has repeatedly stressed that success in forming new connections stems not only from repetition of the same material, but chiefly from the comparison between new and old. Pavlov's thesis should be taken as a foundation for developing a methodology for conducting lessons.

Counting with Various Perceptual Analyzers

Along with the lessons utilizing visual perception, it is quite important to **include other perceptual analyzers in the counting process.** Even for three-year-olds certain techniques of perceiving a set by hearing and reproducing it in movements are recommended. But these assignments can also be employed with four-year-olds, although now the children can count the sounds and remember their overall quantity (the total number of sounds).

What is the significance of counting sounds and movements? Counting by hearing and counting movements deepens children's understanding of the significance of the total number which sums up the sounds in the mind, since the elements themselves in a set of sounds and movements are perceived sequentially—that is, in time. Unlike objects, sounds cannot be counted again. Therefore, the need to remember the total number summing up all the sounds perceived becomes evident and highly significant to the child.

Counting objects by touch actually associates the counting of movements with the counting of unseen objects. But, in contrast to the counting of sounds, the child can check himself by visually counting the objects that he has counted out by touch. Counting a set of objects or movements by touch interests the children, and it becomes more accurate and complete. Let us give several examples of these assignments.

Counting by Touch. The children are given cards with buttons sewn onto them, covered by handkerchiefs. Feeling the buttons, the children count them and determine the total number. It is important to show them the method of counting the buttons from one edge of the card to the other. At first the counting is accompanied by loud talking; this can gradually be replaced by uttering the number-words in a whisper, and then by silent counting.

In another variant of the lesson, the children can be given small homogeneous objects covered by a handkerchief (such as small blocks) and asked to count out a specified number. Here the solution method will be somewhat different: choosing the blocks one by one, the child moves them over to his or her left hand under the handkerchief, uttering the number-word when the transfer of each block is complete. After counting out the number called for by the assignment, the child moves all the blocks out from under the handkerchief. Another child is called upon to count the blocks, to check whether the assignment has been done correctly. The assignment on counting out by touch is given with a model at first: the child counts objects depicted on a card and, based on the number, counts out the blocks or other toys under the handkerchief by touch; the card serves as a model of a visual set for the child. Assignments involved oral specification of a number can also be given later.

Counting by Hearing. The children are asked to count the sounds that the teacher makes, striking first a drum, then a table, then a glass, then a tambourine, and so forth. The sounds are different in nature, and they must be clearly differentiated to be counted correctly.

Counting and counting out can be combined in another assignment: the children count sounds, and then count out an appropriate number of objects by touch. "Count how many times I knock, and count out the same number of blocks under the handkerchief," the teacher suggests.

Three-year-old children have also perceived and reproduced a number of sounds, but their perception was purely sensory; the four-year-olds, however, perceive and reproduce a set by counting its elements—that is, they accompany the sensory perception by a number-word, summing up all the elements in a set of sounds by a total number.

Counting Movements. Three-year-olds reproduce a certain set in movements—for example, clapping hands once for each doll or rapping on the table with a hammer as many times as the teacher rapped, in imitation of her. In the present group, the children can rap to match a quantity of objects presented in a model, and then according to a specified number-word. The nature of the movements can be made more complicated through the year; the children can be asked to toss a ball up three times or to bounce it on the floor as many times as there are triangles on a card shown to them. The child at first accompanies all his movements with counting aloud, but gradually makes the transition to counting to himself.

Different analyzers can be combined in the perception and reproduction of sets and in counting them: the auditory and the visual analyzers, the auditory and the motor, the visual and the tactile, etc.

Counting becomes quite varied, and the very notion of the diversity of sets evolves. All this not only perfects the counting activity and the child's understanding of the significance of number as a definite index of the size of a set, but also promotes sensory development.

Mistakes Made by Children as They Start Learning to Count

Sometimes a child names only the objects in the plural instead of giving the total number of objects. "One, two, all the mushrooms together," the child says. This is evidence that the children do not yet understand the significance of counting as an activity aimed at establishing the precise number of objects. They do not yet understand why they are counting, naming the numerals in order. This kind of mistake is usually encountered in children who, because of certain circumstances, are not yet ready for counting with number-words: they either have had no practice at all in comparing sets by establishing a correspondence between their elements, or else have not studied it enough. It is advisable to work intensively with these children, using the curriculum and methods for the previous age group.

A very prevalent mistake is when the children begin counting with the word *raz* rather than *odin* 'one'.[1] This stereotype usually develops in children who come from families where the parents drill the children in naming the numerals, supposing that they are teaching them to count. The children easily learn such a vocal stereotype, but it is quite difficult for genuine instruction in counting to overcome it. The teacher must not let such mistakes on the child's part pass. "Remember the right way to count?" the teacher says. Or the teacher asks: "Who among the children noticed Nina's mistake—who will help her to correct her mistake?"

It is important to explain the essence of counting to the parents, too, indicating that memorizing the number-words in no way means teaching the children to count, that counting is a complicated activity, which the children cannot learn all at once. Moreover, the word *raz* cannot designate a single object: it can be correlated only with a movement, and then only conditionally. But the children need to be taught to count objects. Thus, they should be taught primarily to compare the elements in sets, to distinguish the equal and unequal numbers of elements.

Some teachers do not take into account the significance of comparing two sets expressed by consecutive numbers. In teaching children to count, they choose only one set of objects, such as two fish. Once they have taught the children to count the two fish, they add one more fish and, counting them, assume that the child will understand that when one fish is added there are three. But the child, after naming three (the numeral), says that there are two fish, as before. Under this teaching method, the child cannot understand why the same fish have stopped being called two: the child does not yet know what role is played by adding one object to the previous set or removing an object from it. This becomes clear to him only on the basis of element-by-element comparison of the two sets.

Some educators, observing the children's difficulties in mastering the significance of the total number when instructed in counting based on one collection, have proposed teaching counting by naming the numerals and the objects themselves: one fish, two fish, three fish. They have supposed that in this case the children would sooner be able to answer the question "How many?" But this method also neglects the meaning of counting and the significance of the total number.

Another error that must be avoided is when, in counting, the children name the numerals properly, pointing a finger at each object, and even identify the total number, but do not name the objects counted. "One, two, three—three in all," says the child, counting roosters. "What are there three of? Three trees?" "No, three roosters." "Here's the way to say it; you have to name the things that you count, and then it will be clear to everyone what you have counted," says the teacher. It is important for the object names to be linked only with the total number, because this helps differentiate the total number and the operation of counting itself.

Another mistake that must be anticipated is when the children, in counting objects of masculine, feminine, or neuter gender, give the numerals only in the masculine form. The children must learn to make numerals agree grammatically in gender and case. It is useful to set up a special assignment for this purpose, choosing objects in the three genders and showing how to make the numerals agree. Then the children themselves can practice numeral agreement.

Using proper teaching techniques in class and in daily life, the teacher anticipates these mistakes, so that the children will not then have to relearn the right way to use numerals.

Sample Lessons in Developing Spatial and Temporal Notions

The development of notions of space and time requires particular techniques. But the results of lessons devoted to them should be combined with what the children learn in other lessons. It is important to organize all the work so that treatment quantity is coordinated with size, shape, and position in space.

Methods for Developing Notions of Size

The curriculum on developing notions of size begins in the previous group, when the children learn about various dimensions in didactic games and lessons. In this group we now refine the notions of the width, length, height or thickness of an object.

At the beginning of the year it is advisable to recall that the children know which strip is longer, which is shorter, which is wider, which is narrower, and so on, and whether they correctly use the superimposition and association techniques.

In the preceding group the children learned to distinguish length and width with different strips; now they must learn to perceive a strip in two dimensions simultaneously: they must be able to find the length and the width.

The lessons can proceed roughly as follows: the children are given two familiar strips (a long and a short one), on which they demonstrate and determine in the customary way which is longer and which is shorter. The teacher's question, "Do these strips have width?" causes perplexity among the children. Demonstrating the width of the longer strip and asking the children what it is, the teacher stimulates the children's thinking. The teacher approves the right answers and asks all the children to outline the width and length of the strip with one finger. Then she asks a new question: "Which is greater—the length or the width of the strip?"

"The length," the children answer. They arrive at the same conclusion when they examine the shorter strip.

Then the children are shown cardboard and paper strips of various sizes, ribbons, segments of various types of material, and so forth. They find the length and width of each object and arrive at the general conclusion that the length is greater than the width in each case. The children can be asked to draw a long, wide path and a long, narrow one on a piece of paper and decide which path is longer or whether they are the same length.

In order to refine the children's notions, they should be asked to pick out from among different strips those which are equal in length and width, or equal only in length but different in width, or equal in width but different in length, and so forth. When the children understand that all strips have length and width and that strips can be different, it is time to provide a series of three types of strips and ask that they be arranged in decreasing or increasing order. Later the number of different-sized strips can be increased to five.

Let us give an example of this sort of assignment. The teacher brings the group three ribbons of different colors, with the same width but different lengths—e.g., one ribbon of 8 cm, another of 14 cm, and a third of 20 cm. These differences are quite perceptible, and the children easily identify the shortest, a longer one, and the longest one. "How can we prove that the pink ribbon is longer than the red one?" "Put one on top of the other." The children check that they have arranged the ribbons correctly according to length.

Then the children can each be given three colored ribbons, which they arrange in order, stating which ribbon is the longest, which is shorter, and which is the shortest. It is important for all this to be reflected both in their actions and their speech.

Four-year-old children should be taught to arrange objects in order by length. To do so the teacher should remind the children that the lower ends of the ribbons should be at the same level when they compare them. They should draw a straight line on paper to serve as a base for the ribbons of different sizes. Their upper borders should form a gradually increasing or decreasing staircase.

To vary the assignment, the teacher can give out three more ribbons of the same sizes and ask the children to choose pairs by size rather than color, arranging them first in increasing and then in decreasing order. It can be made even more complex if the teacher uses ribbons that differ by 2 to 3 cm in length (e.g., 10, 13, 16 cm) but are the same color.

The children can be asked to draw three ribbons of equal width but different length such that the difference in length is roughly constant. The teacher asks that each ribbon be shaded in with a colored pencil. Of course, not all the children do this assignment properly right away; some cannot draw three ribbons of equal width because their attention is focused on the different lengths of the ribbons. The teacher advises the children to cut out these ribbons and check by superimposition whether they have done the assignment correctly. Two or three children demonstrate their work. It becomes clear who has made a mistake and why.

The situation can be further complicated by finding a ribbon of the same length among many others (based on a model), and somewhat later recalling the length of the model, finding a ribbon of the same length by sight, and bringing it to the teacher to compare it with the model.

The contrast can gradually be reduced, increasing the number of ribbons to five, asking the children to arrange all five according to increasing length, and explaining why it was done this way: "This pink one is the shortest, this red one is a little longer, this blue one is even longer, this yellow one is still longer, and this green one is the longest." The children will gradually get better at distinguishing objects by length, their sight estimation will develop, and their ability to reflect the parameter of length in words will be strengthened.

Lessons involving the other dimensions (width, height, thickness) are analogous to the ones described above. It is important at this stage to teach the children to distinguish the different dimensions—for example, showing the length and thickness of round pencils. Placing them on a stand in a vertical position, point out that in this case we speak of the height rather than the length—that is, the length is converted into the height. The children are usually very interested in changing an object's position in space, practice finding its length and height.

Comparing width and thickness also evokes considerable interest. The diameter of a round object can serve as an attribute of thickness. A strip of paper is wide (or narrow), but a stick, rope, or pencil is thick or thin. This, of course, is not completely accurate, for a book, a notebook, and other things can be thick or thin, but at the elementary stage it is appropriate to stick to round objects (collect thick and thin branches, distinguish thick and thin tree-trunks, thick and thin plant stalks, thick and thin rope or strings).

Various play techniques, including didactic guessing games, can be used in exercises on distinguishing magnitude. For example, tossing a ball to one of the children, the teacher says: "A road is wide, and what is narrower?" Returning the ball, the child answers, "A sidewalk is narrower," and so forth.

Methods for Developing Notions about the Shape of Objects

The children should gradually become acquainted with the names of geometric figures through games, lessons, and daily life. It is important for the children to hear how the teacher herself names these figures. When the children build something, the teacher might advise using cylinders or cubes. It is important to do this even in the three-year-old group, and the children gradually become accustomed to hearing the hitherto unknown names for toys, building material parts, etc. As they play, the children's attention can be directed to the fact that a sphere and a cylinder roll easily, but not a cube. The question forces the children to reflect, and it is not important that they may be unable to answer immediately.

"Why do the sphere and the cylinder roll, but not the cube?" the teacher repeats her question. She proposes feeling the figures, outlining their shapes with a finger. "The cube is sharp, but the sphere is smoothed out," the children say. "Why is the cube sharp?" "It has corners—like these."

"Do the cylinder and the sphere have corners?" The children find that the cube has many angles, but that the cylinder and the sphere have none.

Then the teacher proposes comparing the sphere and the cylinder to say which is more mobile and which more stable. The children try placing the sphere and the cylinder in different positions and find that the cylinder can stand up or roll, while the sphere "just rolls." "Why can the cylinder stand up?" The children inspect the object and say that the cylinder has a "floor" and a "ceiling," but rounded sides. "But in the sphere everything is rounded." In this way the children discover the characteristic properties of the geometric objects that exist among their toys.

By using cards depicting various quantities of geometric figures in mathematics lessons, the children learn their names. These figures (circles, triangles, squares, rectangles) are also represented in the distribution material for counting and in a geometric mosaic, and four-year-old children usually can both distinguish and name them.

In the four-year-old group the basic task is to acquaint them with the basic properties of these figures in lessons. Let us give examples of such lessons. The purpose of this lesson is to demonstrate to the children that a geometric figure can vary in size. The teacher proposes comparing the large and small figures by the superimposition technique. The children establish that the figures are identical in shape but different in size and color.

Then the teacher passes out three figures of different sizes to be arranged in ascending or descending order. The children can be asked to examine the figures in their own envelopes, arrange the figures of the same shape in rows, and state how many of which they have.

While all the children get identical kits in the first lessons (circles, triangles, squares, and rectangles in different colors and in only two sizes), later each child gets a special kit of figures consisting of the same four shapes, but each figure in a different size, color, and quantity. The children eagerly sort out their kits, talking aloud about who has which figures and how many of them. "I have three squares the same size, one rectangle, two triangles—a big one and a little one—and four circles of the same size," says one child. "And I have two squares—a big one and a small one, three triangles of different sizes, one big circle and four rectangles of different sizes," says another child. Laying down the figures and naming their shapes aloud, as well as stating how many they have, their size, and their color, the children consolidate and generalize their knowledge.

The same material can also be used as a set consisting of different parts. "We have many different figures in the envelope. What parts does this set consist of? Think, and arrange the figures in rows by shape," the teacher suggests. The children say that there are four parts in the set of different figures: squares, circles, rectangles, and triangles. The teacher proposes laying out the elements in these parts so that it will be immediately apparent which of the parts is the largest and which the smallest. The children place the circles, squares, rectangles, and triangles in rows under one another. Depending on how the geometric figures have been assembled in the individual envelopes, there may be numerical equality or inequality among these parts. Triangles make up the largest part of the entire set for all the children or for one child, and circles the smallest, and so on.

In such an assignment, it is important to emphasize that each envelope contains a set of different geometric figures, but this set consists of different parts—in this case squares, triangles, rectangles, and circles, which are the parts of a whole—that is, the entire set of geometric figures in the envelope.

It is advisable to show that parts in this whole can be found by other attributes as well, e.g., by color or size. Sorting the figures by color, the children clarify the composition of the whole, determining by the same method of establishing a correspondence which part of the whole is largest based on color and which is the smallest.

These exercises teach the children to see a set and its subsets based on various attributes—that is, they are led to understand a set and to perform an elementary mathematical analysis of the relations. Analogous lessons can be conducted with geometric objects of different sizes (a sphere, a cube, a cylinder).

Variants of lessons with plane geometric figures take many forms. For example, it is recommended that a geometric mosaic be used to make the children realize that a square can be made from two triangles, and a rectangle from another two. Then the children themselves can be given two or three different-colored squares so they can cut them to make equal triangles. Let them think for themselves about how it can be done. Then they can put the cut triangles in different ways in space—now with a vertex up, now down, now on the right or left. The children can be asked to count the cut triangles, or to group them on the basis of color: "Four triangles have come from two squares: two red and two green ones, all the same size," the child relates.

Other variants of the lessons have the objective, for example, of transforming one shape into another by removing several sticks: obtaining one rectangle by removing four sticks from five equal squares (Figures 10 and 11), or laying out two triangles in two ways, from five sticks (Figure 12), or placing three sticks in the figure of a lamp so as to obtain four triangles (the three sticks are shown by a dotted line in Figure 13).[2] The children can also be given an assignment such as the following: examine the shape of some objects in pictures and correlate it with a certain geometric figure (glass—cylinder, ball—sphere, box—cube, bottom of a glass—circle, handkerchief—square, page of a book—rectangles).

In the intermediate group, by the end of the year the children can be introduced to certain properties of the square, the rectangle, the circle, and, somewhat later, the triangle.

Figure 10.

Figure 11.

Figure 12.

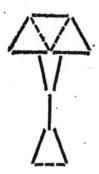

Figure 13.

The children are given these figures and asked to trace the outlines of
a square and a circle, and of a square, a rectangle, and a circle, and to

think about how these shapes differ from one another and what they have in common. The children indicate that the square and the rectangles have corners, but the circle does not. It is recommended that the children who have those figures count the angles in them and state what they have in common. The children count the angles of the square and the rectangle and state that they each have four angles or that they have the same number of angles. The teacher asks them to run their fingers along the figures, reflect, and tell how the angles are formed. The children may respond in various ways or merely demonstrate, not knowing how to put it into words. Now the teacher moves her finger along each of the square's sides and says that they are called sides, and that the square's sides are connected and form the vertices and angles. The children repeat this movement on the rectangle, showing the vertices, angles, and sides; they count the number of vertices, angles, and sides in the square and the rectangle (four angles, four vertices, and four sides in each). Comparing it with the circle, they outline its contour with one finger and draw a conclusion about the absence of angles and vertices in the circle. "The circle has one side—here it is—without angles—it's round," a child states. The teacher corrects the child's answer, explaining that only the figures that have angles can have sides.

Then the children are given a triangle, and by inspection they conclude that it has three vertices, three angles, and three sides. Very often the children themselves say why this shape, in contrast to the square, is called a triangle.

Sometimes the children ask: "Why is it not a quadrilateral but a square?" In this case the teacher confirms their guess and explains that the square and the rectangle can be called quadrilaterals.

In order to show the children that the features they have picked out are characteristic properties of these shapes, the teacher passes out larger versions of the same figures. Inspecting them, the children count the vertices, angles, and sides in the squares, rectangles, and triangles, and come to the general conclusion that all squares and rectangles, regardless of size, have four vertices, four angles, and four sides, that all triangles have only three vertices, three angles, and three sides, but that circles do not have angles, vertices, or sides.

In such lessons it is important to make the children find the answers themselves, and not to merely communicate pre-digested knowledge to them. Let the children themselves inspect the figures, drawing their own conclusions, and the teacher can refine and summarize their responses.

Presenting information in the form of problems confronts the children with questions to which they may not always be able to easily give the answers, but which force them to think and listen to the teacher more attentively. Thus, the teacher should not rush to give the children pre-digested knowledge: their interest must be aroused first. But the teacher should prompt methods or techniques for finding the answer, and sometimes even demonstrate. "Outline the square with your finger—here's how," the teacher explains. "How is it different from the circle? Outline the circle this way." The children arrive at the necessary conclusion.

Methods for Introducing Children to Spatial and Temporal Notions

Lessons dealing with orientation in space and time should be reminiscent of the game "Guess where it is." For example, a girl is called to the teacher's desk and asked to determine what is facing her, behind her, on her right, above her, and below her. The others check her answers. Then the girl is asked to cover her eyes, and she is placed in another position. Opening her eyes, she must again detail what is now around her.

Later the children can be situated in different spots in the room. A child might go to a corner and tell what is in front of him, behind him, on the right and the left, while another goes to the window, and so forth. In all these cases the point of reference is the child's body.

In physical education class there are many opportunities for practicing spatial orientation: lifting a flag, demonstrating the directions forward, back, right, and left, throwing a ball closer or farther than a designated line, etc.

It is also advisable for the children to practice with spatial orientation in other lessons, e.g., placing geometric figures on a piece of paper so that there is a circle in the center, a triangle on the right, and a square on the left, or arranging aids in a particular order: putting the box of counting materials to the right and the box with two strips in front of themselves. To reinforce their knowledge and reflect it in speech, the teacher can ask the children how they have arranged their own school things. These directions regulate the children's behavior and at the same time reinforce their spatial orientation. There are many favorable conditions for this in everyday life; they need only be utilized (putting away clothes while undressing, cleaning up the room, setting the table).

The children can also learn to orient themselves in time in their daily life. But an introduction to various time segments should be accomplished in special discussions along with reading books. For example, the teacher might ask the children to tell what each one did before coming to kindergarten (one woke up, dressed, washed, had breakfast, etc). After listening to several children, the teacher summarizes: "All you children probably did this, it was morning." Then there follows a question about what the children do in the morning in kindergarten, and what they do in the afternoon in kindergarten and at home, and so forth. The children recall their own actions, correlating them with the parts of the day. "Morning, afternoon, evening, and night— these are the four parts of a 24-hour day. Every day always has these four parts," the teacher emphasizes. "The day turns around," one of the children observes. "Right—one day takes the place of another, it is over, and yet another one comes. The days change during the night, when the Kremlin chimes strike," the teacher says, finishing the discussion by reading a story or poem.

Familiarity with the day makes it possible to explain to the children that the day that ends with the striking of the chimes is called "yesterday": the new day which begins after the chimes strike while it is still "night," and in which we distinguish morning, afternoon, evening, and night, is called "today," while the one that we are still expecting, which will come after the striking of the chimes, is called "tomorrow." Tomorrow is what is still to come, and tomorrow is also a day that has the same four parts;

but when they arrive, we name them differently—they are today, because this 24-hour period has now come, and we can do what we had planned to do tomorrow; when the day which we call *today* leaves us, we will start calling it by the word *yesterday*, explains the teacher. "Today we went on an outing in the park, but when the day passes into night, will it be yesterday?" a children inquires. "Tomorrow is never today; it's only that we are expecting it; but when it comes, then it will become today—am I saying it right?" another explains.

If the children are given a preliminary introduction to the day, its composition, and the way days change, they have no trouble learning the concepts of *today*, *yesterday*, and *tomorrow*.

In introducing the children to temporal concepts, the teacher should explain what is meant by *fast* and *slow*, using actual examples. In later groups, when the children study the duration of certain time segments, this concept will be refined. For now, they should be given an idea about the degree of rapidity only by means of contrasting examples: comparing the speeds of a car and a horse, or a cyclist and a pedestrian. Clarifying the degree of speed enables the children to orient themselves in the general significance of the words *faster* and *slower* and use them in everyday life: "Lesha has set the dinner table faster than Misha."

11

Curriculum and Methods for Teaching Elementary Mathematics in the Older Kindergarten Group (Five-Year-Olds)

Organizing Work with Five-Year-Old Children

Observations of five-year-old children who enter the older group from various families and preschools, as well as those who have been in full-program kindergartens, betray wide variation in what they know. But all children of this age display an interest in knowing mathematics—counting in particular. They count everything that passes before their eyes (the stories in buildings, windows, streetcars, cars, etc.).

Children who have not studied the curriculum of the previous groups can often name the number-words (sometimes even up to 15), but do not correlate the number-words precisely with the objects, omit number-words when counting, are unable to name the total number, or do not differentiate the total number from the counting process. The children are unable to count out a specified quantity from a larger aggregate (they may forget the specified number, for example). This is evidence that they have not yet consciously learned to count and do not understand the significance of number as an index of the size of a set; they perceive the specified number only as a signal to stop—that is, as a sort of indicator that they should cease counting or counting out. The children have not learned the technique of physically comparing sets by establishing a one-to-one correspondence between them; they do not notice the spatial relations among the elements of a set in a model; they put down objects by pressing them close together, and therefore they cannot always reproduce the same number properly.

The children are unable to arrange a set according to different attributes. If five pencils of two colors are lying around, the children determine their number separately, based on color ("three red ones and two blue ones"), without being able to generalize on the more general basis of objects (pencils). This means that they have not mastered the operations of generalizing sets and separating out the subsets of a set.

The children often name the numbers properly in sequence and indicate that the number eight is greater than seven, but the only reason they give is that "the number eight is farther, and the number seven is closer." This reason is based exclusively on the sequence in naming them, rather than on the given number's composition from units.

The children most frequently count objects with their right hands in just one direction—from right to left.

They do not see the numerical equality of aggregates if the elements in one group are larger than the elements in another, or if sets that are equal in number occupy different positions or are represented in different forms. This indicates that the quantitative aspect has not yet been differentiated in the children's consciousness from the qualitative characteristics of a set.

The children still make many mistakes in counting sounds, counting objects by touch, and counting their own movements.

Thus, the children's ability to recite the number-words in order up to 12 or 15 should not reassure the teacher. She must analyze more precisely whether the children have notions of specific sets and methods of forming them, and must determine whether they can operate with sets and compare collections of objects—juxtaposing their elements one by one—without resorting to counting.

Many children who have come from their families into the older group do not know the names of the basic geometric shapes and cannot analyze the various parameters of dimension, confusing width and thickness and not differentiating between width and length: they believe height to be only the topmost point, rather than the entire vertical extent of an object. They experience considerable difficulty in the proper use of prepositions and adverbs to designate spatial relations, and their notions of time are not yet adequately developed.

Of course, not all children who come from their families prove to have these deficiencies, but at the start of the new school year the teacher should give first priority to ascertaining the gaps in knowledge and skills among the children in the group. The teacher must also equalize the children's knowledge in order to be able to successfully follow the curriculum for the older group.

It is advisable to allot the first month of work (September) to reviewing the curriculum for the previous group. This provides an opportunity to clarify the need for supplementary lessons with certain children.

The curriculum for the older group outlines a range of knowledge and abilities to promote the children's further mental and mathematical development.

In the intermediate group the children have already achieved practical familiarity with sets and have learned to separate out its parts based on certain attributes (color, size, shape).

The children already know how to compare individual parts of a large set with one another, establishing a correspondence between the elements in these parts, and to determine which of the set's parts are larger, smaller, or equal in number. Since they know how to count up to five, the children can count the elements in each part and express the quantities of these parts in terms of numbers, indicating which part is larger and which is smaller.

Work on sets should continue in the older group. Separating out the parts (subsets) of a set can be diversified in terms of both the attributes used and the number of parts. For example, if a set of toys is to be grouped on the basis of material, some can be wooden, some rubber, some earthenware, and some plastic—four parts to a single set of toys. The total number of toys (ten) and the number of toys in each part (five, two, two, and one) can be counted, taking the first part (five) as basic, with the remaining parts (two, two, and one) added to form the entire set.

Combining all the parts together again forms a single unified set. Such exercises make it easier for the children to understand that a set, as a structurally integral unity with a common attribute, does not always consist of elements with identical qualities. Not just the number of individual elements that make it up, but also the number of individual parts can be counted. The acts of breaking a set into parts and uniting these parts into a single whole also acquaint the children with the relations between part and whole. All this develops children's thinking, sharpens their wits, makes the concept of a unit more profound, and prepares them for understanding the arithmetic operations.

Curricular Material for Children in the Five-Year-Old Group

Teachers of five-year-old children should help the children understand that a set can be composed of elements that vary in quality; an element in a set can be either an individual object or an entire group.

Teachers should drill the children in identifying several parts of a set based on a certain attribute and establishing the relations between a finite set and its parts: a whole is more than (any of) its parts. Children should practice establishing a one-to-one correspondence between parts identical in number, identifying the larger and smaller parts of a set or stating that they are equal, and recombining these parts into a single whole. This practice should come after the children have become familiar with the union of sets.

The children should be introduced to the operation of removing parts of a set and with the meaning of the word *one*, which designates not just one object but also an entire group of objects regarded as one part of a set.

Number and Counting

The teacher should teach the children to count up to ten. The children must strengthen and develop their abilities and skills in counting out objects up to ten given a model and a designated number. The children should be able to determine equal quantity in groups of different objects, summarize a set by means of a number on the basis of counting and comparing sets (here there will be five, eight, or ten objects apiece).

The curricular materials should develop children's ability to count objects in various arrangements in space (not merely in a row).

The children should refine the notion that a number does not depend on the nature of the elements, their qualitative attributes (their size, the distance between them, spatial arrangement), or on the direction in which the counting is done (from left to right, from right to left, from the middle to the sides, etc.)

The teacher should instill a knowledge of the quantitative composition of the first five numbers from units (five is made up of one, another one, another one, another one, and another one) based on concrete material.

The teacher should teach the comparison of consecutive numbers up to ten, based on the comparison of specific sets. The children should know how to turn an inequality into an equality (eight is more than seven; if one is added to seven, that makes eight in each group, equally; seven is less than eight, and there is one less in the set of seven; therefore if we subtract one from eight, we will get seven).

The teacher should teach children ordinal counting up to ten. The children should be able to distinguish the significance of the questions "what kind of," "which," or "how many," and answer them correctly.

Children should begin developing the concept that an object can be divided into several equal parts (e.g., two or four). For example, one apple can be divided in half—that is, into two equal parts, each of which is called one-half; the apple can be divided into four equal parts, each of them called one-fourth of the apple. A square or a circle can be divided into several equal parts in precisely the same way, obtaining half of a square or one-fourth of a square, and so on (the children themselves divide an apple, a circle, and other things).

Size

Children should refine their notions of changes in the length, width, and thickness of objects. The children should be taught to reflect these abilities properly in speech ("It has become longer," "This is thinner," "The rope is thicker than the string").

The curricular material should develop the children's powers of sight estimation, teach them to determine by sight the length or thickness of a stick, the width of a ribbon, the height of a fence or a tree, evaluating the perceived dimensions by comparison with the length of objects or segments known to the child (thickness compared with a finger, height compared with a person, as thin as a string, as thick as a branch, two paces long).

Children should strengthen their notions of a sphere, cube, cylinder, cone, bar (rectangular parallelepiped), square, rectangle, triangle, circle, oval, and trapezoid, and their ability to name them properly.

The teacher should teach the children to count the number of vertices, sides, and angles in various plane figures and acquaint them with the differences between certain figures (rectangle and trapezoid, cone and pyramid).

The teacher should teach them to see geometric shapes in everyday objects: what is like a sphere (ball, watermelon), a cylinder (glass, jar), a cone (funnel, ring pyramid), a circle (saucer, plate), a rectangle (table-top, wall, floor, ceiling, door), a square (handkerchief), a triangle (scarf), an oval (the outline of longitudinal cross-section of an egg, the edge of a dish), and a trapezoid (a child's table, the roof of a house).

Orientation in Space

The curricular material should reinforce the children's ability to specify in words the position of objects with respect to themselves (Andryusha is passing in front of me, the table is on my left) and in relation to another person or thing (the bunny is sitting to the right of the doll, the rooster is standing in front of the doll).

The teacher should drill the children in spatial orientation during movement and teach them to consciously change the direction of their movement during walking, running, and gymnastics.

The children should practice determining their positions among the surrounding objects (for example, I am standing behind the chair; I am standing near the chair; I am standing among the blocks; I am standing in front of Misha, opposite Misha, behind Misha, to the right of Lena and to the left of Kolya. That means that Kolya is on my right, but Lena is on my left, and so on).

Orientation in Time

The teacher should teach the children to name the days of the week in order. They should be able to determine what day today is, what yesterday was, and what tomorrow will be.

Curricular material should develop the children's "sense of time"—acquainting them with the actual duration of particular time segments. The teacher should teach ways to ascertain what can be done in any of these segments.

Orientation in Weight

Curricular material should develop the children's baric sense (the "sense of weight"). Children should be able to find objects of equal and unequal weight, weighing them on their palms, at first for contrast. They should be able to determine the weight of objects and arrange them in increasing or decreasing order.

Sample Lessons: Set, Number, and Counting

Introduction to Sets

In the previous groups the children often dealt with sets in practical terms. They realize that any concrete collection consists of individual objects, but it is also possible to separate out individual parts possessing certain attributes in these collections (or sets).

The teacher in the older group faces the task of rounding out the children's notions of a set, disclosing the significance of the terms *set* and *elements of a set*, and teaching the use of these terms.

The teacher asks the children to give examples of sets. "A set of squares," "A set of doors in a room," "A set of houses on a street" suggest the children. The teacher raps several times on the table and asks, "Now what can we call that?" "A set of sounds," "A set of movements," the children respond. The teacher asks them to think about what constitutes any set. The children answer that a set is composed of individual objects, individual sounds, or individual movements. The teacher summarizes by saying that these individual objects, individual sounds, or individual movements that comprise a set are referred to as the *elements of the set*. She names several sets and asks them to state what can be referred to as a set and its elements in various instances (a set of pencils, a set of children, a set of tables in a group, a set of toys).

Then, with the teacher's assistance, the children find that not all elements in sets are homogeneous—for example, the elements in the set "furniture" are tables, chairs, dresser, shelf, buffet, and other objects— that is, some elements are alike, such as the tables or the chairs, and others are different, like the shelf, the buffet, and the dresser. "What can we say about the elements of a set?" the teacher asks, leading the children to the generalization that a set can consist of elements of various qualities. She asks the children themselves to make up a set from elements of different qualities. The children bring a toy teddy bear, a toy rooster, and a toy horse. "What can this set be called?"—the teacher asks a new question. Some children say that it is a set of toys, but others say it is a set of animals. Both answers are right.

Then the teacher herself places a set of blocks on the table and a set of roosters on the chair, and asks, "What can we say about these sets?" The children state that one is a set of blocks, where the blocks are the elements of the set, and the other is a set of roosters, and the roosters are the elements of the set of roosters. "Can these two sets be combined? What will the set be called then?" "A set of objects, a set of toys," the children answer. "When we combine these two sets, what can be said about each of them?" "Each of them will be a part of the whole set," respond the children. At the teacher's request the children specify that there are two parts in the set of toys, and they name the components of each part. Then the children are asked to compare these parts, determine which has more (or fewer) elements, or whether they have the same number of elements, and state which is larger—the whole set or a part of it.

Thus, the teacher leads the children to understand that **several individual parts can be combined into one entire set**, that **a (finite) set is "larger" than a part of it.** The arithmetic operation of addition is not yet present, but the mathematical foundation is being laid for it in these exercises. In the first lesson the teacher displays two or three various types of small toys, such as a group of ducks, a group of geese, or a group of hens, and asks whether all these groups can be combined into one, and what the group as a whole and each individual group will then be called. The children start to think, and finally agree to combine all the groups, describing it as a set of toys. "What else can we call such a set (these combined groups)?" The teacher stimulates the children to think. "It will be a set of birds," says one of the children. "Now name the parts in this set of birds." "One part is ducks, one part is geese, and one part is hens," the children answer. "How many parts are there in this set of birds?" the teacher poses a new question. The children respond.

In another lesson the children are asked to make up a set from different parts by themselves; for example, they might take two groups of trees, birches and pines. Combining them, the children say that they have made one set of trees from two parts: one part is birches and one part is pines. The teacher points out the relations between part and whole: "Which are there more of, all the trees together or only the birches?"

Various pictures of objects can be used as material for these lessons: saucepans, pots, and ladles as a set referred to as cooking utensils; cups, mugs, teapots, coffeepots, milk pitchers, and saucers as a set referred to as a tea set, and so forth.

Entertaining lessons such as these enable the children to practice various kinds of grouping (classification techniques), which, in turn, leads them to an understanding of both generic and specific concepts and to a more profound mastery of a set—in particular, the relations between part and whole.

In making up combined sets, the children count the number of parts and the number of individual elements in each part. Let us assume that the children have made up a combined set of domestic animals from three groups of animals (dogs, cats, and horses). Counting the number of groups, they name one, two, three—three parts in all. As they determine which of the parts is larger or smaller, or whether they are equal in number, the children count the elements in these parts; in counting the dogs, they explain that there are three of them (one, two, three), and there are more cats (one, two, three, four), but fewer horses (one, two). Counting the elements in the form of individual items and components of the unified set, they use the same number-words. It is important to particularly emphasize this aspect, pointing out that the word *one* is a quantitative index not only of an individual object, but also for the whole group—or parts, if we are interested in the number of parts in the set. The children begin to understand that they can count both the parts of a set and the individual objects within each part. The children's one-sided connection between the word *one* and a specific single entity is gradually destroyed, and this means that they begin to realize the significance of the number one as an index of the size of a set.

The teacher asks the children to enumerate separate entities or groups that can be referred to by the number one. "One big teddy bear," "One group of teddy bears on a shelf," "One group of dolls is sitting on the sofa, and one doll is sitting at the table," "One aquarium," "There are many fish in the aquarium: one part is little fish and one part is big fish," "One cone and one group of blocks are standing on the shelf," the children say.

While drilling the children in recognizing sets and their elements, the teacher asks them to demonstrate a certain set as a whole and the elements in sets composed both of individual objects and of separate parts. For example, a container of red flags is standing on the table. The children say that there are many red flags in the container. "Are there parts in this set?" the teacher asks. They answer that there are no parts here. The teacher puts a group of yellow flags in the same container. The children respond that now there are two parts in the set of flags—yellow flags and red ones. The teacher asks them to think about how to tell without counting which subset has more elements. The children make various proposals: make pairs of the red and yellow flags, or put both kinds in a row, one under the other. Using one technique or another, the children determine which of the comparable parts is larger and which is smaller (there are more red flags than yellow ones, and there are fewer yellow flags than red ones.)

Then the teacher asks the children themselves to compile a set from parts (in whatever way they wish). "I first took a set of circles and joined them with a set of triangles and a set of squares," one child says, "and I got a set of different figures." The other children also establish the quantity of parts in their sets. But here is what one child says: "I combined a set of yellow circles with a set of red circles and took another green circle." The teacher asks, "Did we really count the number of individual circles? In fact, we were counting the number of parts that we have joined together in one set." The child becomes thoughtful. The teacher rapidly spreads out several yellow circles and asks Misha to show on the blackboard the circles he combined to make up his set. Misha puts down several red circles and attaches a green one. "How many individual parts did you combine in one set of circles?" "Three," Misha answers, showing them. "Now that's right: the green circle is an individual part, too, because it is another color, even though there is only one green circle. See, children, how Misha has made a set of three parts in an interesting way. One circle is a part of the big set of circles in just the same way as the others," the teacher says in precise terms.

These lessons arouse the children's interest: they themselves choose an initial set, then combined it with other sets that differ from the basic one in certain attributes. "I combined a set of daisies with a set of bluebells and poppies. I made one total set of flowers out of three parts." "How many individual flowers are in each part?" "There are five in the daisies part, two in the bluebells part, and one in the poppies part." "How many parts in all are in your set?" "Three." "And how many individual flowers are in your bouquet?" "Eight in all." "What do we call the individual objects in a set?" "Its elements." "Which is larger, in your opinion—a part or the entire set as a whole?" the teacher asks. "The part is less than the whole," the child answers.

Later the children can also be introduced to the operation of removing part of a set. It is best to do this at first with a set consisting of three parts. The teacher hangs a set of red, yellow, and green circles on the board, and the children find the number of parts in the set. Then she takes away one of the parts. The children say that "the set has grown smaller": only two parts are left. One child is called upon to remove another part, and the set again grows smaller: now only one part is left. Thus, if part of a basic set is removed, the set becomes smaller. The children practice this operation: taking one part of white mushrooms and combining it with one part of morels, they make up a single set of mushrooms; then they remove any part of it, after which they have only one part left. *The operation of removing part of a finite set serves as a foundation for subsequently learning the arithmetic operation of subtraction.*

Teaching Children to Count and Count Out Objects

Instruction in counting and counting out objects continues in this group as the children compare sets that are equal and unequal in terms of quantity and are expressed by consecutive numbers: five and five, five and six, six and six, six and seven, seven and seven, seven and eight, eight and eight, eight and nine, nine and nine, nine and ten, ten and ten. These 11 cases should not be stretched out over a protracted period of study. At first the children can be drilled in counting to seven in one or two lessons, then they can move on to counting up to nine, and, finally, up to ten. All the intermediate cases are repeated during this counting. The goal of the first lessons is to demonstrate, based on a comparison of sets expressed by consecutive numbers, the principle of forming the number following the number as $n + 1$, and forming the preceding number as $n - 1$—that is, acquainting the children with the principle of the natural number sequence.

Therefore, as before, two strips on which equivalent or non-equivalent sets are placed are used in these lessons. For example, placing seven circles on both the top and bottom strips, Mara shifts one circle from the bottom strip to the top and says, "Now there are more here—here are eight, and on the bottom there are six." "How many must we add to the bottom strip for there to be as many as you now have on the top?" "Seven and eight," says the little girl, meaning the two missing circles. "Do you mean that you will add seven circles, and then eight more?" "No! Only two. Look here: this is seven, and this is eight." "How many in all do you have on each strip when you have added two circles underneath?" "Eight circles apiece—they're equal."

The answer—"Add seven and eight"—shows that the children have not yet differentiated the concept of a number's quantitative significance from its ordinal significance; in naming the quantitative numerals seven and eight, they attach an ordinal sense to them, meaning to add the seventh and the eighth.

The teacher can suggest that the children think about what the number will be if we add another circle to eight circles. In responding, the child must check his answer. Let us assume that the child adds one circle on the top strip, counts the set again, and decides that his answer is correct. Then the child moves one circle from the left end of the row to the bottom strip, and there turns out to be nine circles on it, and eight circles remain on the top.

These practical exercises lay a foundation for understanding recipro- cal relations. This knowledge can be reinforced by conducting different variants of the lessons, in which the children count the objects presented, and must take one more or one fewer, placing the objects under each other so that it will be immediately apparent where there are more and where there are fewer.

Reproducing Sets Based on a Spoken Number

In subsequent lessons the children count out a specified number of objects from a larger set. "Let Misha bring seven boats, and let Irina bring eight roosters," the teacher assigns. She explains to the children in advance that they should remember who has to bring how many of what, and that they must not forget the number of objects in counting out. When the teacher asks, "How many roosters have you brought?," Ira should respond without recounting: "I've brought eight roosters."

The children can also be given an assignment requiring that the children remember the number of objects, their color, and their spatial position. For instance, the teacher asks them to put six green triangles on their left and four red triangles on their right. Then the children say how many there are of each and where they are. "What else can we say about them if you don't know where there are how many?" "On my left is a set of green triangles, and on my right is a set of red triangles." "Can't these sets be combined into one? What can we say then about this set?" The children combine the two groups of triangles and say that they have one set of triangles. But this set consists of two parts: one part is the green triangles, and the other is the red triangles. The teacher asks them to recall how many triangles were included in the red part and how many in the green part.

What should the children consider in carrying out this assignment? That they are dealing with two sets which can be combined into one, consisting of two parts, each with its own color. The children should also remember the connection between the quantity and the color of the triangles, and the location of each group (on the right and on the left).

As the children gain practice, all the connections between the number and the object, its color, and the spatial arrangement of objects become habitual, and the number of errors in carrying out the assignments gradually diminishes. Speaking aloud (counting aloud) significantly promotes this process. Along with the assignment, the teacher should quiz several children. It must be taken into account that the children will not immediately be able to tell what they have done, and therefore the teacher can help with leading questions, such as: "What color are the triangles on your right, and how many are there?" "What color are the triangles on your left, and how many are there?"

Teaching Counting in Various Spatial Arrangements

It is quite possible to vary the arrangement of objects in the older group. The children should learn to count objects "in a circle," vertically, in the form of a number configuration, and arranged in an undefined group (Figure 14). It is important to point out that they must remember what object they started counting with, so that the same object is not counted twice and none is left out. It is therefore advisable to make the spatial form of arranging the set elements more complicated—e.g., in the form of a vertical row, or along a slanted line. The children are inclined to take the object closest to them as a reference point. They can be asked to count away from themselves (from the bottom up or from the top down), thus providing that the result will be the same, and then to count along a slanted line as well. With a horizontal arrangement it is advisable to count from left to right (as they have done up to now), as well as from right to left. Then the children can be asked to count the circles in various arrangements in a number configuration. After showing various methods of counting, the teacher should discuss the most convenient one with the children. She should emphasize that it is possible to count in any direction, as long no element of a set is omitted.

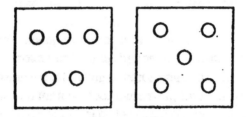

Figure 14

Instruction in the Significance of Number as an Index of a Certain Class or Set

In the older group the children's understanding of number as an index reflecting a certain class of sets continues to develop. This can be promoted by various techniques in lessons. For example, the teacher asks the children to take three or four types of objects, but in equal quantities, and to demonstrate this equality practically, setting the objects in rows beneath one another.

A similar lesson can be conducted in the following way. The children place the same number of toys on two or three tables: six of each on one, eight of each on another, and ten of each on a third (several children can take part in this assignment at once). Comparing the number of toys on their tables, the children arrive at the generalization that there are eight of each type of toy on the given table, independent of the nature of the toys. The number that summarizes these sets becomes concrete: eight roosters, eight trees, eight hens, eight cars, eight squares, eight triangles, eight blocks, and so forth; all the toys are different, but there are eight of each type.

Generalization of objects based on their quantity functions in combination with concretization. Thus, the children learn to abstract number on the basis of a one-to-one correspondence between the elements of equivalent sets.

This generalization can and should be coordinated with the notion of a set. "What can we say about all the toys standing on this table?" the teacher asks. "There are many different toys on the table." "Who can guess how to put it more precisely?" "There are many toys on the table." "Correct. What else can be said about this set?" "The set of toys consists of different parts, different types of toys. There are eight toys apiece in each row, and there are seven parts in all" one child counts the rows of different toys. "All the parts are equal; there are eight toys in each part."

This answer reflects an understanding that a single set can consist of a number of parts, and that all the parts can be identified by a number-word. And this means that for a child, a number becomes an index of the capacity of a set.

In order to vary these lessons, different assignments can be carried out. For example, the children seated at one table are asked to take three types of toys, seven apiece, those seated at another table are to take six apiece, and so forth. The general interest is sustained by different responses from the children in each group. In another variant, each child receives an individual assignment. In this case the assignments are different even for children seated at the same table. (The teacher plans ahead of time who will be given what assignment.) With this variant of the lesson, each child must remember the number given to him and do the assignment independently. It is also important in this lesson to direct the children's attention to the connections between a set and a number.

In another variant of a lesson aimed at generalization, the children are given cards with various numbers of objects drawn on them, such as eight cherries, seven raspberries, six cucumbers, six tomatoes. The children have different collections of cards. The point is to teach the children to orient themselves in these quantities, to remember and be quick at picking up the cards on the teacher's card. The teacher shows a card depicting geometric figures, e.g., six circles, and asks the children to hold up the cards showing the same number of objects. If six objects are depicted on several cards, the child should raise all these cards (children who do not have cards with the given quantity do not raise their hands). The cards that are raised are handed to a neighbor, who checks the answer. If a number of children have the same quantity, they too exchange their cards. Once the cards have been verified, they are set aside, face down. An assignment is given for another number and is checked the same way. In the end the teacher determines who has failed to spot cards, in order to give these children extra practice. The children say of the cards that have been set aside and grouped by number: "We have three cards, with six objects apiece: six tomatoes, six cucumbers, six birch leaves," "We have four cards, with four objects apiece: four acorns, four maple leaves, four balls, four cherries. The objects are different, but there are four of each of them" (cf. Appendix B).

The children gradually learn this method of description: at first they merely name the toys and indicate their quantity, while the teacher generalizes or helps the children do so with leading questions. In order to avoid stereotyped responses, the questions should be varied—for example: "What parts does the set of all your cards consist of, and how many parts are in your set? How many objects are shown on each card? What can be said about all these series of sets?"

Thus, in lessons of this type the children become visually acquainted with equivalent sets named by the same number-word: they combine these sets into one total, and they count up the number of parts. During the exercises the children's understanding of sets becomes more profound, as does their understanding of the significance of number as an index of the size of a certain class of sets.

Studying the Unit Composition of a Number

The following group of lessons is connected with a new curricular objective—the unit composition of a number. The children must not only be shown that any set consists of individual elements (specific objects or groups); the relation of a number to the unit must also be made explicit—that is, the quantity of units in a number should be emphasized.

It is particularly clear that a set is composed of individual elements when every element is distinguished from every other by some attribute (color, size, object content, etc.).

In the initial stages sets for counting were homogeneous in qualitative attributes—eight red flags, for instance. But the children themselves have already made up sets from heterogeneous objects (a teddy bear, a toy horse, a block, and a bunny makes up a set of toys). In subsequent stages (in the intermediate group) the children become familiar with a set as a whole, consisting of different parts, and in the older group they learn to combine individual parts into a single whole. The children learn to differentiate the elements of a set and count them correctly. Now the relations between a unit and a number should be particularly stressed, showing, for example, that the number five consists of one, another one, another one, another one, and another one. This should be accomplished through specific sets, such as five different-colored flags, five triangles of different sizes, five different toys—a rooster, a teddy bear, a duck, a dog, a goose. At first the children count these sets, but the teacher points out the quantitative composition, asking them to name the quantity and color of each flag, or the size of each triangle, or the quantity of each type of toy. After counting five flags, the child indicates how this five is composed, emphasizing its quantitative composition: one red one, one blue one, one green one, one yellow one, one light blue one—five in all.

In the future the children themselves make up sets of various objects and determine their composition. The teacher should be sure that the children name not only the objects, but also their number: "I took four toys: one swan, one turtle, one plate, one fish."

At some point the children can be asked to draw a set consisting of a specified number of various objects. However, as the children get carried away with their drawing, they often forget about the numerical relations between the objects that they were to have drawn, forgetting the number of objects they were supposed to draw. Therefore, counting should be incorporated in drawing only when the children have basically learned to count. Otherwise, a premature combination of two complex composite stimuli can inhibit the unestablished counting connections.

Observations of children and analysis of their mistakes in studying the quantitative unit structure of number show how the children now approach sets in a new way. "How did it happen that you have four?" asks the teacher. Abstracting from all the qualities of objects, a child might answer, "One, another one, another one, and another one." And although he still relies on the objects before him, now he is interested only in the quantitative aspect. The set of elements he has picked out are abstracted into units, which, when added up, constitute the number four. "How many different toys did you pick to make the number four?" the teacher asks, in order to turn the child from the abstraction of the number to the specific set and thereby reinforce the connections. "I picked four different toys: one rooster, one goose, one hen, one duck."

In studying the quantitative unit composition of number, it is important to emphasize again that **a unit is not just an individual object, but can also be an entire group.** The teacher shows the children a set of circles of different colors and asks them to determine the number of parts. The children say that the set is composed of five parts. "Name the color and the number of parts in this set." "There are five different colored parts in this set: one part is the red circles, one is the blue one, one the yellow, one the green, and one the orange circles. There are five parts in all." "How many units does the number five consist of?" "Five individual units." "What can a unit represent?" "It can represent one individual object or one group of objects," the children respond.

Over the course of several lessons the children learn the quantitative unit-composition of number; they understand that a number reflects a corresponding number of units, and realize that a number is an index of the size of a set. "Make a set of four parts," the teacher says. "One part daisies, one part cornflowers, one part buttercups, and one part carnations; there are four parts in all," the children say.

The mechanism for forming these relations involves the development of a series of associations. "When a connection is formed," Pavlov says, "that is, what we call an 'association', it is undoubtedly practical knowledge, a knowledge of certain relations in the external world, but the next time we use it, it is called 'understanding'—that is, the use of this knowledge and these connections is understanding" [4:579-580].

A measured and consistent system of lessons creates conditions for the gradual formation of constant new connections that contribute to the children's store of knowledge. This knowledge proceeds from an elementary notion of sets and an understanding of their interrelationships to an understanding of number as an index of a set.

The Study of the Reciprocal Relations among Consecutive Numbers Based on Comparing Sets

The next curricular task is to acquaint the children, based on comparison, not only with sets containing equal and unequal numbers of elements and the relation between them, but also with relations between consecutive numbers.

In studying the unit composition of numbers using concrete materials, the children have learned quantitative differentiation—the foundation for understanding the connections and relations between consecutive numbers.

Establishing a connection means determining a sequence of numbers (one after another) in forward and reverse order; it means knowing which number is greater and which is smaller. The relations between consecutive numbers imply a precise understanding of how much greater or smaller one number is than another.

At first the children establish associative connections for consecutive number-words; instruction in comparing sets supplements them with concrete notions that make it possible to determine that one number is greater and another smaller, and establish practically and effectively whether sets have equal or unequal numbers of elements. The children acquire this knowledge and these skills in the intermediate group. In the older group, during instructed in counting up to ten, they should also use practical material to learn which of two consecutive numbers is greater and which is smaller (nine is greater than eight, and eight is less than nine). But this is the initial stage in understanding connections, whereby only the sequence of numbers is mastered during counting (first eight, then nine). Children in the older group should ultimately understand the relations between consecutive numbers. How can this be accomplished?

Based on the ability to juxtapose the elements of sets they want to compare, the children should first learn practical methods of turning inequality into equality and equality into inequality. For example, they have seven circles arranged on the top strip on a card, and eight circles on the lower strip. The children see that there are more circles where there are eight and fewer circles where there are seven. From the outset they learn that eight is greater and seven is less.

But even the concepts *greater* and *less* are relative. Is the number eight always more and seven always less? The children should address this question directly: "Eight is greater than what?" "Eight is greater than seven." "Seven is less than what?" "Seven is less than eight." "What do we do to make both strips have equal numbers?" The children start thinking again. Then an answer is usually offered: "We must add something." But this answer is imprecise: it should be specified where something needs to be added, and to what. "If we add one circle to the seven circles, there will be eight circles on the top strip." "That's right, but a conclusion about the number with which we are comparing the number eight should follow from this. Think—eight is greater than what number?" "Eight is greater than seven," the children respond. "And what number can eight be less than?" The children's thinking functions once more: "Nine, nine," they say.

The teacher brings the children back to the circles laid out on the strips. "You were right to say that eight is greater than seven. But how do we get equality between the circles on both strips?" "We added another circle to the seven circles, and so there were also eight circles on the top strip," the children say. "If eight is greater than seven, what can we say about the number seven?" the teacher poses a new question. If the children have trouble answering, the teacher adds, "Seven is less than what number?" "The number eight," the children answer. "Now repeat everything about the numbers seven and eight," the teacher proposes. "The number seven is less than eight, and the number eight is greater than seven," the children say, expressing the relations between these numbers but not yet naming the difference between them.

It has been established that children first perceive number as an absolute rather than a relative concept. Therefore they say, "Seven is later, and six is earlier, and that means that seven is greater"—that is, they draw a conclusion on the basis of the external sequence of numbers. In the older group, however, the children should understand the relative significance of the expressions *greater* and *less*. They should be explicitly shown the relations pertaining to which number is greater and vice versa—which is smaller. These relations should be emphasized in the formulations: "Seven is greater than six, and six is less than seven."

When the child says, as before, "Eight is greater and seven is less," the teacher does not correct the child but turns to the children, asking: "But greater than which number—how can we say it more precisely?"

Thus, achieving a clearer formulation, the teacher strives not merely to help the children master a new sentence structure, as is often supposed, but to reflect the relations between the numbers in speech. Later the children can gradually be led to actually ascertain the different relations between consecutive numbers.

Experience has shown that to do this the teacher must demonstrate the meaning of the words *extra* and *missing* when sets are compared. By creating equivalent sets from nonequivalent ones, the children will comprehend that if there are four objects in a set, and one is to be taken away so that three will be left, that object is extra; if, on the other hand, there are three circles in a set, and one circle must be added for there to be four, one is missing. For different sets expressed by consecutive numbers, the children establish equality using a two-part method: either they add one to the set with fewer elements or they take one away from the set with more elements. These reciprocal relations, when well learned by the children, should be reflected in speech: "Eight is more than seven; therefore, if we take one away from eight, we get seven; there will be equal numbers. But it can also be done another way: seven is less than eight; here one is missing; therefore, if we add one to seven, there will be eight in each group—equal numbers."

After this it is not hard for the children to answer questions on the difference relations between consecutive numbers. "How much greater is the number eight than seven?" "The number eight is one greater than seven." "How much less is the number seven than eight?" "The number seven is one less than eight," answer the children.

Thus, children develop an understanding of the reciprocal relations between consecutive numbers gradually, which requires step-by-step instruction.

What mistakes do we encounter in practice? The children often say in comparing concrete sets: "Eight is more, and seven is less." "How much greater is eight than seven?" "One greater." The following answer is also often heard: "Eight is one more." This occurs because the questions and answers are based on visual material, and the teacher supposes that the answer is right since everything is obvious. But such a response conceals a failure to understand the relations between the numbers. The children are used to the fact that it is never otherwise: it is always either one more or one less (since reciprocal relations are demonstrated to preschool children only for consecutive numbers). Thus when the teacher pays insufficient attention to precise formulations by the children, they develop erroneous conceptions.

Let us give an example of a lesson. The children place five circles and six triangles on two strips. When asked which number is less or greater, Roza answers, "Six is greater, and five is less." "Does everyone understand which numbers are greater or less?" "We didn't understand anything." "What did Roza forget to say?" "She forgot to say that five is less than six, and six is greater than five." "Right. Roza did not compare the numbers and did not say which number the number five is less than. Who can tell us how much the number five is less than six?" "The number five is one less than six," Lesha answers. "Prove this for the other children, Lesha." Lesha goes to the chart with two strips hanging near the teacher's desk, puts five circles on the top strip and six triangles on the bottom one, establishing a correspondence between them, and then says, "Here there are five circles; there are fewer of them than the six triangles. The five circles are one circle short for there to be as many of them as there are triangles. We can make an equal number of circles and triangles in another way: if we add one circle to the five circles, that will make six of them—just as many as there are triangles. But we can also do something else: we take one away from the six triangles, and there will be five of them—just as many as there are circles; there will be five on each of the two strips—equal numbers.

The children should be taught this sort of response with a proof, which develops their logical thinking. At the same time the children can be asked to compare the number five with the number four. This shows the children that the number five is not only less than six but is also greater than four—that is, that **the same number can be both "greater than" and "less than," depending on the number with which we compare it.**

When the children have a firm mastery of the relations between consecutive numbers, it is possible to give even more complicated assignments involving the difference comparison of consecutive numbers without visual material. "Which number is greater, and which is less if I have nine and eight?" the teacher asks. "The number eight is one less than nine, and the number nine is one greater than eight." "What must be done to get equality?"—the teacher asks a new question. "We must take one away from the number nine," Kolya says, "and then there will be eight in each of the two sets—equal numbers. But it can be done another way—add one to eight, and there will be nine in each of the two sets—equal numbers." "Go ahead, Kolya, and show it." Kolya demonstrates what he has just said.

So that the children will think before answering, rather than merely mechanically repeat a memorized sentence, it is sometimes advisable to suggest conditions where the difference is two, for example, rather than by one. "I will name the numbers six and eight, and you think and tell which is greater and which is smaller than the other, and by how much." Sometimes the children are inclined to give a wrong answer, but, when they give a proof based on visual material, they detect their mistakes by themselves. "I made a mistake," says Misha. "Six is two less than eight, but I said one. I was thinking poorly." With such an example the teacher, on the one hand, leads the children to master the diverse relations among numbers, and, on the other hand, trains them to consider these relations, rather than giving a mechanical answer.

It is important to show the children that one number is greater or less than another, not only with individual objects, but also with sets that include several parts. For example, one set of geometric figures is made up of five parts (squares, circles, triangles, and ovals). Comparing the number of parts in the sets, the children conclude that in this instance the number five is greater than four, and the number four is less than five. Thus, the children arrive at the following conclusion: no matter how a number is expressed—by individual objects or groups—it is always one greater than the preceding number and one less than the following number.

All these observations, together with actual comparison of the elements in two sets, develop a stable understanding of the quantitative relations between consecutive numbers. In the child's mind the number five is greater than the number four now not only because it is named later when uttering the standard number sequence, but also because it contains a larger number of units (elements of the set) than the number four.

A number is characterized by two attributes: quantity and order, and the children should learn both of these. In the older group they need not at first give an oral response when asked how much greater or less a certain number is than another ("How much greater is eight than seven?" and the other way around: "How much less is seven than eight?"). Before responding to this question, the children should see visually and repeatedly that the two sets are not equivalent, and should learn to actually establish that they contain equal numbers of elements, and then explain everything. Only then will the above questions become clear to them, and they can give a deliberate answer on the basis of visual material.

Let us give a few more variants of lessons. Individual assignments are offered to provide variety in the children's activity and responses: some assignments are for determining the relations between the numbers three and four, others between six and five, still others between ten and nine, and so forth. Different geometric figures are presented for selection, to be put on the strips: some children will take circles and ovals, others trapezoids and squares, and still others rectangles and triangles.

These assignments are given according to the children's level of preparation. Those who do the assignment tell what they have done aloud, and tell which number is greater or less, and by how much.

The children thus gradually compare all the first five numbers, and then the numbers from six to ten, using concrete materials. The knowledge is reinforced using different groups of objects, showing the children that the relations between numbers are constant (five mushrooms, five trees, five cones, and five trapezoids are always less in quantity than six circles, six squares, six ovals, six fish, or six trees).

Considering that the concepts *greater* and *less* are relative rather than absolute, the teacher must watch the children's responses to see that they name both relations (nine eight and eight nine) and indicate how to obtain equality of the numbers.

This comparison of numbers and determination of their relations should begin with the numbers two and three. When consecutive numbers are compared, the difference will always be equal to the number one. Therefore, it is not a good idea to begin teaching comparison with the numbers one and two, since the children have not yet firmly learned the number one as a number and often still connect it with the concept of a single object. It is easier for the child to see and understand the difference relations of one between other numbers than one and two.

Thus, only as a result of diversified exercises in comparing consecutive numbers using concrete material do the children form an understanding of the relations between them, first based on the ability to actually turn make nonequivalent sets equivalent by adding or removing one object, and then comprehend the reciprocal difference relations between the numbers.

Involving Various Perceptual Analyzers in Counting

The children should have a distinct notion that the sets in the world around them can be represented in various ways, and we perceive them through our various sense organs. By drilling the children in counting by hearing, by touch, and so forth, we not only train the perceptual analyzers, we also provide for simultaneous development of the interanalyzer connections in the cerebral cortex. Counting activity is generalized to apply in any situation, for a systematic quality develops in the activity of the cerebral cortex. The children form a dynamic stereotype of counting, which enables them to respond adequately to highly diversified composite stimuli.

In working with children in the older group the teacher uses the same counting techniques as in the intermediate group.

Ordinal Counting and the Study of Ordinal Numbers

A new goal in the older group is to teach the children to differentiate between ordinal and cardinal numbers, between the questions "How many?" "What kind?" and "Which?", and to answer them correctly. The children usually already use ordinal numbers in their everyday speech, but they do not have a distinct notion of how they differ from the cardinal numbers. Even in grade one the children may respond to the teacher's question, "What number did you and I study yesterday?" by saying, "The first." Thus, they do not understand the distinction between the number one and the ordinal number "first"; these words are synonymous to the children. The following responses by preschool children also indicate a failure to understand the difference between the cardinal and ordinal numbers: "Which number is greater—seven or six?" "Seven." "Seven is how much greater than six?" "Seven," the children answer, although in practice they can properly show than one object is extra in a set consisting of seven objects. By saying "Seven greater" the children mean that where there are seven, there is one extra. They interpret this "extra" as the seventh, but they call it seven.

Therefore, it is quite important to explain the significance of cardinal and ordinal numbers to the children. It is pointed out in the theory of arithmetic that "a cardinal number is a concept of a certain class of equivalent sets...", and that "an ordinal number... is a general abstract concept of the ordinal place of an element in aggregates of a specific type (sequences)." The teacher should know these distinctions clearly and be able to explain them to the children in simple terms.

Various assignments can be done for these purposes. Here is one possibility. The teacher puts ten different-colored flags in a stand on the table. The children first determine the color of each flag and count the total number (ten flags in all). The teacher indicates that when we count one, two, three, and so on, we are finding out about the number of all the flags. But how can we find out about each of the flags? In what place does it stand among the other flags? Here, too, we must count, but in another way: the first, the second, the third, the fourth, the fifth, and so on. For example, the children might count to see the place in which the last flag (a pink one) stands. They find that since it occupies the tenth place among the remaining flags, it is called the tenth flag. The color of the last flag is changed a few times, and the children learn to use the ordinal numbers by counting.

The teacher emphasizes the difference in the responses to the questions "How many?" and "Which?" When "How many?" is asked, we want to find the total number of flags, but when "Which?" is asked, we mean one flag, and we want to clarify the position in counting that it occupies among the other flags.

The teacher drills the children, asking various questions: "Counting from left to right, in what place does the brown flag stand? Which one is the red flag in counting? How many flags in all in a row? What color is the third flag?" and so forth. The children learn to distinguish the significance of the different questions and answer them properly.

Knowledge acquired in one lesson should be reinforced in other lessons, which may differ either in the methods or the material used. For example, the children might lay out ten circles of the same color in a row. The teacher proposes replacing a specified circle by a circle of another color, and she gives it to the children. "How many circles are there in all?" the teacher asks. "Ten," the children answer. "Replace the third red circle from the left with a green one. Now tell which circle the green one is." This lesson can be made more complex by having them replace any red circle with a green one (the third, the fifth, or seventh, say). Then the children count the green and red circles, naming the circles that stayed red or became green. Thus, they gradually begin to understand that when they hear the question "How many?" they are dealing with a cardinal number, and when the question is "Which one?" they are dealing with an ordinal number. The nature of the counting also changes in relation to the question. When responding to the question "How many?" they use cardinal numbers. **The meanings of the questions "What kind?", "Which?", and "Which one in counting?" must be differentiated.**

The teacher also calls the children's attention to the fact that **they should always indicate the direction when finding the place in a series.** For instance, they may count from left to right or from right to left. The ordinal number changes accordingly. Thus, if one circle is the eight out of ten circles, counting from left to right, it becomes the third in counting from right to left.

But when determining the total number of objects, it does not matter in what direction the counting is done—from right to left, from left to right, or from the middle to the ends.

For some time ordinal counting constitutes the fundamental, principal object of weekly lessons. But when it has been largely mastered, part of the lesson can be given over to reinforcing it. Like any other curricular goal, ordinal counting should be repeated throughout the year, although the intervals between lessons for reviewing a certain topic may increase.

Familiarizing the Children With the Division of a Whole into Equal Parts[1]

It was discussed above how children can be taught to single out the parts in a set. (In a set of flags, one part of the flags is red and one part is yellow. There are two parts in the set.) In a discrete set the individual parts were singled out on some basis with ease and could be equal or unequal in number. But a whole, seemingly indivisible object can also be divided into parts, e.g., an apple, orange, cake, biscuit, rope, or strip of paper. In such cases we often try to make the parts equal (identical). If we fold a strip of paper first in half, and then in half again, we see four parts if we open it up.

If we fold a long rope in half three times and then count its parts, there turn out to be eight. In all cases where a whole is divided into parts, the children should notice that we intend to divide it into equal parts, that a part is less than the whole, and that the whole is greater than each of its parts.

We take a circle, for example, divide it in half, and obtain two parts, and if we divide it in half again, there will be four parts. A square is divided in half in exactly the same way—we obtain two parts, each of which is a rectangle rather than a square. If a square is divided in half twice, we get four parts, each of them a small square. But we can fold a square in half differently—diagonally—and obtain two isosceles triangles, and if we fold these triangles in half again, we get four smaller isosceles triangles.

Thus, by folding (but not cutting at this point) various objects, the children themselves dividing them into parts, determining the number of equal parts in a whole.

The children reflect the results of practical exercises in their speech: "I folded a square in half and got two parts—two rectangles; I folded it in half again and got four equal parts from the square—four little squares" (the child counts and holds up these parts as he explains).

As a result of all these exercises the children can be led to the conclusion that every time they obtain two equal parts by dividing in half, if these two equal parts are again divided in half, the result is always four equal parts.

But a whole can be divided by cutting it into parts—as with an apple, pear, cake, or bread—instead of by folding. However, the study of dividing a whole into parts must begin with folding rather than cutting. The point is that as they cut, the children perceive the part as an independent entity, a separate element independent of the whole. "You can't make a whole apple again from the four parts—you can't glue it back together," the children say.

Research has shown that the children interpret the terms *one-fourth* and *one-third* in their own fashion. In counting the four parts of an apple (or a biscuit, cake, or square cut into four parts), the children correlate the words one-fourth only with the last part of the apple, without knowing what the other parts are called. When the teacher asks them to check whether all the parts are equal, it turns out that they do not know what this equality amounts to. Some children determine that the number of parts are equal by establishing a one-to-one correspondence. They find equality when there is an even number of parts and deny it when there is an odd number (when the whole is divided into three parts).

When an object is divided by folding it in half and again in half (into four parts), the children see the parts belonging to the whole. At a subsequent stage these parts can be cut, but the whole must be restored by pasting. And finally, only at a later stage are the parts restored to a whole without being firmly attached—that is, by placing them together.

Paper geometric figures—circles, squares, rectangles or various sizes—can serve as material for dividing a whole into parts in the early stages (that is, material that can be folded or bent).

The children's understanding of the elementary relations between the part and the whole and their ability to make a proper correlation between the words "half of a whole" (or "a second part of a whole") and "one-fourth of a whole" makes it possible to move on to dividing a whole apple, biscuit, cake, or other objects into equal parts by cutting them.

This should be the sequence of instruction, although the children might find it more interesting and simpler to cut an apple into parts than to divide a square. But the teaching objective is not the cutting process itself, but the development of an understanding of the relations between parts and whole, correctly naming each equal part ("half," "one-half," "one-fourth"), and demonstrating these parts.

The children already know that if an apple is cut in half, there will be two equal parts—two halves. "What is a half?" "Two parts equal to one another are halves." "If an apple is cut into two parts that are not equal, can we call them the halves of the apple?" The children respond negatively.

The teacher asks the children to cut each of the halves of an apple into two equal parts. "How many equal parts has the whole apple been cut into now?" "Four equal parts." "What is each of these parts called?" "One-fourth of the whole apple." At the teacher's request the children show all the apple's parts and name each one. Then they are asked to combine all the parts and tell what they have obtained. A child is called upon to take the four apple parts in his hands. "It is as if it has been stuck together and a whole apple is there again," he says. At the teacher's suggestion a child distributes the apple parts to the children and asks what they have gotten. "I got one-fourth of the whole apple," everyone answers. "Sometimes one-fourth of an apple is called a quarter," the teacher says (the children have heard the word—they have been sent to the baker's for a quarter loaf of bread). "What does a quarter of a loaf of bread mean?" "When the loaf of bread is cut into four equal parts." "Correct. Now why do you think they speak of a half of a loaf?" "Because they divide the loaf of bread into two parts," Misha answers. The teacher takes a round loaf of bread and deliberately divides it into two unequal parts. "Into how many parts have I cut the bread?" "Into two parts." "And can each of these parts be called a half?" The children answer negatively, saying that the bread must be cut into two equal parts. They say that Misha's answer was wrong.

On the basis of dividing an apple and a loaf of bread into two and four parts, the children arrive at a generalization: "We can speak of a half when an apple or a loaf of bread or something else is cut into two equal parts, and of quarter when an apple or a loaf of bread or some other object is cut into four equal parts." "If we cut the apple or the bread into unequal parts, what must we say then?" the teacher asks. "The apple has been cut into unequal parts," the children answer.

The children's everyday experience is thus refined and enriched by the knowledge obtained during instruction.

The children can be given independent practice at dividing objects (a rope, ribbon, braid, etc.) into two and four equal and unequal parts, and can be asked what they have obtained (how many parts, what they are, and what they are called). Here, to reinforce the connection between part and whole, the children should be reminded that a part is less than a whole, and a whole is greater than each of its parts.

The Development of Spatial and Temporal Notions

Methodology for Developing Notions of Size and Measurement

During the preceding stage the children learned that objects can change in length, width, height, and thickness. But it is important for them not only to determine these changes using prepared materials, but also to produce them independently. For example, they may be asked to draw or cut out two or three rectangles of the same length but of different widths; to draw two carrots—one longer, the other shorter; to cut out paper squares—one large, the other small.

The children's knowledge of the various dimensions should be properly reflected in their speech: "The white string is thicker than the black one", or "I need a long string for stringing beads" (not a big one, as children often say). The children should also apply their knowledge in various activities: drawing, modeling with clay, applique work, and games. For example, for a game of "train" the children draw the railroad track on the ground, marking the stations at various distances from Leningrad (all on the same side of that city): some closer, others farther away. The children can determine these distances even more precisely; for instance, the Udelnaya station is closer to Leningrad, so they count off four paces from the start of the track, while the Levashovo station is farther away and they count off six paces. "How much farther is it to the Levashovo station?" the teacher asks. Counting the distance between the Udelnaya and Levashovo stations in paces, the children say that Levashovo is two steps farther. Thus, a pace becomes a unit of measure in the children's game.

Another example: in competing to see who can hit a target with a ball or throw a beanbag the farthest, the children want to find out who throws farther than whom, and how much farther. This can be determined by sight or, more precisely, by counting the number of paces from the starting line to the place where the beanbag lands. In this way an everyday need arises for real distance measurement.

The children in the older group must form distinct notions of the relations between the sizes of objects reflected in expressions indicating the object's place in a row of other objects: *long, shorter, even shorter, shortest*. In the intermediate group the children learned to recognize the relations between two or three objects. In the five-year-old group they should learn the relations of from five to ten objects arranged in increasing or decreasing order according to size—that is, they should learn "seriation." Mastering these relations is a relatively complex task related to the children's development of analytic perception of an object (isolating length, width, and height) and to the ability to measure objects by comparing them in terms of given parameters. Sight estimation plays a considerable role here.

Let us consider several pedagogical techniques. To verify the knowledge acquired in the intermediate group, the children can be asked to choose a ribbon according to a model whose size must be remembered. The material can be two collections of five paired ribbons of the same width but of different color and length (from 12 to 20 cm), and the ribbon color can be different in each pair of the same length. The problem is to abstract only one length in the given model and find a paired ribbon to go with it. The child should check the completed assignment. "How can you prove that your red ribbon is the same length as my blue one?" At first the child points out checking techniques, then gives a practical demonstration.

In another variant of the lesson, all the children are given five different-colored strips of the same width but of different length (differing by 2 cm). They are asked to arrange them in order (Figure 15), whichever way they choose (in increasing or decreasing order). Then the children explain, "My longest strip is the red one, the pink one is shorter, the blue one is even shorter, the orange one is even shorter, and the green one is the shortest." Another child enumerates the colors and sizes of his strips, which are arranged in increasing order. This exercise refines the perception of size and color and improves the children's speech.

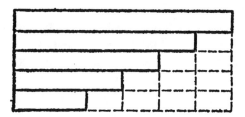

Figure 15.

The assignment can also be given to the children in another form: four ribbons, arranged in order, are compared in length, and the children get a practical lesson in the transitive nature of these relations. For example, the children say that the red ribbon is longer than the pink one, the pink one is longer than the yellow one, and the yellow one is longer than the green one. "Then which ribbons is the red one longer than?" the teacher asks, to encourage the children to think. At first they name only individual ribbons ("The red ribbon is longer than the yellow one," "The red ribbon is longer than the green one"). The teacher asks them to think and list all at once the ribbons exceeded in length by the red ribbon. Looking again at the row of ribbons, one child says, "The red ribbon is longer than the pink one, the yellow one, and the green one. It is the longest of all the ribbons." "And which ribbon is the shortest?" the teacher poses a new question. The children name the green ribbon. "Which ribbon is it a little shorter than?" "The yellow one." Thus all the consecutive ribbons are first compared in order, and then a generalization is made: "Which ribbons is the green one shorter than?"

By repeatedly comparing ribbons, strips, and other objects arranged in decreasing or increasing order, the children gain an essential practical familiarity with the transitivity of the relations ($A > B$, $B > C$, $C > D$, and therefore $A > D$).

It is also quite important to point out to the children how much longer one strip is than another in a seriation row. The children form a seriation row from five given strips of the same color, the same width, and different lengths. The whole thing is like a "staircase," and these are the "steps," the children say, moving their fingers "up" and "down" the staircase. The teacher asks them to think about what to do to make up two consecutive strips equal in length. The teacher introduces several rectangles of various lengths but the same width as the strips, and asks the children to choose the rectangle that would complement one of the consecutive strips and make them equal. By adding the rectangle they chose to their strips, the children establish that the consecutive strips are equal. Then the teacher asks them to think and guess how much longer one strip is than the other. The children show the small rectangle they have added to all the strips when evening up the consecutive strips. "How much larger is one step in the staircase than another?" By adding the rectangle to all the strips in order, the children conclude that the width of the "stairsteps" is the same throughout. "What must we do for all the strips to be of the same length?" the teacher asks a new question. The children start thinking. The teacher gives each one four or five strips and asks them to think about where to put each strip so that the staircase will turn into a rectangle. The children do the assignment and count the number of small rectangles that make up the strip they added to the second stairstep, the third, and the fourth. "What does each little rectangle on the strips mean?" the teacher asks, indicating the size of the strip that shows the length differential of consecutive steps.

The children can also be asked to arrange five long strips in a row, after which they are given another five strips of intermediate size to include in the row they have constructed. The children are asked to explain how the first staircase differs from the second. They say that there were five steps in the first, and they were very high, but there are ten steps in the second staircase, and they have become low.

The children can also be given an assignment to sharpen their wits. Six or eight strips of different length are passed out, such that no strictly regular seriation row can be constructed because two of the strips are equal in length. Many children immediately note that they have two equal strips and ask that one of them be replaced. Others notice it only after constructing the staircase. And finally there are children who do not notice the disruption in the regular arrangement of the strips, detecting the error only after subsequent analysis of their staircase, with the help of the teacher and the other children.

It is recommended that similar exercises be conducted involving relations of width and height. In teaching children sensory perception of size, it is advisable to use the series of didactic materials proposed by Maria Montessori (a long staircase, a short staircase; bars and cylinders—large and small, tall and short, thick and thin).

The children should practice not only in formal lessons, but also during didactic games, using the game "Guess What's in the Sack," for example (the sack is filled with objects of various shapes and sizes).[2] A number of games can be taken from F. N. Blekher's book *Didactic Games and Didactic Materials* [1:102, 104-105, 111-112].

Creating a seriation row for the length, width, and height of objects is fully accessible to four- and five-year-old preschoolers. Here the older children do not merely arrange objects in decreasing or increasing order; they also become aware of the different relations between the elements in a seriation row. These facts disprove the assertion by J. Piaget and B. Inhelder that the perception of equality in difference relations between the elements in a seriation row is accessible only to children at the age of 10 or 12.

An important pedagogical objective is to teach the children to closely scrutinize the various qualities and properties in the objects around them so that their knowledge of the dimensions of objects will also be reflected in their productive activity (drawing, modeling with clay, and building) and so that the size and shape of objects will be perceived interdependently. This is why the recognition of an object always proceeds according to these two attributes in didactic games.

Methods for Introducing Children to Geometric Figures

Six-year-olds can not only easily distinguish a circle, a square, a triangle, and a rectangle, they can also name them, knowing that all these plane figures can be of various sizes and colors. They also know geometric solids: the sphere, cube, and cylinder. The Preschool Curriculum sets the goal of acquainting the children with the oval, and among the geometric solids, the cone and bar (rectangular parallelepiped). All these shapes are widely represented among the objects in the children's surroundings, and they should be taught to name them properly.

The basic task of the teacher for the older group is to make the children more familiar with the elementary attributes and features of the geometric figures that they know as standards for comparing objects by shape.

Let us give some examples of lessons on introducing the children to the new geometric figure.

In order to introduce the **cone**, the teacher sets a toy—the ring pyramid—in front of the children, asks them to outline it with one finger, and then asks what familiar plane figure resembles the ring pyramid. The children remark that the pyramid resembles a triangle. "Take this figure in both hands. How is it different from the triangle?" The children note that it is round and gets gradually thicker from top to bottom, and that it consists of rings stacked on a spindle. The teacher says that such a figure is called a cone. Demonstrating another figure consisting of squares of decreasing size, the teacher explains that this toy can be called a pyramid. As the children take the pyramid and the cone apart and see their elements, they themselves notice their differences: the cone consists of round rings that decrease in size and have no angles, while the pyramid is made of squares that decrease in size; the cone will roll, but the pyramid cannot because it has angles.

Once they have identified that basic feature of a cone, the children find and name objects resembling the cone, as the teacher's indicates (a funnel, vase, lampshade, carrot).

As an exercise, the children name familiar objects that are cylindrical in shape. Comparing the cylindrical shape with the cone, the children establish the similarity and difference between them. A battery is cylindrical—it is identically round and even everywhere, but a carrot is cone-shaped (conic)—it is also round but not even like a cylinder; one of its ends is narrow.

In one lesson the teacher acquaints the children with a **bar** (without giving it the name of "rectangular parallelepiped," which is hard to say). She shows them a bar and asks what it looks like. "The bar is like a brick," the children say. They know this shape well, but they call it a brick because they know no more precise term. At the teacher's request the children outline the rectangles with their fingers (without yet calling them "faces").

Then the teacher asks them to find objects around them that are like the bar (a book, a dresser, box, aquarium, matchbox).

Knowing the five geometric solids (cube, sphere, cylinder, cone, and bar) awakens in the children considerable interest in the shapes of objects around them—the body of a car, a streetcar, a trolley, or a bus; they begin to perceive them in a different way. Shape is identified in these familiar objects. They spot the shapes of a cylinder and a cone in tree trunks and branches. They notice the cylindrical shape in pipes, columns, and wires. "Only the post is thick, and the wire is thin," they observe.

Thus, familiarity with geometric solids strengthens the children's cognitive activity, enriching their notions about life around them, and is also reflected in their productive activity (drawing, modeling with clay, building, and their accounts of what they observe).

Introduction to the Oval, Square, Rectangle, and Trapezoid

The children are usually able to distinguish an oval from a circle. To emphasize the difference, the teacher takes models of various colors, where the height of the oval is equal to the diameter of the circle. Superimposing the circle on the oval figure, the teacher shows the children that the figures are not the same and that it is wrong to call them by the same name. The teacher tells the children the term "oval." The children superimpose the models on one another and arrive at a generalized conclusion about their similarity and differences: "One part of an oval is wide, while the other tapers off like an egg." The children group the models of different color and size according to shape, and place each of the figures in increasing or decreasing order by size, accompanying their actions with descriptions.

In one lesson the children are given pictures of objects (a hoop, steering wheel, wheel, egg, cucumber, plum, etc.). They are asked to group the pictures based on their shape. Examining the pictures and outlining the drawings with one finger, the children conclude that they all consist of curved lines.[3]

In subsequent lessons the teacher asks them to **compare a square with a rectangle**, calling their to the features of the two figures. The children see that the sides of the square and the rectangle are line segments. For comparison the teacher takes a rectangle in which two sides are equal to a side of the square. The rectangle and the square are of different colors (Figure 16). The teacher superimposes the green square on the red rectangle. By superimposing the square in various ways, the children realize that only two sides of the rectangle are equal to the sides of the square, and the other two sides of the rectangle are longer than the square's sides. Part of the rectangle is left uncovered by the square. This difference is even more persuasive if the two figures are drawn on graph paper (a square can serve as the unit of measure for the area of the figures). Counting the unit squares on the square's sides shows the children that its sides are equal. Counting the unit squares on the rectangle's sides leads them to conclude that only the opposite sides are equal.

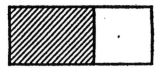

Figure 16.

Then the teacher introduces the children to the **trapezoid,** which is widely represented in the surrounding objects—trapezoid-shaped table-tops are increasingly common in kindergartens, and the children draw trapezoid-shaped roofs for city houses.

The teacher presents this figure by comparing it with the rectangle. The trapezoid also has four sides, four vertices, and four angles. Super-imposing a model of a yellow trapezoid on a model of a red rectangle, the teacher points out that the bottom sides of both figures coincide, but the trapezoid's upper base is shorter than the rectangle's upper side (Figure 17). Since the trapezoid's lateral sides are inclined, connecting the short upper side with the long lower one, two red triangles of the rectangle are visual from underneath; the area of this trapezoid is less than the area of the rectangle. Then the teacher takes a trapezoid whose area is greater than the rectangle's area, and now superimposes the rectangle on the trapezoid (Figure 18). In this case the top side of the rectangle coincides with the short base of the trapezoid, and the lower side proves shorter than the longer base of the trapezoid; the trapezoid's lateral sides remain uncovered, forming triangles.

Based on such comparisons the children conclude that a trapezoid, like a rectangle, has four sides, four angles, and four vertices, but the upper

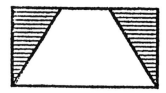

Figure 17.

Figure 18.

and lower bases are not the same: one is shorter and the other is longer; the trapezoid's lateral sides are inclined so that they connect the short upper base with the long lower base. (The trapezoid can be a different size and situated in a different way—for example, with the long base on top and the short base on the bottom.)

The children in the older group can also be led to elementary generalizations of familiar figures according to various attributes. For example, they can group familiar plane figures of different shapes and colors (circles, ovals, various triangles, squares, rectangles, trapezoids) according to generic attributes: (a) identify two groups of rounded and angular figures; (b) identify three groups—rounded figures; figures with four vertices, four angles, and four sides; and figures with three vertices, three angles, and three sides; and within each type arrange the figures in decreasing or increasing order of size; (c) identify three groups of figures (independently of shape and color): large, medium, and small; (d) group the figures by color, regardless of their shape and size.

The children can be shown a triangle and asked why this figure bears that name. The children usually guess easily because they know the basic attributes of this figure (three sides, three angles, and three vertices).

Indicating a group of figures with four angles (a square, rectangle, trapezoid), the teacher can ask the children to think of a name for this group. They ponder for a while, and then offer their suggestions: "four-sided figures," and "four-angled figures." The teacher approves their guesses and ingenuity, and states that these figures are called quadrilaterals. This method of introducing the children to quadrilaterals promotes the **formation of a generalization**. The children are led to the idea that one concept is incorporated in another, more general one. The square, rectangle, and trapezoid are varieties of quadrilaterals. Grouping objects based on the number of sides, vertices, and angles abstracts the children's thinking from other, nonessential attributes. Identifying basic attributes—the number of vertices, angles, and sides—in various figures makes it possible to demonstrate the group of quadrilaterals. But the quadrilateral is not merely a new figure. **The quadrilateral is a generalized concept, which the children learn at a sensory-perceptual level.** This method of learning is valuable for the mental development of the older preschool child.

Various techniques can be used to identify shapes, such as outlining them with one finger. The children can be given cards with outline drawings of various-sized figures, and they must select corresponding figures based on shape and size, and superimpose them on the outline drawing.

Also useful is an aid recommended by E. I. Tikheeva, consisting of paired cards with five models of various-colored geometric figures arranged in different ways. For example, the figures on one pair of cards are arranged in the following way: a yellow circle in the center, a red square in the upper left-hand corner, a blue triangle in the lower left-hand corner, an orange rhombus in the upper right-hand corner, and a green rectangle in the lower right-hand corner. The color and arrangement of these figures change in the next pair of cards. The five colors and five spatial arrangements make it possible to create a considerable number of such pairs (see Color Figure 13), but in the beginning there should be fewer figures to a card.

This aid can easily be used to construct lessons: one group of paired cards is given to the children, and the teacher keeps the other. The teacher shows a card to the children and asks them to find one that will make a pair. The aid requires attention and orientation not only in shape and color, but also in the spatial arrangement of the figure. It is therefore advisable to relate the children's response to a description of the arrangement of the given figures on the card.

The following lesson can also be recommended. The children are each given several pictures of objects. The teacher puts a certain geometric figure on the board or simply names it, and asks, "Who has a square-shaped object in their picture?" The children whose cards show objects similar to this shape hold up their cards to show the teacher and the other children. When there are several objects for a shape, all the cards are raised, and eight are placed next to the described figure or turned face down, to remain with the child.

Exercises on identifying and naming geometric figures and identifying shapes in various objects can be conducted outside of lessons, either in small groups or individually, using various games, such as "Dominoes" or "Geometry Bingo" (see Color Figures 8 and 9).

These exercises can be combined with exercises on dividing a figure into parts. For instance, the children can be given a large circle, a large square, and a large rectangle. These figures are divided precisely into two and four parts. Each figure and its parts are colored a particular color on one side, and on the other side all the figures and their parts have the same color. A set of this type is given to each child, and the lesson content is gradually made more complex. At first the children mix up the parts of all three figures, each of which has been divided in half, sorting them by color and making a whole according to the model. Next the children again mix up the parts and complete them with elements of the same figures which have been divided into four parts, again sorting and again composing whole figures. Then all the figures and their parts are turned over on the opposite side, which is all the same color, and from the combined set of different parts they select those which are needed to make a circle, a square, and a rectangle. This last problem is very complicated for the children, since all the parts are the same color, and they must choose based on shape alone.

Later the assignment can be made more complicated, by dividing the square and the rectangle into two and four parts in a different way—for example, dividing the square into two rectangles and two triangles, or four rectangles and four triangles (diagonally), and dividing the rectangle into two rectangles and two triangles, and into four rectangles, and, from them, two small rectangles divided into four triangles [1:128]. As we see, the number of parts increases, and this complicates the assignment.

Another useful aid has an object drawn in color on one card (e.g., a cup), rendered in silhouette on another card, and in outline on a third. Using this aid, the teacher shows the outline of an object and the children identify it; then those who have a silhouette or a colored picture of it name the object and show the appropriate cards to the other children or place them in a row with the outline picture (see Color Figure 12).

It is very important to drill the children in combining geometric figures and in making various compositions from the same shapes. This teaches them to scrutinize the shape of the parts of any object and read a technical drawing when carrying out building activities. Real objects can also be made from geometric figures (see Color Figure 10) [3:55].

Methods of Introducing Children to Spatial Notions

In the older group the teacher should continue to reinforce the children's awareness of the direction of movements away from themselves and their ability to designate the position of an object in relation to themselves. The principal objective in this group is the ability to determine and describe with words the position of an object with respect to another object—for example, the bunny is sitting on the doll's right, the horse is standing on the doll's left, the teddy bear is behind the doll, and the rooster is standing in front of the doll.

The comprehension and use of words to designate spatial relations between objects is an important factor in helping the child interpret his sensory experience. Outings, excursions, outdoor games, physical exercises, and the children's everyday orientation, both in the classroom and in the entire kindergarten, play a special role in developing spatial orientation. The special lessons have an auxiliary significance.

Good instructional techniques to apply to these problems are to examine didactic pictures and describe the arrangement of objects, and to select paired pictures of homogeneous objects arranged in various ways. For example, three toys in a row are drawn on one pair of paper strips: a teddy bear in the center, a train on the left, and a ring pyramid on the right; another pair has a train in the center, a teddy bear on the left of the train, and a ring pyramid on the right; and so forth—that is, the three objects change places (see Color Figure 14). The teacher shows one pictures, and asks who has the same kind. The child who has its pair holds up the picture, describes it, and matches it up with the teacher's. It is important for the child not only to find the paired picture, but also to describe the spatial arrangement of the objects.

Here is another technique. The teacher puts groups of toys in different corners of the room. The children are called upon to tell what they see as they approach a group of objects; for example, a bunny is sitting in the right front corner, a ring pyramid is on its right, and a doll table is to the left of the bunny; a carrot lies in front of the bunny, and a tree stands behind the bunny. All the toys are different, and there are five in all.

Physical exercises can be used to reinforce spatial orientation; during the exercises the children should be taught to change the direction of their movement on command while walking and running, and to describe their spatial position with respect to a certain object—for example, "I was standing in front of the chair, but I need to stand behind the chair."

Play techniques can be used in which one child is assigned to hide an object *behind* the bookcase, *under* the bookcase, *near* the bookcase, and so forth; another variant is to look for it and tell where it was found. There are many opportunities to reinforce orientation in three-dimensional space.

In the older group the children must be taught to orient themselves freely in the plane, i.e., in two-dimensional space, which not all children are capable of right away, and which many children are not sufficiently prepared for when they enter school; they often do not know the top from the bottom of a notebook page. They should practice this in their lessons. Above all, the children need an explanation of the following expressions: in the center, in the middle, on the right, on the left, at the upper right, at the lower right, and so on; then they should be given a number of practical assignments.

Let us give an example of such an assignment. The teacher asks the children to arrange numerals on a sheet of paper as indicated: put the figure 5 in the center of the page, the figure 6 to the right, and the figure 4 to the left; above the figure 5, on top, put the figure 2, to right of it the figure 3, and to the left the figure 1; under the figure 5, on the bottom, put the figure 8, to the right the figure 9, and to the left the figure 7. The figures turn out in order in three rows. The teacher asks someone to read them, beginning with the first row and going from left to right.

But the arrangement can be different, too—for example: in the upper left-hand corner of the page, in the upper right-hand corner, in the lower left-hand corner, in the lower right-hand corner, in the center, or in the middle, in the middle of the left side, in the middle at the bottom, and so on. Here, too, the children must be taught not only to act according to what the teacher says, but also to tell about the arrangement of the objects so that their practical actions will be reflected in speech.

Methods of Introducing Children to Temporal Notions

In the previous group the children learned about the sequence of temporal segments, including the parts of a day and the way they change, they learned to distinguish between today, tomorrow, and yesterday, and they learned that one day gives way to another. Now they can find out that the days have their own names, that seven days make a week, and that the sequence of the seven days is always the same: Monday, Tuesday, Wednesday, etc.

Every day in the older group the children determine the current day, naming the preceding and following days. The teacher reminds them that, although they are presently saying it in the morning or afternoon, they mean the whole day, which always begins with the sound of the Kremlin chimes. Knowing about the changing days of the week, and then about the change from one week to the next, leads the children to a notion of the periodic nature of time. The children themselves begin saying that "a year makes a circle": it was summer, then it passed, and now summer is coming again. In the same way for the week, it was Monday, then Monday passed, but in another seven days it will again be Monday.

The teacher should also gradually focus the children's attention on the duration of particular time segments in their activity. For example, the teacher might ask the children to think about how much time they spent dressing to go on an outing. Without yet having a notion of the duration of time segments, the children respond in different ways (varying from two minutes to an hour). The teacher specifies that they spent a total of 20 minutes getting dressed. If the children's attention is focused on the length of this procedure in a systematic way, they gradually become aware of the duration of this particular time segment. The children evince an interest in doing things at a quicker pace. "Please watch to see how many minutes I take to get dressed today for the outing—I am trying to get dressed faster," a child tells his teacher. Drawing the children's attention to the continuity in a certain activity gradually develops their "sense of time" (see Color Figure 20).

Developing the Children's "Sense of Weight"

Children's sensory development proceeds along many lines. The many facets of sensory development lay the foundation for subsequent mathematical development by combining the sensory and the logical (in quantitative, spatial, temporal, and other notions). Many scholars have devoted their attention to the development of the "sense of weight," or the baric sense, in many systems of preschool education (E. I. Tikheeva, M. Montessori, and others). This sense is a prerequisite for mastering the concept of mass and methods of measurement. Even small children distinguish the weight of objects, reflecting their perceptions in the words "heavy" and "light." But they first perceive these differences with the participation of the large muscle groups and in sharp contrasts (e.g., the child's chair and the doll chair). In the older group, exercises can be introduced on distinguishing weight with lesser contrasts, involving more restricted muscle groups—weighing objects on the palms, for example. When objects are weighed on the palms, the weight differential can gradually be reduced (from 300 to 50 g). The correlation in mass should also change gradually: $1 : 1.5$—$1 : 2.5$.

The nature of the exercises is basically the same as with exercises on distinguishing dimensions. For example, the children are given beanbags that are identical in shape and size and are filled with various dry materials (one with sand, say, and another with flour). The problem is to determine which sack is heavier and which is lighter. The children are taught techniques of weighing the sacks first on one palm, then on the other. Then the sacks are replaced by small boxes, kegs, and other objects of identical sizes, also filled with various dry materials, and the children continue weighing them on their palms.

Such assignments can be given to several children at once. In doing them, the children put relatively heavy objects on one table and lighter ones on another. Thus, the sacks or boxes on each table will be equal in weight. One child checks whether all the objects on the same tables are of equal weight. The checking is carried out by the same sensory method.

In another variant of the lesson, several pairs of boxes of two different weights are mixed together, and the children are summoned to inspect them and put the light boxes in one place and the heavy ones in another.

As the children's power of differentiation develops, the assignment can be made more complex: three (then four or five) weight differences are introduced, and the children receive three (or four or five) objects of decreasing weight and must arrange them in decreasing (or increasing) order. Then they are asked to find pairs for these three (five) objects—that is, objects that are equal in weight.

Children gradually achieve more sophisticated differentiation in sensory determination of equal or unequal weight. For comparison, the children might be given panels of equal size made out of different kinds of woods (as Yu. I. Fausek has done).[4]

For developing a sense of weight, it is very important to use collections of objects that are identical in size and shape but made out of different materials, such as iron, wood, rubber, or celluloid. It is no less important to demonstrate that weight is independent of an object's size, by comparing, e.g., a large balloon with a small wooden or metal ball.

Finally, the children can be taught to determine the weight of objects more accurately with simple balance scales. Objects that have already been weighed on the palms are put on the pans of a scale, one of which moves down; when the weight (mass) is identical the children note that the pans rest in equilibrium. Although the children are not yet actually weighing or using conventional standards (weights), they begin to understand the significance of scales for more precise measurement of weight. Their interest in weighing grows, and they watch carefully to see how adults use scales in stores. These observations begin to show up more frequently in games as well.

Reinforcing and Using Knowledge in Other Lessons, Games, and Everyday Life

The knowledge children acquire during mathematics lessons should be applied in various activities and everyday life. Thus, in drawing and modeling objects, the children give an object shape by using methods of identifying it by vision, touch, and hand movement, and name the geometric figure that resembles the given shape. For example, in drawing a fish they say that it is like an oval; in drawing an apron, they say that it is like a rectangle.

In making toys for the Christmas tree or getting presents ready for younger siblings, the children count them so that "there will be enough for everyone."

Pasting activities should also come into play, they acquire skills at cutting out circles, triangles, and quadrilaterals (trapezoids, squares, rectangles), making two triangles from a square or a rectangle, and arranging these figures in the plane in various ways.

The children develop their power of sight estimation and a sense of regularity in drawing designs and in pasting work: they place objects in a regular arrangement on paper, compose symmetric designs of leaves and flowers, count berries or the petals and leaves of plants, and then say how and why the elements have been arranged.

In music and physical education lessons, the children should practice their spatial orientations: determining their own positions with respect to other children and objects, as well as their spatial relations to one another (the ball has rolled under the chair, behind the bookcase; it is near the table; and so forth). In the course of a lesson or game, the children run in a certain direction, walk in a straight line, form a circle, and so forth.

The children's knowledge of mathematics should also be applied during outings. They can be asked to compare the length and thickness of stems and leaves, and to make sight measurements of the thickness and height of a tree (for instance, the pine tree is equal in height to a four-story building, they can encircle a tree trunk with both arms), the distance to a specified point, or the width of a road (determined by sight and verified by pacing).

The children's knowledge of the day should be brought to bear in observing the changes that occur during various seasons, pointing out that the days grow longer in the spring, in autumn they grow shorter, and in winter they are very short.

There are many games in preschool establishments that can be used with the children in their lessons and independent activity, such as didactic counting games: bingo, paired pictures showing objects on one card and numerals on another; paired cards showing the spatial arrangement of figures; shape-recognition lottery games such as "What is Like a Circle" (or an oval, etc.)?

In playing building games children need practice in orienting themselves freely in figures, correlating large, heavy parts with lighter ones in a structure (putting the large or heavy ones at the base), and naming them accurately.

In working with tinkertoys or erector sets, the children should be asked to select the parts of the appropriate size by sight and count the holes in the pieces. They should be taught to read a technical drawing, reproduce a structure according to it, and orient themselves in methods of fastening things together for strength.

The children must apply their abilities in their daily life as well: counting objects for setting the table, arranging them correctly (knife and spoon to the right of the plate, fork to the left; the bread dish and the vase of flowers in the middle of the table), and stowing away classroom equipment neatly.

The children must be taught to orient themselves in the kindergarten area, in their environment, and to put things in a definite place; when they go on an outing, they should count the toys they take along and bring back the same quantity.

They must learn to orient themselves on the street: know the name of the street on which the kindergarten is located and the address of their own apartment.

They should use their abilities to orient themselves in time: refine their notion of workdays and days off, the regularity with which certain lessons occur on certain days (music lessons, mathematics class, etc.). They should reinforce their knowledge of their own birthdays, their ages, and the name of the group. They should learn a definite daily routine.

12

Curriculum and Methods for Teaching Elementary Mathematics in the School-Preparatory Group (Six-Year-Olds)

Organizing Work with Six-Year-Old Children

The preparatory group occupies a special place in the kindergarten. The educator's task consists, on the one hand, in systematizing the children's accumulated knowledge and studying their general level of development based on all their previous developmental and educational work and, on the other hand, in giving the children psychological preparation for school, which requires a reorganization of the child's personality. During this period the children's consciousness and behavior should make the transition toward understanding their responsibility as future students and their responsibility for their own behavior. The children have acquired a great deal of empirical knowledge in kindergarten, but the transition to school means that scientific knowledge will gradually be revealed to them in increasing depth, and this requires a readiness to operate with abstract concepts. What is paramount here is not the development of individual functions alone (perception, memory, attention, etc.), but the change in the functional connections and relationships in the child's consciousness. "Consciousness evolves as a whole," L. S. Vygotskii has written, "changing its internal structure and the connection of its parts with each new stage, and not as a sum of partial changes occurring in the development of each particular function. The fate of each functional part in the development of the consciousness depends on the modification of the whole, and not the other way around" [3:242]. This modification in the functional structure of consciousness is fundamental and most essential in the development of the personality.

Children in the preparatory group are aware that they are the oldest children in kindergarten. This senior position, the fact that they are preparing to move on to school, changes their attitude toward themselves and toward the children in the other groups, just as the younger children's attitude changes toward them. "I am only in the older group; next year I will be in the preparatory group, and then I will go to school," a child says, dreaming of occupying a place in the oldest group.

For the preparatory group, the teacher should constantly bear in mind the on-going restructuring of the consciousness of the students, and should change the system of interrelationships to a certain extent. The children should be free from superfluous oversight, and their independent thinking should be encouraged, breeding confidence in their own powers, stability in their choice of interests, and a sense of purpose. It is important to confirm the children's awareness of their responsibility to the younger children and to adults. "The children in the preparatory group are the oldest; they should serve as examples for the other children and show concern for the younger ones," a teacher emphasizes. She advises them to look closely at the students' work and at their lessons at home. In subsequent conversations the children often tell about their brothers and sisters with pride—about interesting books which they are reading or about hard problems they have learned to solve in school.

Therefore, all curricular problems in the preparatory group, including elementary mathematics, must be considered, on the one hand, from the standpoint of generalizing and systematizing the children's accumulated knowledge and, on the other, from the standpoint of the children's preparation for working in school and continuity in their knowledge. But the main goal in preparing for work in school involves the children's mental development: learning mental operations—analysis, synthesis, comparison, generalization, and classification. Curriculum continuity between kindergarten and school in no way means that they do or do not have the concept of trapezoid or a "reverse problem" in the grade one curriculum; rather, it depends on whether a child is able to analyze a given figure or problem, isolate the most essential aspect, and generalize. For example, much of the topic "Numeration" is included in the kindergarten curriculum, and involves review for the children who enter school from kindergarten. But this review is extremely important for these children after the summer break in their instruction.

Thus, the curriculum for the preparatory group acquires particular significance not only for the kindergarten as the curriculum that systematizes the knowledge they have acquired in the previous group, but also as the curriculum that parents can use in preparing their children for their studies in grade one. The school-preparatory group program calls for 14 lessons a week, two of them devoted to developing the children's elementary mathematical notions. The first month of work, as in the previous groups, should be devoted to lessons, providing a repetition of the curricular material in the previous group and permitting the teacher to evaluate the level of knowledge and skills possessed by the children who are just entering kindergarten. It might prove necessary to conduct extracurricular lessons with these children to fill in certain gaps. But such lessons should not be conducted for a prolonged time: during group work the children will not only be instructed but will instruct one another as well.

Curricular Material for the Preparatory Group

Work in the preparatory group is aimed at systematizing and refining the knowledge that the children have accumulated. It encompasses the same sections as the analogous work in the previous group.

Sets. The children should be given practice in the operations of combining and complementing sets, removing a specific part of a set, and distinguishing between the terms *set* and *elements of a set* and using them correctly. The teacher should acquaint the children with the process of breaking a set into groups with an indicated number of elements or into equivalent subsets.

Number and counting. The children's skills in counting up to ten and beyond, counting sounds, counting by touch, and counting off objects from a larger quantity based on a particular number (with eyes open and closed) should be reinforced. The children should be able to count homogeneous and heterogeneous objects in any arrangement (in a circle, a square, a row, etc.). They should know the quantitative composition of a number up to ten as units (that eight is one, one, one, one, one, one, one, one). They should know that a number can be broken down into two smaller numbers, and that one larger number can be made from two smaller ones (using concrete material up to five); this is based on the operation of combining sets.

They should learn to count ordinal numbers up to ten and respond correctly to questions asking "How many?" and "Which one?"; they should distinguish between a "Which one?" question and a "What kind of?" question. They should know the preceding and following numbers for every number up to ten. They should strengthen their awareness of the reciprocal relations between consecutive numbers up to ten (seven is one more than six, six is one less than seven).

They should be able to recite the numbers in order both forwards and backwards, beginning with any number in the natural number sequence up to ten; name the numbers adjacent to a given number; name the preceding and following numbers for a specified number; and understand the expressions *before* and *after*.

They should be able to count groups consisting of two, three, or five objects; name the number of groups and the objects in each of these groups, as well as the total number of objects in all the groups (for example, three groups with three objects in each, and nine individual objects in all).

They should practice dividing a whole object into two or four equal parts (for example, cutting an apple, roll, sheet of paper, etc.). They should be able to correctly name the parts of a whole (a half, a quarter, two quarters), pointing out each of them. They should understand the significance of these terms, and realize that the whole is greater than a part, and a part is less than the whole.

The teacher should introduce the children to numerals. She should teach them to make up and solve simple addition and subtraction problems (addition where less is added to more, and subtraction where the subtrahend is less than the remainder).

The children should be familiar with the structure of a problem (the condition, the question), and should learn to compose problems based on their personal experience and with varying content (using visual materials). They should be taught techniques of adding on a second addend and counting off a subtrahend one-by-one. In problem solving, the children should be taught to reason and prove, thus developing their logical thought.

Magnitude. The children should be taught to measure length, width, and height in everyday objects around them (using conventional units of measure). They should learn to determine the volume of liquid and solid substances using conventional units of measure (for example, measuring the amount of water in a pitcher with a cup, measuring the amount of groats in a package with a mug).

The teacher should continue developing the children's "sense of weight," establishing equilibrium and determining weight by using conventional measuring devices. Sight estimation should continue to be developed, and the children should be taught to verify their sight estimates using conventional measuring devices.

Shape. The teacher should reinforce the children's conception of familiar geometric figures, so that they can name them correctly (circle, oval, triangle, square, rectangle, trapezoid, polygon, cube, sphere, cylinder, cone, bar). The children should learn to draw and compare straight line segments oriented in various positions in the plane and measure them with paper ruled off in squares.

To sharpen the children's wits, they should be taught to modify geometric figures by composing various polygons from several triangles or an entire circle from the parts of a circle. They should analyze the complex composition of a drawing consisting of different geometric figures, and analyze the shape of everyday objects and their parts. The teacher should drill them in grouping objects by shape.

Orientation in Space. The teacher should give the children practice in determining the arrangement both of objects in the classroom and of pictures on a sheet of paper. The children should learn the elementary relationships between the duration of motion and the length of the path covered (the longer the path, the more time is needed to cover it).

Orientation in time. The children should continue to practice determining the day and properly using the words *yesterday*, *today*, and *tomorrow*. They should be able to identify the days of the week and their sequence.

The teacher should develop their "sense of time," providing practice in determining duration (one minute, five or ten minutes). The children should imagine what can be done in one minute, five minutes, 10, 20, or 30 minutes. The teacher should train them to keep within an allotted time for a lesson, in their games, and in private life. The children should know the name of the current month, the sequence of the seasons of year, and the basic attributes of each.

Comparison of the curriculum for the preparatory group and the curricula for the previous groups shows that the children's knowledge is not so much being expanded as being refined, reinforced, and systematized. Comparing the curriculum for the preparatory group and for grade one (the period in which "Numeration" and "The First Ten Numbers" are studied) demonstrates their continuity and the repetition of certain curricular goals in the schools: the principle underlying the natural number sequence, the ordinal and cardinal meaning of number, elementary computation techniques based on a knowledge of the properties of the natural sequence $n \pm 1$, comparison of numbers based on comparison of specific sets or line segments, logical analysis of the text of a problem and the quantitative relations contained therein, the ability to find the necessary arithmetical operation for solving problems, the independent creation of problems from a numerical example, counting various groups and counting objects by tens, and measurement of various quantities in connection with the study of dimensions, spatial and temporal relations.

Sample Lessons in the Kindergarten
School-Preparatory Group: Set, Counting, Number

Working With Sets

In the older group the children became acquainted with the operation of combining sets and removing the correct part of a set, and with the terms "set" and "elements of a set." This knowledge continues to be reinforced in the preparatory group. Let us cite some sample lessons, which are somewhat more complicated than the analogous ones recommended for the previous group.

The children can be given pictures of objects or small toys representing various means of transport (streetcars, buses, trucks), which make up a "transportation" set. They name three parts of the set. Then they are asked to break down each of the parts into rows, give the number of elements in each part, and designate it with the appropriate numeral—for example: four streetcars, three buses, two trucks. Since all three parts have been combined into one set, the total number of elements in the entire set is counted. There turn out to be nine elements.

The teacher asks the children to explain how the total set consisting of nine elements was formed. They name the three parts and the number of elements in each part: four streetcars, three buses, and two trucks have made up the total set of nine elements. "From what smaller numbers has the number nine been obtained?" the teacher asks. "From four, three, and two," the children answer.

Another variant of an assignment on combining sets can start with two sets consisting of quite different objects—for example, one set of pictures of vegetables (one carrot, one turnip, one beet, one cucumber), and another set of pictures of fruits (one apple, one pear, one orange). The children are asked to find the number of elements in each set and "record" it with the appropriate numerals (four and three). Then, combining both sets in to a group of fruits and vegetables, the teacher asks the children to count the total number of elements in the combined set. Once they have carried out this assignment, the children should relate that they did and how they did it. "We combined two sets—that is, we joined three elements of one set to four elements in the other, and we got a combined set of seven elements. The entire set consists of two parts: one part vegetables and the other part fruit."

Thus, by combining sets, the children gradually come to understand the arithmetical operation of addition. This technique can also be used for drilling. The children are asked to make up two sets mentally, consisting of five different elements apiece, combine them, and indicate the total number of elements. For example, Misha says that in his head he has made a bouquet of two sets. One set is made up of five flowering branches (one apple tree branch, one cherry tree branch, one bird-cherry branch, one lilac branch, and one jasmine branch). He has made the other set out of five flowers (one daisy, one cornflower, one carnation, one tulip, and one violet). Combining the two sets, he has obtained a single total set of ten different plants.

As the children carried out such assignments and talk about them, they practice not only in combining parts into a single whole and in counting the elements of the parts and the whole, but also in understanding the quantitative significance of number. The material in these exercises should be varied, thus developing the children's ability to analyze and generalize, and to reflect their own practical actions in speech.

The following technique can be used for practice in removing a specified part of a set. The teacher puts some cups and saucers on the table and asks the children to name the number of objects of each kind (five cups and five saucers), say how many parts the set consists of (two), and finally determine the total number of objects (ten). Then the teacher asks them to collect the saucers and put them away in the doll cupboard. "One part, expressed by five saucers, has been removed from the set. What is left on the table after removing the five saucers?" "Another part—five cups—is left on the table." "Then we have removed five objects from a set consisting of ten objects, and five objects are left, or we have removed one part of the two parts of the set, and the other part is left," the teacher summarizes.

Exercises with sets can be highly varied. They serve as a foundation for subsequent mastery of the arithmetic operations. For example, to prepare for the operation of multiplication, the children can be asked to count the pairs of identical flags that make up a set of ten objects. Let us assume that there are flags of five different colors in this set—that is, it has five parts, and each part contains two flags.

The children can be asked to make up a set of four parts (circles of different colors), taking two circles of each color, and then counting the elements in the combined set. "What is ten equal to?" the teacher asks. "Ten circles are equal to: two, two, two, two, and another two." The children can also be asked to make a bouquet of three kinds of plants, taking three flowers of each type (this can be done on an outing or in the group, using flash cards).

These exercises are recommended for the subsequent mastery of the operation of division (both according to content and into equal parts).

The children are given a set of ten geometric figures in an envelope. They are asked to find the identical figures and break them down by groups, then to count the total number of figures in the entire set and the number of objects in each group, and finally to determine the number of groups. They say that there are ten geometric figures in the envelope, and that there are two of each type of figure. They count five groups in all. "How many elements did the whole set consist of?" "Ten elements." "How many elements were in each part of the set?" "Two elements in each of the five parts."

The children keep this set at their desks, and the teacher gives them another envelope, also consisting of ten figures, but with only two types. As in the preceding instance, the children find the identical figures, counting them in each of the groups and counting the total number of all the figures. In this case, the conclusion is again that the set consists of ten elements, with two parts in all and five elements in each part. The teacher asks them to compare both sets, to think about them ,and tell what is common to them and what is different. "There are ten figures in the first and second envelopes, but there are two figures in each part in the first envelope, and five parts in all in it, while in the second envelope there are five figures in each part, and two parts in all," the children answer.

In another instance a set of nine flags is provided. One child is called upon to divide them equally among three children, after which he relates: "I had nine flags, I gave them out to three children, and everyone got three flags apiece." "How many flags were there in your set?" "Nine flags." "How many parts did you divide the nine flags into?" "Three parts." "How many flags were in each part?" "Three flags apiece." "How else can we name all the flags?" "A set." "How many parts did you divide this set into?" "Three parts." "How many elements were in each part?" "Three elements each."

On the next occasion, the children are seated at their desks and are given two boxes and some envelopes containing ten identical circles. They are asked to count the total number of circles and divide them up equally in the two boxes. The result: the ten circles are divided into two parts, each containing five circles. Then the boxes are left in front of the children, and they are given five small plates and some envelopes containing ten triangles. They are again asked to divide the triangles equally on the five plates. The conclusion is drawn that they have divided the ten triangles into five parts, with two triangles lying on each of their plates.

As the children compare the two operations with sets, they find what is common about them and what is distinct. "I had a set of ten circles and a set of ten triangles. We divided the ten circles into two parts, with five circles in each part; but we divided the other set of ten triangles into five parts, with each part containing two triangles."

As a result of such exercises as these, the children can conclude that the same number of elements in a set, the greater the number of parts into which these elements are to be divided, the fewer elements there will be in each part.

Thus, by performing various practical operations with sets, counting the elements in sets and the number of parts, and expressing all this in speech, the children learn the concept of a set and elementary concepts of correlation among the elements of a set. This is very important for their general mathematical development.

Furthermore, by combining sets, removing part of a set, and identifying the common and different elements, the children analyze the assignment, develop the ability to isolate the most fundamental, essential aspect in it, and display ingenuity. All this is not merely based on verbal exercises, it is also based on actual operation with a variety of sets. The notion of a set is no longer confined to external identity of elements, as in the initial stages: it becomes more mobile, flexible, and sophisticated. Now the children start to understand that they need not always indicate a number: they can confine oneself to enumerating the names of the elements. For example, in comparing the parts included in a set by establishing a correspondence between their elements, the children can determine their equivalence or non-equivalence without resorting to counting.

The children also understand that the concept of an element changes: in one instance an individual object will be an element, and in another a whole group of objects will be an element.

Quantity and counting. Children's skills at counting up to ten, using various analyzers (visual, auditory, etc.) are reinforced in the preparatory group by the same techniques as in the previous group. Here primary attention should be paid to reproducing a set based on a specific number; it is very important for the children to practice remembering several numbers at once, by connecting them with the object names, the qualitative features, and spatial arrangement.

Exercises in remembering numbers can be varied. For example, the teacher might give a child the tasks of counting off six bunnies, three ducks, and two cards, dividing the six bunnies equally between Vera and Misha, giving the three ducks to Roza, and putting the two cards on the shelf. "Remember what I told you," the teacher stresses. At first the child can be asked to repeat the assignment aloud, but later the child must learn to grasp it at once, to think it over without resorting to repetition. After the assignment is done, it is important for the child to tell he did and how he did it. The verbal account reflects in the consciousness the operation that has been performed—that is, it provides for the operation to be transferred onto a mental plane.

In this example, numbers were attributed to various objects, but it is important to teach the children to connect them with the qualitative attributes of the same objects and with whatever measurement operations are involved. Let us give an example of these assignments.

The children are asked to draw six triangles: two red, three blue, and one green. They are given paper ruled off in squares, with the size of the triangles indicated: six squares for the base, and four squares for the height. To avoid imitation, pairs of children who share one desk can be given different assignments. As they do the assignment, the children tell what they have drawn, how they did it, and how many they drew. Of course, there is no need to call on all the children, but everyone should be prepared for an oral response and should learn to reflect his own actions in words.

Counting Objects in any Arrangement. The Development of Spatial Orientation in the Plane

In the five-year-old group children were shown techniques of counting objects in various arrangements. These skills are reinforced in the preparatory group. But what is paramount is to lead the children to the generalization that counting can start with any object, in any direction, and the number will stay the same.

It should be noted that children who have not undergone training in the younger and intermediate groups often attempt to count from right to left and vertically, away from themselves. This tendency, which is characteristic of small children, is sometimes retained for a long time. Even in grade one, as the children make the word "ma-ma" from letters, they might arrange the letters from right to left ("am-am"); the children make the same mistakes in the spatial arrangement of numerals, placing and reading them in order, but from right to left—9, 8, 7, 6, 5, 4, 3, 2, 1. Therefore, while emphasizing that it is possible to count the elements in a set by starting with any element, the teacher should give constant attention to **structuring the hand and eye movements from left to right and from top down.** It is highly advisable to give the children practice in arranging numerals or geometric figures by dictation.

Children who are about to enter school should be able to orient themselves clearly in the plane (in their notebook) and should understand such expressions as "going three squares from the top down" or "moving four squares from the left edge" or "let's make a right margin of five squares."

Assignments for drawing lines from dictation can promote this sort of orientation. For example, the children are asked to draw a line segment "five squares long" on the horizontal (Figure 19), going five squares from the left edge of the sheet of paper, and going ten squares from the top. Then they are to draw a segment in the vertical direction, counting down six squares, and to draw a line segment of five squares horizontally to the right from the end of the vertical line, after which they are again to drop down vertically four squares. Then, turning left, they are to draw a horizontal segment ten squares long and connect the beginning of the first (upper) horizontal line with the end of the bottom horizontal line, and count the number of squares occupied by the last line (ten squares). They can be asked to guess why the vertical line on the left is ten squares long. The children say that its length is equal to the length of the two lines that extend down: one was six squares long, and the other was four squares long. "Who can guess why the bottom line must be ten squares?" the teacher asks. The children compare this line with the top lines and give their explanation aloud.

This sort of dictation gives the children practice in the proper arrangement of lines in the plane, determining the direction of their motion, and remembering the lengths of segments expressed in conventional units of measure—squares. The questions asked at the end of the lesson develop mental activity and the ability to conjecture.

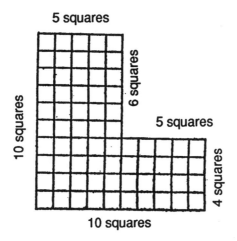

Figure 19.

Introducing Children to Numerals as Conventional Signs of Number

When children have learned to count freely and understand the significance of number as an indicator of the magnitude of a set, they can be introduced to numerals as conventional signs of number, or as symbols. Practical experience has shown that most five-year-old children are well oriented in numerals; they recognize the number of buses, trolleys, houses, and apartments; they distinguish monetary symbols by numerals; and so on. As they remember a picture of a numeral, they do not yet understand that a numeral is a conventional sign for a number, similar to other signs such as + (add), - (subtract), = (equal to), (greater than), and (less than). Therefore, it is advisable to acquaint them with numerals along with other symbolic designations, but to do so only in the preparatory group. This introduction to elementary symbols raises the children's mental development to a new and even higher level. Let us give several variants of lessons on introducing children to numerals and the conventional signs (equals, greater than, less than).

When she asks the children to count any group of objects, such as six dolls, the teacher can call attention to the fact that the number of dolls can be discovered without actually seeing them, but by merely looking at a card showing six circles on a strip. The teacher asks the children to recall when they did this earlier. The children remember that they were looking for a group of toys, putting cards near them that show the same number of circles. The teacher confirms that the children's recollections are correct, and says that dolls can be conditionally represented by circles. "Should the circles always be arranged in a row?" The teacher is suggesting a new idea to the children. After hearing several answers, she shows a number configuration. "Can the number of our dolls be represented by this number configuration?" (Figure 20). The children nod their heads affirmatively. The teacher puts down several groups of toys (e.g., three) asking three children to designate each of the groups of toys by an appropriate number configuration. The children do the assignment. "But the circles in the number configuration have to be counted, just like dolls. Doesn't anyone know how grownups designate number without counting the circles on the card, so that they will know at once that one card is three, another is five, and still another is eight? Who can guess?"

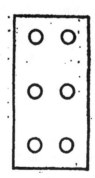

Figure 20.

Of course, there are always children in the group who will say that adults designate numbers (write) with numerals. Confirming the answer, the teacher says that now the children will also designate numbers by numerals, but that they need to learn to distinguish them. "Who already knows some numerals, and where have you seen them?" the teacher asks, to stimulate the children to recall their own experience. "Lesha says that he knows a streetcar with the number 8 on it, but what does the number 8 mean on the streetcar?" The children explain that people determine the streetcar's route by its number, rather than the number of streetcars.

The children go on recalling where and in what circumstances adults use numerals as conventional signs. "Can the numeral signs also show a number of objects?" the teacher asks. The children or the teacher cite some appropriate examples. Then the teacher holds up one object and designates it by the numeral 1, holds up two objects and designates them by the numeral 2, and holds up three objects and designates them by the numeral 3. The children practice distinguishing these three numerals, which are different in their configurations and are easy to remember. Then they silently select an appropriate number of objects for the numeral that has been exhibited (first at the teacher's desk, and later at their own desks).

The children learn the numerals easily. Special attention need only be given to those that are somewhat similar; subtler differentiation is needed to distinguish between them—for example, 1, 4, and 7; 2 and 5; 6 and 9; 3 and 8. Therefore, it is best not to study the numerals in order, but rather to group them according to the way they are written. For instance, the teacher might devote one lesson to the numerals 1 and 4, with the children selecting a quantity of objects accordingly. As they learn numerals, the children pay close attention to their configurations, comparing the way they are written and analyzing their details (establishing what is common and what is different). For example, the numeral 1, which looks like a stick, has a small "tail" going to the left at the top—a small, oblique, straight stick. The numeral 4 also has a stick on the right, while a small corner is connected to its upper left-hand part. In comparing the numerals

1 and 4, the children describe their differences, "drawing" them in the air.

In the next lesson they work with the numerals 1 and 4 and are introduced to a new numeral, 7, comparing they way it is written with the numerals 1 and 4, which they already know. The numeral 7 also contains a stick, like the numeral 1, but it is slanted rather than straight, and at the top left it has what appears to be a short wavy line, adjoining the stick; sometimes the stick is intersected by another small horizontal line.

"How does the numeral 7 differ from the numeral 4?" the teacher asks. The children, examining the 4 and 7, find the similarities and differences. Then come exercises on distinguishing these three numerals and on forming their connections with numbers. The teacher exhibits each of them in turn, and the children name the numerals and collect appropriate quantities of objects at their own desks (one child can work at the teacher's desk as a check).

Then the children are given three numerals apiece. The teacher puts a certain quantity of individual toys on her desk, and the children are to say how many of them there are, holding up the appropriate numeral. But a numeral can also designate the number of parts (subsets) in any one set—for example, there might be seven toys in all, and four parts among them: one group of ducks, one group of geese, one group of hens, and one group of chicks—four groups in all.

The next lesson can be devoted to the numerals 2 and 5, and the way they are written can be analyzed and compared in the same way. The children realize that the 2 has a circle on the top left, and the 5 has a semicircle on the bottom right, that the 5 has a wavy line on top, like the 7, while the 2 has the same sort of line on the bottom.

The numerals 6 and 9 should be analyzed in the same way, emphasizing that the circle is located at the bottom of the 6 but at the top of the 9, and they are turned in different directions. Finally, the children learn the numerals 3 and 8, which differ because the 8 consists of two ovals and the 3 consists of two semi-ovals open to the left.

Lessons with examples are recommended for reinforcing the children's knowledge. The teacher holds up a numeral, and the children count out small objects corresponding to it, putting them on their desks, find appropriate cards with number configurations, or repeat a corresponding number of movements.

A lesson can be conducted in another way. For example, the teacher might knock several times first on one object, then another, or might show quantity in the form of a number configuration or on a card showing objects, or might put several objects on her desk, with the children holding up the corresponding numerals each time.

Becoming acquainted with the numerals creates no particular difficulties for the children, but it is a new stage in the development of the concept of number. Better mastery of the way in which a numeral is written can be promoted by analyzing it and sketching it with broad movements in the air.

No more than one or two lessons are needed for studying each pair of numerals, and six or seven are required for learning all the numerals. Exercises on distinguishing numerals can be given in lessons with other curricular objectives or during outdoor games such as "Find the Pair" or "Cars and Garages."

The Quantitative Significance of Number. Its Unit Structure from Six to Ten

In the five-year-old group, children have already become learned about the quantitative significance of the first five numbers as composed of units. This work continues in the preparatory group with the numbers from six to ten, where the teacher is able to use the techniques the children have already learned. It is also advisable to connect this work with operations on sets.

Since the children have had practice in drawing various objects whose quantity corresponds to a specified number, this technique can also be recommended in the preparatory group. The children can be asked, for example, to draw six different geometric figures on graph paper. They draw one circle, one oval, one square, one rectangle, one trapezoid, and one triangle, and "read" their drawings by naming the shape and the number. "How many different shapes have you drawn? What does the number six consist of?" the teacher asks. "The number six consists of one, one, one, one, one, and another one—that is, six ones," the children answer. They begin to call the number one a unit, and this is reinforced in the study of the other numbers. "How many units are there in the number nine?" the teacher asks. "The number nine consists of nine units: one, one, one, one, one, one, one, one and another one," the children are quick to answer.

Studying the Composition of a Number from Two Smaller Numbers

Children work up to the study of a number composed of two smaller numbers as they do exercises with sets. In determining the number of parts in a finite set, the children learn that a part is less than the whole. As they compare the parts of a set by establishing a correspondence between their elements (without resorting to counting with number-words), they see that these parts can be equal or unequal in number. Finally, by counting the elements in each part of a set, they establish what numbers constitute a certain number. These and similar exercises demonstrate that just as a set can be made up of different parts, so too can a number be made up of smaller numbers.

But a number of studies (L. A. Yablokov, N. A. Menchinskaya, A. M. Leushina, E. I. Korzakova, etc.) have shown that children who have not mastered operations with sets perceive a set or a number as a single, indivisible whole. Even at the age of seven, these children sometimes have trouble answering the question, "How many fish are there in all if there are six fish on the table and four fish in the box?" Counting each group of fish separately, the children usually respond that there are six and four of them. Teaching children to separate out the components of a set helps overcome this narrow notion of a set and creates a sensory basis for understanding number composition.

A qualification needs to be made here: according to the aforementioned monographic method, the breaking of a number down into smaller numbers, like the separating of the parts of a set, has nothing in common with the study of number composition. That study amounted to mechanical memorization that, for instance, the number six consists of five and one, four and two, three and three, two and four, and one and five, as was illustrated using concrete material.

In the present case, children learn that a number is composed of two smaller numbers not by memorization, but by understanding that a set can be composed either of homogeneous or of heterogeneous elements, a series of groups or parts whose number can be counted, so that one group can be compared with another to determine whether or not they are equivalent.

Because a number is an index of the capacity of finite sets, the number serves as an index both for the set as a whole and for its individual parts (subsets), but since the part is less than the whole, a number can consist of smaller numbers. While the children operate with sets, they begin to understand that, just a single set can be made by combining individual parts, so too can a new, larger number be obtained by combining smaller numbers. It is these concepts that are important for the children to form, rather than mechanical memorization of number composition.

Studies by E. I. Korzakova have shown that children also broke down sets into parts when studying number composition by the monographic method—for example, they would put some pebbles on one side and some on the other, and say that at first they had seven pebbles, but now there were four in one group and three in the other. However, they could not connect these small numbers into one because they did not understand the relations between the parts and the whole, between the number and its units.

When children are taught operations with sets or the operation of counting, their development takes quite a different course. Children in the preparatory group know that a number consists of a certain number of units equal to the number itself. They know how the natural number sequence is formed, they understand the reciprocal relations among the natural numbers, and they know each number's place among the other numbers and can substantiate it. All this enables the children to understand easily that every number can be broken down into units or into other numbers.

The study of breaking the numbers up to five into two smaller numbers has practical significance for the preparation for computation in kindergarten. In order to add three to four, the number three must be broken down into units and, using the technique of adding on, the second term must be added one by one: four + (one + one + one). Or it can be done in another way: four + (two + one). At this age it is important to arm the children with both these methods of adding on. To do so, they must know the composition of the first five numbers from smaller numbers.

Various techniques can be used for studying number composition. Here is one of them. The teacher takes some circles that are red on one side and blue on the other. Laying down three circles of one color and counting them, the teacher indicates that the number three in this instance is made up of three circles that are identical in color: one, one, and another one. But a set called by the number three can also be made up of elements of two colors: the teacher turns the third circle over and asks the children what is the color of the circles that make up the set. The children answer that the set identified by the number three consists of two red circles and one blue one. Then the teacher turns another circle over, and the children see that now three is composed of one red circle and two blue ones.

Summarizing the children's response, the teacher stresses that the number three can be composed in various ways: taking two and one or one and two. Three circles can be broken down in another way, too—for example, by placing one circle on one strip and two circles on another strip; taken together there will be three of them, as before. The teacher proposes that all the children do this assignment and, dividing the circles on the two strips as they wish, tell who did what.

The following assignments can be recommended: the children draw four triangles (or any other figures) and color them in two colors as they please. When the children are questioned, the different variants for composing the number four from triangles of two colors are disclosed.

As the children practice, they make sets of three, four, and five elements from two parts differing in color (or shape or size), and on this basis they find out which smaller numbers can make up the numbers three, four, or five.

In addition to color, the attribute of the spatial arrangement of subsets can be used. For example, a child is given five pebbles (or five circles or small toys) and is asked to take some of them in one hand and some in the other. The other children are to guess how many pebbles he has in each hand. Those who guess right go on to a new assignment.

A variant of this assignment can be a request to divide a group of five toys between two children. Those who receive the toys get up and show the children how many they received and how many there were in all. It is important for the teacher to watch the children's answers, which should indicate both the **total number** and its **components**. "I had five flags in all, and I gave three flags to Irina and two to Volodya. Irina and Volodya together have five flags. This means that the number five can be composed of three and two."

As the children gain practice in decomposing sets on a certain basis, they sometimes do not confine themselves to two subsets, but single out three or four parts in a set. But the lessons must be kept gradual and sequential. In the preparatory group the children decompose a number and compose it only from two smaller numbers:

the number 2: 1 and 1
the number 3: 2 and 1, 1 and 2
the number 4: 3 and 1, 2 and 2, 1 and 3
the number 5: 4 and 1, 3 and 2, 2 and 3, 1 and 4.

In studying number composition, it can also be pointed out to the children that the circles in number configurations (which the children use starting in the five-year-old group) are always arranged in small groups. This helps them identify a number configuration not by merely recognizing the external form and its association with a number-word, but by combining and unifying a small number of groups into a single whole.

In such instances, the child will identify the set in any form of arrangement.

Exercises in breaking down the first five natural numbers into two groups and instruction in uniting smaller numbers into a single number prepare children for learning the arithmetic operations, in which we are always working with at least two numbers.

Reinforcing Ordinal Counting Skills up to Ten

The study of ordinal counting is begun in the previous group, but there is a reinforcement of the knowledge acquired in the preparatory group.[1] The principal objective is to teach children to differentiate clearly between ordinal and cardinal numbers, to make conscious use of both cardinal and ordinal numerals, responding properly to questions that ask, "How many?" or "Which one in order?" (not to be confused with the question "Which one?", which is used to clarify a qualitative attribute). The children gradually understand that number has dual meaning: cardinal and ordinal. A cardinal number shows the result of counting objects independently of the order in which they were counted (it is important for all the objects to be counted, and each one only once). But an ordinal number shows the number's place in the natural number sequence, its position among the other numbers.

In the preparatory group it is important to expand the children's notions of the use of ordinal numerals in practical life. The children should be told that objects that have received their numbers are subsequently recognized only by the number—for example, we number the seats in theaters, trains, and airplanes; buildings and apartments within buildings; streetcars and bus routes, etc. Numbering helps us distinguish one object from another, to find the necessary seat or apartment, and so on.

Reinforcing Children's Knowledge of Reciprocal Relations Between Numbers

When comparing sets and establishing one-to-one correspondences among their elements, children already learn to distinguish larger and smaller numbers in the intermediate group. By the age of five, they understand why one number is greater (or smaller) than another and know how to make an equality out of an inequality in sets represented by consecutive numbers. But they have learned all of this in a practical way, using concrete sets. The goal of instruction in the preparatory group is to lead the children to understand the reciprocal relations among numbers: **each natural number** n is one greater than the preceding number and one less than the following number ($n \pm 1$); they can then master the difference relations between consecutive numbers.

Of course, children in the preparatory group still find broad generalizations of the principle for constructing the natural number sequence inaccessible, but this is not essential. Based on the comparison of sets, they can already compare numbers, actually explaining and showing why one number is greater or less than another, and can establish different relations between them, proving that their answers are correct. This is why the work is more complex than in the previous groups.

In the preparatory group it is important to apply the techniques of increasing or decreasing a set by one in practice, enlisting the various analyzers (visual, auditory, tactile, and motor). This can also contribute to the reinforcement of the knowledge of numerals.

For example, the teacher can put the numeral 6 on the display board, asking the children to count out a number of triangles that is one less, and a number of circles that is one more. The children lay out five triangles and seven circles on their desks, and the teacher places six squares on her own table. She asks the children to compare the number of circles, squares, and triangles and show which number is greater than which. "Seven is greater than six, and six is greater than five," Sasha says. "Now what can be said about the number seven and the number five?" the teacher asks. The children start thinking, but then they guess that the number seven is greater than five. "Which of these numbers is less than the others?" The children look at the triangles, squares and circles, and answer that five is less than six and six is less than seven. "What can we say about the numbers five and seven?" The children quickly arrive at the conclusion that "Five is less than seven." Thus, the children gradually come to understand transitive relations, which are quite important and, as research and practice have shown, entirely accessible to the children [1:25].

These assignments on increasing and decreasing a number, as well as on equalizing numbers, can be varied: they can be keyed to knocking, jumping, throwing a ball, taking one step more or less than indicated by a numeral or specified orally. The assignments can be carried out in writing using cards with numerals and signs: "Knock on the desk just as many times as there are circles on the board, and write this in numerals and signs." The child writes $8 = 8$ and reads: "Eight is equal to eight." "Why did you put in the equal sign?" "Because the words *just as many as* indicate equality and are represented by the = (equal) sign," answers the child.

The following lesson can be conducted for comparing numbers. The teacher puts the numerals eight and seven on the board and asks the children to think about which of the numbers indicated by the numerals is larger (or smaller) than which. At this stage it is advisable to acquaint the children with such conventional signs as greater than (>) and less than (<). Knowing the signs, the children can show that $8>7$ and $7<8$. This evokes fresh interest in comparing consecutive and equal numbers. But the assertions that the number eight is greater than seven and, on the other hand, seven is less than eight, should actually be proved by the children. A child who is called upon rapidly places circles on the top and bottom strips one for one, showing that the last circle in the set of eight does not have a corresponding circle in the set of seven arranged on the bottom strip. "What must be done to establish equality between the number seven and the number eight?" the teacher asks. "We must either add one circle to seven, and then there will be eight apiece in the two sets, or else take away one from eight, and then there will be seven in each of the sets," the child answers and, actually carrying out both variants, puts the appropriate numerals and signs under each: $8 = 8$ and $7 = 7$.

Let us give another variant of this assignment. The teacher shows a numeral to the children and asks them to name the number that is one greater (or less). The children hold up the corresponding numeral. The next time, the teacher calls a child to her desk, gives him a card with buttons on it, and asks him to determine their number by touch. The child must find the appropriate numeral and put it near the card of buttons so that all the children can see it. The teacher asks the next child to jump across one fewer button than the numeral shows, and all the children are to select one more small object than the child has picked and designate that set with a numeral. "Why has your answer turned out to be equal to the number of buttons on the card?" the teacher asks, stimulating the children to think. The children start thinking. But some are ready to give an explanation at once: "You told Misha to jump one time less than there were buttons, and you told us that we should go one more than Misha jumped. That brought us back to the same number and the same numeral as on the card of buttons. First the number was reduced by one, and then it increased by one. It remained as before."

The curriculum calls for children to know how to count from any number (up to ten) both forwards and backwards, and name the number adjacent to a specified number. The exercises described above also prepare the children to do this. It should be emphasized that the teacher's task is not to train the children to name the numbers forwards and backwards: it is important for them to understand a number from two aspects—as a cardinal number in its relation to one, and as an ordinal in its relations with the adjacent numbers. If the children have learned this well, they will begin counting forwards and backwards from any number quite consciously.

Another exercise for comparing numbers is oral counting, forwards and backwards from any number. This technique is well known among teachers. The teacher names a number, and the child gives the following or preceding number, as previously indicated by the teacher. "Seven," the teacher says. "Eight," answers the child. "Nine." "Ten." The numbers are recited backwards in the same way: "Eight." "Seven." "Nine." "Eight." "Six." "Five."

Then the teacher asks the child to recite several numbers instead of one—for example, the next three or four after a given number, first forwards and then backwards. The teacher puts up the numeral 5 and asks the children to name the next four numbers. "Six, seven, eight, nine," the children say. The teacher holds up the numeral seven and asks them to name the four preceding numbers. "Six, five, four, three," the children respond.

Where should attention be focused? The children are not saying a number that is spoken or held up by the teacher: they are supposed to immediately name the following or preceding numbers. They should not be trained to search for a number by starting from one (as is often done by children who have not grasped the relations between numbers). If the children still whisper to themselves, naming the numbers, they do not understand the relations between consecutive numbers. Therefore, training in mechanically memorizing the order of the numbers starting from one will do nothing for the children's development. But if considerable attention is given to mastering the relations between consecutive numbers in forward and reverse order during previous work with the children, they will have no difficulty reciting the numbers starting from any number.

The next type of exercise in finding adjacent numbers consists in responding properly to a question asking "Guess what number I have left out." The teacher says, "Six—eight." And she asks, "What number have I left out?" The children answer, "The number seven." The numbers can also be named in reverse order: ten—eight, seven— five, six—four, and so on. For variety, the children might be asked to find the missing number in a sequence of numbers given by the teacher in forward and reverse order, such as "four, five, seven, eight," or "six, five, three, two."

The next assignment is "Name the neighbors." The teacher names one number, and the children are to name those adjacent to it. For example: "Name the neighbors of the number six." The children give seven and five. They can also be asked to omit a number between two specified numbers. They themselves can practice looking for consecutive numbers, using visual aids (cf. Figures 8 and 9 in Appendix B). Practical experience has shown that children who have an inadequate mastery of the relations between consecutive numbers most frequently give only the numbers one—three, and are unable to name the others. These difficulties indicate poor preparation, failure to understand the reciprocal relationships, and a need to return to the curriculum for the previous group. Then the children should be introduced to the expressions *before* and *after* a number, with the explanation that *before* requires that they name a smaller number, while *after* requires a larger number.

The teacher may also not only name the number aloud, but also demonstrate the numeral in such assignments as these. For example, the teacher might hold up the numerals 6 and 8, asking the children to find the missing numeral, or hold up the numeral 7 and ask them to "find the neighbors" (cf. Appendix B, Figures 8 and 9).

It should be recalled that a spoken number and a displayed numeral are not equivalent: a visual image of a numeral and an image reproduced on the basis of words require different efforts. Searching for an answer on the basis of an oral specifications requires greater concentration, attention, and mobilization of what the child knows. But the teacher can use both techniques.

All these techniques (exercises) will be useful only if the children have already studied the relations between consecutive numbers using visual material, since the techniques are geared toward reinforcing rather than revealing the notions of the reciprocal relations between numbers in the natural number sequence.

It should be noted that the children respond to these techniques with interest, but employing only these methods often results in one-sided notions about numbers, as if they were only ordinal. It is important for the children to indicate as they compare numbers that one number is greater than another because its quantity of units is greater than those for the preceding number, or to demonstrate how the numbers correspond by means of physical objects. The teacher cannot be satisfied with the answer that seven is greater than six, since it is important for the children's concept of number to be backed up by proper notions of the magnitude of the set reflected in a certain number, and not merely the order in which the numbers come. This is why special attention is devoted to developing the children's quantitative relations between sets on the basis of establishing a correspondence between their elements throughout the years of schooling.

Counting Groups

In the five-year-old group the children have already learned that it is possible to count groups consisting of several objects, as well as individual objects, sounds, or movements ("individual entities"). In the preparatory group the children can be reminded that adults sometimes count groups all at once, not just individual objects, e.g., eggs in fives or tens; a set of dishes (a tea service or tableware) consists of a group of different objects, but is perceived as a single set. With this experience as a support, the children can be given exercises in counting groups.

Assignments can be varied by increasing the number of objects in a group or increasing the number of groups; for example, some objects are grouped in fives, and there are two groups in all. The teacher asks the children to remember which objects in real life are grouped by fives and what such a group is called.[2] The children count the number of fives. Then the teacher asks, "What must be done to increase the number of groups?" As they carry out the assignment, the children explain, "For the number of groups to be increased in a single set, we must decrease the number of objects in each group. At first I had five objects apiece, and there were two groups, but now I've put two more objects in each group, and there are more groups—five."

In one lesson the children are asked to string some clay beads that have not yet hardened on a wire in groups of ten. The ten-bead chains can be painted different colors and, if the wires are joined, a chain can be made of groups of ten, which number can be either increased or decreased. "Take two groups, with ten objects in each, increase the chain by one group of ten, and tell how many groups you have," the teacher says. "I had two groups, I increased the chain by one group, and then I had three groups, with ten objects in each." "Remember what we call a group with ten objects." "A ten." "How many tens do you have?" "Three tens." "Which is greater—three tens or two tens?" "Three tens is one ten more than two tens." "Take two flags and increase the group by one flag. How many flags will you have?" "There will be three flags," Zhenya answers, "in the same way as on the chain, where we increase the two tens by one ten."

Thus the children are taught to count groups, establishing an analogy between counting individual objects up to 10 and counting particular groups (tens).

Consolidating Techniques of Dividing an Object into Two or Four Equal Parts

In the five-year-old group the children divided squares, rectangles, circles, apples, and other objects into two and four equal parts. They know that a part is less than the whole, they know what the parts are called (a half, a quarter), and they know that an object must be divided precisely in order for the parts to be equal (two halves, four quarters). The same techniques are also used in the preparatory group, and several additional new techniques are gradually introduced. For example, the children draw a segment of 10 squares on graph paper and are asked to divide it in half. "But how can it be done?" the teacher asks. Some say that the segment must be measured with a measuring device, with the measuring device folded in half. Others believe that the middle can be shown by sight (but how can we verify that the eye has not made a mistake?). Still others propose counting off one square at a time on each side to obtain equal numbers of squares. Others say that they know that five and five will be ten, and so they should count off five squares and mark the middle at that point. The teacher approves the children's answers and states that all the methods are correct. "But which one is handier? If a segment is drawn on the graph paper, what is the easiest way to find half of it?" "How do you divide it if there are eight squares, for instance?" "Count off one square apiece from the ends of the line so that the segments will be equal: there will be four and four." "Can a segment set up like a column be divided in this way?" the teacher asks and proposes drawing such a straight-line segment six squares, going vertically. The children draw it, count off one square from each end of the segment, and mark off its midpoint. Three squares from either side of the midpoint. "What do we call these squares? Who can guess?" "Conventional measures," the children answer.

Another possible variant of this kind of assignment involves drawing the segments on unruled paper. The teacher gives all the children a measuring device of roughly 10 cm and asks them to draw a number of segments in different orientations—horizontal, vertical, and inclined— and then find their midpoints. "There are no squares here," the children say. "Think about how to divide it in half using the measure." The children fold the measure in half, measuring and marking off the midpoint on a segment. To provide verbal reinforcement for the operation, the teacher asks them to tell how they have done it. Then she asks them to draw two more segments—one vertical and the other horizontal—and to divide them into four parts. The children themselves guess that the measuring device will have to be folded in half twice. The teacher asks them to tell about the parts into which they have divided the segments they have drawn, what these parts are called, and how many of them there are in each segment.

The parts of equal, one of which has been cut in two and another into four parts, are compared, and the children determine which is larger or smaller.

The children learn not only to divide objects into equal parts but also to understand that the part is less than the whole, and the parts of a single whole become smaller as the whole is divided into a greater number of parts. In this way, the children learn new functional connections and acquire a visual foundation for subsequent understanding (in school) of fractions. The teacher works the children's knowledge into their practical activity as well. For example, as they help a cook make a salad, the children try dividing a carrot, potato, or onion into two or four equal parts.

Let us summarize. In all groups, including the preparatory group, the teacher teaches the children the operation of counting. The teacher develops the first elementary concepts of set, number, the system of the natural sequence, and the reciprocal relationships among numbers; she brings the children to an elementary comprehension of the fundamentals of the number system—counting groups of objects. On a practical level, she acquaints the children with the whole and its parts—that is, she creates a basis for the future understanding of fractions.

Teaching children to count, while always dealing with concrete sets (objects, sounds, movements), is the principal task of pre-school instruction. Counting is the basis for subsequent school instruction in computation, which basically deals with numbers and other mathematical categories. The development of counting and the concomitant formation of certain concepts is very closely related to the development of the children's mental activity and arouses their interest in mathematics, engendering a positive emotional attitude toward acquiring mathematical knowledge. Methods of teaching counting are designed to stimulate the children's thinking and ingenuity, and to instruct them to work with concentration.

When the children have mastered the various operations with sets and counting, and the concepts that are developed at the same time, they can learn a new activity—computation, which is taught primarily in school. But the children should be introduced to the elements of this activity in the preparatory group so that their preparation for learning arithmetic in school can be verified.

What is the basic distinction between these two types of activity? **Counting always deals with specific sets**, whether these sets are made up of objects, sounds, or movements. The elements in these sets are tangible or visible; they are perceived by the various perceptual analyzers. Based on the concrete activity of counting, the children begin to develop an entire system of abstract concepts: number, the natural number sequence, the relations between numbers (cardinal and ordinal), and so forth.

Computation is more abstract, since it deals with numbers, and a number is an abstract concept. Computation is founded on the various arithmetic operations, which are abstract concepts, generalizations of the respective operations on sets. As the child masters computation, his thinking becomes increasingly divorced from the concrete and rises to the level of operating with abstract concepts, symbols, formulas, and schemata.

The success of this transition is depends on how completely the child has learned to count, as he develops, accumulates, and sharpens concepts without which the transition to computation would be impossible. This is why this transition must begin in kindergarten: in this way it is possible to verify whether everything has been done to prepare the children, reveal essential imperfections in the preschool period, strive to eliminate the imperfections, and, as the children go on to school, document the gaps in their knowledge so that the next teacher can attend to them in due course.

Teaching Children Elementary Computation

The issue of how to begin teaching computation has long been a topic of discussion among teachers and methodologists—whether to begin with numerical examples or arithmetic problems. Some have argued that instruction should begin with numerical examples, which makes it easier to demonstrate the computation technique, while others have preferred starting with arithmetic problems.

At present the schools simultaneously give problems and numerical examples on which elementary problems are based. Thus, relying on the children's ability to increase or decrease a number by one, an assignment is given to draw a segment 5 cm long (rather than five squares long), and then increasing its length by 1 cm. Then this assignment is converted into a problem. The question is asked: "What is now the length of the segment?" The children carry out the assignment, explain how they did it, and answer the question.

As another example, the following problem is presented: "A boy was to make three flags, but he made one flag fewer. How many flags did the boy make?" The children analyze the problem's structure and record the arithmetic operation in the form of a numerical example.

In practice, preschools commonly acquaint children with arithmetic operations and computation techniques based on simple problems which reflect the actions of the children themselves. A problem helps them understand, for example, the point of finding the sum of two addends. Diversity in addition and subtraction problems promotes a growing awareness of the meaning of frequent terms such as *add, subtract, is obtained, will remain,* that is, an understanding of the meaning of the arithmetic operations.

How Children Master the Essence of an Arithmetic Problem

Mastering the simplest problem requires that the children analyze its content, isolate the numerical data, and understand both the relations among the data and the operations to be performed. In solving a problem, the children move from simply ascertaining the number of surrounding objects and phenomena to an awareness of the complex quantitative relations among them.

Studies have shown that children are not immediately aware of the structure of a problem. Instruction must promote this awareness. Once they grasp the condition of a problem, as distinct from a story or a riddle, the children must understand the relations between the numerical data.

The statement of the question in a problem presents particular complexity for children. Why is this so difficult? The question determines the problem's essence, directs the child's thinking toward the relations between the numerical data, and helps him understand the nature of the empirical operation and find the appropriate arithmetic operation that must be performed. But a question contains two aspects—a practical, social aspect and an arithmetic aspect. The child does not yet differentiate between them; he perceives the question in a problem as a personal appeal to himself. The child is accustomed to having to answer a question when asked, instead of repeating it. Therefore, when children are repeating a problem, they do not as a rule reproduce the question, but include an answer in the problem; they are in a hurry to provide an answer to the question. They do not yet know any other function for the question. To bring the new aspect of a question for the children—the arithmetic aspect—the teacher should at first rely on what they already know, putting each of them in the position of someone who is inventing a problem which the others are, to solve. In this situation the necessity of the question becomes obvious to the person assigning the problem. Mixing questions of different types also helps children understand the significance of the question in an arithmetic problem. The children should gradually comprehend that **the question directs their attention to the relations between the numerical data and to an understanding of what needs to be found out in the problem.**

Solving various problems should lead the children to understand the essence of the arithmetic operations, to understand that these operations on numbers generalize the multifaceted human practical activity with sets. This activity is reflected in such generalized concepts as *add*, *subtract*, *is obtained*, and *is equal to*, with the numbers themselves the indices of the capacity of sets. Learning all these mathematical terms raises the children's thinking to generalization of the actual empirical operations.

The children do not immediately master the meaning of a sum, either. At first a sum is taken to be the actual union of sets. But a sum is merely a mental addition of numbers. Therefore, the preliminary work in combining different subsets into a single set, isolating a part of a set, and so forth, is essential in preparing children to learn the meaning of the arithmetic operations.

The mastery of elementary computation techniques (adding on and counting off by ones) is promoted by the children's understanding of the natural number sequence and the reciprocal relations between consecutive numbers and the relations between any number and one (the fact that a number is quantitatively composed of units). Therefore, a great deal of attention is also given to these questions when children are taught to count. This is why children who do not understand these relations cannot, as a rule, rise to a mastery of computation techniques, and their counting remains at the level of practical activity (they count both terms again or they count the remainder). Solving problems in representational form is inaccessible to these children, for it requires the ability to break down a number into units mentally and a distinct comprehension of the relations between consecutive numbers.

Methods of Teaching Children to Solve Arithmetic Problems in Kindergarten

Selecting Numerical Data from an Addition Table

To acquaint the children with problems, arithmetic operations, and solution methods, the numerical data on which the problems are to be constructed must first be determined. The "Education Curriculum" indicates that in kindergarten the arithmetic operations of addition are limited to cases where a smaller number is added to a larger one, and the subtraction operations involve a subtrahend that is less than the remainder. In order to understand this stipulation in the curriculum, we must analyze the table of addition within the limits of ten and to established what has motivated these limitations.

The addition table can tentatively be divided into three parts. The first includes cases where the sum does not exceed five. The second part includes cases where the first addend is greater than or equal to the second addend $(3 + 3, 4 + 4, 5 + 5)$. The third part includes cases where a larger number is added to a smaller number.

Addition Table

Part I   Part II

1 + 1	2 + 1	3 + 1	4 + 1	5 + 1	6 + 1	7 + 1	8 + 1	9 + 1
1 + 2	2 + 2	3 + 2	4 + 2	5 + 2	6 + 2	7 + 2	8 + 2	
1 + 3	2 + 3	3 + 3	4 + 3	5 + 3	6 + 3	7 + 3		
1 + 4	2 + 4	3 + 4	4 + 4	5 + 4	6 + 4			
1 + 5	2 + 5	3 + 5	4 + 5	5 + 5				
1 + 6	2 + 6	3 + 6	4 + 6					
1 + 7	2 + 7	3 + 7						
1 + 8	2 + 8							
1 + 9								

Part III

The first ten numbers include just as many cases of subtraction as addition: the second term is subtracted from the sum: $5 + 2 = 7$; $7 - 2 = 5$; $5 + 3 = 8$; $8 - 3 = 5$; and so forth.

The first row in the table is nothing other than a presentation of the relations between the natural numbers in succession in terms of arithmetic operations; when one is subtracted, the relations between consecutive numbers in reverse order are represented. The second and third rows in the addition table basically include cases where a smaller number is added to a larger one in addition, and in the reverse operation the number to be subtracted is less than or equal to the remainder.

For example:

| 4 - 2 | 5 - 2 | 6 - 2 | 7 - 2 | 8 - 2 | 9 - 2 | 10 - 2 |
| | | 6 - 3 | 7 - 3 | 8 - 3 | 9 - 3 | 10 - 3 |

The first part of the table includes cases of addition and subtraction up to five. But children usually have no trouble memorizing these five cases of addition and four cases of subtraction—as the inverse of the corresponding cases of addition— and do not solve them by counting off one by one. If the children are using these techniques, decomposing the numbers two and three into units and adding them on and counting them off present no difficulties. Therefore, the first three rows in the addition table and the inverse instances of subtraction are selected for teaching the children computation.

Since in kindergarten basically only one computation technique is given—adding on and counting off by units, the second addend or the subtrahend, expressed by the numbers two or three, and only in special cases by the number four $(5 + 4, 6 + 4, 9 - 4, 10 - 4)$, is easily broken down into units so that it can be added on and counted off.

As for the third part of the addition table, which will be studied in school and in which a larger number is added to a smaller one, introducing the pupils to the technique of transposing addends simplifies the solution: when the addends are transposed, all of them reduce to cases included in the second or first part of the table $(2 + 6, 6 + 2; 3 + 7, 7 + 3;$ etc.). This is why the study of the first and second parts of the table has special significance, and there is no need to hurry on to the third part in kindergarten.

What laws and properties of arithmetic operations do computation techniques depend upon? **The technique of adding on depends on the associative property of addition.** It is known that the result does not change whether we are add a number right away or whether we break it down into smaller numbers and add them one by one. For example: $4 + 3 = 4 + 1 + 1 + 1 + 1 = 4 + 2 + 1 = 7$.

But adding or taking away by units is easier in the first stages of instruction, since increasing or decreasing a number by one unit depends on counting—on the children's understanding of the reciprocal relations between the natural numbers.

The need to ensure accessible and consistent instruction means that the teacher should select instances of addition where the second addend is the numbers one, two, or three, and they are added to numbers from one to ten, without moving beyond those limits. It should be noted that subtraction is studied parallel to addition, and the same numbers one, two, and three are to be subtracted using the technique of counting off one by one.

Planning the Study of Problems and Arithmetic Operations

Study of how children learn computation makes it possible to plan work with the children so that curricular material will be distributed. Two successive stages have been noted in teaching problem solving.

Stage I. The children are told what a problem is and shown how it is composed, and its components are explained—that is, they are introduced to its structure (the condition, in which the relations between the numerical data in the problem are presented, and the question). The children are taught to repeat both a whole problem and its basic parts, to pose a question independently, and to answer it correctly by solving the problem. They are familiar with problem-solving methods and the arithmetic operations they must perform in order to find a solution, and they learn to formulate these operations (addition and subtraction). They learn to make practical distinctions in the **components of these operations: the addends (the first and second) in addition and the minuend and the subtrahend in subtraction.** In order to focus the children's attention on these issues, it is advisable to stay within the limits of elementary numerical data at this stage, which would cause no difficulties for the children (adding the number one to every number in the first ten, and the reverse operation of subtraction). The children solve these problems with ease, since they depend on a knowledge of the natural number sequence in ascending and descending order.

Within this stage, however, it is advisable to move gradually. When studying the structure of a problem, the children learn at first to give only the correct answer to the problem's question; they are not yet required to formulate the arithmetic operation. Only later do they learn to distinguish and formulate the operations of addition and subtraction and to distinguish the components of these operations, learning to "record" them by means of cards showing numerals and signs. At the **second stage** the problem introduces more complex numerical data, where first the number two, and then the number three, becomes the second addend or the subtrahend. At this stage the principal objective is **to teach the children techniques of computation through adding on and counting off one by one.** They break the second addend into units and, without counting the first addend again (they know the number from the problem), they add the second addend to it one by one. Analogously, in subtraction, they take the subtrahend away from the minuend one by one (to subtract two from six: six take away one is five, five take away one is four. Therefore, if we subtract two from six, we get four).

It should be noted that teachers themselves often make mistakes such as perceiving the expressions *count* and *add on* as synonymous. Counting, as an activity, is geared toward determining all the elements in a set, and always begins with the number one. However, **adding on is a method of computation whereby a number is added to a certain number, as a sort of complement to it.** Therefore, since the first addend is given in advance, the second addend is to be added on in parts (in this instance, in units). Illustrating problem-solving methods should further children's mastery of the technique of adding on (or counting off) rather than counting. Therefore, after showing a set of objects representing the first addend (or minuend), it is recommended that the objects be hidden (putting mushrooms in a basket or pencils in a box, for example), or that the first addend (or minuend) be covered with a handkerchief, as G. V. Bel'tyukova suggests for first-graders, or else that the first addend be left exposed and named, outlining it by a circular movement. This reinforces the need to remember the number in the given set and add the second addend to it by units.

The teacher should also move gradually in the second stage. First the children are taught to add and take away the number two— that is, they study the second row in the addition table and the corresponding cases of subtraction—and then they move on to adding and taking away the number three one by one—they study the third row in the table. The preparatory group need go no further. But, of course, studying the fourth row in the table is not prohibited— adding and taking away the number four—again, first by adding on and counting off one by one. But here the children can be shown another technique—adding on and counting off a group of two all at once, since they have already studied the second row in the addition table and have memorized many of the sums. However, this should not be hurried: it is much more important for the children to develop stable, fully conscious skills in adding on and counting off the second addend one by one.

Gradual and orderly study of computation is best; it provides for systematic mastery of new material by not overloading the children. Children's acquisition of new knowledge and joy at their own success make their interest in counting lessons increase.

Children who master the curricular material in the preparatory group are fully prepared to study grade one arithmetic, since the instruction process in kindergarten promotes not only specific knowledge and abilities, but also general development: an interest in counting and a positive emotional attitude toward arithmetic; stimulation and development of mental operations (analysis, synthesis, generalization in combination with concretization, the ability to operate with elementary concepts and abstractions).

Problems are commonly divided into simple and compound. A simple problem contains one operation, while a compound problem contains several operations. In some simple problems the arithmetic seems to follow directly from the content. For example: "Lesha had four red flags, and he was given another blue flag. How many flags did Lesha have now?" The words *was given* indicate that Lesha's flags have increased in number, and therefore we are to perform the operation of addition.

Thus, while the question in some problems seems to prompt the operation to be performed, in other problems the question seems to contradict the content: it requires the restoration of a previous situation. Nevertheless, both types of problems are quite accessible to children in the preparatory group in a certain sequence. The children should first learn to solve problems of the first kind. But as they understand the essence of the arithmetic operations and learn the solution methods, solving problems of the second kind also becomes feasible, although at first with simplified numerical data (where the second addend or the subtrahend is one).

The children should not be hurried to compose oral problems either: it is most important for the children to understand what a problem is—to analyze its structure.

Types of Visual Material used for Problem Solving

Based on the nature of the material, problems can tentatively be divided into dramatization problems, picture problems, and illustration problems. Each type of problem has its own special features and highlights certain points (the theme or subject-matter, the nature of the relations between numerical data, etc.), developing the ability to select the necessary everyday material and teaching logical thought.

The unique aspect of a **dramatization problem** is that its content directly reflects the lives of the children—what they have just been doing or what they usually do. For example, the teacher has Sasha bring four flags and put them in a container, while Lena brings one flag and holds it in her hands. "What can we say about Sasha and Lena?" The children make up a story to go with the problem's condition. "What can we find out from this story?" "We can find out what color flag Sasha brought and what color Lena brought, and where they took them." "But then it's not a problem, but a story. In a computation problem we always want to find out about numbers. Therefore what question can we put in the problem about Sasha and Lena?" "How many flags did they both bring together?"

The point of a dramatization problem is revealed in a highly visual way. The children begin to understand that a problem always reflects people's concrete lives. K. D. Ushinskii has written: "Problems should be selected to be practical, based on the children's life, and with good teachers it turns out that an arithmetic problem is at the same time an entertaining story, a lesson in agriculture or home economics, a lesson with a historical and statistical theme, or an exercise in language" [2:532-533].

By teaching children to consider real life in the content of a problem, we promote a more profound cognition of life and teach them to consider phenomena in diverse connections, including quantitative relations. Dramatization problems are particularly valuable at the early stage in instruction. The children learn to compose problems about themselves, tell about one another's actions, and pose a question for solution. The structure of a problem becomes accessible to them.

Picture problems are prepared in advance, some of them from published sources. These problems can be quite varied. In some of them everything is predetermined: subject-matter, content, and numerical data. For example, three trees and one stump are drawn in a picture. Only a few problem variants can be composed with these facts. "Three trees are growing in a clearing, and another one has been cut down, leaving only a stump. How many trees were growing in the clearing?" This is how the children frequently formulate the problem. It can also be composed in a somewhat different way: "Some trees were growing in a clearing. When one was cut down, three trees were left. How many trees were there in the clearing at first?"

But picture problems can have a more dynamic character. For instance, a picture panel is provided, showing a lake and a shore; a forest is drawn on the shoreline. Cuts are made in the pictures of the lake, the shore, and the forest, and small drawings of various objects can be inserted in the slots. Collections of ten such things (ducks, mushrooms, rabbits, birds, etc.) are to be placed in the picture. Thus, the subject-matter is predetermined here, but the numerical data and the content of the problem can be varied to a certain extent (the ducks can swim or go ashore, or a hunter can shoot them), just as different variants of problems about mushrooms, rabbits, or birds can be made up (see Color Figure 6).

The teacher can also make a picture problem and ask the children to think up the condition. For example, the teacher might draw a bowl containing five apples, while one apple stands on the table near the bowl. The children can make up an addition and subtraction problem.

Illustration problems occupy a special place in the system of visual aids. While everything is predetermined in dramatization problems, and there are only partial restrictions on the theme, subject-matter, and numerical data in picture problems, illustration problems, with the aid of toys, provide scope for a variety of subject-matter and imaginative play (only the theme and the numerical data are restricted). For instance, five ducks are standing on a table at the left, and one drake at the right. The problem's content (its condition) can be varied to reflect the children's knowledge of their environment or their experience. These problems stimulate recollection of interesting occasions, develop the imagination, teach children to select facts in their logical connections from memory, develop their ability to devise problems on their own, and lead them to solve and compose oral problems. Thus all these visual aids promote mastery of the meaning and essence of arithmetic problems and their structure.

Methods of Introducing the Structure of a Problem

It was indicated above that dramatization problems are most convenient for helping children master the structure of problems, since they reflect the children's own activity. For example, they have just learned to compose a number from two smaller numbers. Vanya is called upon to take four circles in one hand and one circle in the other. The children have to guess how many circles Vanya has in both hands together. This kind of subject-matter can be converted into a problem. "I can make up a problem about Vanya," the teacher says. The children are on the alert, ready to hear something new. "Vanya took four circles in his right hand, and one circle in his left. How many circles are in both of Vanya's hands?" The children answer, "Five." "Right. Now you and I have solved the problem. Like in school! Now we'll make up a problem about what we are going to do, a problem about ourselves." The teachers gives an assignment that the children are accustomed to, calling on a certain child to do it. For example, the teacher might ask Lesha to count the buttons sewn on a card without looking at them. Lesha counts and says that there are eight. The teacher asks Nina to take one more button. Nina does the assignment—taking nine buttons. "I can also make up a problem about Lesha and Nina. Lesha counted eight buttons on the card, and Nina took one more button than Lesha had. How many buttons did Nina take? Who will answer the question?" All the children answer, "Nine." "How many buttons did you take, Nina?" "Nine buttons" (demonstrates). "You see, we not only made up a problem and solved it; we have even checked it."

Then the teacher can have the children make up similar problems. The teacher asks Masha to bring seven flags and put them in one glass, and to put just one flag in another glass. Masha does the assignment. The teacher asks the children to make up a problem about Masha. "Masha put seven flags in one glass and one flag in another glass, and there are eight in all," Serezha says. "Serezha, did somebody really ask you to tell how many flags in all Masha has put down? Repeat what Masha did." Serezha repeats the content of his problem, but does not know how to finish and what to say. "You did a good job of telling the children what Masha did, but the children should find that out from your problem: what color were the flags that Masha put down, or something else?" "I want them to guess how many flags Masha put in the two glasses." "Children, have you understood what you are to find out from the problem that Serezha has thought up?" The children respond. This is generally how instruction in solving and making up computation problems can begin.

At this initial stage it is very important to show the children how a problem differs from a story or a riddle, emphasizing the significance and nature of the question. For this purpose, the teacher gives various assignments.

For example, the teacher calls upon two girls and one boy, puts them on either side of the desk and asks the other children to tell something about these children. Knowing that they are to make up a problem, the children relate: "You put two girls on one side of the desk and one boy on the other side." The teacher immediately observes: "You have not said what can be found out about them. Then I will ask you: what are these children's names?" The children laugh: "That's not a problem; that's a story." "Why isn't it a problem? I've asked a question." "Not that kind," the children say. "Then ask a question yourselves so that it will be clear that this is a problem." "How many children did you call to your desk?" "How many children are standing on either side of the desk?"—the children themselves propose possible questions. "What is being asked about in the problems? Remember the problems that you and I have already solved." "How many in all?" or "How many were left," the children say. "That's true—the question in problems often begins with the words 'how many,' but are 'how many' really the only words in the problem?" The teacher exhibits the numeral 8 and asks the children to place the corresponding number of circles on their desks. "How many circles have you put down?" she asks, turning to the children. "Eight." "Why?" "Because you showed the numeral 8." "Now see, I asked you how many circles you put down, but have you really solved the problem?" "No, it's not a problem, but we can think up a problem," the children observe. "So what is being found in a problem if the question 'How many?' is asked?" "A set... A number...," the children say.

"Yes, a problem often tells about certain sets, which are expressed in numbers. And these numbers are either to be added or, if one of the numbers is to be decreased, we subtract a specified number from it. These sets in problems are called numbers. The question in a problem indicates that an operation is to be done with these numbers (adding or subtracting)." To show how a problem differs from a story and to emphasize the significance of numbers and the question in a problem, the teacher asks the children to listen to it and guess where the story is and where the problem is. "Several girls and boys came to us from the five-year-old group and began to play." The children say that this is a story, not a problem; it cannot be solved since the teacher has not said how many boys and how many girls came into the group, and did not ask a question for a problem. The teacher says something else: "Three boys and one girl came to us from the 5-year-old group and began to play. How many children came to our group?" "Now it's a problem," the children remark with satisfaction.

To teach the children to distinguish a problem from a riddle, the teacher selects a riddle where there are numerical data. "Two rings, two points, and a rivet in the middle. What is it?" "That's not a problem, but a riddle," the children say. "But there are numbers," the teacher says. But the children say that this kind of problem cannot be solved by doing operations with numbers: here something is being described, and one is to find out what it is. "It's a pair of scissors—I've heard that riddle," Mara says.

In introducing the children to the condition of a problem, it is important to emphasize particularly that in a computation problem there are numerical data, and there should be no less than two of them.

For example, after giving several geese and ducks to a child, the teacher proposes the following problem text: "I gave geese and ducks to Lena. How many birds did I give to Lena?" The children laugh, saying that such a problem cannot be solved, since it has not indicated how many geese and how many ducks were given to her. Lena herself makes up a problem, asking the children to solve it: "Maria Petrovna gave me eight ducks and one goose. How many birds did Maria Petrovna give me?" "Now it's a problem; it can be solved. Nine birds in all," the children say.

To demonstrate that there must be no fewer than two numbers in a problem, the teacher intentionally leaves out one piece of numerical data: "Valerik held four balloons in his hands, and some of them blew away. How many balloons did Valerik have left?"

The children start to think. "How many balloons did Valerik have?" Borya asks. "Four balloons." "But you didn't say how many blew away," Ira observes. "You said 'some,' but how many is some? You don't take away 'some' from four balloons." "It can't be solved that way!..." "Two numbers need to be named, not one," the excited voices ring out.

The teacher agrees that the problem was given imprecisely, since the second number was not specified, and says that there should always be two numbers in a problem. Then she repeats the problem in a somewhat altered form. "Valerik held four balloons in his hands, and one of them blew away. How many balloons did Valerik have left?" The children solve the problem with pleasure.

Specific examples from everyday life make the children more clearly cognizant of the need for two numbers in the condition of a computation problem and better master the relations between numbers and the meaning of the arithmetic operations, which they are actually performing without yet formulating.

After such exercises the children can arrive at a generalized understanding of the components of a problem. Every computation problem consists of a condition and a question. There are two numbers in the condition. But what is mentioned in the condition? The condition contains the relation between the numerical data. Analyzing the condition enables the children to understand the arithmetic operations to be performed. Once they clarify the structure of a problem, the children easily single out its individual parts. Then they should practice repeating a problem as a whole as well as its individual parts. Some can be asked to repeat the condition, others the question, and they can be asked to formulate it themselves.

If the children are making up a problem, let some make up the condition and others ask the question. Sometimes they should be asked to pick out the numerical data from the problem's condition and state whether these numbers are to be added or subtracted from one another, and then explain why the child thinks that it should be done in one way rather than another.

Methods of Introducing the Arithmetic Operations (Addition and Subtraction)

At the beginning stage the children find the answer to a problem without yet considering what operation they are performing. They rely on their previous experience in operating with sets and on their knowledge of the reciprocal relations between consecutive numbers.But as soon as they learn the structure of a problem, the arithmetic operations addition and subtraction can be treated explicitly, the meaning of these operations can be pointed out, and they can learn to formulate them. What new problems arise when this is done? Arithmetic operations are performed with numbers rather than sets. Therefore, in leading the children to formulate arithmetic operations, the teacher must provide a gradual transition from operations with objects to operations with abstract numbers.

Let us give several examples of how this can be done. The teacher notes that the children have learned to make up problems, devising the condition of a problem and posing a question to go with it. The teacher proposes making up a problem on the basis of carrying out a practical assignment, e.g., putting five red circles on the top strip, and one blue circle on the bottom. "I've put five red circles on the top strip and one blue one on the bottom," Sasha says. "What can we find out from Sasha's problem—what question should be asked?" Zina formulates the question: "How many circles did Sasha put on both strips?" The children answer. After questioning several children, the teacher assigns a new question: "How did you find out that there are six circles on both strips?" The children respond in various ways: "We counted," "We know that five and one are six," "We were taught long ago that five and one are six," "We know that six is more and five is less," "We added five and one, and that was six." Summarizing their responses, the teacher makes special note of the last one: "Sima was right in saying that we must add two numbers named in the problem—that is, perform addition. We connected the five circles in our minds with one more circle, and we got six circles. But do we need to connect all the circles on one strip? "No, we don't," the children say. "Why not?" The children start thinking. The teacher explains, "Because in our head we add numbers, not circles. We only imagine that we are putting the circles together. Earlier we united two sets into one and counted up the elements again. Now we have added only the numbers in our heads. This is called the operation of addition. And so, **adding one number to another and only mentally connecting two sets that are named with numbers is called the operation of addition.** Now repeat: what is the operation called?" "The operation of addition," the children say.

"Now you and I are not only going to answer the question in the problem, but also explain what operation we are doing." The teacher reminds the children how to talk about this operation. "We must tell about the operation of addition in this way: 'We add one circle to five circles, and we get six circles.'" The teacher asks the children to repeat the formulation of the addition operation in the problem they have solved. "But how do we answer the question? Remember what we are supposed to find out in the problem." The children repeat the question, "How many circles did Sasha put on both strips?" The teacher indicates that the problem's question must be answered in this way: "Sasha put six circles on both strips." The children repeat the formulation of the addition operation and the answer.

Several more problems are composed to go with actual previous operations. The children learn to formulate the operation of addition and answer the question. In the beginning stages of instruction, it is a good idea to illustrate problem-solving with concrete material. "We take five red circles" (the five circles are pointed out with a gesture), "and we add one blue circle" (with a circular gesture around the second addend), "and we get six circles" (with a circular gesture uniting the two addends). But the arithmetic operation should gradually be abstracted from the concrete material: "Which number are we adding to which?" the teacher asks. "We are adding the number one to the number five, and we get six." "How did we get six? How do we answer the question?" and so forth.

Therefore, as the meaning and the method of the operation are assimilated, it can be formulated without naming objects, and, by merely answering the question, the children can return to the specific name of the resulting sum.

When the children have essentially mastered the formulation of addition, the teacher proposes that they create another problem that can be solved by subtraction. Again the problem is based on an actual operation proposed by the teacher, "Yura puts six dolls on the table, and Tamara asks Yura for one doll." The children make up a problem about Yura and Tamara.

Sasha says, "Yura put six dolls on the table, and Tamara asked him for one doll, and he gave it to her." Zhenya repeats the problem's condition, and Natasha poses a question for it, "How many dolls did Yura have left?" The teacher asks Lyusya to repeat the question for the problem. Lyusya says confusedly, "How many were left?" "Were left on what? Blocks?"

Research Library
AIMS Education Foundation
Fresno CA 93747-8120

the teacher asks. All the children laugh. Lyusya says, "How many dolls were left on the table?" "Why have they turned out to be on the table?" Lyusya is confused, she has not followed the actions of Yura and Tamara. Nina helps her, "How many dolls did Yura have left after he gave one doll to Tamara?" Lyusya is asked to repeat the question, "How many dolls did Yura have left?" "How many dolls were left?" the teacher asks. Many children, including Misha, answer, "Five. Five. Five." The children remark to Misha that he has not indicated five of what. "You mean jackets?" they laugh. "Five dolls," Misha corrects his answer. "Is it clear to everyone who had five dolls left?" Misha makes his answer more precise, "Yura had five dolls left." As we see, the teacher works with the children in formulating a precise response.

"How did you learn right away that Yura had five dolls left?" the teacher asks. One of the children says that they see them; others say that they know that five is less than six. "We took away," others say. "We took away one," Serezha says. "But you didn't say what you took it away from," Nina protests. The teacher enjoins the children to learn not only to answer the problem's question correctly, but also to tell what is to be done with the numbers in the problem. "Now you have said that you 'took away' one doll from Yura's dolls, but he might resent that: he gave it away himself. Therefore, it's better to say it another way. But how? Who can guess?" The children begin thinking and are silent. The teacher explains how to formulate the operation of subtraction. "Subtract one doll from six dolls, and you get five dolls. This operation is called subtraction." Then she explains that **in the operation of subtraction we subtract a smaller number from a greater one and obtain a remainder.**

The children should learn to use this precise formulation of subtraction. "What number are we subtracting what other number from?" asks the teacher. "We are subtracting one from the number six, and we get five," the children say. Then the teacher returns to the problem under consideration, asking the children to remember the question, and indicates how to answer it: "Yura had five dolls left."

Thus, instruction in formulating arithmetic operations is a new stage in the children's development. But this new stage depends on all the previous work. The children have repeatedly demonstrated by practical activity that by combining five red flags with two blue ones, they create a set of seven flags. But in the preparatory group they learn to express this operation of uniting sets in the form of the arithmetic operation of addition. Therefore, the transition stage for formulating the arithmetic operation is naming the objects that the problem calls for adding together: two flags are added to five flags, and seven flags in all are obtained. Only at the next stage can they formulate the problem in terms of abstract numbers $(5 + 2 = 7)$. This gradual development is characterized by a transition in their thinking from the concrete to the abstract.

The transition to operating with abstract numerical material must not be hurried. Such abstract concepts as *number* and *arithmetic operation* become accessible only as a result of children's exercises with concrete material over a long period of time, which is precisely what the methods presented here are aimed at achieving.

As they start to learn about arithmetic operations, the children perceive the words "add" and "take away" (but not "subtract") in problem-solving in terms of their everyday meaning. Since the conditions of a problem reflect actual everyday experience in increasing or decreasing a number of objects, a problem can contain other common expressions, such as *gave, arrived* (for the operation of addition), or *flew away, dropped out, ran away, walked away,* or *took away* (for subtraction).

But the words *add, subtract, is obtained,* and *is equal to* are concepts, special mathematical terms reflecting the generalization of varied practical operations performed by humans. In addition, one number is to be added to another; in subtraction, one number is to be subtracted from another, and we say that the result *is obtained* or *is equal to.* Special attention should be paid to the abstraction of the words *add, subtract, is obtained* and *is equal to.* But abstract concepts should always rest upon concrete notions. Therefore, premature operation with abstract concepts can lead to formalism in what the children know.

In working with children, the teacher must show them how to distinguish between problems requiring different arithmetic operations. For this purpose the following technique can be used. The teacher asks someone to put down five chairs at first, and then tells the same child to add another chair. The children make up the text of the problem: "At first he put five chairs around the table, and then he added another. How many chairs has he put there in all?"

The teacher asks them to listen to another problem, compare the two, and tell whether they are the same or different, and how they differ: "The boy put five chairs around the table, and then he took one chair and put it at another table. How many chairs were left around the table?"

The children immediately see that the problems are different: "In our problem we had to add, and in yours we had to take away," Lara says. Directing attention to Lara's brief answer, the teacher asks the children: "Does everyone understand what Lara said?" Rimma notes that it is unclear, since Lara has not said what one chair is to be added to or what one chair is to be taken away from. The teacher asks Rimma to correct Lara's answer. "These problems are different," Rimma says. "They are about the boy, but they are different. In the first problem he has added one chair, and in the other he took away one chair." "Has Rimma said everything?" the teacher asks a new question. "She didn't say what we take away from and what we are adding to," one child observes. "She didn't say what operation is to be performed," another says. "Right. We have to say what operation is to be performed, and tell about it." Kolya gives a complete answer: "In the first problem it is stated that one chair was added to five chairs; that means we are to add the numbers: add one to five, and get six. That is the addition operation. In the second problem it is stated that one chair was taken away from five chairs, and that means we must subtract one from five, and get four. That is subtraction."

"And how will you answer the questions in the first and second problems?" the teacher asks. "In the first problem it asks how many chairs the boy placed around the table. We should answer this way: 'The boy placed six chairs.' In the second problem it is asked how many chairs were left at the table. The answer is like this: 'There were four chairs left at the table.' Are the problems the same or different?" "The problems are different." The teacher stresses in conclusion that these problems are different: one problem involves addition, and the other involves subtraction.

The children's attention should also be directed toward the difference in the questions included in the addition and subtraction problems. The teacher asks them to remember the questions and compare them. Repeating both questions, the children focus their attention on them and perceive the difference between them more precisely. The teacher points out the connection between the question and the operation to be performed.

Based on their analysis of these problems, the children conclude that they are similar, first, in the discussion of the boy and his placement of chairs in both problems, that is, common content, and second, in the fact that the same numbers are involved in both problems. They are different because of the boy's different actions: in one problem he brings another chair, and in the other he takes one chair away from the ones already at the table. The questions in the problems are different, as are the arithmetic operations (addition, subtraction) and the answers.

This sort of comparison and analysis of problems is useful to the children. They show a better understanding of both the problem content and the meaning of the questions conditioned by the content.

Observations show that children learn to formulate the question more easily for subtraction than for addition. This is apparently due to the fact that the formulation of a question requiring subtraction is more stable, since at this stage the children primarily solve problems where they are required to find only a remainder. Therefore, the question in the problem is almost always formulated in the same way: "How many were left?" or "How many will be left?" In addition problems, however, the question will vary; its formulation depends on the actual operation performed in the problem. "How many chairs did the boy place around the table in all?" "How many geometric figures did the children put on the two strips?" and so forth. The necessity of combining the beginning of a question, "How many... in all" with the physical operations (verbs) specified in the condition of a problem diversifies the formulation of the question.

It should be noted that certain children also tend to standardize the formulation of the question in addition. They limit themselves in every instance to something like: "How many were there?" It is advisable to ask the children to think about how to express their ideas more precisely and formulate questions for problems more correctly.

When they understand the point of the arithmetic operations and have learned to formulate them, they can move on to a more detailed though elementary analysis of problem content, without repeating the problem. For this purpose such questions as the following should be asked: "What is discussed in this problem? What is said? What is asked in the problem? What should be done to solve this problem?" or "What should be done to answer the question in the problem?"

At first the children often give only monosyllabic answers. For example, in answering the question, "What is discussed in this problem?" they say, "Chairs," merely identifying the theme of the problem. "But what is said about chairs in the problem?" the teacher asks a supplementary question. "First the boy put five chairs at the table, and then he added another chair." "What question has been posed in the problem?" "How many in all?" "In all of what, apples? Pieces of candy?" The children laugh, "No, how many chairs in all?" "Where—in our group?"— the teacher insists, thus showing the logical necessity for a precise answer. "No. How many chairs did the boy put around the table?" the child refines his question for the problem. "What is to be done to solve this problem?" A monosyllabic response often occurs again: "Add," in which the entire operation is not formulated. "But think about what you have to do in order to answer the question in the problem, what operation you have to perform, how to tell about it." "We must add one chair to five chairs, and we get six chairs." "How will you answer the question asked in the problem?" "The boy put six chairs around the table."

We have cited an example of teaching children to analyze a problem, isolate the numerical data and their relations in the problem, use their ability to properly formulate a question to go with the problem (the arithmetic operation), and give a complete, detailed answer to that question.

The teacher should not accept incomplete answers from the children ("Take away," "Add," and so forth). An incomplete answer can be interpreted in different ways, and someone else might not understand what the child is talking about. The arithmetic operation must be formulated properly.

In analyzing a problem it is very important to get all the children to consider a better, more precise answer, and to hear the children out patiently. When the children use abbreviated answers in a situation that is obvious to them, they sometimes make mistakes in their own conclusions and deductions or are unable to substantiate their opinions. Therefore, even after formulating the operation and the answer to a question, it is sometimes useful to discuss with the children the problem that they have just solved, checking their understanding of its structure, their computation techniques, and their answer to the question. "How many numbers were there in the problem that we solved?" "Two numbers." "Could only one number have been given?" "No, you can't solve a problem with one number; there have to be no fewer than two." "What are the numbers?" "Five and one." "Which number have we added to which?" "We added the smaller number to the larger one." "What question was asked in the problem?" "How many chairs in all did the boy put at the table?" "What operation was used to solve this problem?" "The operation of addition." "Why?" "Problems of this kind are solved by the operation of addition." "How was this operation formulated?" "Add one to five, and you get six." "What answer was given to the question?" "The boy put six chairs at the table."

This conversation trains the children to think logically and construct proper answers to questions about the subject matter and design of a problem, the numerical data and their relations, the choice of arithmetic operation (substantiating that choice), and the formulation of the arithmetic operation.

When the differences between the arithmetic operations have been thoroughly mastered and the children can solve the problem freely, for the sake of variety it is quite acceptable to show the children a few symbols. Since the children in the preparatory group do not yet know how to write, the notation is made with cards showing numerals and signs. The children already know the signs =, >, <, and the numerals; therefore they need to be shown only the signs for "add" (+) and "subtract" (-). It should be explained to them that the point of the + end and - signs is to economize on what has to be written down. It takes a relatively long time to write the words "add" or "subtract," it is inconvenient, and so people have thought of replacing the words by these signs.

The teacher may suggest writing down the aforementioned problem about the boy and the chairs, for example. She shows how it should be done putting the cards for 5 + 1 = 6 on the feltboard and reading the notation. "What operations have we written here?" the teacher asks. "The operation of addition," the children answer and read it, at the teacher's request.

Another operation is recorded: subtraction, considered as a variant of the same problem: 5 - 1 = 4. The children name the operation and read it themselves.

For the purpose of practice in distinguishing the written forms of subtraction and addition, the teacher can write down several numerical examples, putting cards on the display board. The teacher asks the children to read them.

All the children can be asked to "write down" whatever operation they wish in the form of numerals and signs at their own desks, and then read their notation. It is particularly important to call upon those children who have made mistakes in their notation by placing the numerals and signs improperly. If they read the notation, the children will find their mistakes faster.

Recording the arithmetic operations promotes better differentiation of them. Therefore, all the children record a previously solved problem at their seats, and one does it at the display board. The children compare their notations with the notation on the board, and anyone who finds a mistake raises his or her hand. The child tells where the mistake was made and how the notation can be corrected.

Assorted visual materials should thus be used in working on problems. By virtue of the diversity of visual aids, the children learn what is most important: in a problem we are always concerned with things that actually occur in everyday life. The teacher should watch to see that the conditions of the problems do not violate the logic of life and that the children learn to invent problems with different content based on a variety of everyday situations. Using various visual aids and recording the operations convinces the children that there are always two numbers in any problem, by means of which a third—either a sum or a difference—is to be found.

It is very important for the children to be active, solving the problem together, correcting and supplementing one another's answers.

It is also very important to teach the children to learn according to the general curriculum and to focus their attention on general matters, for preschool children are still inclined to concern themselves with what interests them subjectively at a given moment. Teaching them to work together is one of the principal tasks of kindergarten.

Instruction in Computation Techniques

After the children learn the structure of a problem and the arithmetic operations of addition and subtraction, they can be introduced to computation techniques. Although the number one was the second addend or the subtrahend at the first stage, now they can be shown how to add or take away the numbers two and three. However, this transition must also be gradual: first the children learn to add and take away the number two, and only then the number three.

Their attention should be focused primarily on the fact that they need not count the first addend again (it is given by the problem's condition); the number two must be added to it immediately, by being broken down into units. "Who remembers and knows how many units there are in the number two?" the teacher stimulates the children to think. This question might give the children pause at first. "Who knows and remembers how many different objects are needed to make up the set called by the number two?" the teacher asks (she has posed this question repeatedly in the study of the quantitative composition of a number from units). The children are animated, and many raise their hands. "The number two consists of one and another one," they answer.

Comprehension of the techniques of adding on and counting off is considerably refined when the children have learned to record an arithmetic operation; the conventional symbols raise their level of generalization. For example, when it is explained that the second addend must be broken down into units to add it to the first addend, the written notation reveals this operation to the children in a graphic way. Therefore, if the children are familiar with numerals and signs, the teacher can ask them to think about how to record an operation using the signs they have learned. The teacher calls on one child, who arranges the numerals and signs in this way: 2 (followed by a space). "What is the number two equal to if you want to show us how it is made up of units?" The child places the numerals 1 and another 1 next to the 2. "Think about what signs need to connect these numerals so we can read what you have recorded." The child inserts an equality sign, but cannot make up his mind to make further notations, even though he understands that he is not finished. Another boy is called upon to assist him. He takes the "+" sign and puts it between the units, then reads the notation: "It's equal to two if you add one to one: $2 = 1 + 1$." "If two is equal to one unit and another one, then two can be added not all at once, but one by one," the teacher explains.

In order to add the second term to the first one by one, without counting it, the children must have a thorough knowledge of the relations between consecutive numbers. They have had extensive practice in doing this in both the five-year-old and the present groups.

The teacher puts four ducks on her desk to the children's left and two ducks to their right, asking the children to make up a problem. They make up different versions, one of which is selected for solution. "First, a hunter shot four ducks, then two more. How many ducks in all did the hunter shoot?" "What do we have to do in order to answer the problem's question?" the teacher asks. "We need to add two ducks to four ducks," Rufik says. "How will we add them?" "One by one." The teacher asks him first to show how he is going to do the adding, using the ducks that are on the desk.

If the child has trouble, the teacher demonstrates this technique, accompanying it with an explanation. "Four and one are five, and one more is six; that means that when we add two ducks to four ducks, we get six ducks. Now we will do this when we have to add the number two.... What number have we added to what number?" "We added the number two to the number four, and we got six." The children are asked to write down this problem, and it causes them no difficulties. But the teacher asks them to think about how to record it so that the method by which they added the number two will be evident. The children make the following notation: $4 + 1 + 1 = 6$. Then they read, "We add one to four, add one, and get six." "How do we know that we have added the number two? You have shown only the method of solution." The children have trouble responding. The teacher asks them first to record the operation to be performed, and then to show the method. The teacher makes the following notation, reasoning aloud: "We need to add two to four, this is equal to our adding one and another one to four. We get six: $4 + 2 = 4 + 1 + 1 = 6$. First, we recorded the operation that we were to do according to the condition, and then indicated the method by which we add the number two. Regardless of whether we add the number two to the number four right away or break down the number two into units and add them to the number four—in either case we get the number six all the same. This notation should be read in this way: adding two to four is addition; we will add in this way: four and one is five, and another one is six, and therefore when we add two to four, we get six. The answer to the question is: 'The hunter killed six ducks in all.'"

The children should have a clear mastery of the distinction and the interrelationship between the formulation of the addition operation and the technique of adding on. This is significantly promoted by the visual method, as shown in the notation above and by the differences in the verbal description of the addition operation and the method of adding on.

The more graphic and precise the teacher's explanations and the clearer the teacher's requirements, the more clear-cut the children's responses and knowledge will be. They must learn to differentiate the computation techniques from the operations with the given numbers themselves. In practice, however, the teacher may encounter the following types of errors. The teacher asks, "How many mushrooms in all were growing in the clearing?" and the children answer, "We must add one mushroom to four mushrooms, and that will be five mushrooms, and add another mushroom to the five mushrooms, and that will be six mushrooms," They replace the formulation of the arithmetic operation ("We must add two to four") with an account of the computation technique and formulate that technique as two independent arithmetic operations, $4 + 1 = 5$ and $5 + 1 = 6$.

In other instances the children formulate the arithmetic operation properly ("We must add two to four, and we get six"). But when asked, "How did you add?" they answer, "by the unit." They cannot explain this method or demonstrate it with the visual material. It ultimately becomes clear that the result of the solution has been obtained by counting both terms again, which is evidence that the children have not understood the distinction between the arithmetic operation and the computation technique. This is why it is important to acquaint the children with numerals and conventional signs in the preparatory group. Using them, the children acquire a visual perception of the arithmetic operation and the computation methods.

After studying the computation techniques involved in the operation of addition, the technique of counting off one by one in subtraction is also studied. The children's previous knowledge also comes into play here, and the demonstration of counting off is aided by the visual material.

For example, the teacher puts six mushrooms in slots on a picture showing a forest background. She then puts the numerical example 6 - 2 on the display board. The children are asked to invent a problem to go with the picture and the numerical example, and to demonstrate it.

A girl is called on to remove two mushrooms from the picture, and she says, "I went walking in the forest and I saw six mushrooms under the trees. First I picked two mushrooms and put them in a basket. How many mushrooms were left for me to pick?" The teacher asks what must be done in order to answer the question. The children formulate the subtraction operation: "we should subtract two mushrooms from six mushrooms." "What number has to be subtracted from what number? How can we say it in another way?" "Subtract two from six." "We are still not able to subtract the number two right away. Therefore, we will subtract the number two one at a time, just as we did when we added the number two." The teacher reinserts the mushrooms, and demonstrating the technique of counting off a number that is to be subtracted by ones, she teaches the children how to do it and explain it. "To take two mushrooms away from six, I will take them away one by one: take one away from six, that's five, and take away another one, that's four. Therefore, we subtract two from six and get four. The question should be answered this way: 'There were four mushrooms left for me to pick.'" The teacher then asks the children to record the operation with the indicated numbers, and then to record the technique by which the operation was performed: $6 - 2 = 6 - 1 - 1 = 4$.

Thus, in subtraction the word "subtract" is used only to formulate the operation itself. The technique of counting off should be explained in different words: "Take one away from six, that is five, and take away another one, that's four." The aforementioned notation and the different formulations for the subtraction operation (subtract) and the computation techniques (take away one and another one) help the children differentiate between them more clearly, as is demonstrated by the notation.

For the children to learn to differentiate between the computation method and the arithmetic operation with specified numbers, they must be taught gradually, in a logical sequence, and by combining different types of knowledge. It is recommended that the work with the children be divided into two stages. In the first stage, show them what a problem is, and teach them to formulate an arithmetic operation with comprehensible numerical data (adding or subtracting one). In the second stage, demonstrate elementary computation techniques—the techniques of adding on and counting off one at a time.

In the transition to solving addition and subtraction problems involving the number three, its quantitative composition must be remembered and recorded as $3 = 1 + 1 + 1$. Later the children easily learn the technique of adding on and counting off the number three by analogy with adding on and counting off the number two. The rule for computation, which is deductively mastered by the children, is thus repeatedly made concrete by solving various problems.

In the preparatory group, work on arithmetic operations can be limited to these instances from the addition table. The goal is not for the children to learn the entire table of addition and subtraction. It is significantly more important to develop the children's thinking by providing varied problem themes, a diversity of designs involving the same theme, and the possibility of using a variety of visual resources in composing problems (dramatization, content toys, content pictures, problem pictures, the notation of a solution).

Once the children learn that problem content can reflect situations from real life, they can be asked to compare problems by themselves without visual material, using their imaginations (oral problems). In these problems, the children select a theme and a story-line for the problem, along with the operation by which it is to be solved. The teacher regulates only the second addend or the subtrahend, reminding the children that they have not yet learned to add or take away numbers beyond three. But the transition to independent oral problems should not be rushed. In introducing them, the teacher should make sure that they are not hackneyed and that the conditions reflect logical everyday relations. It is essential to develop the children's ability to take a critical approach to the content of problems and to solving them (formulating the arithmetic operation, determining the solution methods, the proper answer to the question in the problem, and the notation used in solving the problem).

It is important to teach the children to prove that their solutions and answers to oral problems are correct using various kinds of visual material. For example, in a problem it is stated that a hunter shot some ducks. The solution to this problem can be proven by means of circles, for example. This makes the children's thinking more abstract, teaches them analysis and synthesis, and improves their ability not only to express their own opinions, but also to prove them.

Solving original problems and problems of increasing difficulty plays an important role in developing logical thought. Until recently it was thought that preschool children could not solve such problems. But research and practice show that this point of view is groundless.

Let us give several examples of such problems. "Some beads were strung on a wire. When three were removed from it, seven beads were left. How many beads were on the wire at the beginning?" The children give the right answer: "There were ten beads on the wire at first." When asked how they found this answer, they say that they had to add what was left on the wire to what had been removed, since the problem asks, "How many beads were there at the beginning?" This meant that they had to return them to the wire, as it were, i.e., they had to add.

Another example: "There was some rice in a package. Mama poured out two cups of rice for porridge, and two cups of rice were still left. How much rice was there in all in the package?" The children answer that there were four cups of rice in all in the package. "Then, in order to find out how much there was before, we have to add another two cups to the two cups, and that will be four cups. There were four cups of rice in the package. What has to be done?" "We have to perform the operation of addition: add two to two, and get four," a child describes the operation.

But these problems should not be brought into play prematurely. They can be offered to the children when the teacher is confident that they have thoroughly learned the mandatory curriculum material. Only when it is necessary to enliven the work by making it more complicated should these problems be introduced. When they are used, they should be presented in the form of a surprise: "Who can think about how to solve the problem that I am about to tell you?" It should be noted that these problems elicit considerable interest among the children. "Here we have to think more," is the reason the children give for their attitude toward these problems.

The children should be taught to reason while analyzing a problem and to prove their answers—that is, they should be taught to think logically.

Problems on increasing or decreasing a number by one or two are fully accessible to children in the preparatory group. They have been prepared for solving them by the entire system of kindergarten instruction.

Foreseeing Possible Problem-Solving Mistakes

When starting out to teach computation, the teacher should have a thorough knowledge of the children's level of knowledge. Children often enter the preparatory group directly from their families with many deficiencies in their knowledge. If the children have received at least two years of training in kindergarten, their kindergarten should be considered responsible for improper school preparation.

Studies of first-graders over the last five to seven years have shown that children coming both from the family and from the kindergarten are largely able to name the numbers. The children often declare that they know to solve problems, that they learned how at home. But it soon turns out that they have merely learned the scheme for constructing a problem. However, it is important to know that a problem reflects various everyday quantitative relations and logical connections. It is also important to understand the meaning of a problem, the interrelationships between its parts, i.e., its structure. But mastering only the outline constrains the theme and the story-line (some think about apples, and all the others repeat the theme without varying its content). This is why the teacher should not hurry to move on to composing oral problems.

Another problem is also encountered frequently. The children know that problems can be composed on various themes. Their imagination has free play, and they rapidly invent various problems about tanks, airplanes, the army, and so on, inventing problems about things they know very superficially. As a rule, they do not invent anything from their own lives or from first-hand experience. The problems they make up often do not correspond to actual reality, although since they are constructed according to the outline, they have an outward appearance of being correct.

Therefore the children must be taught to take an exacting attitude toward the problems they make up and remember that a problem's content should always correspond to real life. This instills a thoughtful approach to facts, teaches the children to analyze them critically, and anticipates the emergence of a "know-it-all" or superficial attitude toward phenomena in life.

The question arises whether a trick problem or "fictitious" problem is accessible. If the children perceive this sort of problem as a joke, it is completely accessible. For example, the teacher might use a certain joke to verify the children's critical attitude toward problem content. She asks them to solve the following problem. "Six birds were sitting in a tree. A hunter came and shot one bird. How many birds were left in the tree?" Some of the children try to solve the problem, but many of them laugh. "They all flew away; they were frightened." Those who were trying to work the problem are embarrassed. "We first have to think about whether it can be this way in life, and then solve the problem," the teacher says. By teaching children to think carefully about whether problem content corresponds to real life, we promote their knowledge of life and teach them to consider quantitative phenomena in diversified relations.

Special attention has been given to mastering the meaning of the arithmetic operations, which are always formulated with the words *add* (in addition) and *subtract* (in subtraction). In arithmetic operations these words have a generalizing, abstract meaning. And it is important for the children to understand this. But it so happens that the words *add* and *take away* (instead of *subtract*) may be perceived by the children only in their practical sense, along with other ordinary verbs. Having superficially learned that these words have a definite relation to the problems, the children begin including them in the text itself.

For example, Nina composes the following oral problem: "There were nine cones in a store. Another cone was added in the store. How many in all?" The teacher analyzes Nina's problem together with the children, and as a result of the discussion the children conclude that it doesn't happen that way in life. "They bring a whole box from the storeroom, but they don't add one," Lena criticizes the problem. Nina changes the text: "Nine cones stood on a shelf in the store. Another cone was found on another shelf and it was put in the right place. How many were there in all in the store?" But now the children criticize the question: "Nine what—apples or people?" Nina corrects the question in the problem: "How many cones in all are standing on the shelf?"

This example offers evidence that the generalized significance of the words *add, take away, is obtained,* and *is equal to* does not always develop immediately in some children. Therefore, when the arithmetic operations are taught at the earliest stage, special attention must be paid to demonstrating the meaning of the arithmetic operations in which people's varied activity with sets is generalized and abstracted. Of course, this process of abstracting and understanding the meaning of arithmetic operations only begins in the preschool years; it will developed further in school. That makes it all the more important to provide a proper direction for this process in kindergarten.

Thus, working on problems not only enriches the children with new knowledge; it also provides rich material for their mental development (for observations of life; mastery of logical connections and quantitative relations; development of analysis, synthesis, and generalization; attention, memory, and speech; mental acuity; etc.). Working on problems teaches children disciplined thinking and behavior—that is, it guarantees an educational and formative effect.

Sample Lessons for Developing Children's Notions of Size and Measurement, Shape, and Spatial and Temporal Relations

The Development of Notions of Size and Measurement

The children have already been taught in the previous groups to distinguish and compare the various parameters of length, reflecting this activity in their speech and in various activities (they have drawn rectangles, circles, and other figures and objects of various sizes; they have determined short distances by pacing, and so forth).

This work continues and becomes more complex in the preparatory group. The children practice isolating various parameters in objects around them: the length of a table, the width of the blackboard, the height of a bookcase. They find the length, width, and height of a box in various positions and the width and length of a picture hanging on the wall or lying on a table.

The children make sight comparisons of objects in terms of length, width, and height, and they verify their judgments by the technique of superimposition or applying one object to another. For example, which is wider and which is longer—a book or a notebook?

The children arrange objects of varying length or height in increasing or decreasing order, and make practical determinations of the difference between the size of the consecutive elements in a sequence.

A new objective in the preparatory group is instruction in techniques of measuring with household measuring devices (distances, length, width, and height for objects, and mass and volume for dry and liquid substances).

Where should attention be focused in teaching the measurement of distance? The children already know the method of measuring by paces, for the most part, and they have used it in play. It applies to the measurement of comparatively long distances (e.g., the length and width of a room or a garden path). The children can distinguish the length and width of the floor and the height of the walls in the room. The teacher asks them to indicate the width and length of the floor in the room during a lesson, and to determine by sight which is greater or whether they are equal. The results might be contradictory when this method of determination is used, and disputes might even arise among the children. The teacher explains that the dispute is easily resolved if they pace off the room's length and width. The teacher makes the children realize that paces must be counted off along a straight line. The number of steps might differ for other children. The children are inclined to see improper counting as the reason. The teacher does not hasten to explain, but asks them to count the paces as the teacher measures the length of the same room. The number of paces proves to be fewer, but the children have counted correctly. "Everyone has obtained a different number of paces. What does it depend on?" "You have bigger paces," the children say.

"Misha has bigger paces, too, but smaller than yours, and Lena's are very small, and so it turns out different," the children guess. "What is a pace?" the teacher asks. "It's the distance from one foot to the other in walking." "That's true. But to count them, what should paces be?" "The same every time, and big," the children answer. "Correct. A pace is a measure, and a measure should be the same in measuring. But can our measure (the pace) be the same for all the children?" The children say that people have different-sized paces. "Here's how my daddy walks—he's tall, and Mommy always lags behind him, because she takes short paces." "What can we say about measuring by paces?" the teacher is leading up to a generalization. "That kind of measurement is possible, but it is not precise." "Who knows how people measure distances more accurately?" "With a kilometer or with a meter," the children answer. "Right. But you will find out in school what a meter and a kilometer are; in the meantime we will learn to measure the length and the width of the room in paces, choosing a point on the opposite wall the room right in front of us and walking in a straight line. And why do we need to walk in a straight line for measuring?" The children start to think. The teacher asks them to try a measurement that is not made in a straight line and then to compare it with the number of paces previously obtained. The children realize that there were more paces; therefore, a straight line segment is the shortest distance between two points (the ends of the segment).

In subsequent lessons the teacher shows the children how to measure the length, width, and height of objects with conventional measures. "Can we measure the table at which you are sitting? What part of the table can be measured?" The children find the table's length, width, and height. "And we can measure the chair," some say. "And the bookcase and the doll's sofa," others add.

The teacher exhibits a flat stick approximately 20 cm long and uses it to measure the length and width of her desk. She observes that it must be measured starting from the very edge, placing the stick on top of the desk, and then, without moving it out of place, by carefully marking the end of the stick with colored chalk and laying it down again, beginning precisely from the colored mark. The stick must be set precisely in a straight line and its end marked every time. Then the number of segments marked in colored chalk is counted. If counting the measures gives the children trouble, a circle can be placed opposite each mark—that is, a one-to-one correspondence can be established between the measures and the circles. The children count the circles and thereby the measures as well. For the first lessons it is advisable to take a measure that can be laid out without a remainder (although it covers the length of the desk). Let us assume that the desk is six measures long. Measuring the width, the children see that they have laid off three sticks, and another small segment of the desk's width remains unmeasured. The teacher explains to the children that in this instance we say, "A little over three measures."

After the method of measuring has been demonstrated and explained, the children are given similar measures, and they begin measuring their own desks. The measuring technique causes no particular difficulties for the children, but accurate measuring requires that the teacher check their work.

"All of your desks are the same size, but Lesha and Lida here have laid off not six measures for the length, like the rest of you, but five measures with a small remainder. Why has it come out that way for them?" "They counted wrong... They did not start laying off the measure from the very edge of the desk... They did not lay off the measure along a straight line," the children speak up. The teacher asks Lesha and Lida to measure their desk again, and the children watch what they do. This time Lesha and Lida also get the correct results, since they carefully lay out their sticks along the length of the desk.

Several typical mistakes can be observed when measurement is being taught: the children determine the reference point incorrectly, shift the ruler, mark the end of the measure wrong with the chalk, fail to use the mark, or superimpose the stick on a length they have already measured, or start too far from the mark. To avoid these errors, the method of measuring must be clearly explained and shown to the children.

The height of a desk can be measured in precisely the same way. It should be remembered, however, that the children sometimes take only the height of the desk top as the height, rather than the entire vertical extent. Therefore, before starting the measurement, it is important to stress that the reference point is the floor, and the measurement marks are to be made on the desk leg.

In subsequent lessons the children can measure other objects—a chair, a bookcase, a bench, a sofa. They should be made particularly aware that the height of a chair or a sofa is the distance from the floor to the seat, while the height of the back of the chair or sofa is not taken into account.

So that the children thoroughly understand the relative nature of measures, they can be asked to measure the same objects with different measures (with a string, for instance). The string is stretched along the length of the desk and cut. Its length is equal to the desk's length. Then the width of the desk is measured with it and marked on the string with a colored thread. By a sight comparison, it is evident that the length of the desk is greater than its width.

Finally, the string itself can be measured by the same stick that was used to measure the length and width of the desk. The string is wound around the length of the stick, and the number of segments will approximately equal the number of segments laid off on the desk in measuring its length with the stick.

But the stick can vary in size. In one class the teacher can supply a shorter stick, 15 cm long. Sticks of different sizes will yield different numbers of measures. Thus, if the desk's length is roughly 120 cm, the children may get 6 measures by measuring the length with one stick and 8 measures when using another, shorter stick.

The teacher can show how to measure the length of the desk by extending the thumb and the index finger. This method of measuring will lead the children to conclude that adults and children obtain different results.

All these exercises lead the children to conclude that distances or the length (width, or height) of an object can be measured by various means (paces, sticks of different sizes, a string, a person's hand, etc.), and that these means are relative units of measure.

"What do you think—when will the number of measures be greater in measuring a certain length—when there is a larger or smaller unit of measure?" the teacher asks. The children start thinking. Then they respond in various ways. The teacher asks them to perform a practical check of their answers. They realize that **the smaller the measuring unit, the greater the number of units obtained in measuring the same length.** The children recall that when they measured the length of the desk, it was equal to six sticks if the stick was long (20 cm) and eight sticks when the stick was shorter (15 cm). Thus, the children gradually arrive at an elementary understanding of the functional dependence between the length of the measure and the number of measures when the same length is measured.

Once they have learned to use various conventional measures, the children themselves start comparing objects. The pine tree at their summer cottage is two houses high, and the jasmine shrubs are taller than the fence; the highway is ten paces wide, and the forest path is narrow—only one pace wide. Their sight comparisons of sizes become more precise, and their powers of sight estimation improve. The comparisons are reflected in speech.

Sample Lessons in Measuring Liquid and Dry Substances

Children are introduced to methods of measuring dry and liquid substances with conventional units of measure for the first time in the preparatory group. To prepare them for measuring volume and vessel capacity, the teacher must first lead them to understand that the volumes of vessels may be equal or unequal independent of their external shape. For this purpose, the teacher chooses vessels of varying shapes but equal capacity, such as a glass, a cup, a bottle, and a test tube of equal capacity. The capacity of the glass can serve as a standard for determining the capacity of all the other vessels. The glass is filled with water, and then the contents are poured into the other vessels. The children conclude that while the shape and size of these vessels are different to the eye, they all have the same capacity (volume). Therefore, it is hard to determine from external appearance which vessels holds more or less liquid.

In order to demonstrate this conclusively to the children, the teacher selects several vessels of different capacities, such as a short jug with a broad base, a tall and narrow vase, a large bottle of different volume, and so on. The children first attempt to determine the capacity of each of these vessels by sight, using the glass as a standard, then all the vessels are filled with water, and their capacity is measured with the glass.

As they compare the results of measuring the liquid with the glass to the predicted capacity of the various vessels, the children realize that vessel capacity must be measured by a single measuring unit—then the results will be more accurate.

In one lesson it is a good idea to demonstrate that the number of measures depends on their magnitude when measuring the volume of a liquid. For this purpose, the teacher asks the children to measure the capacity of a jug, which is equal to two glasses. Then the teacher gives them a half-liter jar and a small cup, asking them first to think about whether there will be more or fewer measures in the jug if the water is measured with the jar or with the little cup. The class checks the various hypotheses, and concludes that the smaller the measure, the greater the number of units there will be when measuring a given volume of liquid.

The volume of dry substances (flour in a sack or in a package, for example) is measured analogously. Dry substances can also be measured with mugs, glasses, cups, or spoons. Again the children conclude that the smaller the volume of the measuring device, the greater the number of units obtained when measuring a single package of flour.

What should be particularly emphasized when the children are learning to measure liquid and solid substances? They should be shown that the measure must be full. A liquid (or flour) must be poured from the vessels serving as measures into another container carefully, without spilling. "And why must we do this so accurately?" the teacher asks, suggesting that the children think and recall the rules for measuring a room by pacing a straight line. "If we don't measure along a straight line, there will be more paces than along a straight line." "And why is it important to be accurate here?" "If you spill it, there will be less water, and you can't measure it accurately with the other measure." The teacher agrees with this answer and adds, "If you spill it, there will be less water in the pitcher, and we are interested in finding out the number of units when there is a certain quantity of water in the decanter."

In the first stages of measuring the volume of a dry substance, each measure should be poured into a separate pile, then the number of piles can be counted. Suppose that Lesha and Nadia get ten piles apiece, but Sima gets only nine piles. Why could this happen? By observing how Lesha, Sima, and Nadia do the assignment, the children conclude that Sima filled the spoon over the top with flour, while Lesha and Nadia filled theirs only up to the edge. The children conclude that for the number of measurements to be identical, the flour must be poured more precisely, by filling the spoon up to the edge.

Generalizing their own experience and observations, the children conclude that when measuring the volume of a substance, a certain mass, length, or whatever, the number of units will always be greater as the measure becomes smaller.

Then the teacher can ask the children to think and state whether the number of piles will be greater, less, or the same if the flour is measured with a teaspoon instead of a tablespoon, and approximately how many piles there will be. The children express various opinions. Everyone says that there will be more piles when the same flour is measured with a teaspoon, but the number of piles is estimated differently. "Who can guess how to determine it more precisely, making only a slight error?" The children start thinking. Some propose measuring a pile equal to one tablespoon with the teaspoon. As they measure, they find that there are two teaspoons to a tablespoon. This means that, instead of one pile apiece measured by the tablespoon, there will be two piles measured by the teaspoon. After stating these hypotheses, the children can give them a practical trial.

By measuring different distances, the length, width, and height of objects, and dry and liquid substances using assorted conventional measures, the children become increasingly aware of the functional relation between the number of units and the size of the measures. These operations provide the children with a more concrete demonstration of the meaning of measurement and prepare them for understanding the significance of the standard units of measure in the future. It is therefore important that measuring with household measures precede measurement with standard units.

The various measures should be connected with the subsequent development of the children's sight estimation. For example, some children began arguing on an outing: was the fence higher than an adult person or of equal height? Attempting to answer the question on their own, the children ask for a long stick with which to measure the fence, then they measure the height of an adult and conclude that the fence is somewhat taller. In connection with their lessons, the children show considerable interest in measuring by various methods. They learn the basic rule for any measurement— **care and accuracy**. They also begin to understand that measuring by sight is very approximate, but its results can be verified with other measures.

The development of the baric sense (the "sense of weight") also continues in the preparatory group. The children practice comparing how heavy objects are by weighing them on their palms and perfecting these movements.

Developing Children's Notions of Geometric Figures

The children's knowledge of geometric figures is not so much expanded in the preparatory group as reinforced and systematized. For those children who have just joined the group, a deficiency must be compensated for, as they have not covered the curriculum for the previous groups. While introducing the children to geometric figures and reinforcing their notions about them, the teacher should use the methods indicated for the previous groups. The principal task in this group is to systematize their previous knowledge and help them master the interrelationships between figures. Therefore, it is very important for the children to become familiar with the concept of a polygon, which is the generalization of the triangle, square, and rectangle, etc.

Before acquainting the children with the polygon, the teacher introduces a model of a new figure, the pentagon, and, without naming it, asks the children to examine it carefully and compare it with the square and the rectangle, to determine what is the same and what is different. The children indicate that both figures have vertices, angles, and sides, but the new figure has five sides, five vertices, and five angles, while the square and the rectangle have four vertices, four angles, and four sides. The teacher asks them to think about what to call this new figure. The children call it a pentagon. Then they are asked to make up a set from the plane geometric figures they know (figures with sides and angles) and arrange them in increasing order of the number of vertices, angles, and sides.

"Do we also need a triangle?" the children are doubtful. So they lay out a triangle, square, rectangle, trapezoid, and pentagon, obtaining a set of figures. They are asked to break it up into groups, combining figures with an equal number of angles in each group. "How many parts are there in your set of figures?" "Three parts: one part is the triangle, one part the quadrilaterals, and one part the pentagon." The teacher calls the children's attention to the parts that have been singled out based on the number of angles, and asks them to think about how the entire set might be named in one word. The children start thinking. One proposes calling them geometric figures, and others say angular figures. "Correct. But how can they be named even more precisely?" If the children cannot guess, the teacher calls them polygons. "Can there be figures with an even greater number of angles?" the teacher asks a new question. One boy says that his father has shown him a hexagon, and others remember that they have drawn hexagons themselves, and that they are easier to draw than pentagons. The teacher exhibits a hexagon and an octagon. The children count the sides, vertices, and angles in these figures. Hexagons and octagons are distributed among the children. They now have many different figures in their envelopes, but they can be divided into two basic groups: rounded figures (ovals and circles) and polygons.

At one lesson the children are given graph paper and asked to draw a polygon with any number of sides, vertices, and angles. In this way the generalized concept of polygon becomes concrete, which develops the children's deductive thinking.

As in the previous group, the children's practice with geometric figures consists in identifying them in various spatial positions, counting the vertices, angles, and sides, arranging them according to size (seriation), and grouping them by shape, color, and size.

The children should not only distinguish, but also reproduce these figures, knowing their characteristics and properties. For example, the teacher might ask them to draw two squares on graph paper: one square's side should be equal to the length of four units, and the other's side should be two units longer.

After drawing these figures, the children are asked to divide the squares in half, connecting the two opposite sides in one square and the two opposite vertices in the other square with a line segment; they should tell how many and which figures they obtained, how many parts they divided the square into, and what each part is called. This assignment combines counting and measurement with conventional measures (the length of a side of a small square), the reproduction of different-sized figures based on knowledge of their properties, identification and naming of the figures after they are divided into parts, and naming the parts of the whole. An assignment with this sort of composite structure system-atizes the children's knowledge acquired in lessons from various units of the curriculum (counting, size, shape, measurement).

At another lesson the children can be asked to compare the sizes of a circle and an oval with a square and a rectangle, and to think about how best to do this. They can be advised at first to use prepared shapes, superimposing them on one another, and to think about which figures are close to one another in size. The oval shape can best be superimposed on the rectangle and the circle on the square, if the circle's diameter is equal to the length of a side of the square and the oval's height is equal to the length of the rectangle's longer side (see Figure 12 in Appendix B).

One important objective in acquainting children with geometric fig-ures is to teach them **to be able to see the form of an object as a whole and the form of its parts.**

In the preparatory group, it is a good idea to use the same techniques of grouping objects by shape as in the five-year-old group. Furthermore, the children can be asked to make up a whole object from parts (using a puzzle depicting an object). For example, a puzzle entitled "Broken Cup" is composed of different-shaped fragments, or a teapot is divided into its constituent parts—the handle, the spout, the cover, the body—which, when connected, create an image of an entire teapot.

Some objects can be formed by combining various geometric shapes. The outlines of objects and geometric figures can be created out of sticks (or matches) as well. The children love exercises on forming geometric figures, and they should be employed (see Color Figures 10 and 11).

The ability to see an object's shape and physically reproduce it in various ways (making geometric figures out of sticks, puzzles, modeling clay, or cut-outs) not only depends the children's perception of the world around them; it also leads them to certain generalizations. The children note, for example, that rounded shapes are typical of the world of animals and plants (leaves, flowers), while a rectangular form is typical of man-made household utensils. All this expands the children's cognitive activity, forms new interests, and develops their attention, power of observation, speech, and thinking (teaching a combination of analysis, synthesis, generalization, and concretization).

As they become familiar with various figures, it is important for the children to develop their power of observation, so that they learn to see the features of the different figures, their similarity and differences; it is also important to lead them to accessible generalizations and syntheses (while triangles, just like quadrilaterals, differ, they are still a variety of polygon, like quadrilaterals).

The children begin to understand the interconnections between different geometric shapes. While in the younger group they looked for rounded or angular objects around them, now their knowledge is enriched by notions of the diverse geometric figures, and these notions are more systematic: the children have learned that some shapes are subordinate to others. For example, the concept of a quadrilateral generalizes such concepts as the square, rectangle, and trapezoid, among others, and the concept of a polygon generalizes all the quadrilaterals, triangles, penta-gons, and hexagons, regardless of their size and appearance. Such inter-connections and generalizations are fully accessible to the children; they elevate their mental development to a new level and prepare them for mastering scientific concepts in school.

The children themselves can draw triangles of assorted shapes on graph paper. To do so they need to select three points in different places and connect them by straight line segments. Or they can draw a segment six units long horizontally, find its midpoint, and, counting off from the midpoint four units down, place a point, then connect it with the endpoints of the segment. An isosceles triangle is obtained. They can be asked to show the vertices and angles in this triangle and to count them, and then the sides.

Then the teacher asks them to draw another triangle (with a right angle): to draw two segments with a common endpoint—one horizon-tally, the other vertically, each five units long—and then to connect the ends of these segments. They obtain a right triangle. Without knowing the names for these shapes, the children spot the similarity and differ-ences. They develop the mental operations of analysis, comparison, and generalization. They can be asked to make new figures out of the triangles and rectangles by combining them. For these purposes it is good to use a geometric mosaic.

The geometric figures can not only be counted, but can also serve as material for arithmetic problems, e.g.: Lesha cut out six trapezoids, and Lena cut out only two trapezoids. How many trapezoids must Lena cut out for them to have the same number of trapezoids?

This sort of connection between quantitative notions and notions of geometric figures creates a foundation for general mathematical devel-opment.

Children's Spatial Notions and their Reflection in Speech

In the younger and intermediate groups the children learned practical orientation in the spatial arrangement of the parts of their bodies and how to determine the location of objects relative to themselves (in front of them, behind, to the right or left, etc.). Then, in the five-year-old group they learned to determine the position of a specific object with respect to any other object and to orient themselves in the various directions of motion, as well as in their own movement.

All these spatial conceptions must be reinforced for the children in the preparatory group, by making extensive use of play techniques in lessons and enlisting the children in various didactic games outside of class (outdoor games, games with aids, etc.).

The students in the preparatory group should learn not only to orient themselves freely in the direction of motion and the spatial relations between themselves and other objects, as well as among various objects, but also to use the appropriate words correctly.

The diversity of spatial relations is reflected in speech by means of spatial prepositions: *in, on, under, over, before, behind, in front of, across from, among, around, between, toward, from, from behind, by, through, along, across*, and others, as well as by adverbial expressions: *here, there, to the left, to the right, far, near, from below, from above*. The teacher should teach the children how to make use of these prepositions and adverbs properly in mathematics and language lessons, as well as in art lessons, games, and daily life.

The teacher can take advantage of commonplace situations or didactic games, and have the children explain where a certain object was found after an assignment, and so forth. Let us give several examples of play assignments. Some children put things away according to the teacher's instructions. The others watch to see whether they do the task properly and described what those children have done.

On another occasion the children cover their eyes, and one child is chosen by the teacher to hide behind the bookcase, and then peek out from behind it later on. Opening their eyes, the children try to determine who is missing and where he has hidden. They do not see the hidden child, but he peeks out from behind the bookcase. The teacher asks someone to say what he has done.

Another variant is also possible: one child goes behind the door, and the other children agree where to hide something. The first child has to find the object and say where it was. He can be helped to look for the object: when he is getting close to it, the children say, "Hot, hot, hot," and when he is far away they say, "Cold, cold, cold."

Orientation in space can be reinforced during outings and playground games. It is important for certain actions to be not only physically performed, but also reflected in speech. Children's stories based on pictures, particularly accounts that require descriptions, also further this end.

Developing orientation on a sheet of paper—that is, in two-dimensional space—is of considerable importance in preparing the children for school. They should be adept at finding the top and bottom lines precisely, the left- and right-hand margins, the middle of the page (its center), the upper and lower left-hand corners, the upper and lower right-hand corners, and they should be able to arrange objects from left to right, from the top down, and so forth. The children have already done a number of exercises of this kind in the five-year-old group.

Visual dictation, as it is called, is one of the more effective techniques. For example, the teacher can ask the children to place a square in the middle of a sheet of paper and arrange eight triangles around the square with their acute angles toward the square, put small circles between the triangles, and place squares over the triangles (angles touching). They have to put circles in the upper and lower left-hand corners and in the upper and lower right-hand corners, connecting them by drawing broken lines. In the early stages of visual dictation, the children inspect a prepared design, analyze it, and reproduce it from memory, using geometric shapes.

Another variant can also be suggested. The children make a design following the teacher's dictation. The teacher tells them where to place each figure, but demonstrates nothing. The children listen attentively to her verbal instructions. They should already be well-oriented in the space of the paper and know the names of the geometric figures and the expressions reflecting the spatial relations indicated by the teacher. One version of this kind of lesson calls for the children to create a design of their own from prepared geometric shapes and then tell how many shapes of each kind they have chosen and how they have arranged them.

Visual dictation lessons simultaneously reflect the children's knowledge of the shape, size, number, and spatial arrangement of figures in the plane and the spatial relations among these figures.

But what must the teacher know in order to develop the children's spatial notions and speech? Above all, the teacher must know the significance of the prepositions and adverbs reflecting spatial relations.

One group of prepositions reflects a multitude of spatial relations among objects and between a person and other objects, indicating position of one object among others. A second group of prepositions conveys the direction of motion toward an object or indicates an object's orientation during motion.

Let us analyze these groups of Russian prepositions. The prepositions *on, in, behind, in front of,* and *across from,* among others, belong to the first group. This group has its own distinctions, which convey nuances in the spatial relations among objects. The prepositions *on* and *in* are used very extensively and in many ways in our speech. *On* reflects an object's position on the surface of another, and *in* reflects its position inside something. (*The lamp is* **on** *the table. The notebook is lying* **in** *the desk drawer. The student's name is written* **on** *the notebook cover. The student wrote the numerals* **in** *the notebook.*) But the same prepositions are also used to indicate the location of a person, animal, or object in space. (*The mushrooms are growing* **in** *the forest. The apple trees are growing* **in** *the orchard. Serezha is standing* **in** *the circle of children. The children are playing* **on** *the floor. The children are sliding* **on** *the ice. The summer cottage stands* **on** *the lake shore.*) Conveyance by certain means of transportation is also expressed by the preposition *on.* (*Daddy came* **on** *a motorcycle and Mommy came* **on** *the train. We crossed the river* **on** *a boat.*)

The Russian prepositions *under, over, ahead, in front of*, and *behind* are used to reflect the spatial relations between objects. On the one hand, they show one object's position with respect to another, and, on the other hand, the direction of movement with respect to another object. (*The lamp is hanging* **over** *the table. The ball rolled* **under** *the chair.*) The same prepositions can convey the dynamics of motion, its direction toward another object. (*Push the chairs* **under** *the table after the flour. You dropped a spoon* **under** *the table. The soap dish was installed* **over** *the washbasin.*)

Although the prepositions *in front of* and *in back of* indicate opposite spatial relations between objects, there are common nuances—they indicate one object's proximity to another. (*A cup of milk is standing* **in front of** *the child. A garden is* **in front of** *the house. The buttons were sewn* **on the back of** *the dress. A hole must be made* **in the back of** *the box.*) On the other hand, another pair of prepositions, *before* and *behind*, which also reflect opposite relations between objects, have a common feature of emphasizing a certain remoteness and direct proximity in the positions of the objects. (*The banner is being carried* **before** *the column of Young Pioneers.* **Before** *the streetcar came the bus. The shed was built* **behind** *the house. We see a pine forest* **behind** *the field.*)

The spatial position of a person or object facing another person or object is expressed by the preposition *opposite* (or *across from*), indicating proximity between them. (*The new kindergarten was opened* **opposite** *our house. The tables in the group room had to be placed* **across from** *the window. The children were lined up in two rows* **opposite** *one another.*)

The location of a person or object surrounded by other objects or people is indicated by the prepositions *among* or *in the middle of*. (*The teacher was standing* **among** *the children. A triangle was found* **among** *the squares in the box. The children made a circle* **in the middle of** *the room.*) But the prepositions *between* and *around* indicate the location of an object in the middle. (*Zina stood* **between** *Serezha and Nina. The chairs were placed* **around** *the table. The presents for the children were placed* **around** *the Christmas tree.*)

Prepositions that convey the direction of motion in space belong to the second group. The prepositions *to*, *from*, and *from behind* reflect the direction of motion toward a certain object or movement from within an object. (*The little girl is going* to *her Mommy. The little girl left* from *the doctor's office. Go* to *the principal of the kindergarten. Your handkerchief has fallen* from *your pocket. Misha has taken the lotto game* from *the bookcase. They poured the milk* from *the bottle into a glass. Someone's head was peeking* from behind *the tree.*)

Movement on a surface is conveyed by the Russian prepositions *through*[1] (along) and *through*[2] (across).[3] The distinction between these prepositions is that *through*[1] does not indicate a definite direction, while the preposition *through*[2] conveys the path of a movement in a confined area. (*We were walking* through[1] *the forest. We returned home* through[2] *the forest. First the children walked* along *the sidewalk, and then they went* across *the street, jumped* across *the ditch, and walked* through[1] *the forest.*)

The prepositions *along* and *across* indicate the orientation of objects during movement or some action. (*We walked* along *the creek. The chairs were placed* along *the wall. The children and I planted the lilac bushes* along *the fence. A log was lying* across *the road. The doll was lying* across *the bed.*)

In addition to prepositions, certain Russian adverbs also serve to designate spatial relations. Some of them show direction of motion and answer the question "where to?" (*to here, to there, to the left, to the right, forward, back, up, upward, down, inward, outward, far, near,* etc.). Others also indicate the reverse direction of motion, answering the question "where from?" (*from here, from there, from the left, from the right, from in front, from behind, from the top, from the bottom, from inside, from without, from outside, from afar, from everywhere,* etc.). A third group of spatial adverbs designates the location of an action, answering the question "where?" (*here, there, on the left, on the right, in front, behind, on top, on the bottom, inside, outside, everywhere, throughout,* etc.).

Children's Orientation in Time

Even in the youngest group the children are taught to orient themselves in time, and youngsters of three and four can correctly use the various grammatical categories to reflect present, past, and future time. They first borrow these grammatical forms from adults by imitation, but later the categories begin to be suffused with a certain content. Even before children begin preschool, they use the words *now* and *next*, which separate the current moment from the immediate future in the child's consciousness.

The use of grammatical categories to reflect the fluidity of time is still not evidence that the children differentiate temporal concepts, just as a child's use of number-words does not show that he possesses the concept of number. Special work is required to develop concepts of time—its movement, periodicity, change, and irreversibility.

As stated above, the children begin to be familiarized with the 24-hour day in the youngest group. Six-year-olds know very well that a new day begins with the sound of the Kremlin chimes in Moscow at 12:00 midnight, and they can distinguish the four parts of a day: morning, afternoon, evening, and night. The notions of these parts are related to the children's everyday existence. Knowing that one day gives way to another, the children start to understand the meaning of the words *yesterday*, *today*, and *tomorrow*. They form a notion of time's motion, the way in which one day is replaced by another.

The expression "day after day" is fully accessible to the children. It enables them to comprehend that the days have names, that there are seven days, and that they make up a week. One week also gives way to another.

The children develop notions about seasonal changes by accumulating personal experience: "It was summer, but now summer has passed; colder days came, it rained—autumn set in; the freezing cold winter follows it; and then spring comes with its warm days and with the buds opening up; after spring, summer will come again."

In the preparatory group the children must form notions of the periodicity of the seasons, their change and at the same time their irreversibility. These notions should be enriched by complete specific attributes that characterize the seasons.

Every period in a year is distinguished not only by natural phenomena, but also by characteristic types of work and public holidays. The conception of time's movement, the way in which one period replaces another, should be distinct, enabling the children to comprehend the conventional units by which the year is measured— the months and the number of days in each months.

The children in the preparatory group can also be told that one year replaces another and that the start of each year is New Year's Day—January 1. The new year begins with January. There are 12 months in a year, each with its own name, and they always come in the same order, just like the days of the week. Familiarizing the children with that order and with the names of the months is quite appropriate, though without insisting that they formally memorize the sequence.

It is important to develop a "sense of time," a concept of its irreversibility, in children of six and seven (cf. studies by T. D. Rikhterman). They should be taught to make the most of time, and thus they should practice distinguishing between the duration of a minute and five or ten minutes, connecting the conceptions of one minute and five or ten minutes with what can be done in that period.

The clock is the visual alphabet of time. Older preschoolers are very interested in the clock, observing the movements of its hands. "Close your eyes and sit quietly for a minute," Yu. I. Fausek, the dean of Soviet educators, told the children, "and I will watch the clock. When a minute has passed, I will tell you." Modern studies also show that a sense of duration, of what is equal to a minute, becomes more precise as the children gain practice.

A device for measuring duration should be introduced in the preparatory group. Sandglasses are one such device. They show time's fluidity in a graphic way, making it possible to consider short periods and regulate one's activity objectively. There should be 1-, 5-, 10-, and 20-minute sandglasses in every preparatory group. They can be used to regulate the children's daily routine and behavior. "The lesson will end when the sand in the 10-minute glass has run through twice," the teacher says. As the children watch the sand, they work more intensively. The sand-glass becomes a unit for measuring the duration of the lesson.

As they gain practice, the children begin to have a more precise idea of just what can be done in a certain length of time. They grow used to having a lesson within certain time limits. They learn to make the most of their time, gradually becoming aware of its irreversibility. It is particularly important to teach the future schoolchild to make the most of his time. When the children come home from school, they should have time to take a walk, rest, do their homework, and visit their clubs. The children's sense of time should be developed so they do not overestimate their time on an outing, so they return home on time. They should do their homework intensively at home, without distractions. With an awareness of time's indefatigable movement, its fluidity and irreversibility, before starting school the children should learn to do everything on time. This is why it is so important to develop the children's sense of time, rather than merely teaching them to "tell" time from the dial of a clock. Developing a sense of time trains the children in a faster work tempo and intensive schoolwork, and cultivates organization.

The children also establish connections between temporal and spatial conceptions. They begin to understand that the longer the path, the more time will be required to cover it; the faster the movement on the path, the sooner they will get there, and therefore, the less time they will take.

Thus, while in the younger group the need to differentiate between the children's quantitative and spatial conceptions was paramount, in the preparatory group connections are established between them, but on a new basis.

Knowledge of number, the ability to operate with numbers, and knowledge of size and methods of using household and conventional measures lay the foundation for subsequent mathematical development. Knowledge of temporal and spatial relations (their interconnections and interrelations and methods of measuring them) and various geometric figures and distinctions between them through number and measurement bring together the notions of quantitative, spatial, and temporal relations and the shape and size of objects. Thus, they too contribute to subsequent mathematical development.

Reinforcing Notions and Applying Knowledge, Abilities, and Skills in Lessons, Play, and Everyday Life

One of the chief objectives for the teacher in the preparatory group is to see that the knowledge, abilities, and skills children acquire in mathematics lessons are applied in various everyday situations—in private life, on outings, in play, and in other lessons. The children must understand that the knowledge they have acquired is really essential. This will make them interested in further expanding their mathematical knowledge.

In drawing, clay modeling, and building the children reinforce their knowledge of geometric figures, the shape and dimensions of objects, their spatial orientation, and quantity. Let us give an example. In the older and preparatory groups the children build and make various items following either a volumetric model or a technical drawing or photograph. They should subject a technical drawing to analysis here: analyze the parts that constitute it, the method of connecting them, think about the material needed for the construction based on the shape, dimensions, and quantity, project the sequence of operations, and comprehend the most efficient modes of operation. Using a metal erector set, the children select parts of the required dimensions, depending on the number of holes in a certain part, and as they make an article of wood, they choose the shape and size of the panels or laths by sight. The teacher instructs the children in planning their operations (the order in which the parts are to be connected) and subsequently analyzing the item they have made, asking them to compare it with the technical drawing or photograph.

But to do so the children should, above all, scrutinize the technical drawing or photograph and properly evaluate the shape and dimensions of the object's parts and their spatial correlation. Knowledge of the various shapes and sizes of objects and of the spatial relations between objects will be of considerable assistance to the children in developing their abilities to "read" a technical drawing and construct an item based on it.

Studies by V. G. Nechaeva, G. V. Grub, Fan I-in, and V. F. Izotova have demonstrated convincingly that inadequate development of spatial conceptions significantly delays the ability to read a technical drawing; the children prefer to make items by trial and error.

At first the children do not usually analyze the technical drawing as a whole, but examine it and reproduce it component by component. But the teacher trains them to analyze the entire project and reproduce the integral spatial structure of the item from memory. The children begin to understand that they should analyze the technical drawing or photograph very carefully before starting to make the article, and remember all the parts and their arrangement (the shape and size of the parts, how they must be joined, etc.). Whereas at first the children examine the technical drawing superficially, and therefore reproduce the articles inaccurately, later they become aware of the value of their own knowledge of shape, dimension, and the spatial relations of objects. They then inspect the photograph or technical drawing with more care. Their visual analysis becomes deeper and better organized; the children display the ability to imagine an object in three dimensions when perceiving a two-dimensional representation of it. This develops versatile thinking, imparts a dynamic quality to the children's notions, and develops the ability to operate with them—all of which together promote the development of constructive thinking.

Whether the children work with drawings of objects or drawings that tell a story, whether it is a design or a piece of applique work, a clay model or the creation of complicated toys—a knowledge of shape and size and the quantitative and spatial relations among the parts of objects or between the objects themselves is universally required. Therefore, geometric notions and measuring skills are developed and reinforced through every kind of representational activity.

Spatial notions and counting skills can be reinforced in **music lessons.** The children learn about the basic properties of musical sound—pitch (register), the rising or falling direction of melody, the duration of sounds (shorter or longer), chords consisting of two, three, or five sounds, and so forth. According to N. A. Vetlugina's data, children associate these basic properties of musical sounds with spatial, temporal, and quantitative notions, such as *farther—nearer, higher—lower,* and *longer—shorter.*

In physical education classes, children often make use of cardinal and ordinal counting in formations and moving around. They line up in two or three columns, they branch off in pairs to the right and to the left, they form circles, one of which may move to the left and the other to the right, and so forth. They march around the gym (forming a rectangle, emphasizing the angles as they turn). They run in a circle, or they play "snaketrain."

Various outdoor games can make extensive use of the children's knowledge about measuring with conventional or standard units (counting off the distance from one "home base" to another by pacing, pacing off distances in throwing or running, or measuring the height of a throw or a jump).

Elementary mathematical notions can and should be reinforced in **nature and language classes.** For example, using their knowledge of the months, weeks, and days, the children can keep a nature calendar more accurately. With an awareness of the fluidity of time, its duration, they can note how long it will be light in the various seasons.

Their spatial notions can be reinforced on nature fieldtrips. "We are going **across** the creek, and we'll go **over** the field, then **along** the narrow path **through** the rye." As they collect leaves and flowers, the children can examine their shapes and structures, count the petals, etc.

The children's measuring abilities should be used while working in the flower or vegetable garden: measuring the width or length of a bed and the distances between beds, measuring parts of the beds for various vegetable crops when they are sown. In caring for plants, the children can measure their growth and count the number of buds and flowers.

In preparing nature materials, the children collect and form groups of ten kernels, pebbles, or acorns, and count the piles they have collected (counting groups).

All these actions and observations by the children should be reflected in their speech. Let the children tell the teacher and each other what geometric figures the leaves or flowers petals resemble; how many large kernels they have collected, and how many small ones; which plants have short stems and which have long stems. When telling a story about a picture, the children should not only describe the action of the plot, they should also learn to see the number and arrangement of the characters and their relationships. The ability to understand means of expression does not come all at once; the children's attention must be directed to the characters' poses (the spatial situation of the individual parts of the body) and positioning, as shown in studies by N. M. Zubareva and R. P. Chudnova.

The diverse spatial, quantitative, and temporal notions can be reinforced in various games. For example, the children might be playing "store." They count the objects to be sold, put numbers on them (the price of the goods), then receive money from the customers, perform arithmetic operations, and "record" their computations. To sell dry goods, they measure them with conventional measures; if they sell fabric or ribbon, they measure them by sight or with a conventional measure. In games along the lines of "Railway Station" or "Our Street," the children establish routes for the trains, buses, and streetcars, assign numbers to them, measure the distance between stations, keep track of the departure times for the trains, subways, and buses (using a sandglass), and determine the cost of the tickets for the different means of transport in various directions.

By reflecting adult activities in their games, the children realize the broad applicability of mathematical knowledge and the importance of knowing how to count, measure, and determine direction precisely.

Didactic games should also be used to reinforce children's knowledge of quantitative, spatial, and temporal relations, and the shape and dimensions of objects. Various lottery games provide practice in counting and computation skills and intensify the children's notions of sets, number, numerals, and the natural number sequence. Object lotteries reinforce their knowledge of shape. Assorted paired cards can reinforce their knowledge of quantity and numerals, the size and shape of objects, and the spatial arrangement of objects. Story cards provide practice in identifying the seasons of the year or parts of the day. Various geometric puzzles, arithmetic rebuses, etc., also reinforce certain knowledge (see Color Figures 3, 4, 5, 7, 8, 9, 12, 13 and 20 at the end of the book).

Didactic recreational games not only reinforce the material that the children know, but also arouse their curiosity and develop mental versatility, initiative, and independent thinking.

The children's elementary mathematical knowledge should also be reinforced in their **everyday life**. Relying on a well-developed "sense of time," the children should be taught to regulate their own activity and behavior: to finish dressing for an outing, eating, or making their beds on time. The children's counting skills and spatial orientation can be extensively used in their chores (setting the table, preparing for class, selecting things to take on an outing).

Quantitative, spatial, and temporal relations pervade a person's entire life. Therefore, what the children learn about these relations, which has been arbitrarily divided up into school subjects, should be introduced rationally in all the children's activity, and should build the conviction that a knowledge of mathematics is important in every person's life. This conviction will strengthen the children's interest in mathematics and in learning more about it in school.

Mathematics preparation for school should thus be considered not so much from the standpoint of the amount of information acquired by the children, but rather from the standpoint of the need to make it systematic—that is, with a view toward the children's mental development and their understanding of the value of a knowledge of mathematics for their lives, the acquisition of an interest in it, and desire to broaden their knowledge in the future.

Appendix A

The Historical Development of Number, Written Numeration, and Number Systems

Development of the Concept of Number

We often use the expression: "It's as clear as two times two is four." Counting and computation have so firmly entered our daily life and we have become so accustomed to them that we cannot imagine an adult who does not know how to count or perform elementary computation. But there was a time when people did not yet have even the concept of number.

For the teacher introducing a small child to the concept of number, it is not only interesting but also essential to know the lengthy course of development of that concept. This helps the teacher better appreciate the difficulties children must overcome to master the concept.

Our remote ancestors did not know about numbers. Precisely when people developed the first mathematical notions is unknown, but there has been a need for counting and for comparing various sets since the beginning of the development of human society. While we can speak of the inventor of a certain machine or the founder of a certain scientific theory, we cannot say who invented counting and measurement. Every nationality independently passed through the first stage in its own development. This stage in human civilization is lost in the depths of history, as remote as the development of language and speech or the use of the simplest tools.

Human beings have always been surrounded by various sets: the stars in the sky, piles of rocks, sets of animals and plants, the limbs of the human body, and the set of homogeneous physiological functions as they occur in time. Humans originally compared these sets with one another without yet knowing about either numbers or counting. By comparing them, they distinguished the elements in a set and its components, observing not only equal or unequal numbers of elements, but also the absence of a certain element or a certain part in a set.

Study of the civilizations of different peoples, the study of different languages, and archeological findings have enabled mathematicians to advance a number of hypotheses about how the first notions of a set developed and how sets were compared in the pre-number period, how the concept of number and the natural number sequence arose, how number systems were formed, and how written numeration developed during the development of human society.

Mathematics arose out of human needs and developed in the process of practical human activity. Unquestionably, it was necessary in the very early stages of development to determine the size of the catch during a hunt and to divide it somehow among the members of the community. With the emergence of agriculture, man had to keep track of the harvest and, in dealing with neighboring tribes, negotiate how many warriors each tribe would supply for joint defense against enemies. And perhaps it was necessary to arrange a time to go hunting together or ascertain how many new moons remained until the start of spring chores. For all these determinations, human beings, who did not yet know any numbers, found methods of establishing quantitative correlations between aggregates.

Indeed, how did people at a primitive level of development perform the complex practical operations involved in the exchange of goods? Let us assume that a primitive man from the forests of Central Africa has until recently carried out all negotiations with only three number-words, counting only up to three. But he exchanged a large quantity of elephant tusks for packages of tobacco without fear of being deceived by the foreign merchants. He compared the number of tusks with the number of packages of tobacco by setting each package of tobacco beside each tusk if the computation was one-to-one. In this way he established equality in number between the collections of objects to be exchanged.

The writer and ethnographer G. Gor describes an analogous example when he cites the words of a representative of the small group of Nivukhi from Northern Sakhalin. "There was an old man among us. He did not know how old he was. He decided to start counting. A year went by—he put a fish head in the storehouse; another year went by—he put a fish head in again, and so forth" [2:175].

T. Semushkin also cites a similar description in the novel *Alitet Goes to the Mountains*. When an American offers a price list for his goods to the peoples in the North, a representative of the Soviet government points out to him that he would have to provide a practical price list—a graphic, living one—rather than a written one. The American does not understand, and Los' tells him: "Here, let's say, we have a bale [bundle] of brick tea—80 bricks. It costs 80 rubles. On top of it we put 2 polar foxes at 40 rubles apiece. The Winchester—two foxes under it, too. The cartridge clip, 20 pieces, put on 2 sealskins, for they cost a ruble apiece, and the cartridges are 2 rubles. This way it will be clear to anyone, even an illiterate hunter" [4:173]. Thus the concepts of *equal, more,* and *less* did not require the concept of number.

Quite varied sets may serve for comparison. Semushkin writes in the same story that the Chukchi Omrytagen was left a string of buttons so that he could remove one of them every morning, and when the string came to an end, he could go to a "talking holiday"—that is, to a conference. Time was accounted for in that way.

The Greeks used a similar method. The Greek historian Herodotus describes how, in the 5th century B.C., the Persian emperor Darius left some Greeks behind to protect a bridge he had built over the Danube when he went off to the South Russian steppes. In doing so, he supplied them with a knotted thong and commanded them to untie one knot each day. When the number of days designated by the knots had passed without his return, the Greeks were entitled to return to their homeland.

Thus, it is known that people who did not know how to count dealt with various sets, comparing them and contrasting their elements. These primitive methods of counting and measuring laid the foundation for later arithmetic and geometry.

Every nationality developed its own techniques for counting and measuring. As a result of thousands of years of experience, people arrived at certain generalizations, forming concepts that became the common property of all mankind.

What were the notions about number in the early stages in man's cultural and economic development? In the beginning man knew no number-words; he did not yet have an abstract concept of number. However, people made the necessary practical distinctions between sets. For instance, one chronicler of life among the nationalities of the North describes how people inspected their dog teams when going hunting, and if one of them was missing, they started to call it. But how did they detect the missing dog?

In the early phase of man's development, a set was perceived not so much by quantitative indices as according to the various qualities of the elements in the set. Quantity still functioned as a bundle of qualities, properties of the set and its elements. The elements and the whole were distinguished by shape, color, size, spatial arrangement, and so on.[1] At this stage, number had not yet been divorced from the sets themselves and their qualitative features.

Consequently, in the first stage of development of the concept of number, people had no generalized concept of number, and there were no special words to reflect these concepts. But the capacity to distinguish and compare sets was reflected in the ability to distinguish the elements of a set and the set as a whole according to qualitative attributes. This stage of development in the history of arithmetic is called the stage of **number as the quality of aggregates**. All of mankind passed through this stage in their development of notions in remote times.

Next came the stage of **counting by hand.** As society subsequently developed, humans not only had to perceive aggregates, they also had to reproduce them. Counting by hand emerged under the influence of this need. The elements of a certain aggregate began to be compared with the digits on the hands and feet, and sometimes even with other parts of the body.

For instance, according to ethnographic accounts, the Polynesians used not only the digits on their hands and feet but other parts of the body, although in a definite order. Counting began with the little finger on the left hand, then passed to the wrist, the elbow, and the shoulder. If the aggregate was not exhausted in this way, they moved on to the right shoulder, elbow, wrist, and digits—from the thumb to the little finger; in this fashion they could count up to 16. Then, if need be, they continued counting from the little finger of the right hand (i.e., 17), back to the little finger of the left hand. If even that was not sufficient, the counting was carried further on another person.

The celebrated Russian traveller N. N. Miklukho-Maklai (1846-1888) wrote that the Papuans counted in this way:

> The favorite method of counting consists in the Papuan's bending his fingers one after another while uttering a certain sound, such as "be-be-be"... Having counted up to five, he says "Ibon-be" (hand). Then he begins to compare objects in pairs with the fingers of his other hand and again repeats "be-be-be"..., and, after making a comparison with the last finger, he says: "Ibon-ali" (that is, 2 hands). Then he can make a count of the objects and later, comparing them first with the toes of one foot, says "samba-be" (one foot), then with the other—"samba-ali" (two feet) [3:280].

Thus, the name for the hand served as an index of the number in an aggregate consisting of five objects; the name for two hands meant ten objects; and the word *man* designated 20 objects at once. So the human body served as a counting device for human beings in the early stages of development. One set was compared with another, element by element. A certain standard aggregate was chosen for comparison, and usually it was based on the parts of the human body. As society developed, a standard set such as the fingers began to be inadequate, and sticks, pebbles, or knots on a cord or thong came into use.

Subsequently, counting by hand could not meet the requirements of a developing economy. It was replaced by the stage of **group counting**. In the process of wider exchange of goods, certain objects began to be grouped into definite aggregates, e.g., baskets, eggs, and canoes. These groups were made up of different quantities—100 coconuts at a time or ten wicker baskets at a time, for instance.

But there were still no words to designate quantity. These aggregates were called by their object names. There was a particular name for a group of one hundred coconuts, or ten baskets, or ten eggs. For example, among one Siberian nationality a set of ten baskets of provisions was called "na banara," and ten eggs-"na-kua." In both cases the particle "na" was involved, but it by no means designated the number ten yet. Echoes of group counting have been preserved to this day: eggs, buttons, and pencils are typically grouped by tens; silverware and furniture may be grouped in dozens or half-dozens. Groups of certain objects retain special terms such as "dozen" or "half dozen," and the precise number of objects, 12 or 6, is not named.

In the early stages, when there was no number-words, this kind of stable group had its own particular name. For example, among the Indians in Western Canada the word "tkha" meant three things, "tkhane" meant three persons, "tkhat" meant three times, and "tkhatoen" meant 'in three places,' and so on. The common sound of "tkh" in all these terms shows incipient awareness of something common, typical of all these cases— that is, an awareness of the quantitative aspect, although number is still not abstracted completely from the object.

It is important to note that at this stage not every aggregate is assigned a special name; a name is ascribed only to groups of objects encountered frequently in the tribe's everyday affairs.

The grouping of objects gradually becomes broader: objects with a flat shape are grouped together, as are round objects, boats, persons, and so forth. And each of these groups receives a special name. As many as seven to ten of these names for groups have been observed among some nationalities.

As we can see, number has not yet been abstracted from object quality—the concept of number is still missing, but there is an awareness of the quantitative aspect of a certain group. Groups of different objects are related to the same name as long as they have, say, a rounded shape. This stage has been called **counting in number-aggregates,** and it advanced the development of abstraction, which made it possible to universalize certain number aggregates.

How does the subsequent development and abstraction of numbers proceed? As the economy and the exchange of commodities developed, **one group of objects came to be a measure for other groups, a criterion for evaluating them,** a distinctive form that performed the function of money. Naming an economically significant group of objects had two functions: on the one hand, it served as a name for the objects themselves, and, on the other, it came to express their standard number as well. Then one group of objects proved to be particularly significant and convenient for comparison with other groups of objects. For instance, a group of animals (livestock) performed such an evaluative function among a number of peoples—it acquired the function of money; groups of shells began to function as money for other peoples. Singling out one of the various groups of objects to serve for comparison and to function as money resulted in an increasing cognizance of the quantitative content of that group. The quantitative aspect, rather than the name of the objects, began to dominate in naming the group. A concept of number and an appellation for it gradually emerged. If the word "hand" at first designated a hand and at the same time five fingers, now the word "hand" increasingly came to take on the significance of quantity. But since different objects were grouped in various sets when aggregates were counted, the standard groups of objects with which the comparison of the other groups took place now usually corresponded to the conventional groupings.

This meant that all other aggregates of objects could be compared with given standard groups: a concept of number based on a standard set gradually began to develop. In the history of mathematics these standard groups are called **nodal numbers**. The standard sets expressed by nodal numbers served as a means of comparison for aggregates of objects.

But these universal, standard aggregates which found reflection in human consciousness and speech in the form of nodal numbers did not develop according to the familiar natural number sequence. There was still no connection between the standard aggregates and, therefore, between the nodal numbers. Let us assume that there were the universal sets and nodal numbers two, five, and ten, but there was still no clear awareness of the number of sets intervening between them, and therefore those quantities had no names. This stage in human development is called the stage of **counting with nodal numbers**. But a developing economy required increasing precision in determining quantitative groups. This necessity contributed to growing awareness of the intermediate numbers as well. For example, there were the nodal numbers five and one; the intermediate numbers began to be expressed by combinations of these. This process is clearly shown by the written Roman numerals: III is the number I repeated three times, and IV is five minus one. The nodal numbers were isolated islets, so to speak, around which new numbers clustered to connect the nodal numbers with one another. These intermediate numbers between the nodal numbers are called **algorithmic numbers**.

But how did they actually emerge? This can be traced by studying the languages of the North American Indians or the tribes of British America. Scholars have delineated the special role of verbs in counting as an aid in classifying sets. Therefore such verbs are called **verb-classifiers**. These verbs were not used by the Amerindians while they collected, say, two groups of objects into accepted, stable aggregates, like ten and ten. But if the Amerindian had to deal with more than ten and 10—26, for example—he would put down ten and ten and several more things, but now his movements would be accompanied by a verb. He would say something like: "I will put another six on top of two times ten fruits (or other objects)." This was an algorithmic number created as a result of the actual counting operation, where a stable collection of objects was first chosen and then supplemented by a certain quantity accompanied by a gesture and a verb. There are traces of this formation of algorithmic numbers in many languages, including Russian. Thus, the numbers from ten to 19 are pronounced like "one on ten," "two on ten," "three on ten," and so on. The particle *on* indicates that something is to be put on top of ten, or added to ten.

Later this motor-action ingredient began to disappear, and counting assumed the character of an arithmetic operation, as reflected vividly in the Roman numerals: VIII = V + I + I + I or XC = 100 - 10, LX = 50 + 10.

The arithmetic method of forming an algorithmic number by adding or subtracting was also reflected in the names of the numerals; for example, in the Roman numbering eighteen was called *duo de viginti*, twenty minus two, and in French the number eighty is *quatrevingt*, four twenties.

This, briefly, is the scientific hypothesis about how the concept of number developed in human society.

The natural number sequence took a long time to develop, and was long perceived as finite. Thus, a number of primitive peoples had only two or three number-words in their languages. But this by no means meant that they were unable to express large sets. The islanders of the Torres straits perceived everything over six as many, and in their language it was called something like "incalculable." Apparently, for our ancestors as well, the number seven, for instance, must have seemed quite large at one time, as is indicated by numerous sayings and proverbs ("Seven do not wait for one," "Measure seven times, cut once," "A baby with seven nurses can't see"[2]).

With the development of economies and science, the notion of "incalculability" moved on to larger and larger numbers, up to 100, 1000, and so forth, until the concept of infinitude in the natural number sequence developed. Consequently, the notions of sets, counting, and number developed in proportion to economic development and the expansion of trade. The numbers did not emerge all at once, nor did they arise in sequence. First nodal numbers were created, and algorithmic numbers were formed on their basis. The concept of the natural number sequence as a definite system of relations $n \pm 1$ (where n is a natural number) also developed gradually.

It took thousands of years for humans to differentiate in their consciousness various sets according to quantity and for special names to arise from this differentiation or abstraction of the quantitative aspect—that is, for the concept of number to be formed.

The conventional sign for a number, the digit or numeral, developed considerably later than number. Many millennia were likewise needed for man to learn to represent a number by a sign.

The numerals originated in different ways for each civilization. For instance, in ancient Egypt the numerals first took the form of actual pictures of the sets of objects concerned. A pole designated a one, and a person with uplifted hands stood for a million. These drawings took a great deal of time to execute. The drawings became increasingly schematic, turning into special signs, or **hieroglyphs** (some peoples use hieroglyphs to this day).

The ancient Babylonians had different written signs which resembled wedges. These ciphers were called **cuneiforms** (from Latin *cuneus*, meaning 'wedge'). They were carved on clay tablets, placed either horizontally or vertically, and the tables were baked for permanence. The variously arranged signs stood for different numbers: ⟨ stood for one, ▼ was read as ten.

Among some peoples the numerals were designated by letters. Sometimes (among the ancient Greeks and Phoenicians) these were the letters for the initial sounds of the number-words. This is called Herodian numeration, after the historian who discovered it. For example, for the Greeks the number five was named *pente* and was designed by the letter *p*, and the number ten was called *deka* and was designated by the letter *d*. Later the letters of the alphabet in sequence began to replace the initial sounds of the number-words. Thus, in Slavic and Greek numeration the first nine letters of the alphabet designated the numbers from one to nine, and the next letters in order designated the tens, then hundreds. This kind of system of designation bears the name **alphabetical numeration**.

Alphabetical numeration was more convenient than Herodian, and it gained a foothold in Greece.

An alphabetical numeral system was also adopted in Russia, and is called **Slavic numeration**. It was created for the South Slavic peoples (present-day Bulgaria, etc.) by the monks Cyril and Methodius in the 9th century. This alphabetical numbering system consisted of 27 letters in the Graecoslavic alphabet; to distinguish the numerals from the letters in their ordinary significance, the symbol   , called a "titlo" (abbreviation), was placed over the numerals.

Roman numeration was used in Western Europe in the Middle Ages. It consisted of seven symbols, I—one, V—five, X—ten, L—fifty, C—one hundred, D—five hundred, and M—one thousand. The other numerals were combinations of these symbols according to the following rules: if the symbol of higher value stood on the right of the symbol of lower value, the latter value was to be subtracted from the former one—IV (4), IX (9), XL (40), XC (90), CD (400), CM (900). If the symbol of higher value preceded the symbol of lower value, the latter value was to be added to the former one—VI (6), XI (11), XIII (13), LX (60), CX (110), CXL (140), DC (600), and MCXX (1120). Only one sign could be subtracted, but up to three signs could be added, VIII, XIII, MCCC, etc. It was impossible to judge the size of a number by the number of signs in the notation. For example: 1500 was MD (two symbols), while 1488 was MCDLXXXVIII (eleven symbols).

The various types of written numeration were gradually supplanted by the highly convenient **Arabic numeration and decimal number system**, in which there are ten digits to designate each of the first nine natural numbers and zero (the absence of units): 1, 2, 3, 4, 5, 6, 7, 8, 9, 0.

The brilliant Uzbek Mahomet, the son of Musa al-Khwarizmi, first developed a number system based on designating all the natural numbers by ten numeral signs in the 9th century. His work was written in Arabic, the scholarly language of the peoples of the Near East at that time. His work was based on the practical experience of mathematicians from India.

Only in the 12th century did Europe become acquainted with this work, and the numeral signs came to be called Arabic or Hindu, but they might equally well be called Khwarizmic [1:22]. The Arabic numerals had a somewhat different form than they do today. Their original form has been preserved to this day in the Near East—among the Turks and Iranians. The Tartars, Uzbeks, Turkmen, and Azerbaijanis, and others, also used them previously.

The Russian word *tsifra* ('digit, numeral') was borrowed from Arabic. Among the Hindus, zero was called *suniya*, which meant 'empty.' The Arabs, borrowing the Indian system, translated the word *suniya* into their language, calling zero *sifr* (cf. Arabic *safara* 'empty'). When the Hindu numeration was transferred to the West, the word *sifr* was not translated, and until the 18th century this word was used for 'zero' in Europe and in Russia. In the 19th century the word *sifr* for zero was replaced by the Latin *nullus*. Since then, the zero sign has come to be called null or zero, and the other nine signs have come to be called ciphers (or numerals). Until the 18th century in Russia, all the written signs except zero were called **expressions**.

Thus, written numbers varied among the peoples of different countries: hieroglyphic numbers among the Egyptians; cuneiform among the Babylonians; Herodian in Phoenicia and Attica; alphabetical among the Greeks, Slavs, Hebrews, Georgians, Armenians, and Arabs; Roman in the Western countries of Europe in the Middle Ages; and Arabic (or Hindu or Khwarizmic) in the Near East. Subsequently, all civilized peoples adopted the last system.

Characteristics of Various Numeration Systems

Various numeration systems have been created and used by different nationalities at various periods in their development. In the history of mathematics, numeration systems are divided into **positional** and **non-**

positional systems. The hieroglyphic, alphabetical, and Roman systems are nonpositional.

What kind of system is said to be positional? The word *positio* is Latin, meaning 'position.' Therefore, a positional system is one in which the significance of the numeral designating a given number depends on its position with respect to the other numerals.

The decimal system is a strictly positional system. Let us analyze it. We can write a very large number with any one numeral; for example, the numeral four written 12 times (444, 444, 444, 444) means four hundred forty-four billion four hundred forty-four million four hundred forty-four thousand four hundred forty-four units. As we can see, the single digit occurring in different places represents different numbers. Thus, the significance of a numeral depends on its place in the written form of the number. This method has been termed the method of "place (or positional) value of numerals." This principle characterized the Arabic system, which became prevalent among the European peoples.

What is the advantage of a positional system? The same digits are used to express the same quantity of units in any place. This enables us to use only a small number of numerals in number notation. The positional system makes it possible to greatly simplify the arithmetic operations. The decimal number system enables us to express very large numbers with a small number of words or numerals. For example, 786,325,432,831 is expressed by a total of fifteen number-words. In the Russian spoken number system we use fifteen basic terms: one (unit), two, three, four, five, six, seven, eight, nine, ten, forty,[3] hundred, thousand, million, billion. The names for the numerals rest on the following bases: the decomposition of a finite set into tens leads to the concept of **place** in the decimal number system, and composing a set from units, tens, and hundreds leads to the concept of **class**.

Counting by tens consists in regarding **every ten elements in the set that is being counted as one element in a new set.** Every ten elements in the new set are again regarded as **one element in a subsequent new set,** and so on. The numbers one, ten, and hundred in the decimal system are called units of the first, second, and third places. Every ten units in any place form a unit of the next higher place. For instance, ten hundreds make a unit of the fourth place, a thousand; ten thousands make a unit of the fifth place, one ten thousands; ten units of the fifth place make a unit of the sixth place; and so forth. The numbers one, ten, hundred, thousand, ten thousands, etc., are called **place units**.

Each three sequential places are combined into one class. The first class is the class of simple units. One thousand is the unit of the second class, and one million is a unit of the third class, one billion is a unit of the fourth class, one trillion (a thousand billion) is a unit of the fifth class, and so forth. There are three places in each class. Each successive place is ten times greater than its predecessor, and each successive class is 1000 times greater than its predecessor.

In order to name any natural number, we must identify the place units of the first, second, and third places in each class, and then give the number of units in each class and indicate the name of the class.

The place system enables us to use only fifteen basic terms to name any number from the immense set of numbers in the first four classes. A number can be read in full detail by naming each place of the number, or more briefly by naming every class of the number, or even more briefly with an abbreviated name for every class of the number. Thus, because we have the decimal system to express any number, no matter how large, we need only a few words. If there were no such system, the infinite set of natural numbers would require an infinite set of different words. The place principle of notation is possible because we break down the units into places and classes.

The positional decimal number system is currently the most widely used. The reason for its general acceptance is that it is so convenient to use. It was pointed out above that in the Roman system it is impossible to tell how large a number is by its external appearance. The differences between multi-place numbers are easily identified in the decimal system.

There are two ways to determine which of two natural numbers is the larger. If the decimal expansion of the one number contains more digits than the decimal expansion of the other, the former number is the larger.

For example, 4,374,655 is greater than 456,846, since there are seven digits in the first number and six digits in the latter.

Suppose the decimal expansions of two natural numbers have the same number of digits. Begin comparing corresponding digits from the left. When we reach a pair of digits that are different, the expansion containing the digit that expresses the greater number represents the larger of the two given natural numbers. For example, 2,345,786 is greater than 1,978,467 since 2 >1; 2,345,786 is greater than 2,278,467 since 2 = 2, but 3>2; 2,345,786 is greater than 2,345,127 since 2 = 2, 3 = 3, 4 = 4, 5 = 5, but 7>1.

Notation with ten signs is extremely simple when there are places and classes. But this simplicity is the product of protracted effort in the historical development of mankind. The invention of the written decimal system and the place value of digits is one of the most important events in history.

The well-known French scholar and physicist of the 18th and 19th centuries P. Laplace evaluates the decimal number system and ten-digit notation: "The idea of expressing all numbers by ten symbols, assigning them a significance in place in addition to their significance in form is so simple that, by reason of this very simplicity, it is hard to understand how amazing it is. That it was not easy to arrive at this method we see by the example of the greatest geniuses in Greek scholarship—Archimedes and Appollonius, from whom this idea remained hidden."

The decimal system belongs among the digit-based systems. But there are other digit-based systems, base five and base twenty. Counting, as was indicated above, has always been object-based and visual. Human fingers and toes were the closest and most visual material for counting. Digit-based systems were therefore very prevalent. Many peoples (e.g., the Indians) had a base five system, one of the most ancient systems. Later on people began to combine the fives into pairs and to count by tens. As for the base twenty system, it was encountered very seldom, and then in combination with the decimal system.

But other systems are known besides the digit-based systems: for example, the base twelve system, whose origin has not been established. However, it has echoes in our own time. Some objects are counted in "dozens"; there are 12 hours in half a day; there are 12 months in a year; a tea service usually consists of 12 pieces; $12^2 = 144$ is called a "gross," and $12^3 = 1728$ constitutes a "mass." The base twelve system was used by the Romans. The base sixty system, as indicated above, was used by the Babylonians. The influence of this system has been preserved in astronomy to this day. The Babylonian astronomers gradually came to divide the day into two sets of 12 hours, and divided every hour into 60 minutes and each minute into 60 seconds. They also divided a circle into 360 degrees, a degree into 60 minutes, and a minute into 60 seconds.

The positional decimal system has proved the most enduring of the many systems. But positional systems are also possible on the basis of counting by twos, threes, fours, and so on, rather than on the basis of the number ten. Thus, one of the most ancient systems was the binary number system, in which two digits were used, zero and one, and the number two was a unit of the second place.

Every positional systems depends on its own second-place unit, which serves as the base of the system; in the decimal system the base is ten, while in the base sixty system it is sixty and in the base twelve system it is twelve (a dozen), while in the binary system it is the number 2. Any positional system requires the same number of numerals for written notation as there are units in the base. A system with a small base requires few numerals, but on the other hand written notation takes up a great deal of space. Notation with a large base is terser, but requires more numerals.

The decimal system became so customary that people forgot about the existence of the other systems. But the very ancient binary system has taken on a great importance in our days of advanced technology; all computers are constructed on the basis of the binary system.

Mathematics and the Other Sciences

The development of mathematics has promoted the development of other sciences, such as astronomy in Babylon five thousand years ago.

Three centuries ago Galileo and Lomonsov, Newton and Lavoisier began to "mathematicize" physics, chemistry, and mechanics. The mathematicization of the sciences began to intensify in the early 20th century, and has burgeoned since the 1950's. Such disciplines as mathematical economics, mathematical linguistics, mathematical biology, and mathematical logic have emerged very recently. At present, science is striving to learn to measure human knowledge and express it mathematically. Thus, new mathematical discipline of information theory was born very recently, in the 1940's. It is concerned with the possibilities and methods of making quantitative measurements of information contained in various communications (reports, lectures, works of art, and conversation, among others). The less knowledge a person has, the greater the scope of information. It is very important to learn to express information in quantitative indices. This provides for considerable rationalization in thought, permits more accurate construction of "thinking machines," and rationalizes the activity of such machines.

The need to perform large computations increases as the economy and the civilization develop. These computations become increasingly cumbersome and wearisome when many scientific and economic problems are being solved. For example, to predict the next day's weather would require months of work for a computing bureau. The less perfect the computer technology, the more mistakes there will be. Thus, human beings have an increasing supply of new requirements, which conflict with their actual potential. Human beings have wanted to swim like a fish, fly like a bird, see farther and more profoundly, and become acquainted with the other worlds in the universe. Thus, motivated by increasing needs, human beings long ago began devising various computing instruments and machines.

Various civilizations have invented devices to assist computations at different times. For example, the ancient Chinese invented a device called a "suan-pan," which they use up to this day.

The abacus (the "Russian abacus") was invented in Russia, and we still use it today. Other counting machines were created later, e.g., the "Felix" arithmometer was invented in 1874 by the Russian engineer V.

T. Odner. This arithmometer can do as much work as ten to twelve persons do on paper in a certain time. The Russian abacus works at approximately the same speed for addition and subtraction, but performing other operations on the abacus is more complicated than on the arithmometer.

As the requirements of society grew, the machines became increasingly precise but at the same time more complicated. Today we have created punch-card equipment and electronic computers, which operate at a speed inaccessible to man. Thus, a computer takes a week to solve a complex mathematics problem, whereas a person might need two hundred years of daily labor.

A new science called cybernetics emerged in the mid-20th century. The American mathematician Norbert Wiener published a book in 1948 under the title *Cybernetics, or Control and Communication in the Living Organism and the Machine.* Wiener's service consisted in being the first to synthesize the achievements of a whole set of related scientific disciplines: information theory, which was founded by the American mathematician and engineer Claude Shannon, who based his work on data from research in probability theory by the Soviet mathematician A. N. Kolmogorov; the theory of automata, developed by John von Neumann; and the physiology of higher nervous activity, founded by the Russian scientists I. M. Sechenov and I. P. Pavlov. Wiener also took into consideration the achievements of modern computer technology and automation.

Only several decades old, cybernetics is one of the youngest sciences, but its perspectives for its development are immense. Cybernetics is introducing human beings to a new era. The development of this science can be compared with primitive mans' transition to agriculture. I. A. Poletaev, the author of *Signal,* the first Soviet book on cybernetics, has given an eloquent statement of its perspectives:

> If a cave man who made stone axes had been asked what tools man
> would use in the future, even the most skillful expert in stonework
> of the time would hardly have been able to tell about the steam-
> hammer, the hydraulic press, and other machine tools of our day.

And this would not be his fault. He had inadequate information at his disposal for making such far-reaching conclusions. In our day we can also ask ourselves, "What will cybernetic machines provide for us and our descendants?" And it must be acknowledged that we can hardly give a better answer to this question than would the cave craftsman.

But human beings themselves have created and built all these machines. All are the products of human activity, created by human hands and the human brain. All are the result of man's continuously developing knowledge, in which mathematics plays a leading role.

The mathematicization of the sciences is the objective of our time, and everyone needs a profound knowledge of mathematics. This is the reason for the attention devoted to mathematics in the entire system of public education.

Appendix B

Visual Material for Mathematics Lessons and Children's Independent Games and Lessons

There should be two types of visual material in a group: large-scale, demonstration material for exhibition to the entire group, and smaller distribution material for children to work with at their desks.

For demonstration a display board (Figure 1) is needed, 60 cm x 30 cm in size, with two felt strips on which various pictures can be placed. For each child there should be cards with two strips, 21 cm x 8 cm in the younger and intermediate groups and 30 cm x 10 cm in the older and preparatory groups (Figure 2).

In the younger group two types of cards are needed. For one type, various geometric figures (squares, circles, triangles, pentagons, etc.) can be drawn on one strip, and these figures can be arranged in a row (linearly), with a different number of figures drawn on each card in a set (two, three, four, or five squares, circles, etc.). The children put the appropriate number of small objects on the blank strip on the same card (bottom or top). The other type consists of cards with two blank strips for placing objects according to the teacher's instructions, both one and many.

On cards for the intermediate and older groups, the elements in the sets can be arranged in various ways: in a row, in the form of a geometric figure, or randomly, i.e., asymmetrically. Thus, on one of two cards some

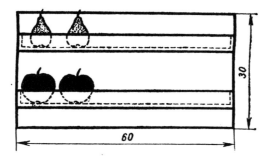

Figure 1. Board for Demonstrating a Quantity of Objects

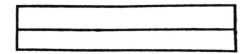

Figure 2 Individual Card with Strips

circles are situated near one another, while on another the same number of circles are set far apart. The two cards are the same size.

The cards can also show shapes of different sizes but equal in number, or small figures in large quantity. Working with these cards, the children conclude that numbers are independent of the size of the figures and their spatial arrangement.

Didactic aids should be designed so that sets are perceived by means of various analyzers (visual, tactile, auditory, and motor): small objects in the form of spillikins, buttons, or small blocks, which the child counts out, or buttons sewn on a piece of cardboard, whose number he or she determines by touch.

Musical sounds and noises should be used to establish the number of elements in a set by hearing: striking on a triangle, tambourine, or drum; playing chords on the piano and mandolin (or guitar); tapping on wood, glass, or the wall; drops of water, the chimes of a clock, the sound of a cuckoo clock, and other noises.

The motor analyzer plays no less a role in forming the activity of counting and in developing the notion of a set. Children count movements and can reproduce them if a number or a certain pattern is indicated—for example, jumping the same number of times as the number of circles drawn on a card, or knocking on a table, clapping hands, jumping, counting out a specified number of steps, throwing a ball, bouncing it on the floor or the wall, jumping a specified number of times through a hoop, and much more. The diversity of motor actions and at the same time their repetitiousness promote the development of the activity of counting and the formation of the general notion of a set.

A set cannot always be assigned ready-made. Sometimes the children create it themselves from subsets, or pick out subsets from a given set and establish the number of elements in them. For example, a set of circles might contain green, red, and blue circles. The set therefore consists of three subsets, each of which has "its own color."

To familiarize the children with numerals in the older and preparatory groups, the teacher needs sets containing numerals of small and large value [1], as well as cards with the following conventional symbols: +, -, =, <, and , (Figures 3 and 4). The numerals are stored in a numeral box, 46 cm x 36 cm in size. A panel is needed for familiarization with numerals (Figure 5).

Other sets are also needed for familiarizing the children with shapes: rectangles, squares, rhombuses, trapezoids; isosceles, equilateral, right, and obtuse triangles; pentagons and hexagons; circles and figures bounded by ovals; three-dimensional solids: cubes, spheres, cylinders, cones, bars (rectangular parallelepiped). The plane and solid geometric figures should be of various sizes. Collections of small toys are also needed for comparing their shape with the geometric figures.

For the study of size, various objects of different length, width, height, and thickness should be selected (ribbons, strips of cardboard or wood), as well as collections of toys: *matryoshki*, kegs, cones (ring pyramids), small boxes, tiny cups, etc. (Appendix C Figures 15, 16, 17, 18, and 19).

Figure 3. Demonstration Numerals

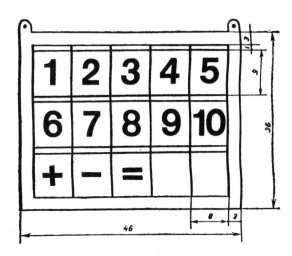

Figure 4. Display Board for Numerals and Pockets for Holding Numerals

Figure 5. Panel for Familiarization with Numerals

For the study of spatial relations the teacher should make special collections of aids, which are also used in conducting various didactic games such as "Where is the doll hiding?": under the bookcase, behind the bookcase, on the bookcase, between the two chairs (see Color Figures 13 and 14).

It is advisable to use a feltboard for displaying geometric figures. A piece of cardboard is covered with felt; felt is also applied on the back of cut-out geometric figures; when the figures are placed on the board, the felt fibers become intermeshed and hold the card tightly.

For learning about time, it is good to have in the group a wall clock, a sandglass, a stopwatch, a dummy clock, a designer clock, and a calendar (Appendix C Figure 20).

Aids for Teaching Children to Count

Among the classroom aids there should be small toys for counting: celluloid, rubber, plastic, wooden, papier-mâché, and other kinds (in the form of cups, fish, roosters, ducklings, mushrooms, rings, small blocks, counting sticks, flags, etc.). Colored beads threaded five or ten at a time on a wire or thick string can be made out of clay.

Demonstration and Distribution Material for Counting

The *number staircase* is a card with ten strips on which circles can be put in the form of a "number staircase" within the range of the first five or first ten numbers (Figure 6). Two-sided circles are provided which can be placed in increasing order on the staircase.

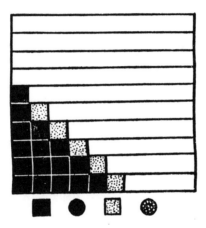

Figure 6.   The Number Staircase

The purpose of this aid is to provide a visual image of the natural number sequence and to help the children understand the connections between ordinal and cardinal numbers (ten circles on the tenth strip, seven circles on the seventh strip, etc.).

The assignments can be twofold: placing the circles in increasing or decreasing order. The aid is meant for four-year-old children (up to five) and for five- and six-year-olds (up to ten). The number of cards should correspond to the number of children in the group.

Each *aid* consists of ten objects: dolls in identical dresses, little Christmas trees of the same size, geese and goslings, *matryoshki* in different dresses and different-colored shawls, circles in three colors (with ten of each color), mushrooms of the same kind and size, drawings of apples and pears, bunnies, colored balls, and colored ring pyramids. These aids (both drawings and full-color pictures) are exhibited to the children and should be stable. A support can be attached to the back of a picture, or it may be made from clay (Appendix C Figure 1). The children work at the teacher's desk: they count and compare sets, establishing correspondences between their elements (geese—ducklings; Christmas trees—mushrooms); the *matryoshki* are used for ordinal counting ("Which *matryoshka* has a blue dress on?") and for learning the unit composition of numbers ("How many matryoshki in different costumes will you take if I name the number four?") [1].

There should be enough cards showing between one and five mushrooms in a row that each child can have five. Mushroom toys or objects the children have made out of clay should also be provided, approximately eight to a child. The child is to superimpose the mushroom toys on the picture, selecting the number drawn on the card from a large set. There should be 125 cards and 200 mushrooms, circles, and other figures in different colors, for a class of 25.[1] This aid is recommended for a group of two- or three-year-old children (see Chapters IX and X). It is intended to teach them to see each picture and correlate the object superimposed on it with the object itself—that is, to assist in mastering the superimposition technique. With three-year-olds, this aid can be used for practice in counting and sharpening the ability to generalize. Different shapes and different colors help the children to gradually abstract away from the attributes of an object and to be guided only by number ("There are five green circles on my card, and I put five red squares on them. The circles and squares are equal, five apiece").

There should be five cards with two strips for each child. Between one and five small objects are drawn on the top strip of each card. The children are first given ten toys like the ones drawn on the cards, and then other toys, to be placed on the bottom strip. A group of 25 children will need 125 cards and small objects of two or three types, 250 of each type. This aid is recommended for three-year-old children (without counting the objects) and for four-year-olds to use in counting objects and establishing a one-to-one correspondence between the elements in sets.

There should be five other cards with two strips for each child. Anywhere from one to five circles are drawn (or placed by the children) on one strip on each card. With them go circles of the same diameter (ten to a child) but of different colors, or buttons (ten to a child) of the same size as the circles, or circles of another, larger size. A group of 25 children will require 125 cards. Circles of another color, buttons of the same size as the circles, large buttons of another color, green triangles, blue squares, etc., should be available in sets of 200.

The purpose is to enable the children to practice seeing quantity, disregarding the color and size of the buttons or geometric figures. The aid is recommended for three- or four-year-old children. The cards are placed in front of the child so that the circle will be sometimes on the upper strip and sometimes on the lower on.

A total of 300 outlines of various objects of graduated size are needed for a group. These may be, for example, rabbits, balls, mushrooms, pyramids, ducklings, etc. (Appendix C Figure 1).[2] The diversity of material means that it can be varied in the lessons, and the children's interest can be maintained.

Another aid consists of paired pictures with three varieties of objects drawn in a row; there are anywhere from one to five objects on each card. Objects in equal quantity but different in shape and size make a pair (Appendix C Figure 2). For example, a long carrot and a shorter carrot, small tomatoes and large tomatoes, maple leaves and birch leaves. The purpose is to teach the children to see equal quantity independently of size and variety.

Groups of objects based on number (Appendix C Figure 2). "Here all the objects are distributed one apiece, and here by twos, by threes, by fours, by fives." Assignments for the children could be: "Find another card where there are just as many as on this card," or "Where's the pair?" the teacher says, holding up a card. The child who has the same number of similar objects runs to the teacher's desk and puts it in the row. This aid is recommended for four-year-old children. Nine sets of aids are required in order to carry out the lessons with an entire group. It can also be used in the children's independent games. Cards are distributed to the children. They take their neighbor's card and put down its pair. In such a game one card should not have a pair (but the children do not know about this). The loser is the one left with that card in his hand.

In a second variant of the game the cards are given out to ten players, e.g., three cards apiece. As the first player puts a card on the table, he says, "I have three maple leaves. Who has another three?" Everyone who has a card with the three objects puts it down. Anyone inattentive is left with cards. No single number can be repeated twice (Appendix C Figure 2).

Lotto consists of seven cards with four windows in which apples, pears, cherries, and plums are arranged. The same fruits are depicted on small covering cards (28 of them), but in increasing order by number (Appendix C Figure 3). The first card has one apple, two pears, three plums, four cherries. The second card has two apples, three pears, four plums, five cherries. The third card has three apples, four pears, five plums, six cherries. The fourth card has four apples, five pears, six plums, seven cherries, etc. The purpose of lotto is to drill the children in counting from any number and enable them to practice seeing an equal number of objects when they are arranged differently and recognizing what numbers are not represented in a certain group of objects if they count from one to ten (there is no card with eight and nine apples; there are no cards with one or two plums; and so on). The game is meant for the older and preparatory groups. It is good to have two or three sets of the game in the group.

"Dish" Lotto consists of ten cards with four windows in which plates, forks, spoons, and cups are shown. One of all four types of objects are represented on the same card, two of each on the second, three of each on the third, and so on. There are also 40 covering cards with the same objects arranged differently (see Color Figure 4). The purpose of the games is to provide practice in counting and seeing equal quantity as expressed by the same number in different groups of objects and when arranged differently. The game can be used in the older and the prepara-

tory groups, and, if limited to the first five cards, in the intermediate group as well. It is advisable to have two or three sets in a group.

Another aid consists of cards with various objects (from one to five on a card). There should be six varieties of cards with objects for each of the five numbers, for example: four maple leaves, four drums, four balls, four beetles, four radishes, four cherries; five butterflies, five drums, five balls, five beetles, five radishes, five cherries; and so on. The purpose is to practice counting objects and grouping objects on the basis of number, and to find which quantities of a given type of objects have been omitted from among the first five numbers. For examples, the teacher passes out cards depicting two radishes, four radishes, and five radishes, or two beetles, three beetles, and five beetles. The children arrange the cards in increasing order of the number of objects and determine which number is missing in the sequence (for example, one radish and three radishes, one beetle and four beetles). This aid can also be used another way: "Hold up the cards—whoever has the same number of any objects," the teacher says, and the children raise their cards.

A third variant is to place cards with anywhere from one to five objects on five tables. The other cards (25) are distributed to the children. They are asked to find the table where they should put his cards. Then the teacher generalizes: "The cards on this table have one object apiece: one chick, one rooster, one cucumber, one bucket, one rabbit, one mushroom" (see Chapter 10 and Chapter 11).

A fourth variant is to give each child one card. The children pair off with whoever has a card showing the same number of objects. The children run around the room to music or clapping, and must form pairs at a signal. When the game is repeated, the children can form a pair with cards showing sets expressed by consecutive numbers—for example, four beetles and five butterflies, one duckling and two chicks. The aid is recommended for the intermediate, older and preparatory groups. But the number of objects on a card can be increased up to ten in the older groups. A group of 25 persons needs two sets of cards.

This assignment uses a set of three cards with three windows. Each window depicts a numerical figure with three, four, or five red circles.

Circles of three other colors go with the cards (15 circles of each color). The assignment is to count the red circles on the card and superimpose the yellow circles on them. Count out the same number of blue circles and place them in a row in the middle window of the card; count out the same number of orange circles and arrange them in any way in the third window of the card. Then exchange the circles' places, and check by superimposing them on the circles in the first window to determine whether the red, blue, and orange circles have been chosen properly. The purpose of the assignment is to show the children that the number of objects does not depend on their arrangement. This aid is recommended for children in the intermediate group. There should be nine or ten sets in a group.

The next assignment uses a set of four cards with three windows. From two to five different objects are pictured in the first window of each card. Individual cards on which the same objects are represented, but in decreasing order by number, go with them. For five butterflies, provide cards with four butterflies and three butterflies; for four fish, provide cards with three fish, two fish, etc. The purpose is to teach the children to find cards with one less object. This aid is recommended for the intermediate group. It is advisable to have ten sets for a group of 25 children (Appendix C Figure 5).

This assignment uses sets of eight cards with three windows. From three to ten various objects are pictured on the left in the first window of each card. These cards are accompanied by individual cards showing the same objects but in decreasing order by number. For ten acorns there should be cards with nine acorns and eight acorns; for seven radishes, cards with six radishes and five radishes; for four carrots, cards with three carrots and two carrots. The purpose is to drill the children in looking for cards with one less object and to provide practice in describing the objects on cards and ascertaining their number.

The following assignments can be conducted: (a) place on the empty windows cards with the same objects, but one fewer; (b) place on the empty windows cards with other objects, but in decreasing order by quantity; e.g., nine radishes, eight acorns, seven radishes, or five carrots, four cucumbers, three carrots; (c) arrange cards in increasing order according to the number of objects, and determine the number of objects (Appendix C Figure 5). All the assignments are geared toward practice in naming numbers starting with any number, in forward and reverse order. This aid is meant for children in the older and preparatory groups. There should be seven to ten sets to a group.

The next assignment uses sets of eight cards with windows. Each cards depicts the following quantities of circles in the extreme left and right windows: one—three, two—four, three—five, four—six, five—seven, six— eight, seven—nine, eight—ten (Figure 7). The middle window on the card is empty. The children have to find the card with the missing number to go with it. The purpose is to practice finding a consecutive numbers.

The assignment can be done in two ways: (a) arrange the cards so that the circles fall in increasing order by number: one—three, two—four, eight—ten; or (b) place the cards so that the circles are in reverse, decreasing order: ten—eight, four—two, three—one, and so on. The aid is meant for the older and preparatory groups; there should be seven to ten sets of the aid for 25 children.

The following assignment requires eight cards with three windows. Anywhere from two to nine circles are pictured in the middle window of each card. Accompanying these cards are 16 individual cards with circles drawn on them (Figure 8). This aid, entitled "Find the Neighboring Numbers," is designed for practice in finding consecutive numbers to go with the one shown on the card. It is intended for children in the older and preparatory groups. There should be seven to ten sets of this aid for 25 children.

This assignment uses five sets of from one to ten buttons sewn in a row. The purpose is to practice counting by touch. The aid can be used in the intermediate, older, and preparatory groups; the children in the intermediate group are given cards with from one to five buttons; children in the older groups can have from one to ten buttons (the buttons from six to ten are sewn in a second row). There should be five sets to a group.

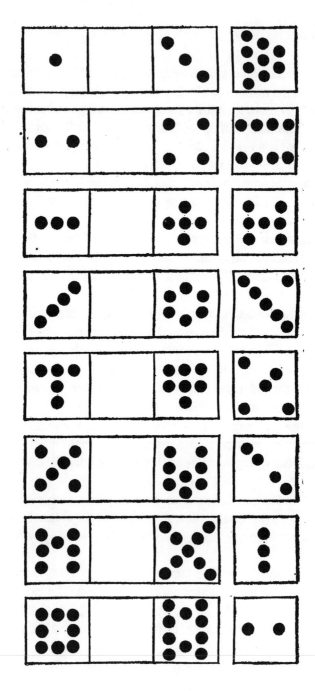

Figure 7. Find and Name the Missing Number

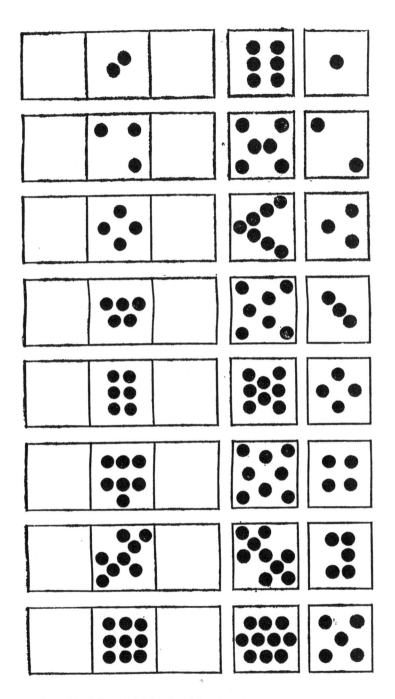

Figure 8. "Find the Neighboring Numbers"

A set of small cards with numerals from 1 to 10 provides another assignment for children in the older and preparatory groups [1]. The purpose is to practice recognizing the numerals. This aid can be used both in lessons and in children's games. For example, one group of children is given numerals and another is given cards showing a certain number of objects or circles. The children disperse, but at a signal they pair up: one child has a card with circles and the other has the corresponding numeral (five circles and the numeral 5).

In a second variant of the game, the children form two lines. In their hands they hold cards with a certain number of objects or circles. At the head of each line is a table with some numerals lying on it. At a signal the children run in turn to the table, find the numeral corresponding to their picture, and go to the end of their line. The winning line is the one in which the children select the numerals faster and most accurately. There should be 25 sets to a group.

Two other assignments use cards with three windows. In "Find the Neighbors," a numeral is shown in the middle window, and the outer windows should be covered with numerals consecutive with the given number. In "Find the Missing Number," the first and third windows show a numeral, and the middle window is empty (Figure 9).

The following assignments use cards with from two to five red circles arranged in a row. They come with 90 cards on which black circles are arranged in various ways. The basic assignment is to make up a number from one to five out of two smaller numbers, using the cards with the black circles.

One variant is to post a card with red circles on the display board. The children are given cards with various numbers of black circles. They are asked to make up a number from two smaller ones to match the card posted on the board.

A second variant is to hang up a numeral on the board instead of a card with red circles. Given this number, the children are asked to make up a number from two smaller ones on cards with black circles or numerals.

A third variant is to post cards with red circles on the display board and give the children cards with numerals. They are asked to make up a

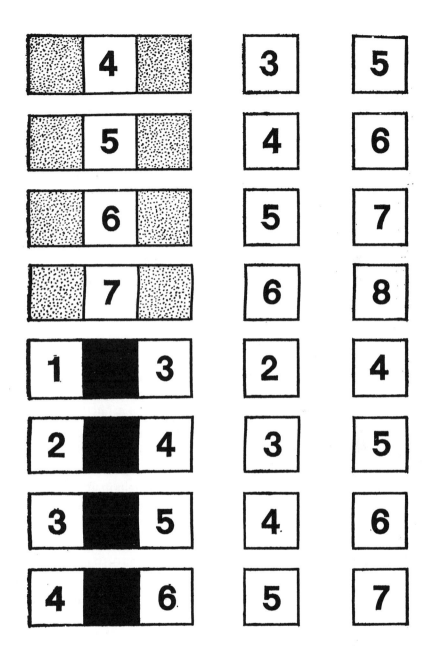

Figure 9. "Find the Neighbors" or "Find the Missing Number"

number from the numeral cards equal to the number of red circles. There should be two or three sets of this aid in a group.

Other assignments use *sets of figures*. One card shows familiar geometric figures, in different shapes, colors, and sizes. A card might depict two circles of the same size, but one red and the other yellow; three circles larger than the first ones, but one yellow, one green and one red one; three squares—one large red square and two smaller ones (one green, the other yellow); four rectangles—two large (but one green, the other yellow) and two small (one red and one blue); and two oval figures (one large blue one and one small red one). All these figures are drawn or pasted at random intervals on a sheet of paper. The children name the figures, grouping them mentally based on a certain attribute (shape, color, size). The number of these sheets of figures should correspond to the number of children in the group.

Similar sets of shapes can be distributed in envelopes. Each child is given a set of shapes for practical grouping. For example, the small red oval might be included first in a group of red figures (independently of its shape and size), then in a group of ovals (independently of size and color), and then in a group of small figures (independently of shape and color). The children count the sets accordingly based on a certain attribute and can represent the result by numerals provided in other envelopes.

A chart can show a set consisting of different objects arranged vertically and horizontally. For example, from left to right in the first row: a teddy bear, a doll, a top; in the second row: a pencil, a dress, a notebook; in the third row: a ball, a book, a skirt. As the children examine the horizontal and vertical rows, they pick out objects in them according to various attributes—e.g., only the toys and their number, only the school objects and their number, or kinds of clothing and the total number of articles of clothing. The children can group the objects on the basis of color as well: e.g., a doll in a red dress, a red ball, and a red top are included in the group of red toys.

Another chart depicts a combined set of various objects arranged in vertical and horizontal rows. For example, from left to right in the first row: a cherry, a notebook, a pencil, a chick; in the second row: an apple, a pencil, a notebook, a duck; in the third row: a pen, a book, a cat. The assignment is to find the identical objects in the combined set in a horizontal row and at the same time in certain vertical columns (the notebook and the pencil occur in the first and second rows of the second and third columns). These objects constitute an intersection of sets—but they are also included in the union of sets, together with the cherry, the apple, the notebook, the pencil, the pen, the book, the chick, the duck, and the cat. These aids are recommended for use in the preparatory group (see Chapter 12).

Other assignments can be based on pictures for making up problems. For instance, a forest can drawn on a 60 x 30 cm piece of cardboard. Slits are cut in the trees, and flat outlines of rabbits, birds, and mushrooms (no more than ten of each object) are inserted in the slits. This picture serves as a springboard for making up a problem or checking a pre-existing problem. The solved problem is recorded on the display board with cards showing numerals and signs (Appendix C Figure 6). The content of these pictures can be highly varied: ducks swimming on a lake, with other ducks on the shore; people in boats and reclining on the shore; a squirrel perching in the branches of a pine tree, with mushrooms sprouting under the tree; assorted vegetables in a basket; apples and pears visible in a bowl.

Aids for Developing Spatial and Temporal Notions

Aids for Working with Shape

Sets of cardboard geometric figures in assorted sizes and colors should be provided for every child: a square, a rectangle, triangles of various types, a trapezoid, a rhombus, a quadrilateral, a pentagon, a hexagon, a circle, and an oval. The purpose of this aid in the younger group is to acquaint the children with the figures and their names. In the older and

Figure 10. Assorted Quadrilaterals

preparatory groups one purpose is to acquaint the children with the properties of figures (counting the vertices, sides, and angles). Other purposes are to enable them to group a set of various figures by shape, size, and color, determine the number of subsets, find everyday objects resembling certain geometric figures, and put together geometric figures to make other objects (see Chapter 11 and Chapter 12).

The following assignment requires a set of large geometric figures and a set of smaller figures, each containing a square, rectangle, trapezoid, rhombus, circle, oval, triangle, hexagon, and octagon. The dimensions of the figures in each set should be such that they can be inscribed in one another—for instance, the circle in the square, the oval shape in the rectangle, the isosceles triangle in the square, and so forth (Figure 12)

Figure 11. Assorted Triangles

[1]. The purpose is to introduce the children to the basic properties of these geometric figures by comparing them by means of the superimposition technique, teach them to find paired figures independently of color, and teach them to capture the properties of geometric shapes when sketching them on graph paper. The aid is intended for the older and preparatory groups. A group should have three sets. In two sets the models should be of the same color, and in the third they should be different.

Other assignments are based on a *Lotto* of five cards, each of which has six windows. One figure is drawn in the upper middle window: a rectangle, a square, a circle, an oval figure, or a triangle. The other five windows are empty. They should be covered by cards depicting objects

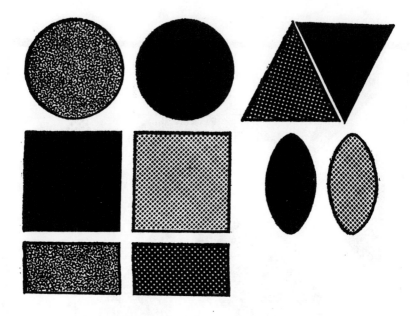

Figure 12. Assorted Geometric Figures

that resemble a certain geometric shape (Appendix C Figure 7). There
can be a similar lotto with five solid figures (Appendix C Figure 8). The
purpose of the game is to correlate a familiar object with a certain
geometric figure (plane or solid). The aid is intended for children in the
intermediate, older, and preparatory groups. There should be three sets
to a group.

The teacher should provide sets of solids: cubes, spheres, cylinders,
cones, and bars (rectangular parallelepipeds) of various sizes and colors.
These aids are designed to acquaint the children with the names of the
solids, provide practice in fitting solid figures into holes on a board or in
a box, introduce them to their basic properties, permit them to group
models of figures according to various attributes (shape, size, color),
acquaint them with three-dimensional figures, drill them in making
measurements with conventional and standard units (a centimeter tape

or a ruler), and practice finding everyday objects that are similar to a certain solid geometric figure (Appendix C Figure 8). This aid can be used in various groups according to the curricular goals.

The class can work with domino cards depicting different geometric figures, using them just like the dotted tiles in ordinary dominoes (Appendix C Figure 9). Other valuable aids are various objects that can be constructed out of plane geometric figures: e.g., a clown, a house with a fence, a sun, a moon (Appendix C Figures 10 and 11).

Another useful aid is wooden boards with windows cut in them for inserting thick plywood geometric figures (Figure 13) can be used. These aids can used for individual exercises with two- or three-year-old children.

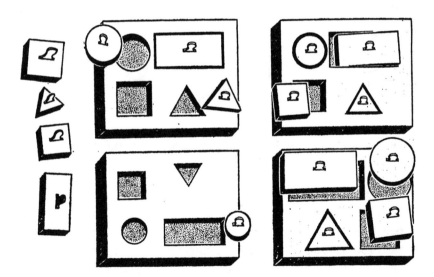

Figure 13. Insert the Geometric Figures

For individual play in the two- and three-year-old groups it is good to have a wooden box with openings for inserting solid geometric figures: a cylinder, a block, a bar, a cone, a sphere, a trihedral prism (Figures 13 and 14).

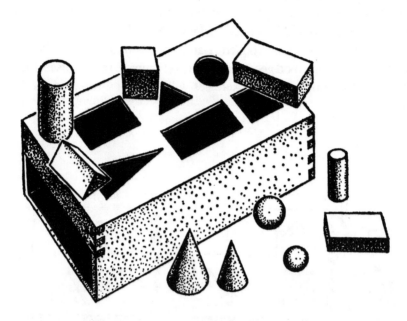

Figure 14. A box for inserting geometric solids in the holes

Ten familiar objects are depicted on 40 cards. Each object is repre-sented in four forms: two different-colored pictures, a silhouette, and an outline (Appendix C Figure 13). This aid can be used in various ways: (a) select four pictures representing a single object; (b) guess an object from its outline or silhouette, and name it; (c) put together pairs of two colored pictures or drawings, e.g., one silhouette and one colored picture, and so on; find an object in a colored picture using the silhouette or the outline, and vice versa; (d) group silhouettes and outlines while naming the objects. This aid can be used in the younger and intermediate groups. A group of 25 children will need three sets.

Aids for Orientation in Space

For determining the spatial arrangement of objects it is advisable to use one of the aids recommended by E. I. Tikheeva.

One aid consists of 15 pairs of cards on which colored models of geometric figures are arranged in various ways. Pairs are made up of two cards where the shape, color, and arrangement of the models fully coincide (Appendix C Figure 13). The purpose is to develop orientation in space, attention, and concentration. The aid is recommended for use in the older and preparatory groups. A group will need three sets.

A game of pairs consists of six pairs of cards, each showing three toys arranged in a row but in different places, or ten pairs of cards, each showing five of the same toys in various places (Appendix C Figure 14). The purpose of the game is to drill the children in distinguishing the spatial relations between objects and develop attention and observation. The game is recommended for the younger, intermediate, and older groups. One group will need three sets.

Another aid is a series of cards for inspection and describing the arrangement of objects in space: (a) a table with a ball in the middle of the table; (b) a table with a ball on the edge; (c) a table with a ball on it between a doll and a teddy bear; (d) a ball under a table; (e) a ball near a table leg; (f) two trees in a clearing, a boy hiding behind the tree and peeking out, a woman sitting under tree, a little girl running toward her, a bow on the girl's head, a handkerchief visible in her dress pocket. The purpose of the aid is to work on spatial orientation and use spatial prepositions and adverbs in speech.

An aid for comparing length consists of five paired yellow strips of identical width but increasing length. Five pairs of red and blue strips of precisely the same dimensions go with them. This makes it possible to combine the pairs by selecting strips of equal length and of the same and different colors (Appendix C Figure 15). This aid is recommended for the intermediate, older, and preparatory groups. A group should have five sets.

The five-year-old group employs certain conventional measuring devices for measuring length: cardboard strips and wooden rulers of various sizes; while the preparatory group uses the meter and the centimeter.

An aid for comparing width consists of five paired red strips of the same length but increasing width. Five pairs of blue and yellow strips of the same length and width go with them, thus making it possible to make up various pairs: (a) combining strips of identical color and equal width into a pair, (b) combining strips of the same width but different colors into a pair, combining the colors first red with blue, then red with yellow, and finally, blue with yellow (Appendix C Figure 16). The purpose of the aid is to emphasize the difference in width and teach children to compare width by association and superimposition. The aid is recommended for the intermediate, older, and preparatory groups. A group will need five sets.

An aid for comparing depth includes a set of cups of various depths, a half-liter jug, a mug, a cup from the doll set (small nested wooden bowls can also be used). The children measure the depth of these objects by lowering a vertical stick into them and marking it to designate the top edge of the vessel. The vessels can be filled with water and thus serve as a means for comparing their capacity. A graduated test-tube can be provided for comparing the volume of liquid in the various vessels. The aid is recommended for the older and the preparatory groups.

To measure the weight of dry substances and other substances, a preparatory group needs a set of scales and weights (500 g, 1 kg, 2 kg). The following objects can be used to measure dry substances: a teaspoon, tablespoon, ladle, cup, and glass.

Aids for Learning the Size of Objects

Paired outline pictures of *matryoshki* in five sizes are useful. A pair consists of two *matryoshki* that are the same size but are dressed differently: their frocks and shawls are of different colors (Appendix C Figure 17). The purpose is to teach the children to focus their attention on the size of an object, ignoring the attribute of color. The specific assignments can be varied: (a) the children must arrange the *matryoshki* in increasing (or decreasing) order of size; (b) five *matryoshki* of different sizes are put in different parts of the room; the children are given one *matryoshka* apiece and asked to find the *matryoshki* of the same size; (c) the children are asked to bring a *matryoshka* of the same size to the teacher, but from memory ("Watch carefully, hold it in your hands, show its height with your finger, put it on the table, and go find the *matryoshka* that is the same height"). The aid can be used in the younger and intermediate groups. It is good to have five sets of *matryoshki* for 25 children.

Pairs of ring pyramids in five sizes can be useful for comparing height: (a) five pairs of ring pyramids with different colored rings; (b) five pairs of pyramids with rings all the same color, but one pyramid is red and the other blue. Pairs can be made up of: (a) ring pyramids which are the same size but have different-colored rings; (b) ring pyramids that are the same size but have one red ring and the other blue; (c) ring pyramids that are the same size, but one has rings of all different colors and the other has rings of the same color (Appendix C Figures 18 and 19). The children can arrange the ring pyramids in increasing or decreasing order of height and count the rings. The purpose is to teach the children to be guided by the size of an object rather than its color when choosing pairs, and to distinguish a gradual increase or decrease in object size. The aids are intended for children in the intermediate and older groups. A group of 25 children will need five sets.

Appendix C

Color Figures[1]

Figure 1. Demonstration and handout material for counting.

Figure 2. Selecting pictures on the basis of number: (a) "Select the pair," (b) "Group the objects by quantity."

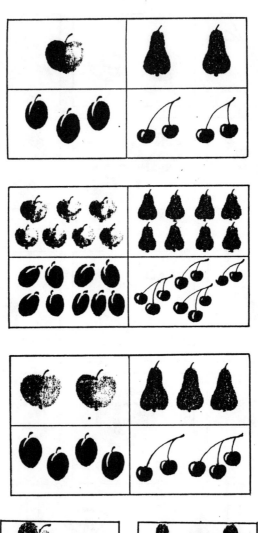

Figure 3. "Counting from any number" lotto.

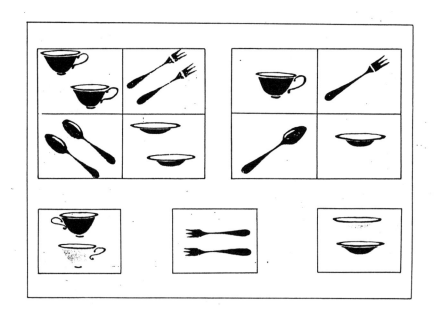

Figure 4. "Dishes" lotto (generalizing objects on the basis of number).

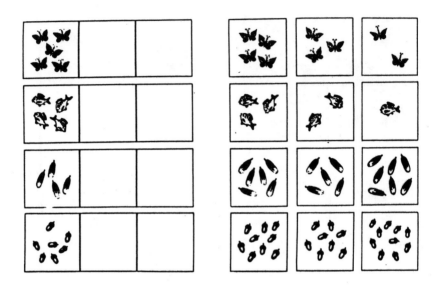

Figure 5. "Arrange the pictures in descending order or ascending order."

Figure 6. Pictures for making up problems.

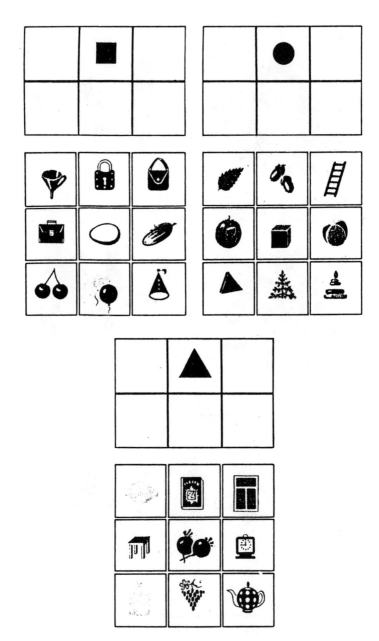

Figure 7. "What looks like the geometric shape?" lotto.

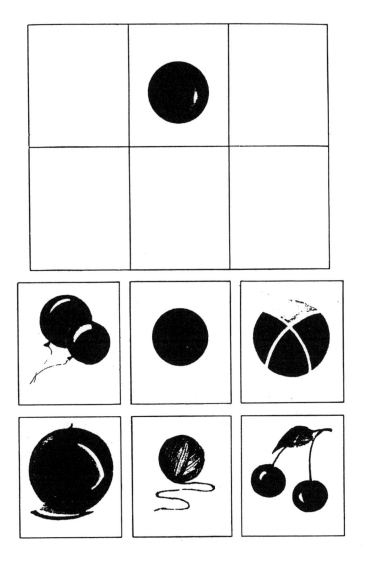

Figure 8. "What looks like the solid?" lotto.

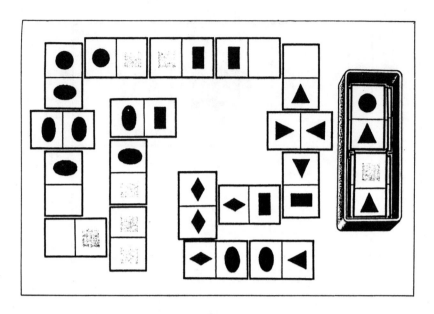

Figure 9. Dominoes with geometric shapes.

Figure 10. Making objects from geometric shapes.

Figure 11. "Name the geometric shapes that make up this picture, and count them."

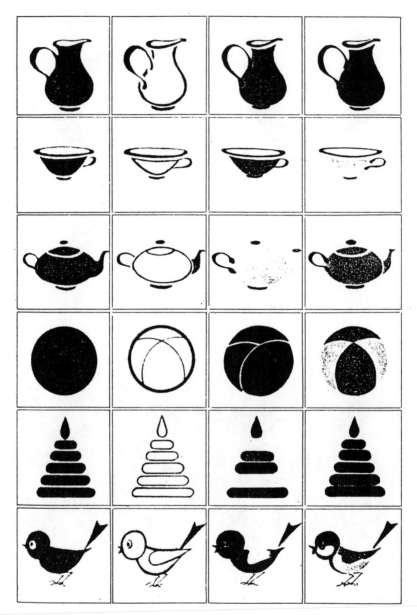

Figure 12. "Find the silhouettes, outlines, and colored objects."

Figure 13. "Choose the matching cards (by the arrangement of the geometric shapes)."

Figure 14. "Choose the matching pictures (of three objects)."

Figure 15. Paired strips for decreasing length.

Figure 16. Paired strips for decreasing width.

Figure 17. Models of *matryoshka* dolls for counting and size comparison.

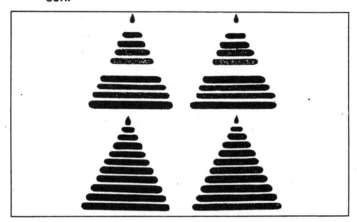

Figure 18. "Find the ones that have the same number of rings."

Figure 19. "Put the pyramids in decreasing order."

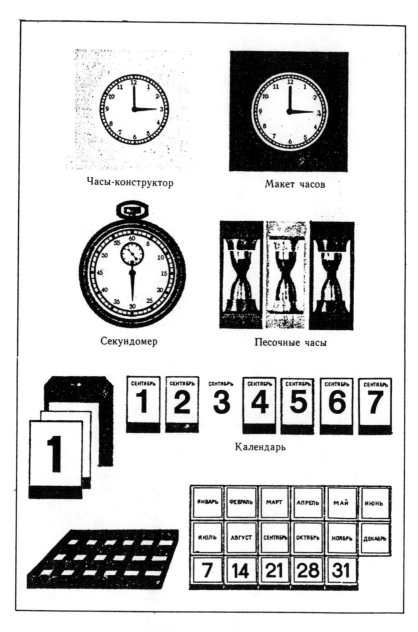

Часы-конструктор

Макет часов

Секундомер

Песочные часы

Календарь

Figure 20. Aids for developing conceptions about time.

Notes

Note to the Preface

1. The Soviet preschool educational system encompasses children between the ages of three and six.

Notes to Chapter 2

1. An archine is a unit of length equal to 28 inches.
2. Even now we find adherents of the monographic method, who erroneously consider it suitable for working with young children.

Notes to Chapter 3

1. We shall use this word for a collection of homogeneous entities (objects or phenomena, sounds, movements, etc.) as perceived by different means of perception.
2. Numerical figures are cards on which a certain number of figures are arranged in different shapes. Different authors have proposed various forms of arrangement (cf. Lay's square figures).
3. A set is said to be seriated, or ordered, if for any of its various elements a rule has been determined by which one of these elements precedes another. A discrete set is one consisting of individually represented objects, unlike a continuous set such as length, volume, etc.

Note to Chapter 4

1. This technique of inspecting geometric figures according to their contours has also been envisaged in the Montessori system (children were asked to outline with their finger

a geometric figure and a window in which the figure was to be placed, or to find a card with a broad outline of a figure).

Note to Chapter 7

1. The problem of how children start to learn verbs with various time inflections still needs special study.

Note to Chapter 8

1. Mathematical knowledge should be developed in children by both the inductive and deductive methods. Thus, it is necessary to create models that will promote the development of the children's deductive thought.

Notes to Chapter 9

1. The content of the work given for this and the following groups goes beyond the curriculum; it is based on a number of new studies which have not yet been incorporated in the curriculum.

2. It is also possible to give out strips of the same color with different-colored circles. On one strip the child places one red circle, and on the other he places many blue circles, or vice versa.

Notes to Chapter 10

1. As mentioned earlier, *raz* 'once' is frequently substituted for *odin* 'one,' especially in colloquial speech.

2. These recreational problems are cited from studies by Z. A. Gracheva.

Notes to Chapter 11

1. Here we consider dividing a whole into equal parts, which will lay the foundation for the children to understand fractions.

2. See the games developed by M. M. Barbashinova (Leningrad Methodological Department).

3. Since the representations of objects are given in the plane, their outlines are represented in the form of circles and ovals.

4. To develop the baric sense, Fausek provided a box with several compartments for holding 6 x 8 x 0.5 cm wooden panels of various kinds of wood: whitewood, alder, ash, redwood, walnut, etc.—twelve of each kind. The difference in weight for two consecutive panels was between 6 and 8 grams [2].

Notes to Chapter 12

1. The assignments for reinforcing skills in ordinal counting can be the same as for the previous group.

2. Translator's note: In Russian there are special words to designate groups of five or ten.

3. Translator's note: These prepositions under discussion, *po* and *cherez*, have no exact English translations.

Notes to Appendix A

1. Even a young girl who does not know the quantity or number of her dolls remembers each of them by their qualitative attributes (one has red shoes, another has a little bow on its head, and a third has a broken nose).

2. Translator's note: The point of the last proverb is the same as our "Too many cooks spoil the broth."

3. Translator's note: The word *forty* in Russian is not formed by analogy with *twenty*, as are *thirty*, *fifty*, etc.

Notes to Appendix B

1. In addition to mushrooms on a card, the same cards can be given out with circles glued to them. For superimposing on the circles, the children can also be given circles, but of another color, or else squares or triangles of a different color—for example, 10 red squares, 10 light blue circles, 10 blue squares, 10 yellow triangles, etc.

2. These objects are suggestions; they may be replaced by other pictures.

Note to Appendix C

1. The following twenty figures were printed in color in the original Soviet edition. As color is in no case crucial to the understanding of the figures, they have been reproduced here in black and white.

References

References for the Preface

1. El'konin, D.B. and V.V. Davydov (Eds.) *Age Potential in the Mastery of Knowledge*, Moscow, Prosveshchenie, 1966.
2. Gal'perin, P.Ya. and N.F. Talyzina (Eds.) *The Formation of Knowledge and Abilities on the Basis of the Theory of Step-by-Step Mastery of Mental Operations*, Publishing House for Moscow State University, 1968.
3. Gal'perin, P.Ya., A.V. Zaporozhets and D.B. El'konin. "Problems in Developing Knowledge and Abilities in Students and New Methods of School Instruction," *Issues in Psychology*, No. 5, 1963.
4. Gorbunov-Posadov, E. and I. Tsunzer. *Lively Numbers, Lively Thoughts and Hands at Work*, 3rd ed., Moscow, GIZ, 1921.
5. Lebedintsev, K.F. *The Development of Numerical Concepts in Early Childhood*, Kiev, 1923.
6. Markushevich, A.I. "On the Reform of the School Mathematics Course," *Mathematics in the School*, No. 6, 1964.
7. Neshkov, K.I. and A.M. Pyshkalo. In A.I. Markushevich (Ed.) *Mathematics in the Elementary Grades*, Part 1, Moscow, Prosveshchenie, 1968.
8. Piaget, Jean and Bärbel Inhelder. *The Genesis of Elementary Logical Structures*, Moscow, Publishing House for Foreign Literature, 1963.
9. Salmina, N.G. "On the Study of Numbers and Operations with Them in Elementary School," in P. Ya. Gal'perin and N.F. Talyzina (Eds.) *The Formation of Knowledge and Abilities on the Basis of the Theory of Step-by-Step Mastery of Mental Operations*, Publishing House for Moscow State University, 1968.
10. Zankov, L.V. *What is New in First-Grade Arithmetic Instruction*, Moscow, Prosveshchenie, 1964.

References for Chapter 1

1. Blonskii, P.P. *Selected Works on Psychology*, Moscow, Prosveshchenie, 1964.
2. Krupskaya, N.K. *Pedagogical Works*, Vol. 3, Moscow, Publishing House of the RSFSR Academy of Pedagogical Sciences, 1959.

3. Krupskaya, N.K. *Pedagogical Works*, Vol. 9, Moscow, Publishing House of the RSFSR Academy of Pedagogical Sciences, 1960.
4. Kostyuk, G.S. In A.A. Smirnov (Ed.) *Issues in Child and Educational Psychology at the 18th International Congress of Psychologists*, Moscow, Prosveshchenie, 1969.
5. Vygotskii, L.S. *Selected Psychological Studies*, Moscow, Publishing House of the RSFSR Academy of Pedagogical Sciences, 1956.

References for Chapter 2

1. Blekher, F.N. *How to Work with an Aid in Mathematics*, Moscow, Uchpedgiz, 1932.
2. Blekher, F.N. *Let's Learn to Count*, Moscow, Uchpedgiz, 1932.
3. Blekher, F.N. *Mathematics in Kindergarten and the Null Group*, Moscow, Uchpedgiz, 1934.
4. Blekher, F.N. *Didactic Games and Didactic Materials*, Moscow, Uchpedgiz, 1948.
5. Evtushevskii, V.A. *Methods of Arithmetic*, 15th ed., St. Petersburg, 1902.
6. Gnedenko, B.V. *Essays on the History of Mathematics in Russia*, Moscow, Gostekhizdat, 1946.
7. Goldenberg, A.I. *Methods of Elementary Arithmetic*, St. Petersburg, 1892.
8. Grube, A.V. *Arithmetic in the Elementary School on the Foundation of the Heuristic Method*, St. Petersburg, 1892.
9. Gur'ev, P.S. *Practical Arithmetic*, 3rd ed., St. Petersburg, 1881.
10. Lay, W.A. *A Manual for Initial Instruction in Arithmetic, Based on the Results of Didactic Experiments*, 2nd ed., St. Petersburg, 1910.
11. Marx, K. and F. Engels. *Works*, 2nd ed., Vol. 1.
12. Marx, K. and F. Engels. *Works*, 2nd ed., Vol. 20.
13. Pestalozzi, J. "How Gertrude Teaches Her Children," *Selected Pedagogical Works*, Vol. 2, Moscow, Publishing House of the RSFSR Academy of Pedagogical Sciences, 1963.
14. Shleger, L.K. *Working with Seven-Year-Old Children*, Leningrad, GIZ, 1925.
15. Shokhor-Trotskii, S.I. *Methods of Arithmetic*, 5th ed., Moscow, Uchpedgiz, 1935.
16. Tikheeva, E.I. *Counting in the Life of Small Children*, Petrograd, Publishing House of the "Child's Life" Museum, 1920.
17. Tikheeva, E.I. *The Modern Kindergarten*, Petrograd, 1920.
18. Tolstoi, L.N. "On Public Education," *Notes of the Fatherland*, No.9, 1874.
19. Vil'dauer, G. *The Mental Development of Older Preschool Children During Activity*, Berlin, 1968.

References for Chapter 3

1. *Encyclopedia of Elementary Mathematics*, Vol. 1, Moscow, Gostekhizdat, 1951.
2. Piaget, J. and B. Inhelder. *The Genesis of Elementary Logical Structures*, Moscow, Publishing House for Foreigner Literature, 1963.
3. Sechenov, I.M. *Selected Works*, Vol. 1, Moscow, Publishing House of the USSR Academy of Sciences, 1952.
4. Sechenov, I.M. *Selected Philosophical and Psychological Works*, Moscow, Publishing House of the USSR Academy of Sciences, 1947.
5. Zaporozhets, A.V. *The Development of Voluntary Movements*, Moscow, Publishing House of the RSFSR Academy of Pedagogical Sciences, 1960.

References for Chapter 4

1. Fausek, Yu. I. *The Montessori Kindergarten. Experience and Observations During Seven Years of Work in Montessori-System Kindergartens*, RSFSR GIZ, Berlin, 1923.
2. Lenin, V.I. "Materialism and Empiriocriticism," *Collected Works*, Vol. 18.
3. Sechenov, I.M. "The Physiology of the Sense Organs," St. Petersburg, 1867.
4. Sechenov, I.M. *Selected Philosophical and Psychological Works*, Moscow, Gospolitizdat, 1947.
5. Sechenov, I.M. *Selected Works*, Vol. 1, Moscow, Publishing House of the USSR Academy of Sciences, 1959.
6. Venger, L.A. "The Formation of Perception in the Preschool Child," *Education*, 1968.

References for Chapter 5

1. Glagoleva, L.V. *Mathematics in Null Groups*, Moscow-Leningrad, GIZ, 1930.
2. Marx, K. and F. Engels. *Works*, Vol. 20, Moscow, Gospolitizdat, 1961.
3. Piaget, J. "How Children Form Mathematical Concepts," *Issues in Psychology*, No. 4, 1966.
4. Samarin, Yu. A. *Essays in the Psychology of Mind*, Moscow, Publishing House of the RSFSR Academy of Pedagogical Sciences, 1962.
5. Tikheeva, E.I. *Counting in the Life of Small Children*, Moscow-Leningrad, GIZ, 1931.

References for Chapter 6

1.Elkonin, D.B. *Child Psychology*, Moscow, Uchpedgiz, 1960.
2. Shemyakin, F.N. "Orientation in Space" in *The Science of Psychology in the USSR*, Vol. 1, Moscow, Publishing House of the RSFSR Academy of Pedagogical Sciences, 1959.

References for Chapter 7

1. Rubinshtein, S.L. *Fundamentals of General Psychology*, Moscow, Uchpedgiz, 1946.
2. Sechenov, I.M. *Selected Works*, Vol. 1, Moscow, Publishing House of the USSR Academy of Sciences, 1952.

References for Chapter 8

1. Bruner, J. *The Process of Education*, trans. from the English, Moscow, Publishing House of the RSFSR Academy of Pedagogical Sciences, 1962.
2. Komenskii, Ya. A. "Great Didactics" in *Selected Pedagogical Works*, Moscow, Uchpedgiz, 1955.
3. Latyshev, V. *A Manual for Teaching Arithmetic*, 3rd ed., St. Petersburg, 1904.
4. Makarenko, A.S. *Works*, Vol. 5, Moscow, Publishing House of the RSFSR Academy of Pedagogical Sciences, 1958.
5. Pavlov, I.P. *Works*, Vol. 3, Book 2, Moscow, Publishing House of the USSR Academy of Sciences, 1951.
6. Ushinskii, K.D. *Collected Works*, vol. 5, Moscow, Publishing House of the RSFSR Academy of Pedagogical Sciences, 1949.

Reference for Chapter 9

1. Krupskaya, N.K. "On Preschool Education," Moscow, Prosveshchenie, 1973.

References for Chapter 11

1. Blekher, F.N. *Didactic Games and Didactic Materials*, Moscow, Uchpedgiz, 1948.

2. Fausek, Yu.I. *The Montessori Kindergarten. Experience and Observations during Seven Years of Work in Montessori-System Kindergartens*, Berlin, RSFSR GIZ, 1923.
3. Gracheva, Z.A. "The Significance of the Mathematics Game 'Tangram' for the Mental Development of Preschool Children" in *Preschool Education*, No. 1, 1971.
4. *The Pavlovian Environment*, Vol. 2, Moscow-Leningrad, Publishing House of the USSR Academy of Sciences, 1949.

References for Chapter 12

1. Levinova, L.A. *On the Understanding of Transitivity of Relations by Children in Their Preschool Years. Theses of Reports. All-Union Scientific Conference on Present-day Problems in Public Preschool Education and the Preparation of Children for School, January 20-23, 1970*, Vol. 2, USSR Ministry of Education and USSR Academy of Pedagogical Sciences.
2. Ushinskii, K.D. *Collected Works*, Vol. 3, Moscow-Leningrad, Publishing House of the RSFSR Academy of Pedagogical Sciences, 1948.
3. Vygotskii, L.S. *Selected Psychological Studies*, Moscow, Publishing House of the RSFSR Academy of Pedagogical Sciences, 1956.

References for Appendix A

1. Andronov, I.K. *The Arithmetic of the Natural Numbers*, Moscow, Prosveshchenie, 1954.
2. Gor, G. *The Youth from the Far River*, Leningrad, "The Soviet Writer," 1958.
3. Miklukho-Maklai, N.N. *Travels*, Vol. 1, Moscow, Publishing House of the USSR Academy of Sciences, 1940.
4. Semushkin, T. *Alitet Goes Away to the Mountains*, Moscow, Khudozhestvennaya literatura, 1970.

References for Appendix B

1. Leushina, A.M. *Illustrative Counting Material for Kindergarten*, Moscow, Prosveshchenie, 1965.